Religious Transformation in the Late Pre-Hispanic Pueblo World

Amerind Studies in Archaeology

Series Editor **John Ware**

Trincheras Sites in Time, Space, and Society
Edited by Suzanne K. Fish, Paul R. Fish, and M. Elisa Villalpando

Collaborating at the Trowel's Edge: Teaching and Learning in Indigenous Archaeology
Edited by Stephen W. Silliman

Warfare in Cultural Context: Practice, Agency, and the Archaeology of Violence
Edited by Axel E. Nielsen and William H. Walker

Across a Great Divide: Continuity and Change in Native North American Societies, 1400–1900
Edited by Laura L. Scheiber and Mark D. Mitchell

Leaving Mesa Verde: Peril and Change in the Thirteenth-Century Southwest
Edited by Timothy A. Kohler, Mark D. Varien, and Aaron M. Wright

Becoming Villagers: Comparing Early Village Societies
Edited by Matthew S. Bandy and Jake R. Fox

Hunter-Gatherer Archaeology as Historical Process
Edited by Kenneth E. Sassaman and Donald H. Holly Jr.

Religious Transformation in the Late Pre-Hispanic Pueblo World
Edited by Donna M. Glowacki and Scott Van Keuren

Religious Transformation in the Late Pre-Hispanic Pueblo World

Edited by **Donna M. Glowacki**
and **Scott Van Keuren**

The University of
Arizona Press

TUCSON

The University of Arizona Press
www.uapress.arizona.edu

We respectfully acknowledge the University of Arizona is on the land and territories of Indigenous peoples. Today, Arizona is home to twenty-two federally recognized tribes, with Tucson being home to the O'odham and the Yaqui. The university strives to build sustainable relationships with sovereign Native Nations and Indigenous communities through education offerings, partnerships, and community service.

© 2011 by The Arizona Board of Regents
All rights reserved. Published 2011
First paperback edition published 2025

ISBN-13: 978-0-8165-0398-8 (cloth)
ISBN-13: 978-0-8165-5554-3 (paper)
ISBN-13: 978-0-8165-9972-1 (ebook)

Cover illustration: Mural from Pottery Mound showing kiva interior with cloud terraces and anthropomorphic rainbow from *Kiva Art of the Anasazi at Pottery Mound* by Frank C. Hibben, courtesy of KC Publications

Publication of this book is made possible in part by a grant from the Amerind Foundation.

Library of Congress Cataloging-in-Publication Data
Religious transformation in the late pre-Hispanic Pueblo world / edited by
    Donna M. Glowacki and Scott Van Keuren.
p. cm. — (Amerind Studies in Archaeology.)
Includes bibliographical references and index.
ISBN 978-0-8165-0398-8 (cloth : alk. paper) 1. Pueblo Indians—Religion.
    2. Pueblo Indians—Rites and ceremonies. 3. Pueblo Indians—Antiquities.
    4. Social archaeology—Southwest, New. 5. Southwest, New— Antiquities.
    I. Glowacki, Donna M. II. Van Keuren, Scott.
E99.P9R293   2012
299.7'840902—dc23   2011027209

Printed in the United States of America
♾ This paper meets the requirements of ANSI/NISO Z39.48-1992 (Permanence of Paper).

To Michael Kabotie, who inspired so many of us with his humor, passion, and profound interest in all things cultural

CONTENTS

Preface   ix

1   Studying Ancestral Pueblo Religion   1
    Scott Van Keuren and Donna M. Glowacki

2   Pueblo Religion and the Mesoamerican Connection   23
    Randall H. McGuire

3   Ritual and Cosmology in the Chaco Era   50
    Stephen Plog

4   The Role of Religion in the Depopulation of the Central Mesa Verde Region   66
    Donna M. Glowacki

5   Bowls to Gardens: A History of Tewa Community Metaphors   84
    Scott G. Ortman

6   Iconography, Space, and Practice: Rio Grande Rock Art, AD 1150–1600   109
    Marit K. Munson

7   Plazas, Performance, and Symbolic Power in Ancestral Pueblo Religion   130
    Matthew A. Chamberlin

8   Spectatorship and Performance in Mural Painting, AD 1250–1500: Visuality and Social Integration   153
    Elizabeth A. Newsome and Kelley Hays-Gilpin

9   The Materiality of Religious Belief in East-Central Arizona   175
    Scott Van Keuren

10 North, South, and Center: An Outline of Hopi
Ethnogenesis   196
Wesley Bernardini

11 Getting Religion: Lessons from Ancestral Pueblo
History   221
Timothy R. Pauketat

Notes   239

References   245

About the Contributors   299

Index   305

Preface

This book project began as a conversation between friends about the topic of religion in the late pre-Hispanic period Southwest (our designation for the Pueblo IV period, AD 1275–1540). At the time, we wondered if archaeological research on Ancestral Pueblo religion was at a crossroads, and we tried to think about how it could benefit from broader theoretical discussions about practice, agency, power, gender, and meaning. More than anything, we realized the need for greater attention—regardless of the challenges—to the ways in which religious expression and practice were deeply enmeshed in the social, political, and historical processes that shaped the modern Pueblo world. This volume is the culmination of those early exchanges. It realizes our vision for a set of forward-thinking essays that grapple with these complex histories by using novel analytical and interpretive frameworks.

From the beginning, we recognized the need for a broad dialogue among a range of scholars, given the scale of the historical processes and the broad geographic area in which religious change occurred during this time period. To address this breadth and depth, we assembled a group of scholars to present case studies in a session entitled "Tension and Transition: Religious Ideologies in the Prehistoric Southwest, AD 1250 to 1450" at the 73rd Annual Meeting of the Society for American Archaeology (SAA) in Vancouver, British Columbia, in 2008. The charge was to bring perspectives that would break new ground and expand the interpretive scope of the role of religion in Southwest archaeology. The original session included the authors in this volume as well as valuable contributions that could not be included in the subsequent Amerind seminar. The latter included presentations by E. Charles Adams on ritual deposits at Chevelon Pueblo, Greg Schachner on shifting religious practices in the Cibola region, Todd and Christine VanPool on the role that women and war may have had in the Salado phenomenon, and Severin Fowles on the manifestations of katsina religion in the northern Rio Grande. Steve Lekson and Randy McGuire also served as valuable discussants for the session.

Based on the success of the SAA session, John Ware, Executive Director of the Amerind Foundation, invited us to reconvene in Dragoon, Arizona, to have an extended conversation about the complexities of religion in the ancient Southwest. The authors in this volume came together for five days in April 2009 in the beautiful setting of the Chihuahuan Desert. Our purpose was to address not only historical questions about the Greater Southwest but also to consider the broader frameworks that we as archaeologists use to study religion. The discussions were spirited, critical, and enormously productive, exploring themes ranging from the historical connections between past and present Pueblo religious practices to the challenges of reconstructing the meaning of religious objects and media. These in-depth conversations ultimately enhanced our individual contributions and the chapters in this book are the outcome of the synergies that were created during the seminar.

From the beginning, our vision for the seminar was to explore archaeological perspectives on religion in the Pueblo Southwest. In doing so, we realized that it is essential to engage native community members and consultants to achieve a deeper understanding of the dynamic role of religion in the Pueblo past. In our initial attempt to do this, Kelley Hays-Gilpin and John Ware conducted postseminar discussions with several Pueblo community members on a range of issues including the central themes of the seminar. Those meetings brought to light critical dimensions of Pueblo religion that are not represented in the volume: they include issues of migration histories, multiple and sometimes divergent Pueblo worldviews, differences between eastern and western Pueblos, and the sensitive nature of Pueblo religious knowledge. These valuable conversations could not, unfortunately, be included in this volume but they demonstrated that our archaeological inquiry on religion must rely on imaginative and inclusive collaborations with descendant communities. Until that happens, a full understanding of Pueblo historical complexity will continue to elude us. That said, we feel confident that the chapters in this volume chart new directions for the study of past religion and, especially, the awareness of how central religion was to the changes that reshaped the Southwest during the late pre-Hispanic period.

We extend a special thank you to John Ware and his team at the Amerind Foundation for hosting an intellectually stimulating event in an immensely tranquil and relaxing setting. The wonderful staff graciously provided all our necessities, including magnificent meals. We want to also thank the Amerind Foundation for securing funding to support the seminar series and this publication. John supported our vision of this project early on, and without this, the volume would not have been possible. Two anonymous peer reviewers provided invaluable, detailed comments on the volume chapters that further strengthened the contributions. We owe a debt of gratitude to Allyson Carter, Scott De Herrera, and the staff at the University of Arizona Press for their efforts and guidance in seeing this volume through the publication process. The index was prepared by Linda L. Tucker-Burfitt, a technical editor and National Environmental Policy Act (NEPA) publications expert for SWCA Environmental Consultants in Salt Lake City. Her work was funded by The Institute for Scholarship in the Liberal Arts, College of Arts and Letters, University of Notre Dame. Last but certainly not least, we thank the authors of this volume for their lively discussions; insightful contributions; tolerance of the numerous, harried requests for editorial changes; timeliness in meeting deadlines; and overall good humor.

Donna M. Glowacki
Scott Van Keuren

Religious Transformation in the Late Pre-Hispanic Pueblo World

1

Studying Ancestral Pueblo Religion
Scott Van Keuren and Donna M. Glowacki

The northern Southwest was fundamentally reshaped by regional depopulation, long-distance migrations, and resettlement into large plaza-oriented villages by the late pre-Hispanic period (ca. AD 1275/1300 to 1540), also known as the Pueblo IV period. These historical events forever altered community life and set the stage for the emergence of the modern Pueblo world. Archaeological research on the demographic, economic, and political dimensions of this important period has focused on ways in which Pueblo peoples experienced climatic and environmental factors, migration, resource scarcity, social strife, and so on (e.g., Benson et al. 2007; Dean et al. 1985; LeBlanc 2000). The in-depth treatment of the role of religion has been, until recently, absent from many explanatory models of cultural change in the Southwest. Archaeologists have not, however, ignored the diverse array of ritual or religious material culture from the period. Attention to religious features and paraphernalia has a deep tradition in both archaeological and ethnographic settings (e.g., Cushing 1886; Fewkes 1904). For example, ceremonial structures, ritual deposits, and the religious subject matter of a wide range of decorated media have been systematically described (see Haury 1950; Kenagy 1986; Schaafsma 1980; W. Smith 1952; Woodbury and Woodbury 1966). However, the centrality of religion to social and political dimensions of ancient Pueblo life has at times been overlooked, partly due to skepticism about our ability to access the "spiritual life" from the record (Hawkes 1954: 162–163).

The chapters in this volume reflect a new interpretive leaning in our discipline. Pueblo scholars now talk about *how* religious institutions, beliefs, and practices figured into and facilitated the major changes that characterize the late pre-Hispanic period (Adams 1991, 1994; Crown 1994; Hays 1989; Walker et al. 2000). This attention to religion in the ancient Southwest is tied, in part, to a new intellectual interest in ideology, meaning, and symbols among archaeologists, especially those working with ancient ritual and religion (see Fogelin 2007, 2008; Hodder and Hutson 2003; Insoll 2004). In the Southwest there is renewed attention to the dynamics of ritual (e.g., Reid and Montgomery 1999; Spielmann 1998; Walker 1995; Walker et al. 2000), the organizational structures of religious life (Ware and Blinman 2000), symbolism (Adams 1994; Crown 1994; Hays-Gilpin and Hill 2000; Schaafsma 1994b; VanPool 2003; VanPool et al. 2006a), and other dimensions of past religious experience (see papers in Schaafsma 2007b; VanPool et al. 2006b; Whitley and Hays-Gilpin 2008a). Within the past decade, scholars who research the late pre-Hispanic period have increasingly delved into meaning and semantics to study the symbolism of pictorial imagery; the experiential dimensions of kivas, plazas, and other ritual spaces; and the metaphorical references in Pueblo religious expression and practice.

In the Southwest, this interpretive reorientation has also come from renewed attention to ethnographic literature and increasing collaborative work with tribal groups. The 1990 Native American Graves Protection and Repatriation Act (NAGPRA) and its impact on the working relationships between archaeologists and contemporary Pueblo people have enriched our understanding of the links between ancient and modern culture (e.g., Naranjo 1995; Suina 2002). Although we cannot assume past religious ideas and practices were the same as those in the historic or modern era, cross-cultural research illustrates that core ritual practices and religious ideas endure across vast time periods (Fogelin 2007:57). One of our overarching objectives in this volume is to explore both historical change and continuity. Several chapters examine continuities and differences between pre- and postcontact religious structures (see Bernardini, this volume; Ortman, this volume). These authors make use of existing ethnographic literature (Dozier 1970; Parsons 1939; Titiev 1944), which, when paired with contemporary oral narratives, allows us to map out long-term processes in a way not possible in many other parts of the world.

The cultural setting and data-rich archaeological record of the northern Southwest, paired with theoretical frameworks that emphasize social practice, contingency, historical process, and materiality, create a strong foundation for examining religious change in the past. We think that this critical period of change during the late pre-Hispanic era must be understood in terms of the social origins and outcomes of religious expression and practice. The archaeological remains reflect social decisions, actions, and outcomes that unfolded against the backdrop of the Pueblo worldview and understanding of sacred concepts, the otherworldly, and the relationships between human and nonhuman agents. The historical processes that garner the most archaeological scrutiny—namely migration, aggregation, and depopulation—were all deeply and intimately connected to religion (Glowacki, this volume; Pauketat, this volume). Thus, we would go so far as to say that all historical processes at both regional and local scales in the Pueblo Southwest must be understood with reference to religious beliefs and practices.

The volume addresses not only historical questions about the Ancestral Pueblo world but also, whenever possible, the broader study of religion in our discipline (see Pauketat, this volume). We use this opening chapter to outline an alternative model of religious experience, taking our cue in part from scholars working well outside the field of archaeology (e.g., Asad 1993). Scholars who work in the Ancestral Pueblo world are well positioned to add to this theoretical dialogue, both because of the remarkable preservation of ritual deposits and other religious materiality in the Southwest and because of the potential for examining issues of long-term change.

Religion Defined

Notions of Pueblo religion in the the history of southwestern research are influenced by the content and scope of classic ethnographic texts (e.g., Dozier 1970; Eggan 1950; Fewkes 1891, 1892; Parsons 1939; Stevenson 1904). Without assuming that the ethnographic present defines religion as it existed in the past, many of the authors in this volume use these data to generate new archaeological inferences. In this introduction, however, we neither review all of what has been written on Pueblo religion past or present, nor do we comprehensively outline archaeological scholarship on religion and ritual. A number of excellent review essays and books thoroughly summarize what we know about the Pueblo Southwest (Adams 1991; Hegmon 2000; VanPool et al. 2006a, 2006b; Whitley 2001; Whitley and Hays-Gilpin 2008b) and broader archaelogical concepts on the subject (Boivin 2009; Fogelin 2008; Insoll 2004; Renfrew 2007). Our goal instead is to outline a theoretical framework drawn from broader studies of religion that emphasizes themes of practice, discourse, and historical contingency.

A survey of anthropological literature quickly reveals the multiplicity of definitions that can be applied to the study of religion in the past (Bowie 2006; Durkheim 1965; Evans-Pritchard 1965; Firth 1996; C. Geertz 1973; Insoll 2004; Meslin 1985; Rappaport 1979; Spiro 1963; Turner 1967). This body of work yields no universal, concise definition of religion, but Geertz's (1973:125) assertion that religion at its core involves a "system of meanings embodied in symbols" has greatly influenced modern anthropological perspectives. This model has also shaped archaeological research over the past two decades (e.g., Chilton 1999; Hodder 1989), but most scholars are still perplexed in their efforts to characterize religion and belief in the past, sometimes opting to focus on ritual aspects of prehistory rather than to interpret largely intangible, metaphysical aspects of past ideologies. Given the obvious hurdles, how do we realize a model that is useful for archaeological analysis? The most useful characterizations, as Insoll (2004:150) eloquently puts it, acknowledge that religion is "a possible component underlying all the use and meaning of material culture" (see Pauketat, this volume). In the same vein, Asad (1983:252) notes that we should not be "identifying essences when we should be trying to explore concrete sets of historical relations and processes." These perspectives are particularly applicable to the Pueblo Southwest, where religious beliefs and practices, to borrow a phrase from Insoll (2004:22), were the "structuring principles" in the lives of individuals. Both southwestern ethnographies and conversations with modern Pueblo peoples (e.g., Naranjo 1995) underscore this idea. As Parsons (1939:xi) put it:

> Pueblo religion is far from being a system external to the rest of life. What the outsider from another age or culture calls religion is felt by

the insider as an integral part of his life. Description of religious complexes or particulars as borrowed or disintegrated or marginal is the outsider's classification.

In this volume, religion is not treated as somehow external to social life, but rather viewed as deeply embedded within a wide array of social practices. The discussion that follows outlines a working definition of religion that emphasizes as much, and underscores the broad materialities of religion in the Pueblo past. Religion must be understood both in terms of the things people believe (tied to sacred doctrine, canons) and the things people do in practice to reify these beliefs. Such beliefs are often understood as overarching, externalized bodies of knowledge and canons, but religion is lived, even internalized, through the practice of individuals. Religion in action is simultaneously personal and communal, cultural and cognitive. As Meslin (1985:48) notes, beyond referencing sacred ideals, religion is "an ensemble of ritual practices inserted into the fabric of day-to-day society." Both belief and practice entail complex dialectics between the overarching knowledge that shapes and is shaped by experience and action. Moreover, religion is not acted upon or experienced by any one person in the same way. We conceptualize religion as the composite of symbols, meanings, and practice by which people negotiate their lives and actions while realizing that which is held as sacred. At the core of this definition is the idea that religion is lived and transformed as sacred concepts and other bodies of knowledge are shaped through social practice.

In his analysis of Geertz's classic definition of religion, Asad (1983: 252) usefully reorients the anthropological questions of religion and its role in society:

> to seek an answer in terms of the social disciplines and social forces which come together at particular historical moments, to make particular religious discourses, practices and spaces possible. What requires systematic investigation therefore are the ways in which, in each society, social disciplines produce and authorise knowledges, the ways in which selves are required to respond to those knowledges, the ways in which knowledges are accumulated and distributed.

Asad thus allows for the ways in which religious practice simultaneously draws upon the past and envisions the future (see Asad 1993:35). Drawing on Asad's (1983, 1993) writings, Lincoln (2006:5–7) has recently identified four domains of religion that, according to him, go beyond overly broad characterizations or "meta-narratives" that deemphasize local historical processes: discourse, practice, community, and institution. Discourse is situated above "the human, temporal, and contingent" and is predicated on what Lincoln calls "transcendent authority" (e.g., an expression of religious canon grounded in tradition). This discourse "frames the way that any content will be received and regarded" (Lincoln 2006:5–6). Practices put religious belief in action, but they are not "inherently religious" as Lincoln noted; this point is especially important for archaeological analyses, which often focus on rituals with explicit religious connotations (e.g., the use and display of sacred objects). Belief and practice constitute the "individual and collective identities" that form Lincoln's "communities" (2006:7); his use of the term brings to mind recent essays that define "communities of practice" (Lave and Wenger 1996). Finally, "institutions" keep watch over and in many cases control the other three domains. Although Lincoln (2006:7) is quick to assert that institutions diverge in their organization and scale, for him, it is in this domain where we find the "leaders who assume responsibility for preservation, interpretation, and dissemination of the group's" ideologies and actions. With the concept of institutions, he clearly envisions the formal hierarchies of Western religious movements, but Lincoln's model also allows for the type of informal management and power relations that underlie Pueblo societies.

Lincoln and Asad warn against the notion that religion can be reduced to a body of externalized, fixed ideologies and symbols or other "cultural patterns" that portray aspects of the sacred or supernatural worldview. Rather, religion must be viewed as a composite of thoughts and practices that are in turn complexly intertwined with (and contingent upon) broader webs of social processes and events. All of this entails not only shared knowledge and communalistic behaviors but also the dialogue between individuals and their social settings, experiences, and traditions. As Pauketat emphasizes in the final chapter, through these actions religion is deeply and fundamentally "entangled" within human experience.

Despite the complexities of inferring the meaning of sacred beliefs and other aspects of past ideologies, archaeologists are well situated to understand religion in terms of how it was experienced by people in the past through practice, social interactions, and the creation and use of material culture. Much of this material evidence, as Pauketat (2001:87) puts it, reflects the "undirected and creative negotiations of people whose dispositions were affected by their experiences," and practice-oriented approaches allow us to more broadly discuss the complex dialectic between religion and ritual, belief and practice in the Pueblo Southwest. The chapters in the volume examine: the dialectical relationships between religious canons versus what is acted upon through Pueblo ritual and other practices; broad-scale ideological movements versus expressions of these religious beliefs at local scales; public versus private performance; and, perhaps most important, the social relations of those who lack religious beliefs versus those who enjoy access to knowledge, space, or other dimensions of religious experience. The volume authors thus move beyond sweeping statements about regional patterns and consider religious belief and materiality at multiple scales. The premise of this volume is simple: we cannot understand the late pre-Hispanic period without acknowledging the centrality of religion (things, practices, beliefs) in every aspect of the Pueblo historical process.

Elements of Religious Change in the Late Pre-Hispanic Period

The central goal of this volume is to examine how the reorganization of religious life figured into cultural changes during the late pre-Hispanic period, but why is this particular episode important, and what evidence do we have that suggests that religious belief and expression shifted? A thorough overview is beyond the purview of this chapter, but we highlight two key archaeological trends that are central themes of many of the chapters that follow and are arguably the most visible markers of religious change during the time period in question: (1) the reconfigured design and use of ceremonial spaces and (2) the elaboration and presentation of visual imagery on painted ceramics and other media. Our review of these aspects of late pre-Hispanic religious life also serves to highlight the scope of new scholarship on ancient Pueblo religion.

In many areas of the northern Southwest, Pueblo towns were built around large plazas that served as the central stage for ceremonial events. Smaller ceremonial spaces (including kivas) were built into room blocks and occasionally incorporated into large plazas (Adams 1989a, 1989b; Adams and Duff 2004; Haury 1950; Kintigh 1985). The expansion of plaza space implies that the social arenas for religious practice became increasingly public and participatory (see Chamberlin, this volume). For many scholars, this increase in the size and configuration of plazas points to the expansion of ritual events and behaviors that reinforced cooperative ideals. In a widely cited model, and one that draws on the historic period and modern Pueblo use of plazas, Adams (1991, 1994) ties the expansion of these ceremonial spaces to the emergence of a pre-Hispanic Katsina religion. For Pueblos today, plazas are the central performance space for Katsina rituals that, by nature, ensure and evoke community well-being. Plaza expansion in the late pre-Hispanic period is thus seen as clear evidence that this suite of religious beliefs (and perhaps others) functioned to integrate Pueblo peoples (wherever these archaeological features appear). This notion by no means implies that all Pueblo individuals or groups had equal access to the religious knowledge or paraphernalia that were central to these plaza ceremonies. Adams (1991) recognizes this in his discussion of Katsina cult origins, and the point has been greatly elaborated on in recent discussions of power relations during this time period (Graves 2002; Graves and Van Keuren 2011; McGuire and Saitta 1996; Potter and Perry 2000) as well as ethnographic literature (E. Brandt 1980, 1994). This topic is discussed by several authors in this volume who explore the dichotomistic ways that religious knowledge was accessed in the late pre-Hispanic period, including the separation of public and private spaces for religious practices.

The elaboration of painted media and rock art by the early fourteenth century is the other explicit archaeological marker of religious expression (see Munson, this volume; Newsome and Hays-Gilpin, this volume; Van Keuren, this volume). Perhaps the most widespread and apparent shift in media representation is seen in painted ceramics, both in the use of new slips and paints and in the subject matter that is portrayed. Pinedale-style designs cross-cut wares across the northern Southwest at the end of the 1200s; the decorative layout includes distinctive features and, as some would argue, a specific suite of associated icons (Crown 1994). This stylistic "horizon" parallels key changes in manufacturing technologies. Polychrome bowls eclipsed the use of bichrome (black-on-white) forms; in some areas, potters began to experiment with glaze paints (Habicht-Mauche 2005). By the 1320s, Fourmile-style pottery appears in portions of the Western Pueblo area, a precursor to later Sikyatki style (Hays-Gilpin and LeBlanc 2007). Both the appearance of elaborated imagery (e.g., masked figures) along with the enhanced suitability of these vessels for feasting (Spielmann 1998) hint at the articulation of new religious ideas through the display and use of certain forms of pottery. The stylistic shifts were by no means limited to ceramics. In fact, the latter media may mimic much more elaborate visual subject matter painted on the walls of kivas and other interior spaces (Hays-Gilpin 2006; Hays-Gilpin and LeBlanc 2007; Schaafsma 2007b; W. Smith 1952). Distinct changes in rock-art styles across the Southwest at the beginning of the 1300s also suggest the emergence (or restructuring) of religious beliefs and practice (Munson, this volume; Newsome and Hays-Gilpin, this volume; Schaafsma 1980, 1994c; Whitley 2001). This body of scholarly work and the archaeological patterns noted above are too extensive to review here, but suffice to say that these media offer solid evidence of new ideologies and modes of religious expression in the late pre-Hispanic period. Much of this recent literature focuses on regional scale changes. For instance, Hays-Gilpin and Hill (2000) examine some of the pan-Southwest distributions of flower imagery and their possible meanings. Crown's (1994) Southwestern Cult model (see below) takes a similar big-picture approach. Here, we simply summarize some of the central themes and the broader investigations of iconography and other visual imagery, and underscore the popular notion that fourteenth- and fifteenth-century religions enhanced communalism and harmony following periods of social upheaval.

Building on Jon Young's (1982) earlier research, Crown (1994, 1996) has interpreted the decorative patterns and iconographic presentation of Pinedale-style Roosevelt Red Ware (or the Salado Polychromes) as a signal of the spread of a Southwestern Cult (her term) by the early 1300s. Like Adams, Crown associates the cult with the spread of new idealistic concepts tied to cooperation and social cohesion in Pueblo society. Adams (1991) makes a similar argument by identifying early visual markers of the Katsina cult on painted murals, rock art, and ceramics in fourteenth-century contexts (Ferg 1982; Hays 1994; Schaafsma 1994a). Drawing on Pueblo ethnography, Adams suggests that the appearance of the Katsina ideology by the fourteenth century "served to integrate both the immigrant and the indigenous segments within" these large aggregated villages (1991:155). Masked figures on Fourmile-style pottery and rock art, the expansion of large ceremonial plazas, and other evidence are interpreted as the material expression of these religious ideals. His Katsina cult model and Crown's Southwestern Cult are presented as large-scale religious belief systems that served primarily integrative purposes. That is, they functioned to emphasize "social harmony" and to counter "disequilibrium" within a Pueblo world that was in flux (Adams 1991:150–151; Crown 1994:215). Plog and Solometo (1997) have reexamined late pre-Hispanic period iconography, identifying shield imagery in kiva murals and other visual referents to social conflict. For them, some of these visual cues refer to "warfare and weather control and fertility" (1997:175), patterns that are typically understated in historic-period and modern Pueblo ceremonialism and religious belief.

In an important essay, Ware and Blinman (2000) outline a related scenario for the emergence of Pueblo ceremonial organizations in the late pre-Hispanic period. They suggest that the complex ritual organization of historic-period Pueblos arose from the social upheaval of the postmigration period. The latter set the stage not only for Katsina ceremonialism but also a range of sodalities and societies, particularly in the Eastern Pueblo region. As they put it, "the instability that followed . . . resulted in an adaptive opportunity for the expression of behavioral novelty, the establishment of new system configurations, and the incorporation of exotic elements into Pueblo social-ceremonial systems" (2000:401). Ware and Blinman illustrate how the syncretic qualities of historic-period (and modern) Pueblo religion are tied to migration, resettlement, and other transformative events that characterize the late pre-Hispanic period. More important, their interpretations provide a strong framework for examining the contingencies of religious and social processes that authors in this volume explore in detail.

Several themes are evident in our brief summary of recent treatments of Pueblo religion. First, a good part of this scholarly work examines religious change at regional scales, outlining what are essentially meta-narratives that attempt to model pan-southwestern processes based on the spread of style events (e.g., the Southwestern Cult). This, of course, reflects the historical centrality of "big picture" analyses in Southwest archaeology (à la Cordell and Plog 1979). These efforts notwithstanding, historical ties to areas beyond the Southwest have yet to be thoroughly explored (Brew 1943; McGuire 1989, this volume). The second thematic current concerns the functional role of religion (Fogelin 2008:2), which implies that ceremonial rituals, painting and displaying key symbols on painted objects, feasting, or other activities that evoked religious beliefs were designed to promote social cohesion and harmony. In the Pueblo Southwest, many archaeologists argue that new ideologies and practices in the early 1300s were enacted in response to social upheavals and, as such, were socially adaptive behaviors. By way of example, for Crown (1994:215), the Southwestern Cult "emphasized the well-being of community larger than the village, [and] stressed peaceful relations." The idea that the cult functioned as such has been modeled on ethnohistoric narratives about religion, and more specifically, the "structures" of Pueblo religious belief (see Whiteley 1998). On the other hand, there has been little effort to use late pre-Hispanic period archaeology to identify and critically examine discontinuities between the Pueblo past and present (Plog and Solometo 1997; cf. Upham and Reed 1985).

There seems little doubt that by the late thirteenth century new religious beliefs reshaped Pueblo life across the Southwest. The themes outlined in the next section stress the need for a new perspective on Pueblo religion in the late pre-Hispanic period that emphasizes historical process and practice over functional explanations, that assumes a complex state of flux as individuals and groups negotiated beliefs through practice, and that acknowledges religious beliefs and ritual practice were deeply embedded in Pueblo daily life. Several key questions are posed: Do regional-scale models overshadow important local patterns, and how are the latter relevant to our interpretations? What elements of late pre-Hispanic period religion are tied to earlier periods, and, in turn, how did they shape the emergence of the modern Pueblo world? What elements of religious belief from other regions (including Mesoamerica) were influential, and how were these modified? How were these religious changes effected through performance, and how were the theatrics of religious expression altered from earlier periods? How was meaning complexly construed and perhaps even altered through ritual activities? How did Pueblo individuals create, transform, or even misinterpret core religious beliefs? How was access to these bodies of religious knowledge and associated paraphernalia restricted, and how were these tensions played out in the expression of various bodies of religious knowledge? The chapters in this volume offer new interpretive frameworks for addressing these questions and for thinking about the social and historical dimensions of religious experience in the Pueblo past.

The Main Themes of This Volume

Archaeologists face the daunting task of inferring the complex fabric of religious belief, meanings, and actions—all fairly intangible constructs—via material means. This interpretive challenge requires not only careful documentation of ritual items, ceremonial spaces, and religious iconography but also dynamic theoretical frameworks and a deep understanding of the origins and historical processes of religious practice for the areas in question. The chapters in the volume shift away from the premise that religion *functions* to one that examines religious practices as they embody historical processes and outcomes.

There was no singular narrative of late pre-Hispanic period religious expression or change. Visual media and other archaeological evidence do not simply reflect ideas understood or acted upon by individuals in the same ways, and these cultural manifestations did not spread as simple packages of beliefs that proscribed all the ritual practices, power relations, or other aspects of the Pueblo world after 1300. Rather, there were intricate origins, pathways, and effects, which shaped complex histories of religious experience that we must closely examine to truly understand the processes underlying the social changes among the Ancestral Pueblo.

The volume contributors bring with them expertise from various areas of the Southwest (see figure 1.1) and examine changes in late pre-Hispanic religion by focusing on several themes: origins and outcomes, religious performance, practice, and meaning, and networks of interaction. These themes relate to several questions: How did religious concepts and practices that characterize the late pre-Hispanic period arise? Where did they come from? What are the continuities and discontinuities relative to historic and modern Pueblo religion? And, more generally, how was religious change in the late pre-Hispanic period intertwined with other dimensions of social change, namely social conflict, power relations, and other aspects of community reorganization? Several chapters discuss webs of historical contingencies, associations, and social networks. These topics are not only deeply connected to questions of origins and outcomes but they also reveal important patterning in the scales of religious expression (from individual and local to regional). Perhaps most important, these deep relationships and links widen our awareness of the centrality of religion in past lives, especially with regard to the central topics of late pre-Hispanic period research (e.g., the social dimensions of migration and aggregation, including power relations and evolving identities). With this in mind, we highlight context and performance as fundamental to archaeological studies of religion, especially interpretive models that reconstruct historical processes rather than simply assume a broad functionality of shared ideologies. We call attention to the complex ways that religion is presented and experienced because religious actions involve actors, audiences, and theatrical scripts

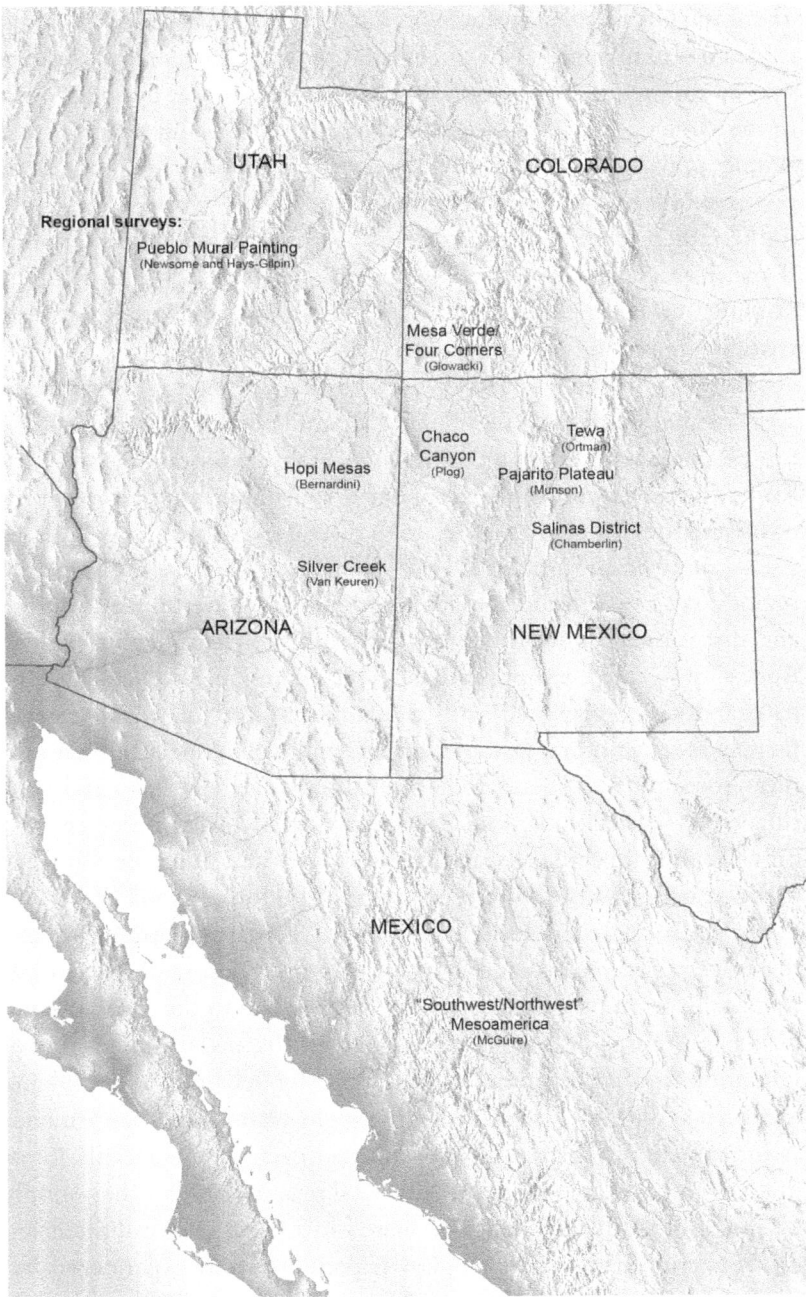

Figure 1.1. Map of the Greater Southwest that shows the locations of the research presented in this volume.

(ritual) that happen in architecturally defined spaces, prominent natural features, and other places. We must not lose sight of the fact that religion is lived by both individuals and groups with various needs, motives, and, most important, diverse understandings of sacred and secular knowledge (Bell 1997).

Origins and Outcomes

How did new or reformed religious practices, rituals, and other aspects of the late pre-Hispanic period historically relate to the Pueblo world prior to 1300? And are these linkages related to the Pueblo world that was encountered during the historical period? From the standpoint of history, changes in religious belief and expression did not emerge within a geographical or temporal vacuum; they were deeply rooted in the Chaco regional system and earlier developments and were further shaped by post-Chaco trends. In chapter 3, Stephen Plog revisits the complex ritual caches at Pueblo Bonito, Chaco Canyon, as a way of elucidating the nuances of late pre-Hispanic period religious expression. In a valuable discussion of the "cult" concept as it used by post-Chaco archaeologists, he outlines the materialities of Chaco religious experience (specifically ritual deposits), suggesting that there was important continuity in practices and belief through the late pre-Hispanic period. Plog details evidence for color-directional symbolism and other material referents to sacred concepts, and he notes the complexity of continuities (or lack thereof) between Chaco and post-Chaco landscapes, raising the possibility as others have (Lekson 1999:160–161) that the latter may have emerged as a rejection of Chaco ideology.

Glowacki (in chapter 4) touches on a similar theme in her discussion of Mesa Verde during the 1200s, examining the prelude to major migrations out of this area by 1300. She outlines a scenario in which revitalization movements along with schisms between the "core" religious beliefs and practices of groups set the stage for outmigration. In some portions of the Northern San Juan, communities reincorporated Chaco ideologies within their religious practices for the purpose of "symbolically reconnecting" with Chaco itself. In this chapter and others, we see the complex maintenance and expression of memories and engagement with the past, or what Mills and Walker (2008) refer to as memory work. Glowacki persuasively argues that the social and economic disruption of Pueblo communities in the Four Corners region must be understood in terms of the religious transformations that occurred in the post-Chaco Southwest.

Beyond the connections with Chaco, it is critical to examine the social and historical links between Mesoamerica and the Pueblo Southwest. These ties are poorly understood despite early interest in Ancestral Pueblo ties to Mesoamerican ideologies (Brew 1943; Parsons 1933). In chapter 2, McGuire expands on his earlier work (1980, 1989). He elucidates connections between Mesoamerica and the Pueblo Southwest (or geographically more inclusive, within the "Northwest/Southwest" as he calls it), and he emphasizes the need to go beyond simple lists that identify which Mesoamerican traits are present or absent in the American Southwest. For him, a "relational" perspective is better able to tease out the nuances of social relationships between these two areas, as opposed to traditional "regionalists" versus Mesoamerican "advocates." His detailed discussion expands our understanding of the Mesoamerican elements that shaped Pueblo religious experiences in the late pre-Hispanic period.

But what of the other end of the temporal spectrum: the links between late pre-Hispanic religion and both historic period and present-day Pueblo beliefs? Several authors revisit Pueblo ethnographies, oral histories, and other sources to illuminate these connections. For better or worse, Pueblo archaeologists have always mapped the present onto the past, assuming important correlates between pre-Hispanic patterns and those observed during the modern period. Chapters in this volume bypass earlier debates about drawing such parallels (cf. Upham 1989) and go well beyond simple direct-historical frameworks. Building on his earlier work with metaphors (Ortman 2000b), Ortman (in chapter 5) outlines a novel approach in his exploration of modern Tewa religious terminology and practice. He demonstrates how it is possible to examine the "content of religious discourses that are no longer lived" through the examination of conceptual metaphors. He draws distinctions between the origins of Tewa religious "discourse" in the Mesa Verde region and modern concepts that are revealed through linguistic structure, as revealed between the metaphorical referents of "the community as a garden" versus the "community as a bowl." These distinctions intimate important religious divergences in the emergence of modern Tewa communities.

Bernardini (in chapter 10) examines the transformational aspects of Hopi history in the Western Pueblo area in light of late pre-Hispanic period religious experience. Following a trajectory established in his previous recent research (Bernardini 2005), he advocates a mode of inquiry by which we infer religious practice and belief through new comparative analysis of historic and modern oral knowledge and archaeological evidence. Citing Wylie's (1989) clever notion of "tacking" between queries and evidence, he seeks to illuminate the late pre-Hispanic period origins of two central Hopi religious frameworks. He outlines a viable scenario for the religious divergences of fourteenth-century (and earlier) traditions that eventually came together on the Hopi mesas by the contact period. As an alternative to mapping Hopi "history" onto the archaeological record, he deftly "tacks" between oral knowledge, historic patterns, and archaeological evidence.

Practice, Performance, and Meaning

Painted pots and plazas were actively engaged by people—as such these and other materialities were cues of religious experience and action (Mithen 1998; Renfrew 2004). How was religion experienced, and what were the social contexts of religious action? Several chapters examine the contexts of religious practice in the thirteenth through fifteenth centuries. By context, we mean both the ways in which ideology is expressed through ritual practice and use of material culture, and the organizational settings in which these activities were performed (from households to entire villages). Chamberlin (in chapter 7) examines the performative aspects of Pueblo ceremonialism in the Salinas Pueblo area in New Mexico. He links changes in plaza space and configuration to changes in the theatrical control of events by religious leaders. The movement of public ceremonial events from "near-phase" to "far-phase" spaces by the early fourteenth century reflects for him a deeper shift in the social orchestration of religious ideologies. In these new settings, specific individuals came to "influence the communication of" religious concepts through their "practical mastery" of ceremonial performance in these much larger performance spaces. Van Keuren in his chapter also examines the broader topic of knowledge production and control as part of the religious experience in the late pre-Hispanic period.

The semantics of Pueblo ideologies are complexly imbued within the material record in imagery on painted pottery and other media, the design of architectural spaces, and the residues of ritual activities. How do we infer the meaning of ideological movements through these contexts and other lines of evidence? With the topics of meaning and knowledge in mind, several chapter authors explore cognitive approaches as a means for expanding our analyses of religious ideologies. Their efforts have included innovative studies of metaphorical expression, comparative work with linguistic structures and graphic behavior, and analyses of the structural execution of decorative media. As part of this, the authors assess hermeneutic and phenomenological approaches and their utility for understanding Ancestral Pueblo ritual landscapes, painted media, and other material evidence. Munson (in chapter 6) explores the visual dimensions of rock art in the Rio Grande area by the late pre-Hispanic period, and specifically the content, design, and "proxemics" of both rockshelter and open-air sites. She demonstrates that with the appearance of new religious concepts by the 1300s, rock art in the northern Rio Grande became an increasingly important and more exclusive mode of religious expression. The placement of etched images in increasingly sacred localities that were repeatedly visited and transformed over time speaks to the same social paradoxes between public and private religious experience that others in the volume note (see Chamberlin, this volume; Glowacki, this volume; Newsome and Hays-Gilpin, this volume; Van Keuren, this volume). Newsome and Hays-Gilpin (in chapter 8) outline a phenomenological approach to understanding visual changes in mural painting during the late pre-Hispanic period. They suggest that changes in mural design and content from the pre- to postmigration periods were tied to the emergence of different embodiments (as "cultural subjects") of Pueblo religious ideals and worldviews. As they put it, new modes of mural painting and presentation reflected—as visual experience and "spectatorship"—new "ways of thinking, being" in the Pueblo world.

Here, they go well beyond the reading of icons, identifying the deeper layers of meaning that pertain to how murals were perceived and seen in the past.

The appearance and spread of religious ideologies played out at a variety of scales, but they are most archaeologically discernible at a regional scale. Thus, our historical reconstructions of religious ideologies in the Pueblo Southwest can overlook the relationship between local versus regional patterns and the real possibility that widespread ideologies were modified and politically manipulated at local scales. What do intra-regional, even intra-village patterns, imply about the transformation of widespread ideologies? Have our models overemphasized pan-southwestern continuities? What were the organizational and institutional frameworks structuring religious practice and how did they vary? Chapters by Hays-Gilpin and Newsome, Van Keuren, Pauketat, and others examine the extent to which religious ideologies coherently spread across the Southwest and how they were incorporated into the existing ceremonies, practices, and beliefs of local groups.

Another dimension to this topic is the social consequences and contingencies of religious change. Nearly all of the chapters link ideological developments to other social dimensions of Pueblo societies, from social cooperation to conflict, the emergence of social inequality, to the role of ideological movements as pulls and pushes in cycles of aggregation and abandonment. Recent literature has popularized the notion that rituals and other religious activities that emerge in this period integrated Pueblo communities, both at local and at pan-southwestern scales. There is substantial merit in this interpretation, based in part on the ceremonialism of historic and modern Pueblos, and in particular, the ritual dimensions of Katsina ideology (Dozier 1970). Yet, at the same time, factionalism and other social processes acted to undermine broader social, communal, and even religious ideals. These occasionally splintered whole communities in recent Pueblo history (Levy 1992; Whiteley 1998). Van Keuren (in chapter 9) examines the production of red ware pottery and plaza spaces at early fourteenth-century villages in the Silver Creek area. Based both on the diversification of pottery styles, especially Fourmile Polychrome copies, and the inconsistency of large plaza construction, Van Keuren argues that the circulation of religious "knowledge" was increasingly fractured. In the Silver Creek area, a highly communal Pueblo community was never achieved, despite the expansion of large public ceremonial spaces and the increased access to painted bowls with religious iconography. Katsina religion, the Southwestern Cult, or other religious ideologies may have emphasized communal well-being in some ideal sense, but the archaeological evidence points to competition for bodies of knowledge, perhaps resulting in factionalism. Broader religious traditions were thus experienced and acted upon very differently in these local settings.

Networks of Interaction

The material residues of Ancestral Pueblo religion also reflect composites of nodes and networks of social relationships, exchanges, knowledge sharing, and passages of peoples and ideas. At a fundamental level, people in the past came "to know the world through a process of enculturation . . . [a] personal coming-into-being" (Renfrew 2004:24). From then on, all cultural knowledge is in play, transformed by the networks of information exchange and interaction that continuously reshape the contexts of religious expression and performance. One can also think about religious belief and practice as complex biographies of social, economic, and political networks of engagement (Renfrew 2004). Religion contributes to creating these complex networks—"engagements" between people and their material settings. Religious change during the late pre-Hispanic period is thus very much a matter of changing scales of social interaction, exchange, and modes of transfer. Some of this occurred at large-scale, pan-southwestern scales; others pertain to the social dynamics within individual settlements and the extent that individuals or households participated unequally in the ritual manifestation of religious ideologies. By working toward a better understanding of this variability, we can not only improve our knowledge of individual pueblos but also comprehensively delineate the fundamental differences in religious practice and belief between Eastern and Western Pueblo landscapes and how they developed historically. In the final chapter of the volume (chapter 11), Pauketat weaves together concepts of social practice, networks, and performance and reminds readers that these discussions involve "thickly entangled relationships" that are continuously engaged through the materiality of religious experiences and practices. He characterizes religious experience—from an archaeological perspective—as something to be understood as connected to large-scale processes through the collective, complex raveling and unraveling of "bundled fields" of social engagement, contact, and action.

Summary

The late pre-Hispanic period marked a seminal period of change in Pueblo religious expression. This historical transition was intricately tied to the departure of groups from the Four Corners area and elsewhere, the changing relational networks with Mesoamerica and other geographical peripheries, and the postmigration historical processes through which large plaza-oriented villages appeared throughout the Southwest. New materialities of religious expression and belief—seen archaeologically through ritual activities, architecture, ceremonial performance, and forms of painted pots and other communicative visual arts—mark the emergence of the modern Pueblo world. It is impossible to investigate this period (or any other in the Pueblo past) without examining historical changes through the lens of religious expression. This requires both increased attention to how people viewed their worlds and how they acted within them, and also compels us to write archaeological narratives that examine both large-scale processes and small-scale, local patterns. The archaeological record of religious expression (painted objects, ritual debris, and ceremonial architecture) embodies entangled networks and webs of social actions (knowing, learning, and doing). As Pauketat notes in the final chapter, Pueblo people made their world through religion, and to study religion as archaeologists, we must assume that in this "making," there is no way to completely separate daily life from religion. As he so succinctly puts it, Puebloan history is religion. The religious beliefs that spread across the Southwest by the fourteenth century were not static entities; they were made, (mis)understood, and transformed through a multiplicity of historical processes. By working toward a better understanding of these processes, we can not only improve our knowledge of individual pueblos but also comprehensively delineate the fundamental differences in religious practice and belief between Western and Eastern Pueblo landscapes and how they developed.

Pueblo Religion and the Mesoamerican Connection
Randall H. McGuire

The late thirteenth-century religious ideologies that transformed the Pueblo world sprang from far-ranging beliefs, rituals, and social relations inextricably linked to Mesoamerica (see figure 2.1). Indigenous peoples living in the Southwest of the United States and the Northwest of México clearly share many aspects of cosmology, iconography, belief, and ritual with peoples living in Mesoamerica. But Pueblo religion also differs from Mesoamerican religion in many ways. It did not diffuse north in neat packages of cosmology and ritual, nor did Mesoamerican missionaries, traders, or conquerors impose a new religion on Pueblo peoples. We need more complex models of this relationship that consider the historical dynamics of similarity and difference between the Pueblos and Mesoamerica.

The Pueblo world at the end of the thirteenth century participated in religious changes that occurred across the Southwest/Northwest and that involved multiple archaeological traditions, including Casas Grandes and the Salado. These new religions of the fourteenth century also integrated Mesoamerican beliefs and rituals that had entered the Southwest/Northwest hundreds of years before. Thus, our analyses also need to historically contextualize Pueblo religion within the Southwest/Northwest.

Here, I unpack the historical and spatial relationships that created the Mesoamerican connection to Pueblo religion. My approach challenges analyses that treat the Southwest/Northwest and Mesoamerica as bounded units and that paint Mesoamerican ideologies with too broad of a brush. I instead focus on historically shifting networks of social and cultural relationships. The starting point of the analysis is a review of the Mesoamerican elements in contemporary Pueblo religion and a reflection on how the Pueblos differ from Mesoamericans. The history

Figure 2.1. Map of the Southwest/Northwest and Mesoamerica.

about how these elements came to be, that is, the history of the Mesoamerican connection, occupies the bulk of the chapter. Finally, I examine how the Pueblo Katsina religion differed from and resembled the other major religious, ideological movements of the late thirteenth century at Casas Grandes and in the Salado religion (also known as the Southwestern Cult).

Approaches to Studying Pueblo Religion

Archaeologists have often produced explanations for Pueblo religion that are both too specific and too general. Specific explanations tend to focus on unique aspects of Pueblo religion and on religious variation between the Pueblos. They usually acknowledge Mesoamerican components but they rarely look further south than Casas Grandes (Adams 1991; Adams and LaMotta 2006; Crown 1994). Broad similarities between Mesoamerican and Pueblo religions entrance other researchers (Mathiowetz 2009a, 2009b; Schaafsma 1999, 2000, 2001; Taube 2001). Their analyses of iconography, cosmology, and ritual leap great expanses of time and space as they take specifics from Olmec, Aztec, or Maya religion as representing all of Mesoamerican belief, and they then find parallels in the Southwest/Northwest. For example, Taube (2001:18) equates Post-Classic Mexican wind temples, such as the Caracol at Chichén Itza, to Pueblo kivas simply because both structural types are round. These scholars tend to favor event-oriented explanations that populate the Southwest/Northwest with Mesoamerican traders, missionaries, and rulers. A multiscalar, relational approach suggests that the Southwest/Northwest and Mesoamerica were both more connected and less connected than either specific or general explanations suggest and that the nature and degree of this connection varied greatly across time and space (see also Lekson 2009).

Scholars often have treated the Southwest/Northwest and Mesoamerica as bounded units that exchanged cultural traits. This view structures archaeological thinking in negative ways (McGuire et al. 1994). By defining their objects of study as categorical units, archaeologists do not allow for the ebb and flow of people, things, and ideas in time and space. Cultural traits reduce everything to equivalent units. Thus, warrior twins, metaphors of wind and breath, copper bells, masked dancers, and pole-climbing rituals all become equivalent markers of the Mesoamerican connection. Yet these things significantly differ in their roles, impacts, and connotations for society, culture, and change. Societies may share cultural traits but the lived experiences of these traits may be quite different. From a relational perspective, such categorical thinking is counterproductive. A relational approach does not attempt to reduce our understanding of the Mesoamerican connection and its role in Pueblo religion to a specific cause such as migration or trade. Rather, it asks how relations among actors and societies constructed and remade this connection (see also Pauketat, this volume; Plog, this volume).

The Mesoamerican connection with Pueblo religion involved relations at a macro scale that stretched from the Yucatán to Taos and at a regional scale from Casas Grandes to Hopi. Yet in the end, real people made this transformation in their local communities, in the world that they knew through their particular experiences.

What Is Mesoamerican About Pueblo Religion and What Is Not

At the end of the sixteenth century, the first Spanish settlers called the Pueblo world *Nuevo México* because it reminded them of *Mēxihco*, the land of the Mexica or Aztecs (Hammond and Rey 1966:141). Like the Spanish friars, twentieth-century Pueblo ethnographers observed numerous parallels between Pueblo religion and Mesoamerican beliefs (Broda 2004). These parallels occurred in iconography, cosmology, metaphors, and rituals (see table 2.1) (Parsons 1939:1016–1025).

Some contemporary scholars link these parallels to the worship of Tláloc and Quetzalcóatl, the feathered serpent. Polly Schaafsma (1999: 165) argues that the Katsina religion is the northernmost manifestation of the Mesoamerican rain god, Tláloc. She proposes that Katsinas per se derived from Mesoamerican concepts that integrated the spirits of ancestors with natural forces in order to transform the deceased into rainmakers (Schaafsma 1999:184). The feathered serpent appears as a puppet in Pueblo kiva ceremonies related to the Katsina religion. In Mesoamerica, Quetzalcóatl cosmology included notions of fertility and regeneration, the legitimation of political power, underworld waters, earth and sky, militarism associated with the planet Venus, human sacrifice, and control of water-bearing winds (Philips et al. 2006; Schaafsma 2001; Taube 2001). In the Southwest/Northwest, Pueblo peoples associated feathered and horned serpents with the unity of the earth and sky as manifest in floods, rain, earthquakes, and landslides. Especially in the Rio Grande, Pueblos associated horned serpents with Venus and warfare. Human sacrifice occurs in Pueblo myths with the killing of twin children to appease the feathered serpent.

The similarities between Pueblo and Mesoamerican religions, however, existed in very dissimilar social contexts. The scale of Puebloan towns pales in comparison with even minor Mesoamerican cities that had monumental architecture and tens of thousands of people. In

Table 2.1. Some parallels between Pueblo and Mesoamerican religion.

Iconography and Cosmology

Warrior Twins associated with the planet Venus	(Riley 2005:10; Thompson 2007)
Color-directional symbolism	(Schaafsma 1999:175)
Multitiered cosmos with a watery underworld	(Schaafsma 1999; Taube 2001)
Cyclic destruction and rebirth of worlds	(Parsons 1939)
Ritual maintains the cycle of the world	(Parsons 1939)
Migration histories begin with emergence from a previous world	(Parsons 1939)
The Flower World	(Hays-Gilpin 2006; Hays-Gilpin and Hill 2000)
Feathered or horned serpents associated with fertility, floods, and earthquakes	(Philips et al. 2006)
Young sun god who would later be called Montezuma	(Mathiowetz 2009b)
Common astronomy and star lore	(Riley 2005:88–89)
Salt woman and Aztec goddess Huixtocihuatl	(Broda 2004:283–284)

Metaphors

Serpent mouths stand for cave openings and water issues from both	(Taube 2001)
Clouds stand for ancestors	(Schaafsma 1999; Taube 2001)
Cruciforms stand for planet Venus and associated with warfare	(Schaafsma 2001:147; Thompson 2007)
Flowers, butterflies, and parrots for the Flower World	(Hays-Gilpin 2006:67–68)
Mountains associated with watery underworld	(Schaafsma 1999:173; Taube 2001)
Wind as source of rain and equation of wind and breath	(Taube 2001)

(continued)

Table 2.1. *Continued*

Water jars stand for rain	(Taube 2001:104)
Cotton as clouds	(Broda 2004:290)
Rituals	
New Fire Ceremony	(Parsons 1939:1021)
Swallowing of sticks and handling of snakes	(Parsons 1939:1020)
Pole-climbing rituals	(Beals 1944)
Ritual contests, racing, and ball games	(Parsons 1939:1017)
Blessing with cornmeal and water	(Parsons 1939:1022)
Prayer offerings (sticks, feathers, and gum paper)	(Parsons 1939:1022)
Human sacrifice (mythic and symbolic in Pueblos)	(Parsons 1939)
Ritual clowns or jesters	(Parsons 1939:1019)
Masked dances to bring rain	(Schaafsma 1999; Taube 2001)
Priests with esoteric knowledge	(Parsons 1939:1020)

Pueblo society, everyone farmed while in Mesoamerica; peasants specialized in farming, artisans in crafts, merchants in trade, and warriors in conflict. Noble elites ruled over Mesoamerican cities supported by castes of priests, merchants, and warriors. Elite and upper classes lived in palaces and controlled resources and people by force of arms. Iconography and texts served to legitimate elite power. By contrast, Pueblo elites lived in houses that were comparable with everyone else's and elites' power came from the control of ritual knowledge. In Mesoamerica, hierarchy was overt, while in the Pueblos a constant tension between egalitarianism and ranking maintained more communal societies (McGuire and Saitta 1996).

Each region actualized parallel rituals and metaphors in very different ways. Both peoples believed they must perform rituals to maintain the cycle of the world. In Mesoamerican rituals, priests dragged war captives to the tops of pyramids and cut their hearts out. In Pueblo ritual, Katsinas danced in the plazas. All people living in a pueblo participated in the Katsina religion and usually all were initiated in the Katsina sodality. In Mesoamerica, elites maintained the cults of the state, while the common people had their own rituals (Gonlin and Lohse 2007). In both contexts, priests controlled esoteric ritual and cosmological knowledge. But in Pueblo society those elites lived humbly like everyone else. In Mesoamerica, priests formed one of three or four elite classes living in opulence, and common people gave them great deference. The Post-Classic Quetzalcóatl cult legitimated elite power, while the rituals of the Katsina religion redistributed food and sacred clowns ridiculed hubris.

We thus have a paradox. We can identify a profound degree of shared cosmology, iconography, metaphor, and ritual between the two regions. As Schaafsma (1999:165) said, "The Southwest and Mesoamerica are undeniably and inextricably linked." Yet the societies of the two regions remain qualitatively different. Ben Nelson's (1995) comparison of Chaco Canyon and La Quemada suggests that the Southwest and Mesoamerica are like two languages with many cognates, but different grammars and syntaxes. The task before us is to ask how the making and remaking of these cognates contributed to the advent of the Katsina religion.

We can start to answer this question by realizing that the parallels between the two areas have varied histories and origins. North American Indian religions share a wide range of iconographies and beliefs (Hirschfelder 1999). Peoples all across the continent use serpent symbolism. Color-directional symbolism has an equally wide distribution. The twins of Mesoamerica and the Southwest/Northwest find parallels in the twins of Iroquois origin. Many western North American cultures begin their history with their emergence from a previous world. These symbols and beliefs clearly transcend both Mesoamerica and the Southwest/Northwest and must reflect a more widespread commonality on the continent as a whole (Wilcox 2008). There can be little question that Mesoamerican peoples first cultivated the corn, beans, and squash upon which Pueblo peoples later built their economies. We would expect that these crops arrived with beliefs and icons related to their cultivation. The Spanish conquest also led to similarities between Pueblo and Mesoamerican religions. Pueblo Catholicism and rituals such as the Matachine Dance, have Spanish origins. Mesoamerican Indians who came with the Spaniards probably inspired some Pueblo rituals such as pole climbing (Beals 1944). The historical question is how the Mesoamerican parallels in Pueblo religion came together from the beginnings of agriculture to the intrusion of Spanish conquerors.

History of the Mesoamerican Connection

For more than a millennium, the social relations that defined the Southwest/Northwest and Mesoamerica ebbed and flowed over the landscape. The most dynamic spaces in this process were West México and the Chalchihuites. West México stretched along the Pacific coast from Michoacán Sinaloa and the Chalchihuites Tradition occurred in Durango, Zacatecas, and Jalisco (figure 2.1) (Williams 2009). This discussion approaches the history of this ebb and flow from a southern perspective, looking at processes in Mesoamerica and how they reverberated to the north. I have used the Mesoamerican chronology to organize the discussion beginning with the Formative, followed by the Classic, Epiclassic, and Post-Classic Periods.

Formative Beginnings

In Mesoamerica, the conjunction of agriculture, pottery making, and village life marks the Formative Period. The spread of agriculture precedes this concurrence by almost 2,000 years. It is several hundred years after a full Formative pattern appears that it is possible to distinguish developments in the Southwest/Northwest from developments in the Chalchihuites and West México.

Several researchers link the northward spread of Uto-Aztecan languages to the adoption of agriculture and the spread of shared cosmologies, symbols and rituals (Gregory and Wilcox 2007; Hays-Gilpin 2006; Hays-Gilpin and Hill 2000; LeBlanc 2008; Mabry et al. 2008). Many of the most fundamental parallels between Mesoamerican and Pueblo religions may spring from this linguistic linkage. Kelley Hays-Gilpin and Jane Hill (2000; Hays-Gilpin 2006) use linguistic analyses to suggest that Flower World cosmology came to the Southwest/Northwest with proto-Uto Aztecan speakers and agriculture.

In the Bajio region of México (figure 2.1), the Formative begins by 250 BC at the site of Chupícuaro (Braniff 1974; Florance 1985; J. Kelley 1976). Chupícuaro and its derivatives spread first westward into West México and then northward into Guanajuato, Jalisco, Zacatecas, Durango, and then later—leaping a gap of arid and rugged territory—into Arizona and New Mexico, edging finally into Utah, Colorado, Chihuahua, and Sonora. J. Charles Kelley (1966) and Beatriz Braniff (1974) have traced striking ceramic similarities from Chupícuaro through the Chalchihuites to the Hohokam. Foster (1982) identifies a continuum in brown ware styles running from Zacatecas, to Durango, to Chihuahua, and to New Mexico. These parallels include red-on-brown decoration, common vessel forms, and quartered designs with bilateral symmetry. In West México, the development of early village life, pottery making, and agriculture look much like the Pioneer Period Hohokam. In southern Sinaloa, archaeologists date the first formative tradition from 250 BC to AD 500 (I. Kelley 1938). The pottery has broad-lined, crude red designs that artisans painted in quarters with bilateral symmetry over a buff slip.

The Classic Period and the Hohokam, Mogollon, and Ancestral Pueblo

Great urban centers, including Monte Alban, and Teotihuacan dominated the highland Mesoamerican Early Classic Period (AD 200 to 600). Politics, economics, ideology, and culture all flowed from these centers. In the Southwest/Northwest, during the same period the distinctive Hohokam, Mogollon, and Ancestral Pueblo traditions developed.

During the Classic Period, West México had its own trajectory of cultural development (López Austin and López Luján 2001:86–88, 123). By the 600s, West Mexican towns had planned mound-plaza complexes oriented to the cardinal directions and domestic residences clustered into courtyard groups (Weigand 2007). Excavations of towns and shaft tombs reveal elaborate figurine styles, effigy vessels, molded spindle whorls, red-on-brown or red-on-buff pottery, and shell jewelry dominated by bracelets. In Durango, Zacatecas, and Jalisco, the beginnings of the Chalchihuites culture appear between AD 300 to 500 with villages and towns and red-on-buff and red-on-brown pottery (Hers 2001).

Hohokam aesthetics with their use of anthropomorphic and zoomorphic figures on ceramics and shells and their ceramic figurines differed markedly from other areas of the southwestern United States (Meighen 1999; McGuire and Villalpando 2007). Both the iconography and style of these images greatly resemble the iconography and style of West México and Chalchihuites art (A. Johnson 1958). Shell jewelry manufacture (especially shell bracelets), the use of ball courts, and effigy vessels also connect the Hohokam with West México. Patricia Carot and Marie-Areti Hers (2008; Carot 2001) have proposed that the Hohokam migrated from Michoacán to Arizona.

The dearth of these parallels from pre-900 Mogollon and Ancestral Pueblo traditions suggests that the Hohokam were related to West México in ways the other "southwestern traditions" were not (McGuire and Villalpando 2007). When viewed from the north, the Hohokam look like an island of Mesoamerican influence, but when viewed from the south they become the tip of a peninsula. In Sonora, recent research has documented Trincheras and Huatabampo traditions linking the Hohokam to West México (figure 2.1) (Carpenter 1996, 2008; McGuire and Villalpando 2007).

Before 900, social relations in México and the southwestern United States did not break down into two parts—Mesoamerica and the Southwest/Northwest—but instead into three social webs (figure 2.1). These would include (1) an Early Classic Mesoamerican core developing in the highlands of central México, the Gulf coast lowlands, and the coast of Oaxaca; (2) a West México and Chalchihuites web that links cultures along the Gulf of California north of Michoacán, through the highlands of Durango, Zacatecas, and Jalisco, on to the Sonoran Desert of Sonora and Arizona; and (3) a Southwest/Northwest that included the Ancestral Pueblos of the Colorado Plateau with the Mogollon in the mountains of Arizona, New Mexico, Sonora, and Chihuahua (figure 2.1). Few, if any, of the things that make the Hohokam part of West México (iconography, ball courts, shell bracelets, etc.) ended up in the post-thirteenth-century Pueblo world. The linkages that connected

Mesoamerica to the Pueblos did not become apparent until the Mesoamerican Post-Classic Period.

The Epiclassic, the Post-Classic and the Hohokam, Mimbres, and Chaco Canyon

The Epiclassic, or Late Classic, Period of Mesoamerica spanned the time between the fall of Teotihuacan around 600/700 and the beginnings of the Post-Classic ca. 900 (Kowalski and Kristan-Grahm 2007; Smith and Berdan 2003). By the end of this period, Mesoamerican elements began to show up in Chaco Canyon, the Mimbres, and the Sedentary Period Hohokam.

During the Epiclassic, Mesoamerica expanded, becoming more economically interconnected, more politically divided, and more cosmologically uniform. The Chalchihuites centers of La Quemada and Alta Vista in Zacatecas were the northernmost points of this expansion. Toward the conclusion of this period, the growth of the Aztatlán tradition drew West México more firmly into the Mesoamerican economic, religious, and political orbit. The Aztatlán tradition was part of a pan-Mesoamerican Mixteca-Puebla horizon that marks the emergence of a reorganized Mesoamerica in the Post-Classic Period.

Classic Period trade had focused on the great urban centers of Teotihuacan, Monte Alban, and the major Mayan cities. In the Epiclassic, trade became decentralized and it thrived in the peripheries (López Austin and López Lujan 2001:22; Smith and Berdan 2003:4). In the Mesoamerican core, a merchant class developed commercialized marketplaces. The volume of trade increased with a greater diversity of trade goods, including more bulk commodities. Late in the Epiclassic, copper objects (mainly bells) from West México entered the trade networks of Mesoamerica and the Southwest/Northwest. Turquoise from the Chalchihuites region and the Southwest/Northwest also became a notable commodity that reached all the way to the Maya lowlands (Weigand 2008).

A proliferation of small polities and city-states grew from the collapse of the urban centers (B. Nelson 2000, 2006). These centers of power were diverse and contained ethnically defined classes of rulers, merchants, priests, warriors, and commoners. Artisans migrated between these centers to serve the needs of the new elites and this movement produced a uniform set of prestige goods and symbols that identified and legitimated the elite. Nomadic peoples and agriculturalists from the north, the famed Chichimecs, entered core Mesoamerica. Increased levels of violence, warfare, and human sacrifice accompanied Epiclassic political instability and change.

Epiclassic elites legitimated their position, power, and conquests through the worship of Quetzalcóatl. The cosmology of Quetzalcóatl employed metaphors of watery underworlds, rain, breath, wind, sacrifice, and regeneration to speak of transformation, regeneration, and fertility (Taube 2001). It incorporated militaristic symbols and its priests practiced human sacrifice. Quetzalcóatl conveyed leaders from the underworld to positions of power in this world and during the Epiclassic and Post-Classic; elites across Mesoamerica mobilized the Quetzalcóatl cult to provide mythological charters for the political order (Ringle 2004; Ringle et al. 1998; Sugiyama 2005). Elites used war, trade, and migration to spread the cult, and they adorned their cities with Quetzalcóatl shrines to establish pilgrimage routes.

Many archaeologists argue that a Mixteca-Puebla Horizon Style marks the transition from the Epiclassic to Post-Classic Periods (ca. 900). Some archaeologists contend that Mesoamerican traders brought this Horizon style to the Southwest/Northwest (Di Peso 1974; Foster 1999; J. Kelly 1966; Riley 2005). Scholars call the West Mexican regional manifestation of this style the Aztatlán Tradition (Williams 2009) (see figure 2.2). Michael Smith (Smith and Heath-Smith 1980; M. Smith 2003, 2007) noted that the concept of a Mixteca-Puebla Style lumps together several separate phenomena that overlap imperfectly in time and space.

Boone and Smith (2003) distinguish between iconography and style. Iconography refers to symbols or icons that occurred together while style references how craftspeople produced that iconography. Within the Mixteca-Puebla Horizon, they identify an Early Post-Classic International Symbol Set that dates from the tenth to the thirteenth centuries. This iconography occurs principally on polychrome ceramics exchanged in regional trade. The symbol set includes representations of Quetzalcóatl and the stepped-fret design (see figure 2.3). Boone and Smith identify the Early Post-Classic International Symbol Set as the iconography of the Quetzalcóatl cult. After the thirteenth

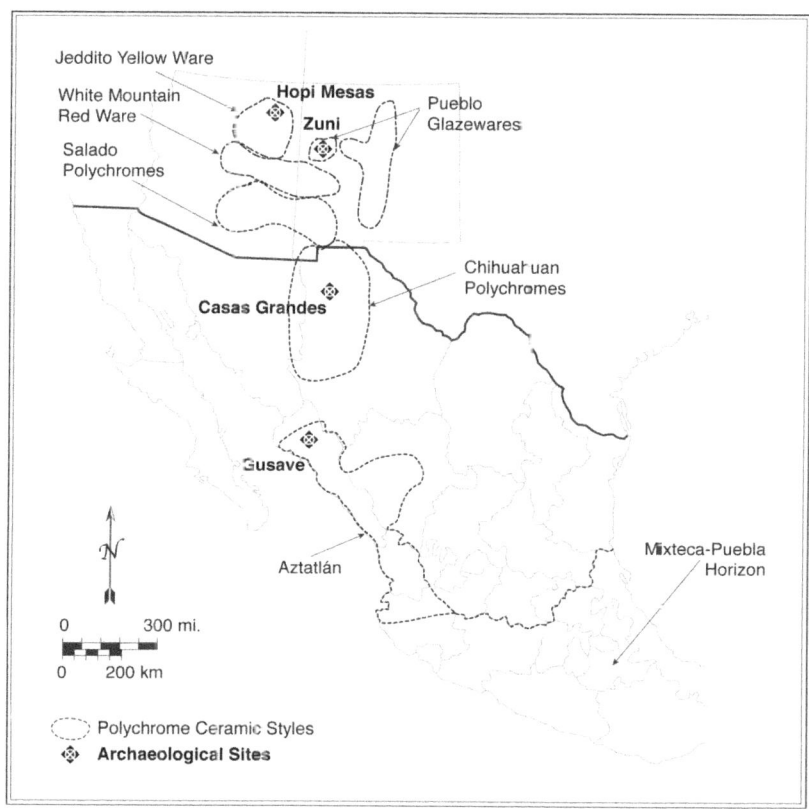

Figure 2.2. Map of late Post-Classic polychrome traditions in the Southwest/Northwest and Mesoamerica.

century, a new Late Post-Classic International Symbol Set appeared with calendric and codex symbols. Mesoamerican artisans executed both of these symbol sets in the Post-Classic International Style. This style incorporated stocky, flat figures with stiff lines and almost geometric, crisp edges (figure 2.3).

The Epiclassic witnessed the massive expansion and growth of the Chalchihuites centers of Alta Vista and La Quemada in Zacatecas (Hers 2001; B. Nelson 1997). These were Mesoamerican cities with ball courts, pyramids, human sacrifices, and ancestor veneration (Nelson et al. 1992; Pérez et al 2008). Hers (2001) argues that Post-Classic rituals of human sacrifice, skull racks, colonnades, and chacmools originated

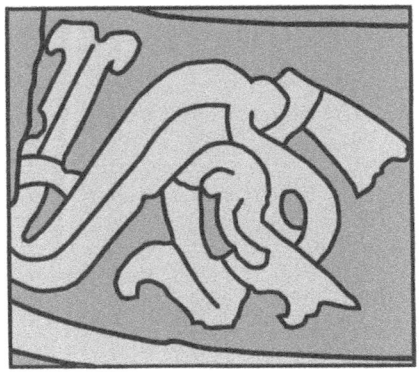

Feathered Serpent and Step Fret Design in
Early Post-Classic International Symbol Set

Codex Bodley – Late Post-Classic International Symbol Set

Figure 2.3. Examples of the Early Post-Classic International Symbol Set and of the Late Post-Classic International Symbol Set.

here and spread south; she also believes that when agriculturalists abandoned the region around 900, they traveled south into the core as invading Chichimecs. J. Charles Kelley (1976) maintained that the Chalchihuites Culture survived in Durango until the fourteenth century but more recent investigations suggest that the Chalchihuites red-on-buff sequence ends at 900 but that there is an Aztatlán development (on a Chalchihuites base) that probably goes up to 1300. Clear evidence exists to connect the Chalchihuites regional centers with Mesoamerica, West México, and the Southwest/Northwest. The icon of the humpbacked flute player originated in the southwestern United States and spread to the Chalchihuites (Hers 2001). Southwest turquoise occurred in Chalchihuites along with West Mexican copper bells and scarlet macaws.

Many archaeologists interpret the appearance of the Aztatlán Tradition (ca. 900) along the west coast as the Mesoamericanization of West México (López Austin and López Luján 2001:86–88, 123). It first appeared south of Guadalajara at around 850. It spread north integrating previously unrelated areas in West México until reaching Gusave in northern Sinaloa by the tenth century. It persisted in northern Sinaloa until the abandonment of Gusave in 1350 (Carpenter 1996, 2008). Polychrome ceramics decorated with the Early Post-Classic International Symbol Set marked the appearance of the Aztatlán Tradition. Tláloc and Quetzalcóatl appear on rock art (Mendiola 2006: 35–36). By the thirteenth century, craftspeople executed these symbols in a Post-Classic International Style. West Mexican artisans used the pseudo-cloisonné technique on pottery and on sandstone backs for iron pyrite mirrors. Copper objects (principally bells) and metallurgy spread from West México to other parts of Mesoamerica.

The Aztatlán Tradition did not spread into the Sonoran Desert, leaving what had been the West Mexican Huatabampo, Trincheras, and Hohokam Traditions un-Mesoamericanized (Carpenter 1996, 2008). These Sonoran traditions became more integrated into networks of cultural and economic relations extending north and west to the Pueblos and Casas Grandes. Thus, after 900, for the first time, two distinct cultural networks existed: the Southwest/Northwest and Mesoamerica.

The iconography and cosmology of the Mesoamerican Epiclassic reached the Southwest/Northwest by the end of the tenth century.

With it came scarlet macaws, copper bells, pseudo-cloisonné mirror backs, and cocoa from a Mesoamericanized West México. Scarlet macaws live in the Gulf Coast lowlands of México but small populations survive today in West México (Wilcox 2008). The iconography and objects appeared most commonly among the Phoenix Basin Hohokam, in the Mimbres and at Chaco Canyon.

The Hohokam remained linked to West México at the end of the tenth century. During the Santa Cruz Phase (550–900) the Hohokam looked like a West Mexican tradition with red-on-buff pottery, shell jewelry (especially bracelets), ball courts, platform mounds, bird and snake motifs, humped-back flute players, and thick-billed parrots. A Santa Cruz red-on-buff sherd from Snaketown has the earliest representation of a horned or feathered serpent in the Southwest/Northwest (Haury 1976:235). During the Sacaton Phase (900–1100), additional items from the now-Mesoamericanized West México, including copper bells, iron pyrite mirror backs, and ceramic vessels, appear. Zooarchaeologists have also identified the remains of dozens of scarlet macaws. Hohokam style, however, remained similar to pre-Aztatlán West México and the Chalchihuites; it did not reflect the Post-Classic International Style.

By 900, Mimbres people were building pueblos with open plazas and hundreds of rooms. Most of the evidence for Epiclassic Mesoamerican iconography comes from Mimbres Classic ceramics (dating 1000–1150). These vessels displayed the first solid evidence for feathered serpents and masked dancers in the Southwest/Northwest. They also portrayed macaws or parrots, possible human sacrifice, twins, Tláloc, and other icons that may reference Mesoamerica. The presence of shell bracelets and fish imagery indicates that Mimbres people actually visited the west coast of México (Jett and Moyle 1986; Wilcox 2008).

Ben Nelson (2006) summarizes the evidence for Mesoamerican contacts at Chaco Canyon. He suggests that Chacoan developments were synchronous with the broad outline of cycles of change in north México. Most of the parallels he identifies, including shell bracelets, roads, colonnades, and copper bells, originate from West México or Chalchihuites. Residue analysis indicates that Chacoan cylinder vessels contained cacao, a drink consumed by Mesoamerican elites (Crown and Hurst 2009). This cacao may have originated from the Gulf Coast of México or more probably from Colima and Nayarit in West México. Nelson notes that archaeologists cannot trace any of these things to specific Mesoamerican empires or capitals. He suggests that Chacoan notions of power and legitimacy may have been cloaked in references to distant places, landscapes, and celestial phenomena.

At the end of the tenth century, some elements of the Early Post-Classic International Symbol Set, specifically the feathered serpent and step fret designs, appear in the Southwest/Northwest. We do not, however, see the Post-Classic International Style. Hohokam style most closely resembles that of pre-Aztatlán West México and the Chalchihuites and the same might be said for the iconographic painting on Mimbres Classic pottery. Copper bells, pseudo-cloisonné mirror backs, parrots, and possibly bracelets indicate trade with West México. Scarlet macaws and cocoa may demonstrate connections that reach directly or indirectly to core Mesoamerica but these things also occurred in West México. It might be tempting to propose that these developments represent Chalchihuites rulers, priests, and artisans migrating to the Southwest/Northwest, even as some of their Chichimec brethren descend upon core Mesoamerica. I, however, find little proof for this. In each case, we have evidence of in situ development, no evidence of foreign intruders, and the parallels seem too generalized to result from a wholesale importation of cosmology, aesthetics, and artesian skills. Most noteworthy is the absence of the Post-Classic International Style. It seems more likely that emergent Southwest/Northwest elites exploited already existing connections to West México to draw on goods, beliefs, iconographies, and rituals that would legitimate their status. In the Southwest/Northwest, the Early Post-Classic International Symbol Set becomes more apparent and widespread in subsequent developments (Nelson 2006, 2007).

Polychromes, Elites, Migrants, and Cults in the Southwest/Northwest

By the early twelfth century, the regional centers of the Hohokam, Mimbres, and Chaco Canyon were in decline or had been deserted (Wilcox 2008). Over the next 50 to 100 years, the social networks of the Southwest/Northwest reorganized in ways that erased the boundaries between the Hohokam, Mogollon, and Ancestral Pueblo and established new webs of social relations. Archaeologists struggled for years to understand these new webs in terms of cultures or traditions such as the Salado, Casas Grandes, Western Pueblo, or Pueblo IV period but these new networks do not fit easily within such categories (Clark et al. 2008; Gregory and Wilcox 2007; J. Hill et al. 2004; Lekson 2009).

In the late pre-Hispanic period, several polychrome ceramic wares developed that crosscut the black-on-white, red-on-brown, and red-on-buff traditions that had defined the Ancestral Pueblos, Mogollon, and Hohokam (figure 2.2). Chihuahuan Polychromes appeared south of the old Mimbres region. Salado Polychromes occurred in an arc anchored in the Phoenix Basin on the west and rising easterly to the Mogollon Rim and down through the Mimbres area of southern New Mexico. White Mountain Red Ware occurred along the Mogollon Rim. North of the rim, Jeddito Yellow Wares extended from the Little Colorado River to the Hopi mesas. Glaze-ware traditions developed at Zuni and along the Rio Grande in New Mexico. All of these new wares express a rich iconography replete with parrots and other birds, horned serpents, water imagery, butterflies, flowers, the sun, stars, and masked dancers.

Numerous authors link the polychrome traditions to new religions (Adams 1991; Crown 1994; Di Peso 1974; Mathiowetz 2009a, 2009b; Rakita 2009; VanPool and VanPool 2007). Minimally, these religions would include one centered on Casas Grandes, a Salado religion, and the Katsina religion that originated along the upper Little Colorado River and then spread to the Rio Grande. All of these religions incorporated icons from the Early Post-Classic International Symbol Set, most notably feathered or horned serpents. The iconography does not, however, manifest the wholesale adoption of the Post-Classic Quetzalcóatl cult. Rather, it exhibits a convergence of select elements from it, from older Mesoamerican beliefs such as Tláloc, from earlier Southwest/Northwest beliefs, and probably from West Mexican cosmologies as well.

Several common factors mark the reorganization of the Southwest/Northwest at the beginning of the fourteenth century. Trade expanded with a shared set of prestige goods that included turquoise on shell mosaics, conch trumpets, parrots and macaws and their feathers, and copper bells. Whole communities migrated and merged with others to form multiethnic towns that would break apart and lead to more migrations (Bernardini, this volume). Pueblo peoples describe this time in their stories of emergence and the migrations they undertook to find the center place (Lekson 2009). There is evidence for increased violence and warfare, including marks of violence on human bones, fortified communities, vacant buffer zones, icons of warriors, and cruciforms representing Venus (LeBlanc 1999; Nichols and Crown 2008; Schaafsma 2000; M. Thompson 2007).

The Mesoamerican elements of post-thirteenth-century Pueblo religion arrived in the region via many routes, from many sources, and over a time span of more than a millennium. Archaeologists see these movements in the Mesoamerican objects traded north such as copper bells and macaws, and in the turquoise traded south. People seldom trade for goods based solely on their rarity or aesthetic appeal. They develop ritual contexts for the display of these goods and apply formal mechanisms for absorbing new symbols. The Pueblos did this in the creation of the Katsina religion. They did not, however, simply import a Mesoamerican religion but instead created something unique to Pueblo culture. As Beals (1944:248) noted, no ethnographic evidence exists for a Katsina-like religion between the valley of Mexico and the Pueblos.

Making Sense of the Mesoamerican Connection and Regional Transformations

Archaeologists have tried to explain the changes of the late thirteenth-century Southwest/Northwest in terms of migrations, or elite interactions, or the spread of cults or intrusions from Mesoamerica. The resemblance of these changes to transformations in Mesoamerica from the Classic to the Post-Classic suggests a more complex scenario. Before the change, cultural developments centered on large regional centers (in the Southwest, these include Chaco, Sedentary Hohokam and Mimbres; in Classic Period Mesoamerica, they include Teotihuacan and Monte Alban). A period of dislocation, change, and shifting boundaries followed that reorganized social networks. The new sets of relations propagated new political centers and elites, along with new commodities and cults to link and legitimate these power centers and form a greater uniformity across the culture area (B. Nelson 2006). This process in Mesoamerica does not reduce to migration, elites, cults, or long-distance intrusions but rather it arose from the relations among migrations, commerce, conquest, religion, and elites through time and across space.

Mesoamerican-derived rituals, cosmologies, and iconographies provided common threads that ran through Casas Grandes religion, the Salado religion, and the Katsina religion. The three movements, however, wove these threads into different designs and patterns that varied in how much they resembled the patterns of Mesoamerica. They also differed in how these threads wove together other aspects of society and culture in lived experience.

Casas Grandes

Casas Grandes (1250–1450) is the most Mesoamerican of all the archaeological sites in the Southwest/Northwest (Dean and Ravesloot 1993; Di Peso 1974). The community included effigy mounds, elaborate elite burials, two I-shaped ball courts, and many other Mesoamerican architectural features. Chihuahuan Polychromes exhibit a rich and complex iconography that includes many elements of the Early Post-Classic International Symbol Set (Di Peso 1974; Mathiowetz 2009a, 2009b; Rakita 2009; VanPool and VanPool 2007). Moreover, archaeologists have found more Mesoamerican objects, including copper bells, macaws, shells, and ceramics, here than anywhere else in the cultural area. Di Peso (1974) also found evidence of human sacrifice and the ritual use of human bones.

Charles Di Peso (1974) initially proposed that *pochteca* traders from a Mesoamerican sovereignty established Casas Grandes as a trade outpost in the Southwest/Northwest. Other researchers (McGuire 1980; Whalen and Minnis 2001, 2003) have dismissed this interpretation and argued instead that Casas Grandes was a regional center in its own right. I would expect that a Post-Classic outpost of a Mesoamerican polity would directly reflect the symbols and styles of its homeland. Thus, an outpost at Casas Grandes should have the Late Post-Classic International Symbol Set of post-thirteenth-century Mesoamerica executed in the contemporary Post-Classic religious style. Casas Grandes iconography exhibits neither of these things. Mathiowetz (2009a, 2009b) has proposed that elites from West México in northern México established Casas Grandes and introduced the Mesoamerican cosmology of the Flower World, Flower Mountain, and the complex of the sun youth to legitimate their rule. Western Méxican elites are more plausible as founders of Casas Grandes than as agents of a core Mesoamerican polity. Alternatively, a Southwest/Northwest elite at Casas Grandes may have used Mesoamerican beliefs to legitimate their power by references to distant places, landscapes, and celestial phenomena.

Of the three Southwest/Northwest religions, the Casas Grandes religion most closely resembled the Mesoamerican Post-Classic Quetzalcóatl cult. The horned serpent is common in Casas Grandes iconography. The use of this iconography in the context of elite burials connects the Casas Grandes rulers to the horned serpent (Phillips et al. 2006: 241). VanPool and VanPool (2007) hypothesize that Casas Grandes priests embodied the horned serpent to undertake shamanistic journeys between worlds. In Mesoamerica, the Quetzalcóatl cult emphasized the transformation between worlds and the deity conveyed leaders from the underworld to positions of power in this world. Mathiowetz (2009a, 2009b) argues that Casas Grandes cosmology, like that of the Quetzalcóatl cult, incorporated notions of fertility and regeneration, the legitimation of political power, waters of the underworld, earth and sky, militarism, and control of the winds that bring water. Finally, archaeologists have found the clearest evidence of human sacrifice in the Southwest/Northwest at Casas Grandes.

Several analysts suggest that all things Mesoamerican did not enter the Southwest/Northwest through Casas Grandes and that the Salado had their own connections to the south. Ronna Bradley's (1993) analysis of shell jewelry from Casas Grandes indicates that the raw materials originated from West México, while Salado shells came from the coast of Sonora. Victoria Vargas (1995) found that Casas Grandes copper bells differed morphologically from Salado copper bells and suggested that each area got its bells from a different source. VanPool et al. (2006a) argue that the Casas Grandes religion and the Salado religion represented distinct but overlapping developments. Each emphasized different aspects of Mesoamerican cosmology, and practiced different rituals: for example, the horned serpent played a lesser role in the Salado religion than at Casas Grandes. They see masked dancers as the core ritual of the Salado religion in contrast to shamanic journeys within the Casas Grandes.

The Salado Religion

Crown (1994) defined the Salado religion based on her analysis of Salado Polychromes. Kayenta migrants living in settlements along the Mogollon Rim apparently created this polychrome ceramic ware in the 1270s (Clark et al. 2008:3–4). The ceramic ware and Kayenta migrants spread from this area to much of southern Arizona, including the Phoenix and Tonto basins, and to southwest New Mexico. Salado Polychromes incorporate symbols from the Mesoamerican Early Post-Classic International Symbol Set, including horned serpents, the sun and stars, and parrots or macaws. Crown (1994) interprets many designs as indicating masked dancers and suggests that people practiced the religion to ensure fertility and to control the weather. In these ways, the religion resembles the Mesoamerican Post-Classic Quetzalcóatl cult and the Katsina religion.

The largest concentrations of people producing and using Salado Polychromes lived in the Phoenix Basin, the Tonto Basin, the San Pedro River Valley, the upper Gila, the Safford Basin and in the Cliff Phase towns and villages of southwest New Mexico (Clark et al. 2008:14). These people laid out their communities in courtyards that were defined by rooms and walls. In Arizona, they built platform mounds in the largest settlements. In these communities, archaeologists find evidence for elite residences and burials (Clark et al. 2008; McGuire 1991; Wilcox 1987:172, 2008). These community plans more closely resemble Casas Grandes than they do pueblos.

Some researchers have suggested that since Kayenta migrants first made Salado Polychromes along the Mogollon Rim that they also introduced the Salado religion (Clark et al. 2008). Kayenta migrants may well have created the Salado ceramic tradition, but the Mesoamerican Early Post-Classic International Symbol Set elements that they added to their Cibola-style decorations did not originate in northern Arizona. They also did not introduce the rituals, beliefs, and cosmology that these symbols embodied to the Southwest/Northwest. I find it equally unlikely that this religion originated from Casas Grandes. Salado Polychromes either predated or were coeval with the founding of Casas Grandes. In the Southwest/Northwest we see the earliest evidence of the Mesoamerican Early Post-Classic International Symbol Set among the Hohokam and the Mimbres peoples. Their descendants lived in the Phoenix Basin, the Tonto Basin, the San Pedro River Valley, the upper Gila, the Safford Basin, and in the Cliff Phase towns and villages of southwest New Mexico where Salado Polychromes were produced or more importantly used. Thus, the Hohokam and Mimbres, instead of Kayenta potters, would appear to be the most likely origin points for the Salado religion.

Researchers have suggested four models to account for the distribution of Salado Polychromes: They were (1) elite symbols of authority or items of exchange, (2) indicators of participation in an economic alliance/regional system, (3) objects associated with the spread of a religious ideology, or (4) markers of a migrant group (Crown 1994:vi). These explanations for the Salado set up a series of oppositions and mutually exclusive propositions (politics versus ritual versus migration). Yet archaeologists find good evidence for all four models. This suggests that, rather than asking which of the four possibilities account for the Salado, we should instead ask how all four were interrelated in the lived experiences of people.

The relational question reveals that the Salado and their religion looked a lot like the religion practiced in the Mesoamerican Epiclassic. In the Salado region, a large area became more economically interconnected, more politically divided, more ethnically diverse, and more cosmologically uniform. Trade became more decentralized and the volume of goods increased. Artisans (Kayenta potters at least and maybe others) moved from community to community in order to set up separate villages or barrios to practice their craft. In Epiclassic Mesoamerica, the movement of goods and artisans produced a uniform set of prestige goods and symbols that identified and legitimated the elite. Salado elites used a common set of objects and symbols (including conch trumpets, turquoise on shell mosaics, copper bells, and macaws) to legitimate their power (Clark et al. 2008:14; McGuire 1991; Wilcox 1987, 2008). Similarly the Salado religion provided a shared ideology that both unified diversity and legitimated social differentiation and inequality. This cult incorporated many Mesoamerican elements but lacked others, such as the Post-Classic International Style, the Late Post-Classic International Symbol Set, extensive human sacrifice, and common ritual uses of human bone.

Katsina Religion

Pueblo IV period religion developed on the margins of the Mesoamerican connection to the late pre-Hispanic Southwest/Northwest. Its iconography appears on Pueblo Glaze Wares, White Mountain Red Ware, and Jeddito Yellow Ware (Adams 1991; Van Keuren, this volume). Archaeologists find more evidence of Mesoamerican connections among the Salado (including the Classic Period Hohokam) and Casas Grandes than in the Pueblo IV period pueblos. Salado and Casas Grandes sites with their compounds, platform mounds, elite residences, and elite tombs are more similar to Mesoamerican communities than are Pueblo IV period and Late Mogollon pueblos, and they contain more Mesoamerican goods than the pueblos. It appears that both the Salado religion and the Casas Grandes religion more greatly resembled Mesoamerican religion than did the Katsina religion. These resemblances included cosmology, ritual, belief, and, most important, the relationship of religion to other aspects of society, especially the legitimation of elite rulers and, in the case of Casas Grandes, human sacrifice.

I would suggest that the Katsina religion was not simply an offshoot or variant of the Salado religion. Some scholars have asserted that Mesoamerica connected to the Pueblo IV period world through the Salado religion (Crown 1994). E. Charles Adams (1991; Adams and LaMotta 2006) argues that the Katsina religion developed in the upper Little Colorado River drainage area and was based directly on the Salado religion. The Mesoamerican components that are key to the religion, however, existed first among the Hohokam and the Mimbres, and the earliest representations of masks occur within Jornada Mogollon rock art in southeast New Mexico (figure 2.1). Lekson (2009) claims that Katsinas originated with the Mimbres, and Schaafsma (2000) places their origin among the Jornada Mogollon. The ethnographically known Katsina religion probably also incorporated Mesoamerican features via Casas Grandes. Mathiowetz (2009a, 2009b), for example, has proposed that the Mesoamerican cosmology of the Flower Mountain and the complex of the sun youth passed from Casas Grandes to the Pueblos. He also contends that the Pueblos transformed the complex of the sun youth into the post-conquest hero Montezuma who remains a part of Pueblo ritual and belief today. Pueblo IV period religion clearly has a more complex origin than simply being the Pueblo version of a Salado religion.

Why the Pueblos were not Mesoamerican societies, and why the Katsina religion was not a Mesoamerican religion can be summarized in a single observation. The Katsina religion was (or is) a form of asceticism. It advocates a communal life of hardship, humility, and hardiness. Individuals are expected to subordinate themselves to the interests of the group in order to maintain the balance and cycle of the world (Parsons 1939). A hierarchical body of esoteric knowledge and ritual lies at the core of the religion. Control of the esoteric sets a few priests off from the mass of the people. Yet the priests manifest their sacred position and power by living modestly and by not standing out from others in the material world. People sacrifice their individuality, possessions, food, and individual desires to feed the Katsinas and advance the common good.

Post-Classic Mesoamerican cosmology also prescribed ongoing sacrifice to maintain the universe. Individuals committed many ritual sacrifices on a daily basis. In popular rituals, people would break or bury objects, discard food and drink, slaughter animals, and kill butterflies as sacrifices to the gods (Aguilar-Moreno 2007:172–174). The sacrifices of objects, food, and even of animals have parallels in Pueblo religion but at least two important differences exist.

Mesoamerican religions believed that soil, crops, the moon, stars, and people sprang from the severed or buried bodies, fingers, limbs, heads, and (most importantly) blood of sacrificed gods (Aguilar-Moreno 2007:172–174). Thus, people had to maintain the earth, the sky, and fertility through blood sacrifice. Individuals, both commoners and elites, let blood from their fingers, tongues, and earlobes as personal sacrifices. In elaborate state rituals, priests killed, beheaded, skinned, dismembered, and cut the hearts out of sacrificial victims. Similar sacrifices as well as the use of trophy heads and human femur rasps appear at Casas Grandes, but not among the Salado.

The Pueblos lacked this fascination with blood and slaughter (Parsons 1939). Instead of spilling blood on altars and offering still-beating human hearts to the gods, they put out prayer feathers and offered pollen and corn meal to the Katsinas. A common Pueblo legend tells of the sacrifice of twin children to appease the feathered serpent and to stop a great flood (Tyler 1964:111). In the Pueblo legend, priests do not dismember, behead, or skin the children, or they do not cut the children's hearts out. Rather, the twins disappear into the waters as the serpent sucks the flood back into the underworld. Some researchers have interpreted this story to indicate that the Pueblos did practice human sacrifice during their history (Riley 1995:110), but archaeologists have found no evidence of human sacrifice in the Pueblo IV period world. Also, the Spanish reported no occurrences of human sacrifice among the sixteenth-century Pueblos (Riley 1995:110). Susan James (2002) has argued that Hopi Powamu rituals have parallels with and mimic Aztec rituals of child sacrifice but she also notes that there is no evidence that the Hopi ever killed their children in these rituals.

Second, state rituals of Post-Classic Mesoamerican religion did not promote asceticism (Aguilar-Moreno 2007; Ringle 2004). Religious beliefs did not mandate that elites live close to the common people and that they should reward reciprocity and humility. With great pomp and spectacle, Post-Classic ritual glorified the elite. The Post-Classic cosmology provided mythological charters for a hierarchical political order. This also seems to have been the case at Casas Grandes and within the Salado religion where religion legitimated explicit expressions of elite power and privilege. Numerous researchers (Adams 1991; Lekson 2009; Schaafsma 1999) have noted that in contrast the Katsina religion leveled social distinctions, included all people, punished hubris, and redistributed food and other resources between households. This leads me to wonder if perhaps this social leveling had something to do with why the Pueblos survived into the sixteenth century while the Salado and Casas Grandes declined and disappeared by 1450 (Clark et al. 2008).

Pueblo IV period and modern Katsina religion incorporated many aspects of Mesoamerican cosmology, belief, and metaphor. However, the practice of this religion in its ritual, its proscriptions for daily behavior, and its role in social relations differed from Mesoamerica in significant and important ways. This means that Pueblo priests may have been able to argue theology with Aztec priests but that the lived experiences of their religions would have been profoundly different for them and their peoples. A Pueblo man dancing in the plaza as the masked embodiment of a Katsina experiences his religion in a very different way than an Aztec war captive who is draped over a stone and waiting for his heart to be cut out. By the same token, the experience of the Pueblo priest laying corn-pollen blessings on the masked dancer is very different than that of the Aztec priest who wielded the obsidian blade.

I have suggested that the Southwest/Northwest and Mesoamerica were both more connected and less connected than many archaeologists have maintained. From a relational perspective, we understand how Pueblo religion developed by setting aside bounded units like the Southwest/Northwest or Mesoamerica. Instead we need to historically examine how relations and networks between different groups of peoples formed and changed over time. In this examination, we would do well to examine the historical contingencies that affected these relationships and how they were realized in the lived experiences of people. In this way, we may come to better understand why Aztec priests wielded knives while Pueblo priests scattered corn pollen.

Acknowledgments

I want to thank Donna Glowacki and Scott Van Keuren for inviting me to participate in the Amerind Foundation seminar and in this volume. I gained much from the seminar and from the other participants in it. John Ware and the staff of the Amerind have created an intellectual oasis in the desert that enabled our engagements. Several individuals reviewed earlier versions of this chapter and helped me greatly in writing it. They include Ruth Van Dyke, Ben Nelson, Donna Glowacki, Michael Mathiowetz, and Scott Van Keuren. Ann Hull drafted the figures for this chapter.

Ritual and Cosmology in the Chaco Era
Stephen Plog

Much of the renewed focus on religion in the Pueblo Southwest over the last two decades has addressed the post-1300 era (hereafter, the late pre-Hispanic period), which is characterized by elaborate kiva murals, red and orange wares with representational designs, and fascinating rock art (Adams 1991; Crown 1994). Associated transformations of village aggregation and layout and remarkable demographic transmogrifications have been the basis for new models that often emphasize the spread of what unfortunately have been labeled "cults" (e.g., the Southwestern Cult or the Katsina cult).

"Cult" has many possible definitions, but one that typifies how the term is used in contemporary popular literature is "a religion or sect considered to be false, unorthodox, or extremist" (*Random House Webster's College Dictionary* 2001:324). Katsina ritual certainly was neither unorthodox nor extremist, but rather it was a major component of Pueblo religion. I believe when "cults" have been discussed in late pre-Hispanic ritual, the intention of the authors has been to convey not a lack of orthodoxy, but a change from prior practices. Documenting change after 1300, however, requires a good understanding of prior ritual and cosmology, a topic that has received considerably less attention. In this chapter I therefore attempt to provide a foundation for discussions that are more central to this volume by discussing the nature of ritual and cosmology before 1130.

Much of my discussion will focus on Chaco Canyon in northwestern New Mexico. The density in the canyon of atypically large 50–600+ room pueblos with unusual architecture (great houses) (see figure 3.1), the existence of multiple roads connecting great houses to each other and to the hinterland, and the abundance of such material as turquoise and macaws have stimulated more than a century of intense study.

Ritual and Cosmology in the Chaco Era

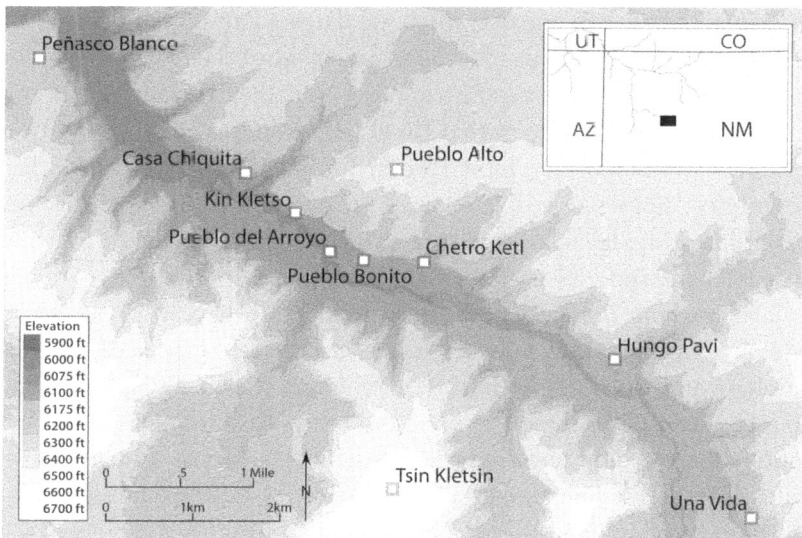

Figure 3.1. Chaco Canyon topography with locations of major great houses. Illustration by Edward Triplett.

Chaco also is one of the few regions occupied before the fourteenth century where archaeologists have highlighted the importance of ritual. Moreover, some (e.g., Lekson 2006:29, 2009) have argued that much of what happened in the Pueblo world after 1130 was a reaction to and rejection of Chaco. Contrary to such claims, I suggest there were both fundamental continuities and differences between Chaco and the late pre-Hispanic era. Rather than the radical disjunction proposed by Lekson or suggested by terms such as "cults," I argue, following Rappaport (1979:154; see also Plog and Solometo 1997), that while some aspects of religion may have been dynamic, others may have been constant and continued to be dimensions of Pueblo ritual from the pre-Hispanic era to the present. Understanding history and evolution requires a focus on both continuity and change.

Ritual in Chaco

It is no exaggeration to say that, in most models outlined in the last 15 to 20 years, Chaco is defined by ritual. The spotlight, however, has been on ritual as a general practice, ritual writ large. Countless discussions of the area refer to the canyon as the ritual center of the Pueblo region in the eleventh and early twelfth centuries, but they provide few if any details about the nature of that ritual (e.g., Kantner 2006; Van Dyke 2008; Yoffee 2001). The more specific formulations suggest that Chacoan great houses served as settings for periodic pilgrimages that involved feasting, fairs, and major ceremonies (e.g., Judge 1993; Malville and Malville 2001; Neitzel 2003:145).

What about the nature of Chaco ritual and beliefs? If Chaco was a ritual center, should we not try to understand key aspects of the cosmology and ritual of the Pueblo inhabitants? Relatively few have attempted to address these questions and others have implied we do not, and perhaps should not, study such beliefs.[1] In contrast, I maintain we must consider belief systems and meanings in order to interpret artifacts and contexts and to understand culture history and change in the Southwest (Helms 1998:6).

I also believe that there is ample evidence of Chaco religion and cosmology, despite claims to the contrary. Renfrew (2007:112, 113) has written that we have found little evidence in places like Chaco "as to an explicit belief system that might with confidence be recognized as a 'religion.'" He further asserts that absent in Chaco is "any abundance of very elaborate iconic symbolism—there is no wealth of iconography, few rich deposits of offerings of valuable material" (2001:19; see also 2007:112). In contrast, I believe there is a wealth of evidence regarding iconography, symbolism, and offerings in the canyon.

Archaeologists excavated Pueblo Bonito, the largest and probably the most important site in the canyon, between 1896 and 1927, and they published most reports prior to 1965. Detailed study of artifacts and contexts in Pueblo Bonito (and many other Chacoan sites excavated prior to 1950) has been difficult based on these publications alone for neither Pepper's (1920) nor Judd's (1954, 1964) monographs describe many of the rooms they excavated and they primarily mention the most remarkable artifacts recovered rather than providing complete inventories. Judd's monograph, in particular, focuses on material types rather than contexts, a pattern that was common at the time in which Judd wrote.

As I have suggested elsewhere (Plog 2010:380), throughout the history of research in the canyon there has been a tendency to emphasize either artifacts or architecture rather than integrating both types of data to study particular contexts. Most statements about the lack of iconography or the alleged empty rooms in Pueblo Bonito (Kantner 2006:32; Lekson 2007:14)[2] are therefore based more on the absence of published information than on the actual absence of materials and features in rooms. Neitzel (2003:124) is one of the few who have delved into archival records and museum collections to examine room-by-room artifact frequencies in Pueblo Bonito and she concludes that her study "should lay to rest the notion that with the exception of a few highly prolific burial and storage rooms, Pueblo Bonito was an empty site artifactually." Similarly, Reyman (1989:51) observes, "More hearths were found than reported in the published literature and when these are added to those reported by Pepper (1920) and Judd (1954, 1964), few archaeologists are likely to conclude there is a paucity." More recent studies have demonstrated the tremendous potential of studies that incorporate published and archival information and integrate both architectural and artifactual data (e.g., Ashmore 2007; Heitman 2011; Plog and Heitman 2010).

A Closer Look at Data and Context

In order to make it possible for scholars to more easily study the archaeological record of Chaco Canyon and to examine structure contexts, I have directed the Chaco Research Archive (http://www.chacoarchive.org), a project supported by the Andrew Mellon Foundation with the goal of collecting archival information—unpublished reports, field notes, journals, photographs, material inventories, and correspondence—regarding key settlements in Chaco Canyon excavated during the late nineteenth or early twentieth centuries. Collection has been only the first step, however, as we are now building room-by-room descriptions and inventories for the settlements, with the information stored in an online relational database that allows scholars to more effectively explore questions about room content and function, demography, organization, and ritual.

As we have entered information into our database, we quickly understood that the archaeological record of the canyon is not only remarkable but that it also offers tremendous potential for building a more solid foundation for the study of pre-Hispanic Pueblo religion during the Chaco era. Here, I offer some suggestions for how we can construct that foundation and what some of that evidence suggests. To do so, I take advantage of the database we are creating. In addition, I outline some of the ways these new insights might impact our approach to late pre-Hispanic ritual change in the Pueblo region.

Understanding Ritual and Cosmology in Chaco

Although the focus of this paper is on ritual and cosmology, I begin this section by noting that my discussion should not be read to imply politics and economics were unimportant in Chaco. As anthropologists, we should be aware that in most preindustrial societies, "church" and "state" were not separated as is sometimes true today, but rather they were related dimensions of the behavior of individuals and groups. Social ties often were ritual ties. Political relations typically were socially and ritually based.

Pueblo ethnographic studies and Pueblo peoples have not only long emphasized this interrelation (e.g., Bunzel 1932a:480; A. Ortiz 1969; Parsons 1939; Whiteley 1988) but they also have shown that ritual is central to understanding Pueblo society. Whiteley (1988:68, 288), for example, has argued that "previous anthropological analyses of Hopi social structure have neglected the ritual order as its key articulating principle" and "ritual action, because of its intent to affect instrumentally the conditions of existence, is simultaneously political action." In *The Tewa World*, Ortiz (1969:130) states, "while this work has had less to do with kinship and marriage—and therefore, with social structure, insofar as it is defined in these terms—than with religious ideas and practices, it is because ritual shapes social relations to such a tremendous extent. Thus, we have not descent, but ritual, not exogamy, but ritual again."

Directional symbolism. Multiple ethnographers and archaeologists (e.g., Marcus 1989; A. Ortiz 1969; Parsons 1939:99, *passim*; Riley 1963; Schaafsma and Taube 2006:232–235) have highlighted the importance of directional symbolism in historic Pueblo cosmology and throughout much of Latin and North America. As Parsons (1939:99) notes, "the cardinal directions are often a frame for the conduct of ceremonial or for securing repetition in song or narrative." Associated with the key directions typically are colors, plants, animals, and birds (e.g., Lange 1959:230; Parsons 1939:99; Stephen 1936). Ortiz (1969:128–129) argues that directional symbolism is so important the Tewa landscape reveals "not a circular village structure but one of four parts in which the corners are always kept open. So pervasive is this tetramerous aspect of Tewa symbolic classification that it reaches from the distant sacred mountains, hills, shrines, and plazas right into the home itself, where sacred objects are buried in the four corners of at least one room."

Heitman and I (2010) also have noted the occurrence of artifact concentrations in the corners of at least one key room at Pueblo Bonito, a room I will examine in greater detail below. Similarly, caches in room corners have been found throughout the Mesoamerican world, including Paquimé in northern Mexico.

Several scholars (e.g., Fritz 1978; Van Dyke 2004, 2008) also have noted key aspects of the layout of individual Chacoan settlements and of the broader cultural landscape are aligned with specific compass directions. Most salient are north-south alignments that include patterns of feature distributions in kivas; the wall dividing the plaza of Pueblo Bonito in half; the relation among Tsin Kletsin, Casa Rinconada, and Pueblo Alto; and the North Road that runs from Pueblo Alto to the San Juan River. Cardinal or intercardinal orientations of room blocks, kivas, and middens in individual settlements characterize a broader area of the north Southwest. North-south also is an important directional reference throughout Mesoamerica (Marcus 1989; McGuire, this volume), with buildings often aligned along that axis.

Mountains, viewed as the source of clouds and waters, as potential entries to the underworld, and as the "houses" of deities or supernaturals, typically are key elements in directional symbolism and in oral traditions, both in the Southwest and in Mesoamerica (e.g., McGuire, this volume; Schaafsma and Taube 2006). Van Dyke (2008:15, 97, *passim*) recently has highlighted the importance of visibility in the layout of sites and shrines on the Chacoan landscape. Pueblo Alto, Tsin Kletsin, and Peñasco Blanco—defining the northern, western, and southern limits of the concentration of great houses—all lie in elevated settings with excellent views of the mountains that rim the San Juan Basin. Even some great houses on the canyon floor such as Kin Nahasbas and

Una Vida "are positioned with excellent views of . . . Hosta Butte and Mount Taylor" (Van Dyke 2008:97).

Less obvious, but possibly equally important, in regard to the significance of mountains, is the Chacoans' apparent focus on wood. As Wills (2000:35) has argued, the tens of thousands of beams harvested in the mountains south and west of Chaco—much more wood than was necessary to build the great houses—suggests there was a symbolic connection between the architects of the great houses and the mountain areas. Moreover, Chacoans expended considerable effort in finishing wooden beams or crafting planks (Vivian 1949; Windes and Bacha 2008). Wills (2000:35) suggests this may have "expressed some degree of corporate affiliation by association with upland zones." However, I see little reason to tie corporate groups to the mountains and instead suggest the emphasis on wood from distant mountains is simply one important indication of the heightened focus on landscape and cosmology in the Chacoan world (Plog and Heitman 2010). Stephen (1936: 438–439), Bunzel (1932b:862), and Schaafsma and Taube (2006:244) note the association of spruce (common in upper elevations of southwestern mountains) and "green things," with spirits, deities, Katsinas, and ancestors who bring rain.

We do not have evidence to support an association of colors and directions in Chaco, but it would be surprising if such a relationship was absent because we have clear evidence from contemporaneous areas of the Pueblo region (Hegmon 2010; McGuire, this volume). One of the most underemphasized aspects of the material record from Chacoan settlements is the abundance of painted wood, pigments, minerals such as azurite or hematite that could be ground into pigment, and manos and metates that have red or yellow "stains" suggesting they were used to grind minerals into powder suitable for pigments or paints. The best documented cache of painted wood is the incredible collection from one room in Chetro Ketl (Vivian et al. 1978). However, our growing inventory of material from Pueblo Bonito shows at least thirty-six occurrences of painted wood (or corn in at least one case) in twenty-four different rooms. Painted wood also was abundant at Aztec Ruin and has been found at Kin Kletso and Bc 50 (Brand et al. 1937:96; Vivian and Mathews 1964:101–102). Kiva murals in Chaco were simple and rather colorless when compared with late pre-Hispanic murals and pottery vessels (but see Plog 2003), but the frequency of pigments and painted material in other media demonstrates color was important in the Chacoan world. I suggest it is a reasonable step to conclude that color-directional symbolism also was significant.

Agriculture, rain, and fertility. Some have questioned the extent to which the people of Chaco were farmers, but I see little reason to believe they were not. Seeds and other food remains are common in Chacoan settlements. At Pueblo Bonito, squash seeds were found in at least fifty rooms, and corncobs, husks, or silks were in at least forty-five rooms, hardly what one might expect at a ceremonial center with allegedly empty rooms. Equally important, we have R. Gwinn Vivian's (1984, 1992, 2004) excellent studies of water control in the canyon, including excavations that have uncovered canals, head gates, and gridded fields. Furthermore, Judd provides documentation of Navajo floodwater fields in the canyon and irrigated fields just to the south in the Kin Bineola Valley. Hyde Exploring Expedition photographs also reveal abundant harvests in the canyon itself. Is it possible to farm in Chaco and did the Chacoans successfully do so? Absolutely. They likely received some food from groups in the immediately surrounding areas (e.g., Cordell et al. 2008), but we should remember that to date studies of where Chacoan corn was grown are based on small samples and on analytical results that are not unequivocal.

Given the agricultural focus of Chacoan society, we should not be surprised to find evidence that at least some components of Chacoan ritual focused on moisture as suggested by the following:

- jet or turquoise frogs or tadpoles: at least sixteen occurrences,[3] concentrated in Room 33 at Pueblo Bonito (Pepper 1905:190–192; 1909:236–238; 1920:75)
- ceramic frog effigy pots or handles: at least three examples at Bonito
- jet, "green stone," shell, or wood ducks and birds:[4] at least twenty examples (Pepper 1905:186, 194–195; 1909:224, 228, 239, 242–244; 1920:134–135, 173)

- ceramic bird/duck pots or handles: at least twenty-two examples
- three cloud blowers[5] and four clay pipes or pipe fragments (one with a snake painted on the stem) from five Pueblo Bonito kivas and at least fifty-five pipes or pipe fragments from twenty-four rooms
- occasional plumed or horned serpents in Chaco rock art

In Pueblo and Mesoamerican cosmology, ducks, frogs, tadpoles, and plumed serpents are all, not unexpectedly, closely associated with water and fertility (Schaafsma and Taube 2006:245). Thus, Furst (1973:107) notes that "in the American Southwest, especially, the duck figures [were] 'seed bearers' (a symbol of agricultural fertility), protector of the Corn Maidens, messenger or explorer of the gods in the underworld, and avatar of the supernaturals themselves when they travel." Stephen (1936:470) reports the duck Katsina "is the uncle (*ta'*), ancestor, of all the kachina and also of the Hopi. He will listen to our songs, see our acts, and go direct to Cloud and ask him to send clouds and rain to the Hopi." Additionally, Zuni Katsinas may assume the forms of ducks "when they travel to and from Zuni" (Schaafsma 1994c:2). Ducks are also the most abundant category of zoomorphs in the Antelope Mesa kiva murals in the Hopi region (W. Smith 1952:127).

In one kiva mural from Antelope Mesa, a frog has a cloud terrace for a head, another has a cloud terrace for the tail, and multiple examples have "tails" made of "zigzag lightning" (W. Smith 1952:123). Schaafsma and Taube (2006:239) emphasize such terraces are multivalent and reference "not only clouds, but mountains and the rain-bringing spirits of the deceased." Stephen (1936:306–307, 470) lists frogs among the various pets of Cloud or Katsinas and notes there is a Duck Katsina song named "*Pa'kwa* (Frog)." He also reports that "frogs constantly pray for rain and hence are held sacred" (1936:707). Moreover, a particular type of small prayer stick made of willow or cottonwood without the bark removed may be stuck in mud spheres (Stephen 1936:651, 707). "The rain comes and washes these apart, dissolves them, and the woody fragments becomes tadpoles" (Stephen 1936:651–652), which then become frogs (1936:707). A song of the Good Katsina at Zuni also refers to the relationship of frogs and rain:

> "Guess, younger brother,
> Whose fine track go all about here?
> All over my water-filled field
> He has walked about
> Can you not guess?"
> Thus he said to his younger brother,
> "The child of the rain-makers,
> The water frog,
> Goes about hurrying his fathers, the rain-makers."
> (Parsons 1939:410)

At Zuni, frogs also may be viewed as dead children who have entered the watery world (Bunzel 1932a:596; D. Tedlock 1994:166–167).

Pipes and cloud blowers are common implements in Hopi ritual and are shown in kiva murals with cloud terraces emanating from them (W. Smith 1952:126, 237). Parsons (1917:174; see also Schaafsma and Taube 2006:251, 263–265; W. Smith 1952:237; Stevenson 1904:315) mentions that tobacco smoke symbolizes clouds and rain. Other studies emphasize that smoke conveys prayers for rain. Thus, Bunzel (1932a:491) states, "At many points in ceremonies tobacco smoke is blown to the six cardinal points that the rain makers may not withhold their misty breath." Stephen (1936) describes smoking as a consistent element of Hopi ritual. He (1936:668, 681, 704, *passim*) also reports that pipe smoke is connected to clouds and rain, although at Hopi "cloud tobacco" may consist of the "tip leaves" of spruce, fir, red willow, and aspen, each species representing one of the four important directions. Also of interest, the ashes of the pipe may be "preserved till after the end of the ceremonial smoking day, and deposited . . . in the main drainage on the east of the mesa" (Stephen 1936:581).

Several other objects of importance in historic Pueblo ritual also occur in Chaco. These items include conch shell trumpets (Mills and Ferguson 2008), flutes (Pepper 1909, 1920), frequent occurrences of ritual caches of shell and turquoise in structures (Heitman 2011), and possible prayer sticks. Given space limitations, I refrain from discussing these in greater detail, but I mention them simply to reinforce the extent of historic and pre-Hispanic similarities. Some aspects of these objects have been, or will be, explored in other papers (e.g., E. Brown 2005; Heitman 2011; Mills and Ferguson 2008; Plog 2003).

The parallels mentioned here suggest that many aspects of Pueblo cosmology and ritual had roots at least as early as the Chaco period and probably much earlier. Beliefs in the importance of directions, colors, mountains, and ancestors living in the underworld did not begin with the Katsina cult (Adams 1991) or the Southwestern Cult (Crown 1994), and ritual designed to increase rainfall and fertility or to communicate with the ancestors did not begin during that era. Indeed, I concur with many others (e.g., McGuire, this volume; Reyman 1971; Schaafsma and Taube 2006) who have proposed that groups throughout the Southwest and Mesoamerica shared significant aspects of cosmology and ritual, and these aspects had deep historical roots. These roots deserve greater attention from archaeologists who work in the Southwest than they have received; such studies will help us make major strides toward discarding nebulous views of Chaco as a "dream" (Renfrew 2001) or a "metaphor" (Stein and Lekson 1992), and replacing such concepts with more nuanced understandings that will enhance our ability to comprehend the pre-thirteenth-century history of the Southwest.

Ritual and the dead. Along with the continuities noted above, studies also should attempt to identify important *differences*. Only by exploring both similarities and differences between Chaco and post-Chaco ritual will we uncover new information such as the use of cylinder vessels to drink chocolate (Crown and Hurst 2009) and, more importantly, better understand the nature of societies in the canyon and how they changed over time. I suggest one of the most salient differences is that Chacoan mortuary treatments were more varied compared to most areas and time periods in the Pueblo Southwest. In 1924, for example, Morris (1924:224, 225) noted that whereas burials almost always had been discovered in the middens of small ruins, "the builders of the great houses of the Chaco period buried practically never in refuse heaps, rarely within their buildings, and that the discovery of their customary method of disposing of the dead remains a problem for future solution."

Those great house burials that have been discovered were interred not in external cemeteries, but in room interiors, with only a few exceptions. Interior burials are known from other regions of the Southwest, but the Chaco burials stand out because many are disarticulated and are occasionally incomplete with portions of the skeleton missing. Judd (1954) and Pepper (1909, 1920) found concentrations of burials in separate areas of Pueblo Bonito; in both clusters a significant number of the interments were disarticulated (Akins 1986, 2001, 2003; Plog and Heitman 2010). Pepper (1909:209–210, 1920) attributed the scattered skeletal remains to water flowing through rooms, while Judd (1954:338–339) concluded that raiders had been the cause

The room in Pueblo Bonito that has received more attention than any other is an extremely small (ca. 2-m-square) masonry structure in one of the earliest portions of the site. In this tiny room, Pepper found one of the most remarkable assemblages ever discovered in the Southwest, including several flutes and more turquoise than has been recovered from all other excavated sites in the Southwest combined. Few other rooms in Pueblo Bonito produced such a large number of individual remains.

Pepper discovered much of the turquoise in the room in association with Burials 13 and 14, both of which were likely interred in the early to middle ninth century based on radiocarbon dates and ceramic styles (Plog and Heitman 2010). A wooden floor composed of shaped planks was then laid across the entire room and twelve individuals were subsequently buried. Such burial coverings are rather rare; the only other example I know of was found at Paquimé (Di Peso et al. 1974:327, 387) where in one instance the grave pit included "no less than 12 persons and was the most complex burial discovered at Casas Grandes." Pepper (1920) found most interments above the floor in Room 33 to be at least partially disarticulated.

Using published data (Pepper 1909) and unpublished field notes, we have been able to map the distributions of some of the skeletal remains and the associated artifacts in Room 33. Several aspects of the distributions are significant, but here I emphasize a few characteristics. First, a plot of the depth of skeletal remains, in combination with new AMS radiocarbon dates and the diversity of ceramic styles, demonstrates that deposition of the skeletal remains occurred over a significant period of at least 200–250 years (Plog and Heitman 2010). No other crypt in the

American Southwest, except perhaps the other cluster of burials found by Judd, has revealed evidence of such long-term, repeated use. Second, the horizontal distribution of material in Rooms 32 and 33, along with the remarkable preservations of wooden artifacts and some cloth, is inconsistent with water flowing through and into the room through the doorway (Plog and Heitman 2010). Third, Pepper's unpublished maps of specific burials reveal clear associations between some remains and artifacts, contrary to his claims of disturbance by water.

Although I have not examined the information on Judd's interments as closely, it is noteworthy that in one of his letters to John LaGorce of the National Geographic Society, Judd (1924) wrote that in one of his burial rooms "a curious feature, and one which I cannot account for, is that most of the skulls lay in one corner of the room among the pieces of pottery and quite separated from the bodies to which they belong." He later (1924) suggested "portions of the bodies were torn from the remainder and the heads."

Four inferences may be proposed based on the burial data and radiocarbon information. First, the remains of some skeletons may have been scattered as the result of continued use of the room over centuries. Taphonomic analysis by Marden (2009) found that the skeletal elements of most individuals discovered in Room 33 are present. Marden suggests that the skeletons were articulated when initially interred and had decomposed prior to disarticulation. Interring a series of twelve individuals in a shallow deposit above the wooden floor of Room 33 over a period of centuries, and in such a small space with no natural sources of light, almost certainly resulted in the latest burials impacting the earlier, decomposing burials. Such long-term use is the most likely explanation of the disarticulated skeletons above the wooden floor.

Second, it also is possible that some of the Bonito burials could have been secondary interments (Plog and Heitman 2010). The fragments of cloth found adhering to many skulls (Pepper 1909) raise the possibility that the bodies were wrapped in cloth and could have been moved from one burial location to another without the loss of skeletal elements. The burial clusters at Bonito thus may in part be Pueblo examples of charnel houses that were common in other parts of North America and Mesoamerica but were infrequent at best in the Southwest.

Third, the frequency of isolated skulls, mandibles, and long bones, some possibly intentionally placed in certain locations, along with data from other sites such as a femur with six bands of dark paint from BC 50 (Senter 1937:147), suggests that human skeletal elements may have been used in Chacoan ritual, perhaps in manners somewhat similar to those reported for an earlier time period at La Quemada in Zacatecas, Mexico (Nelson et al. 1992).

Possible ritual use of skeletal elements in the Pueblo Southwest may be underemphasized by archaeologists, as there are also indications of such behavior post-Chaco. Fewkes (1909) discovered human skulls in four ventilator tunnels at Spruce Tree House, for example, and LaMotta (1996) has documented the use of human skeletal material at the Homol'ovis after 1330, in abandonment rituals.

Fourth, the association of Burial 14—one of the richest burials ever discovered in the Southwest—with both a remarkable assemblage of artifacts and at least thirteen other interments deposited over a period of two to three centuries suggests rituals devoted to ancestors played a more central role in Chaco religion and politics than elsewhere in the Southwest (Plog and Heitman 2010).

I suggest aspects of the human remains from Bonito, particularly the frequent interment of individuals in two burial clusters and in one instance, a clear concentration, of skulls and long bones, may be best understood from the perspective of recent ethnographic and ethnohistoric research that has emphasized the potential cosmological and political power of these skeletal elements. Helms (1998:27), for example, has argued that "the long-term viability of the living is often perceived to depend on the role played by the dead, directly or indirectly, in perpetuating the flow of energies that activate the universe." She further stipulates, "One of the major sources of this most necessary and beneficial gift of the dead is the bones of the deceased (*particularly the skull and long bones*), which in general are believed to be the seat of life" (Helms 1998:27, emphasis mine). Similarly, in their discussion of the Andes, Arnold and Hastorf (Helms 1998:45) suggest "it appears that through their access to and possession of heads, certain ayllu groups might institutionalize . . . political claims." Furthermore, "the possession of certain heads would literally give 'title' to certain privileged descent lines, shaping their land claims within defined boundaries, and allowing them to speak to, and for a larger political grouping."

Given the association of the interments at Bonito with a wealth of cosmological and iconographic symbols, Heitman and I (2010) have proposed that rituals dedicated to ancestors may have been a key component of Chacoan religion and political power from the time the first great houses were built in the early to mid-ninth century to the decline of Chaco in the late eleventh or early twelfth centuries. Such rituals, however, need not be viewed as distinct from ritual to promote fertility and rainfall. Pueblo ancestors reside in the underworld, the source of water. As Arnold and Hastorf (2008:203) note for the Andes, the "vital dimension of heads as channels for rituals centered on water and fertility in general, as well as their potent association with leadership, may explain why, at both Tiwanaku and Wari, the central place of heads is celebrated in important buildings, hosting ceremonies with political if not sacred dimensions." Chaco was not Tiwanaku, but I nevertheless believe it is plausible that Room 33, with its wealth of burials and iconography, its association with nearby rooms filled with cylinder vessels and ceremonial staffs, and its north-central location in Pueblo Bonito (north often being the most sacred direction), may well have been viewed as a source of cosmological power to the people of Chaco.

Ashmore (2007) has presented a similar argument based on a somewhat different analysis. She stresses, for example, that Room 33 was one of the least accessible rooms in the northern section of Pueblo Bonito because it was necessary to pass through Rooms 40, 28, and 32 in order to access the single door to the burial chamber (185). Ashmore (2007:179, 183) proposes that the northern section of Bonito may have been "an *axis mundi*, perhaps for the Chacoan world as a whole," a place of "emergence or return, known to people in the pueblo but, for most, with origins and destinations concealed from active view."

Summary

After the initial depopulation of Chaco in the early 1100s, the Pueblo world witnessed a continuation, and perhaps intensification, of the demographic fluctuations that had begun centuries earlier. People constructed hundreds of new villages, large and small, and then left them behind. We can readily identify these demographic fluctuations, but change and continuity in social, political, and religious trajectories have been much more difficult to measure.

To date, most studies of post-Chacoan religion have focused on change and the possible introduction of new rituals and beliefs. In this chapter, I have argued that there also was substantial continuity from Chaco to the late pre-Hispanic era to the historic era described in ethnographies. To fully understand how and why the Pueblo world was transformed during the centuries before the Spanish arrived, we must study *both* religious change and continuity. Given the dramatic changes in the social landscape of the Pueblo world between 1030 and 1540, for example, why do we find continuities in the importance of directional symbolism or the relation of ancestors and fertility? Moreover, we must understand those statics and dynamics in relation to political, social, and economic dimensions of Pueblo life with which they were so intertwined. A difficult challenge lies ahead, but the renewed focus on ritual in recent years is a promising sign, as the chapters of this volume attest.

Acknowledgments

I thank Donna Glowacki and Scott Van Keuren for inviting me to participate in the Amerind seminar and for their helpful comments on an earlier version of this chapter. I also thank John Ware and the staff and volunteers of the Amerind Foundation for their incredible hospitality. Carrie Heitman, Abigail Holeman, Wolky Toll, Adam Watson, and the seminar participants, particularly Randy McGuire, offered helpful suggestions on an earlier draft of this chapter.

The Role of Religion in the Depopulation of the Central Mesa Verde Region
Donna M. Glowacki

The AD 1200s in the central Mesa Verde region have been described by Lipe (1995) as a turbulent time, and indeed it was, for within 60 years sweeping demographic and social changes during poor climatic conditions resulted in widespread depopulation. The circumstances prompting the Mesa Verde migrations involved multiple factors. One of the most obvious was that the 1200s were climatically difficult for Ancestral Pueblo farmers because there were intermittent periods of mild to severe drought (Van West and Dean 2000; Wright 2010), cooler than average temperatures (Kohler 2010; Wright 2010), and changing precipitation patterns (Cordell 2000; Cordell et al. 2007; Dean 1996a) that reduced agricultural productivity across the region (Kohler 2010).

In the context of these climatic challenges, archaeologically we see evidence of increased aggregation into large pueblos (Glowacki and Ortman, in press; Lipe 1995; Varien 1999a; Varien et al. 1996), localized depletion of resources (Driver 2002:158–160; Johnson et al. 2005; Kohler 1993), intraregional population movements (Glowacki 2006, 2010; Varien 1999a; Varien et al. 2007), ongoing emigration from the region (Ahlstrom et al. 1995; Duff and Wilshusen 2000), and increased violence (Haas and Creamer 1993; Kuckelman et al. 2000; LeBlanc 1999). These changes tend to be interpreted as responses to worsening agricultural circumstances. Consequently, it is tempting to take a somewhat Malthusian tack and conclude that the depopulation of the region was a result of the co-occurrence of increased aggregation and decreased agricultural productivity due to climatic hardships that created an untenable situation. It was a system pushed to its limits.

This narrative, however, only accounts for the *external* factors involved, which had to be mitigated by Pueblo people through social and cultural means. Their actions were further influenced by historical contingencies and individual, household, and community-level concerns. Determining how the demographic and climatic changes were culturally accommodated in the Central Mesa Verde region requires understanding religious practice and how it was affected by the turbulent conditions of the 1200s. Religion is fundamental to how Pueblo culture—both past and present—is organized and how Pueblo society is governed. It affects where people live, how villages are organized, who people can marry, and its rituals maintain world order and ensure the successful completion of subsistence cycles (Bernardini 2008; Dozier 1970; Eggan 1950; A. Ortiz 1969; Parsons 1939; Titiev 1944; Ware and Blinman 2000; Whiteley 2008:24–31). Religion permeates everything and thus is inextricably enmeshed in political and economic considerations. Archaeologists cannot understand the broad sweeping changes taking place across the northern Southwest without it (see also Pauketat, this volume; Plog, this volume).

When it comes to studying religion in the ancient Southwest, most archaeologists have focused on the materialization of the Katsina religion and the pan-southwestern developments of the fourteenth century (Adams 1991; Adams and LaMotta 2006; Crown 1994; McGuire 1986, 1989; VanPool et al., 2006b; Ware and Blinman 2000). Much less attention has been given to Pueblo religion prior to 1300 and how it might have affected these later developments (see also Plog, this volume). When religion has been addressed, the discussion is either about Chaco Canyon and its influence (Kantner 2006; Plog, this volume; Van Dyke 2008) or about ritual during the Pueblo I period (Blinman 1989; Potter 1997; Schachner 2001). The role of religion in the depopulation of the Central Mesa Verde region, however, has been largely neglected. Although archaeologists have recognized that religion must have contributed to prompting the Mesa Verde migrations (B. Bradley 1996; Lipe 1995:163, 2002; Varien et al. 1996:105–106), we have yet to account for the ways that Pueblo religion and religious change affected, and was affected by, the conditions leading to the depopulation. Though difficult to identify archaeologically, the role of religion and religious change was as important as climatic and demographic changes in structuring the circumstances of the 1200s, if not more so, because religion shaped how climatic, environmental, and social changes were perceived and acted upon.

Here, I explore how religious change—inferred from architectural and artifactual evidence—may have played a central role in prompting widespread emigration from the Central Mesa Verde region (see figure 1.1). I suggest that one way people coped with circumstances during the 1200s was through the formation of new religious societies and practices. These religious changes, evident in the Mesa Verde archaeological complex, would have had deep historical roots (both in Chaco and pre-Chaco) that influenced how religious practice and ideology were altered to accommodate immediate needs and agendas in the 1200s. The adoption of new beliefs and practices could have increased social fragmentation at various scales, making communities particularly vulnerable to any negative impacts from poor agricultural yields and increased aggregation. The consequences of religious change in central Mesa Verde, in turn, affected the changes in religious ideologies that characterize the late pre-Hispanic period and beyond (Bernardini, this volume, Pauketat, this volume). Thus, the changes in thirteenth-century Mesa Verde religion were part of an ongoing transformative process happening across the Pueblo world.

Religious Change and Revitalization

I use Anthony Wallace's (1956, 2003) seminal work on revitalization movements as a heuristic framework to better understand how religious change might have contributed to regional depopulation. The concept of revitalization provides a means for describing how religious change happens by accommodating the action of individuals and the social and cultural contexts within which their actions take place, while accounting for external influences and pressures (Vokes 2007:315–316). It also allows for the tensions inevitably involved with change because intrinsic to revitalization is opposition between those seeking to change their circumstance—an innovative minority—and those seeking to retain their power and status—the traditional establishment (Harkins 2004; Lepowsky 2004).

Although I use Wallace's framework, I do not share his structural-functionalist interpretation of how it works. Revitalization is not an inevitable outcome of environmental or cultural crises nor is it an isolated "event" (i.e., lacking historical contingencies) that only served to return balance to a system. Nonetheless, revitalization and religious movements—"a pervasive rearrangement of a field of social relationships at any scale" (Pauketat, this volume)—do happen. In addition to crises (e.g., war, drought, famine, immigration, economic downturn), people, places, objects, and events (celestial, natural, or interpersonal) are all nodes (Pauketat, this volume; Plog, this volume) or points of articulation around which revitalization and religious change can occur (Dowd 1992:169–190; Harkins 2004:xxvi; Lepowsky 2004; Rainbird 2002a:437, 439; Vokes 2007:317–318; Wallace 2003). Thus, revitalization movements can take a variety of forms, depending on the node that prompts it (Vokes 2007:318; Wallace 1956:275–276), and they can be implemented at a variety of scales. Movements can be extreme and can incite violent uprisings; they can be prophetic, particularly when moral failure is blamed for dire circumstances; they can be nativistic and rely on revivalism to renew traditional connections; or they can engage all of these tactics. Regardless, they are all embedded in historical processes and complex social networks, and these movements had long-reaching effects, both across space and through time.

Revitalization movements are most often associated with colonial contexts (Lepowsky 2004; Liebmann and Preucel 2007; Wallace 1952). This is largely due to two factors: (1) colonial contact increased the occurrence of revitalization; and (2) most of our examples of revitalization come from ethnographers who, by default, study postcontact contexts (Vokes 2007:314). Colonial contact, however, is not requisite because, as noted, any number of catalysts may cause religious revitalization including intergroup interactions that have nothing to do with colonialism. Wallace (2004:ix) himself calls for going beyond cases of colonial contact by examining manifestations of revitalization in "the belly of the beast" (i.e., within cultures rather than between them).

Revitalization most readily occurs when people are predisposed to adopting new traditions because they perceive inadequacies in existing practices, they need to cope with uncertain times, or they were convinced of its necessity—whether needed or not—by a persuasive individual or group (Harkins 2004:xxiii; Lepowsky 2004:42; Vokes 2007; Wallace 1956, 2003). Often initiated by an individual or a small group, movements quickly take hold and have widespread influences—both positive and negative—that affect the whole community or culture (e.g., Pop'ay's role in the Pueblo Revolt and subsequent nativistic revitalization; see Liebmann and Preucel 2007).

Politics, the contestation of power, and personal aspirations pervade the social negotiations that allow movements to form and proliferate. Thus, conflict, social tension, and resistance are inherent in the process because there are differing, and possibly contradictory, agendas, beliefs, and viewpoints at play (e.g., innovative versus conservative). This is particularly true when religious movements are first taking hold, for it is an acutely volatile time that increases vulnerability to additional crises or problems (Wallace 1956, 2003). Indeed, not all revitalization movements attain momentum and coherence, but even failed attempts at revitalization can be socially and politically disruptive (Harkins 2004). Moreover, prolonged stress can be particularly detrimental because it forces people to take extreme actions that go against their normative cultural practices (Wallace 1956, 2003; Vokes 2007). These actions can lead to drastic outcomes such as long-distance migration, regional depopulation, and cultural decline.

Religious movements are most frequently realized through the development of new religious societies, the creation or importation of new rituals and practices, or the revival of old ways (Harkins 2004; Vokes 2007:318; Wallace 1956:275–276). They are not only embedded in history but the movements themselves are also historical events—a sequence of contingent occurrences—that transform space and objects (Beck et al. 2007; Harkins 2004:xxi; Sewell 2005:248–257; Vokes 2007; Wallace 1956, 2003). It is the spread of a new ideology or religious practice from its genesis to a cultural group that constitutes revitalization. Consequently, material correlates, such as changes in ritual objects or iconography, and architectural changes, such as the construction of new structures or the modification of existing ones to accommodate new practices, can be indicators of new religious movements and practices.

McGuire (1986:258–261, 1989:57–59) was the first to apply a revitalization or "crisis cult" model to late pre-Hispanic Pueblo contexts. Using this framework, he explained the development of the Katsina religion as a revivalist movement drawing on kiva mural imagery that depicts rituals with masked figures and objects, such as copper bells and macaws, which were widely circulated during the heyday of Chaco.

Bruce Bradley (1996) subsequently applied Wallace's framework to the Central Mesa Verde region when he focused on revivalism that was potentially apparent in a resurgence of Chaco-esque attributes at Sand Canyon Pueblo in the late 1200s. I add to these previous discussions by suggesting that revitalization and religious change, ever-present at a variety of scales, was one of the primary responses to the severe conditions of the mid- to late 1100s. As I argue in this chapter, the new religious movements introduced in the early to mid-1200s did not ameliorate conditions and may have actually exacerbated them to the extent that widespread migration—yet another means of revitalization—became the best strategy to resolve the situation.

Revitalization and the Central Mesa Verde Region

In the wake of the decline of Chaco, the mid- to late 1100s was a particularly stressful time in the Central Mesa Verde region. Climatically, this period was characterized by colder than average temperatures, low water tables, and extreme drought conditions (1130–1180), all of which decreased agricultural productivity (Kohler 2010; Van West and Dean 2000:37; Wright 2010). There was also an unusually high frequency of violence that was characterized by dismemberment and postmortem processing (Kohler et al. 2009; Kuckelman et al. 2000). This violence was widespread because there are at least eleven sites dating to the 1100s that have evidence of conflict (Billman et al. 2000; Kuckelman et al. 2000:table 1; Morris 1939:105; Toll 1993).

The severity of these conditions would have tested the ideologies and institutions of Ancestral Pueblo communities, particularly if the severe drought and violence were perceived as a sign of ritual or moral failure. That Chaco itself was in decline by the early to mid-1100s suggests a loss of faith in the power of the Chaco ideological system, and this may have accompanied or possibly preceded the environmental downturn and resulting challenges. This circumstance would have also made it difficult for groups at Aztec, for example, to flourish because it was so closely tied to Chaco. As a case in point, the construction of Aztec in the early 1100s may have been an effort to revitalize the Chacoan ideological system for it was built in the mold of a classic Chaco Canyon great house (Brown et al. 2008; Lekson 1999), at least initially. After 1130, however, large-scale, planned construction episodes at Aztec ceased, the use of local juniper wood rather than distant ponderosa pine increased, and the frequency of long-distance exchange decreased (Lipe 2006). Thus, it seems that Aztec too was struggling in the wake of the mid-1100s drought and the failing Chaco ideological system that initially legitimized Aztec. There is also regional evidence of the waning influence of Chaco and Aztec because new great house construction decreased after the late 1100s (Glowacki and Ortman, in press; Lekson and Cameron 1995; Lipe and Varien 1999).

New religious societies or practices would have been one way to address perceived shortcomings of the established ideology. And, indeed, by the early 1200s, we see evidence that the severity of the conditions during the preceding decades may have caused people to shift away from established patterns and to rethink their religious practices and social organization. Changes in settlement pattern (i.e., size, configuration, and location), the construction of new types of architecture and elaboration of old forms, the production of new pottery vessel forms, an increase in decoration on the exterior of bowls, and new types of perishable objects all suggest social reorganization that, given the nature of Pueblo culture, had to be negotiated through religious change.

Changing Settlement Patterns

Following the intense drought and social unrest of the mid-1100s, aggregation into existing large pueblos, such as Yellow Jacket Pueblo, increased (Glowacki and Ortman, in press; Varien et al. 2007), and during the early 1200s at least twenty-five new large villages were established in the eastern portion of central Mesa Verde (Glowacki 2010: table 9.1). Many of the newly established villages were also situated in canyon-head or canyon-rim settings, which were often near springs (Glowacki and Ortman, in press; Lipe 1995; Lipe and Ortman 2000; Varien 1999a:148–149; Varien et al. 1996). These new pueblos were built closer together than they were in previous periods, which caused new challenges because resource catchments may have begun to overlap creating competition over resources (Varien 1999a:158–160, fig. 7.9; Varien et al. 2000). Moreover, by the mid-1200s, much of the regional population was consolidated in the eastern part of the region and a majority of that population was living in large aggregated villages

(Glowacki 2010; Glowacki and Ortman, in press; Varien et al. 2007). This increased consolidation and aggregation, even among local populations, is also stressful and likely created new opportunities and challenges that caused people to continue modifying their existing practices to accommodate the increased number of people living together (Varien et al. 2000). These dynamics were further affected by evident immigration into the eastern portion of Central Mesa Verde (Glowacki 2010; Varien et al. 2007:fig. 5b) of people that came from southeast Utah (Glowacki 2010). The integration of these immigrants into existing or new aggregated villages via mechanisms of acculturation and syncretism likely added to social tensions.

The spatial configuration of the aggregated villages constructed between 1225 and 1260 differed from the existing, long-lived pueblo villages. The conventional layout, best exemplified at Yellow Jacket Pueblo, consisted of dispersed, linear pueblos that were front-oriented, often along a north-south axis (see figure 4.1). The new spatial layout, however, was more aggregated, inwardly focused, and had a bilateral layout (e.g., Sand Canyon Pueblo, Big Spring, and Yucca House; see also Glowacki 2006, 2010; Lipe and Ortman 2000; Varien et al. 1996). The transition from linear, dispersed pueblo villages to an aggregated village likely changed the relationships between households and communal organizations, potentially promoting community-level arrangements over kin-based ones (Bernardini 1996; Ware and Blinman 2000). A social reconfiguration of this nature likely involved associated changes in religious practice. Ware and Blinman (2000), for example, suggest that it is evidence of the proliferation of nonkin, religious sodalities. Regardless of the underlying causes and implications, these organizational changes were part of the kinetic chain of events that produced the large-scale transition from an upwardly focused Chacoan ideology to the inward focus of the fourteenth-century pueblos (see Newsome and Hays-Gilpin, this volume; Pauketat, this volume).

Changes in village layout also hint at an increasing control of power by individuals or groups (i.e., clans, lineages, descent groups, or sodalities). Evidence of planned construction at some of the new aggregated pueblos, for example, suggests a level of centralized leadership not apparent at earlier large pueblo villages in the region (Ortman and Bradley 2002:48–49, 52–53). Access to resources within the pueblos also

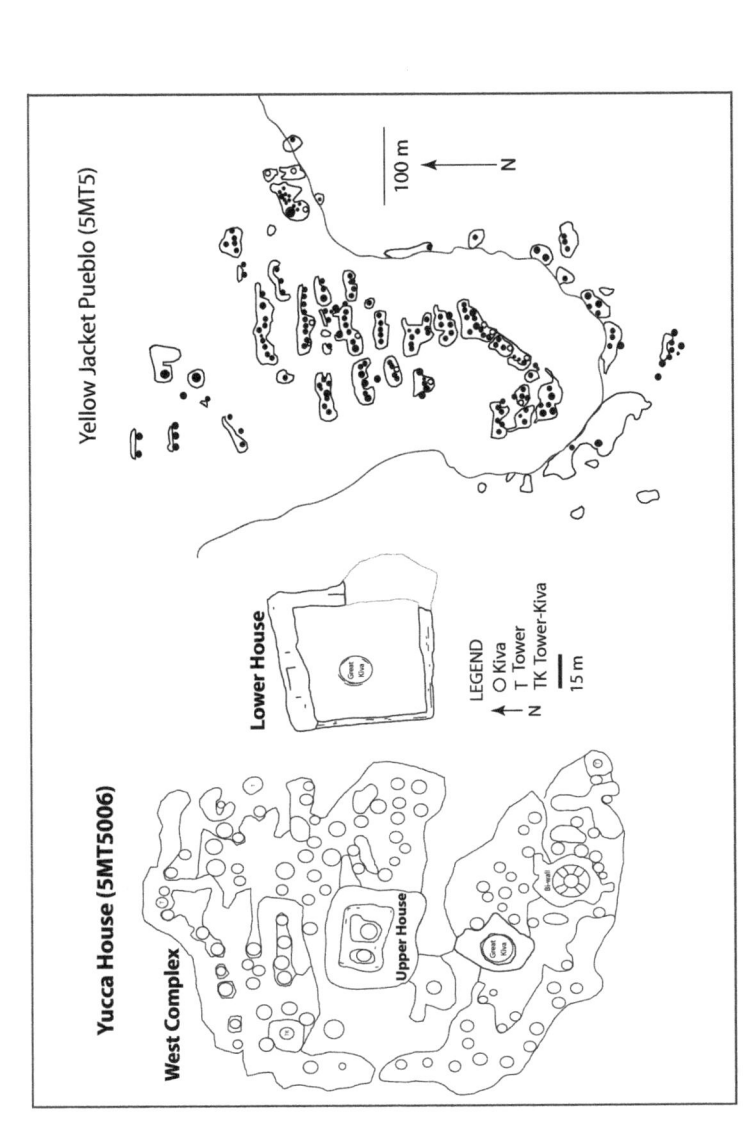

Figure 4.1. Comparison of a linear pueblo village layout, illustrated by Yellow Jacket Pueblo (5MT5), and an inward-focused, aggregated pueblo village layout, represented by Yucca House (5MT5006).

pueblo villages indicates the simultaneous development and modification of inclusive and exclusive ritual organizations, which have a long history among the Pueblo people (Fowles 2004; Plog and Solometo 1997; Potter 2000).

Pottery and Perishables

Changes in pottery production also point to innovation and ritual change during the early to mid-1200s. For example, large-sized bowls became more common than in previous periods (Mills 1999; Ortman 2000a). Evident at a number of late thirteenth-century sites, including Yellow Jacket, Castle Rock, and Woods Canyon pueblos, this trend suggests a widespread need to display more food than in previous periods (Mills 1999; Ortman 2000a, 2002). Highly visible exterior bowl designs also became more common (Hegmon 1991; Mills 1999), particularly at the large, aggregated villages with public architecture (Robinson 2005). Exterior bowl designs can symbolically communicate affiliations (e.g., Bowser 2000) and have been linked to the proxemics of communal feasting in the Southwest (Mills 2007; Potter 2000; Robinson 2005; Spielmann 2004). These changes in bowl production suggest an increased need for vessels that could be used at communal events and rituals, and they were part of the long-term trend in the increasing importance of communal feasting and associated rituals that occurred across the Colorado Plateau (Mills 2007; Spielmann 2004).

Vessel forms, such as mugs, kiva jars, and canteens, also increase in frequency during the 1200s (Breternitz et al. 1974; Lipe and Lekson 2001), and their use may have been associated with the development of new rituals or the modification of old ones. Kiva jars and mugs, in particular, are unique to the Mesa Verde archaeological complex (Lipe 2010). Both forms probably had multiple uses; one of which was likely in rituals. For example, Kidder (1962) observed that kiva jars were commonly, although not exclusively, found in ceremonial rooms (kivas). Putsavage's (2008) use-wear and spatial analyses of Mesa Verde mugs suggest that they were frequently used for both domestic and ceremonial purposes. Bruce Bradley (1996) has equated mugs with the distinctive cylinder jars of Chaco Canyon that were recently found to contain cacao used politically and ritually in Mesoamerica (Crown and Hurst 2009). Although mugs differ markedly from cylinder jars in form and context of use, both of these vessel forms were presumably used for liquids. As of yet, we do not know what was contained in Mesa Verde mugs, but, given their widespread use and frequent association with burials (Putsavage 2008), it seems likely that mugs and the liquids they contained were periodically used for rituals. Most importantly, both kiva jars and mugs were no longer used after the depopulation of the Northern San Juan region (Lipe 2010), which suggests they had particular associations, probably ceremonial, that were no longer popular.

The perishable record also points to the development of new religious societies and practices in the mid-1200s. Hide clothing, including moccasins, a hide shirt, and a hide cap that was nearly identical to that depicted in rock art, found in both the Galisteo Basin and Tsegi Canyon, have been discovered on Mesa Verde Proper and a few decorated buckskins have been recovered from Aztec (Laurie Webster, personal communication, 2009). Schaafsma (2000) has associated hide clothing with the rise of a warrior ritual sodality across the Southwest. This inference may also be supported by the recovery of contemporaneous coiled basketry shields. Only three shields have been recovered, but they were widely distributed as one was found at Aztec (Webster 2008: 178), one on Mesa Verde Proper, and one at Mummy Cave in Canyon del Muerto (Morris and Burgh 1941: 51–52; Schaafsma 2000:9). I believe the trends in pottery and the appearance of new forms of perishables during the 1200s represent materialisms of religious change.

Revitalization and the Regional Depopulation

The changes in settlement, architecture, pottery, and perishable items found in Central Mesa Verde during the early to mid-1200s are all material evidence of changing social arrangements. Pueblo social organization and culture is governed by religion and thus cultural change is often the product of religious change through various mechanisms, including religious movements and revitalization. These changes came on the heels of a difficult time with severe drought, violence, and a breakdown of key aspects of the Chaco system. Even though revitalization is not an inevitable outcome of crises, periods of crises, both natural and social, do create disjunctions that are often addressed through religious change and revitalization in one kind of religious change. This practice is even more likely in cultures, such as the contemporary Pueblos, where religion and ceremonies are interrelated with seasonal and subsistence cycles and their efficacy requires the proper performance of rituals by appropriate community members (Connelly 1979). Assuming similar ideals were prevalent in the past, it would seem that at least some of the social changes evident in the Central Mesa Verde region during the 1200s evolved from an effort to overcome perceived deficiencies through religious change and revitalization movements.

These cultural changes and religious movements did not happen uniformly, however, for the composition and networks of each village arose from differing complex circumstances deeply embedded in historical contingencies and from varying configurations of social groups, personalities, and agendas. This reality is well illustrated by the simultaneous occupation of the traditional, long-lived linear aggregated pueblo villages and the new, inwardly focused ones. The linear pueblo villages were deeply rooted in long occupation histories and the organizational changes of the 1200s were adapted to fit the existing arrangements, whereas the new type of pueblo village layout physically embodied the contemporaneous cultural changes taking place. Thus, these different histories of development present diverse contexts within which religious change was realized. Accordingly, religious change and revitalization during the thirteenth century must have involved a number of elements including the importation, creation, adaptation, and revival of religious practices and societies. The experimentation with communal gathering space and the variation in multiwalled structures, noted above, are evidence of the different ways that villages accommodated the changing ideas about inclusive practices and exclusionary ritual societies.

The varying ways that revitalization was put into practice likely caused stress and a fragmented social landscape, particularly when conservative and innovative agendas clashed (see also Chuipka and Fetterman 2009). Cultural resistance is an inevitable outcome as revitalization movements develop (Wallace 1956:274) for there are oppositions inherent in maintaining continuity while accommodating innovations that moved away from traditional practices. Indeed, it may have been one of the underlying causes for the widening field of violence that becomes apparent by the mid- to late 1200s (see also Plog and Solometo 1997). Competition for resources—both natural and social—was an integral part of the social landscape (Lipe 2002:230–232; Varien et al. 2000), and religious revitalization and the proliferation of new ritual societies would have contributed to this dynamic.

The changing role of Chaco and Aztec in Mesa Verde society and the varying influence of the Chacoan ideological complex in shaping religious practice at pueblo villages further complicated the nature, timing, and scale of the changes taking place. For example, the absence of multiwalled structures and the limited use of exterior designs on Mesa Verde black-on-white bowls in west-central Mesa Verde suggest a different level of participation in the networks and organizations developing in the eastern portion of the Northern San Juan region (Glowacki 2010). It also suggests that people living in west-central Mesa Verde may have become more aligned with developments further west in the Northern San Juan region and beyond (Glowacki 2010), where there were minimal to no Chacoan influences (Dean 1996b, 2010). This patterning indicates that there were broad-scale differences in the perceived importance of Chaco that also likely played out on a village level throughout Central Mesa Verde (e.g., the variation in multiwalled structure form).

Although after the mid-1100s, village organization in the eastern part of Central Mesa Verde seems to have moved away from traditional Chacoan characteristics, increased pressures from climate, aggregation, and settlement change in the mid-1200s may have spawned a revivalist movement (see also B. Bradley 1996). For example, at some sites, great houses were remodeled and reoccupied (Cameron 2005; Lekson and Cameron 1995; Lipe 2006:303; Lipe and Varien 1999), signifying renewed connections to key locales associated with Chacoan influence. Additionally, even though multiwalled structures proliferated in Central Mesa Verde during the early to mid-1200s and appear to be tied to the developments here, there are circular tri-walled structures at Pueblo del Arroyo in Chaco and at Aztec (Lekson 1999), which suggests that in addition to the reinvention of this architectural form there were also underlying continuities referencing aspects of Chacoan practices being expressed. These architectural shifts suggest that by the mid-1200s, at least on the part of some, there was a renewed desire to symbolically reconnect with Chaco. By the end of the 1200s, however, the trajectory of ideological change definitively shifted away from Chaco-associated practices (Lekson 2006:29) for there was a distinct break from former practices evidenced by the regional depopulation itself, the discontinued use of Mesa Verde–style artifacts and architecture (i.e., towers, multiwalled structures, mugs, and kiva jars; see Lipe 2010), and the subsequent developments in Pueblo organization during the fourteenth century.[1]

By the early to mid-1200s, religious movements in the eastern part of Central Mesa Verde may have attained some degree of coherence as evidenced by the proliferation of the hallmarks of a Mesa Verde style (e.g., mugs, towers, multiwalled structures). Thus, although there were a variety of ways that religious change and revitalization were being implemented at each village, there appears to have been a broadly shared understanding of the emergent Mesa Verde ideologies. However, the adoption of new religious practices may have been contentious at certain times or among certain groups and other problems must have persisted because, by the mid-1200s, notable numbers of people were emigrating from the region (Glowacki 2006, 2010). Even though the changes in religious practice and social organization were intended to help mitigate instability in the aftermath of the difficulties experienced during the late 1100s, they actually may have contributed to exacerbating social tensions such that emigration from the area became an increasingly appealing option to counteract untenable circumstances. This initial population loss likely made it difficult to maintain ritual cycles and religious institutions, which further contributed to the disintegration of their social order.

Then things really fell apart. The early 1260s were another agriculturally difficult period and, of course, there were the infamous drought conditions of the late 1270s and 1280s (Kohler et al. 2008; Van West and Dean 2000; Varien et al. 2007:fig. 8). Not surprisingly, violence also increased (Kuckelman 2002; Kuckelman et al. 2000; LeBlanc 1999). Consequently those remaining in the Central Mesa Verde region found themselves in all-too-familiar territory living through conditions that were not unlike those experienced during the aftermath of Chaco, a history deeply embedded in their cultural memory. Indeed, it is remarkable that the complete depopulation of the region results from this "familiar" context, shortly after the apparent revival of practices linked to Chaco. The regional depopulation, which resulted in the loss of nearly all of the material cultural signatures associated with the Mesa Verdean occupation (Lipe 2010), was likely intentional distancing from, if not outright rejection of, direct material and ideological links to Chaco because of Chaco's association with two stressful periods of intense drought and violence. The desire to materially disassociate from the Mesa Verde religious complex of the 1200s would have allowed people to more readily adopt and contribute to the religious practices and social organizations at their destinations.

Many recognize that religious change and revitalization were the outcome of the Mesa Verde migrations (e.g., McGuire 1986, 1989; Ware and Blinman 2000), but they were also central to creating the circumstances that led to the depopulation of the Central Mesa Verde region and adjacent areas. Moreover, the transformations in religious practice and organization happening in the region during the 1200s were part of a kinetic chain of events and actions that not only were shaped by the past (Chaco) but also created historical contingencies that affected the materialization of the Katsina religion and other religious practices of the fourteenth and fifteenth centuries, as well as influenced the shift to plaza-oriented pueblos and the adoption of social mechanisms that emphasized the group over the individual. The Mesa Verde migrations were more than just a response to increasing population and severe climatic challenges; they were also part of the ongoing, long-term arc of religious change across the Pueblo world.

Acknowledgments

This chapter is much improved due to thoughtful comments from Wes Bernardini, Margie Connolly, Linda Cordell, Steve Lekson, Randy McGuire, Scott Van Keuren, John Ware, Laurie Webster, the participants of the 2009 Religious Ideologies Amerind seminar, and two anonymous reviewers. My heartfelt thanks to the Amerind Foundation and their wonderful staff for not only providing exceptional hospitality and support during the seminar but also for putting up with me for a few extra days in March 2008 and April 2009 while I was researching and writing this paper. The foundation for the ideas presented here came from research supported by the Florence C. and Robert H. Lister Fellowship (Crow Canyon Archaeological Center), the Joe Ben Wheat scholarship (CU-Boulder), a Dean's Fellowship (Arizona State University), and an NSF Dissertation Improvement Grant (BCS-012487).

5

Bowls to Gardens
A History of Tewa Community Metaphors
Scott G. Ortman

As noted by Van Keuren and Glowacki in their introduction to this volume, comparative religion scholars today define religion as a social phenomenon with four components: (1) *discourses* whose concerns transcend the human, temporal, and contingent, and claim a similarly transcendent status; (2) a set of *practices* whose goal is to produce a proper world and proper human subjects, as defined by the religious discourses to which these practices are connected; (3) *communities* whose members construct their identity with reference to religious discourses and their attendant practices; and (4) *institutions* that regulate religious discourses, practices, and communities, reproducing them over time and modifying them as necessary while asserting their eternal validity and transcendent value (Lincoln 2006:5–7). From this perspective, the changes in architecture, artifacts, and symbolic imagery that accompanied the thirteenth-century reorganization of the Pueblo world suggest that this reorganization involved, at minimum, a transformation in religious institutions, communities, and practices (Adams and Duff 2004; Cameron 1995; Cameron and Duff 2008; Habicht-Mauche 1993; Lekson 2009; Lekson and Cameron 1995). This chapter seeks to examine the extent to which underlying religious discourses were also transformed during this period. In my view, previous work has not provided satisfactory answers to this question because the methods used to study past religious discourses—ethnographic analogy and the direct historical approach—have focused on aspects of religious discourses that have *not* changed from the past to the present. These methods do not allow one to delve into the content of past discourses when they were *different* from those of the present, or to understand how present-day discourses relate to earlier ones.

I suggest that a good way to study the histories of religious discourses is to focus on the building blocks of these discourses and their varied expressions in language and the archaeological record. According to the comparative religion scholar Edward Slingerland (2004), these building blocks consist of conceptual metaphors—cognitive models through which relatively abstract domains of experience are conceptualized in terms of more concrete domains. This is an important insight from a methodological standpoint because conceptual metaphors underlay many forms of human action (Kövecses 2002; Preston Blier 1987; Sandstrom 1991; Shore 1996; Walens 1981), they can be deciphered from material expressions in the archaeological record (Hays-Gilpin 2008; Ortman 2000b, 2006, 2008a, 2009; Ortman and Bradley 2002; Potter 2002; Potter and Ortman 2004; Sekaquaptewa and Washburn 2004; Tilley 1999; Whitley 2008; Whittlesey 2005), and the metaphors of past speakers of a language can be identified through studies of compound words, polysemy, and semantic change (Campbell 1998: 254–273; Pinker 2007:235–278; Sweetser 1990:23–48; Traugott 1989). So if one agrees that conceptual metaphors constitute an appropriate currency for studying religious discourses, it would appear that appropriate methods are already in place.

In this chapter I apply these methods to examine some of the metaphors through which Tewa-speaking Pueblo people have "imagined" their communities over time (*sensu* Anderson 1983; Isbell 2000). I begin by examining contemporary Tewa songs to identify metaphors that present-day speakers use. Then I turn to linguistic analysis to show that some of these concepts are also embedded in Tewa and in related languages, and thus have considerable time depth. Importantly, this analysis will also reveal residues of imaginings that are not expressed in contemporary song, or even in the archaeological record of the Tewa Basin. At this point, archaeological analysis comes to the fore and suggests that these "dead" metaphors were expressed in Mesa Verde–region villages that were likely inhabited by Tewa speakers before they moved to the Tewa Basin. In addition, the archaeological evidence suggests that this older style of imagining the community was replaced by the style that is dominant today as Tewa speakers settled in to their current homeland.

Through these analyses, I will argue that the community concepts of present-day Tewa communities are different from those of their ancestors. I will also show that the community concepts of present-day Tewa communities arose in dialectical relation with new experiences of architecture and agriculture *after* speakers of this language migrated to the northern Rio Grande. In other words, the methods I employ allow me not only to trace present-day conceptions back to the fourteenth century and to reconstruct the semantic content of earlier conceptions but also to examine how present-day conceptions took shape over time. Based on these results, I suggest that conceptual metaphors, and associated methods for deciphering their varied expressions in archaeology and language, are central to understanding the transformation in Pueblo society that took place between AD 1200 and 1400.

The Tewa Pueblos and the Tewa Language

There are seven pueblos at which Tewa is the dominant native language today. Six of these (Ohkay'owinge, Nambe, Pojoaque, Santa Clara, San Ildefonso, and Tesuque) are located in the Española Basin in New Mexico, which is bounded by the Santa Fe divide on the south, the Jemez Mountains on the west, Mesa Prieta on the north, and the Sangre de Cristo Mountains on the east. The seventh village (Tewa Village), on Hopi First Mesa, Arizona, formed as a result of migration from the Rio Grande in 1696. Based on evidence from place names, oral tradition, historic Spanish documents, and archaeology (Anschuetz 2005; Harrington 1916; Marshall and Walt 2007; Mera 1935; Schroeder 1979), it is clear that Tewa-speaking peoples once occupied a much larger area of north-central New Mexico. In the north, ancestral Tewa sites occur throughout the Española Basin and northward into the lands upstream of the confluence of the Rio Chama and Rio Grande. To the south, ancestral Tewa settlements also extend across the Santa Fe divide and into the Galisteo Basin southeast of Santa Fe. I will focus here on ethnographic, linguistic, and archaeological evidence related to Tewa communities of the northern area, which is often labeled the Tewa Basin (see figure 5.1).

The Tewa language is part of the Kiowa-Tanoan language family. This family includes Kiowa, a language of the southern plains; Towa,

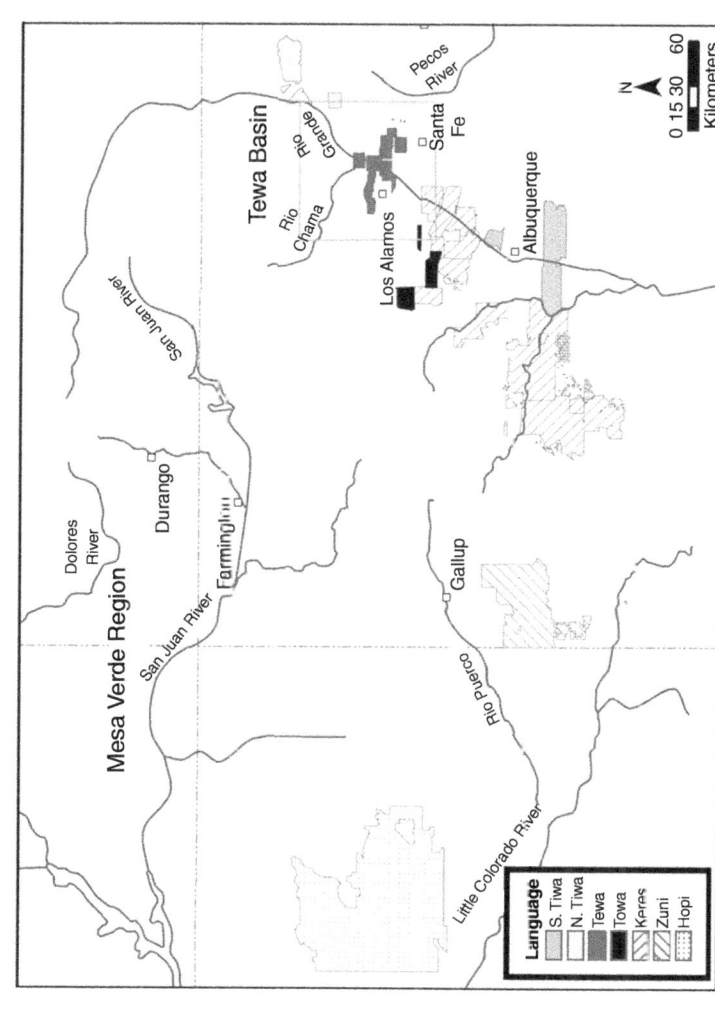

Figure 5.1. The Pueblo area, with tribal lands and languages indicated.

which is spoken at Jemez; Northern Tiwa, which is spoken at Taos and Picuris; Southern Tiwa, which is spoken at Sandia and Isleta; and Piro, an extinct language that was once spoken along the Rio Grande south of Albuquerque (Davis 1959; Hale 1967; Harrington 1909). The internal relationships among these languages have been questioned at times (Hale and Harris 1979; Kroskrity 1993:55–60; Watkins 1984), but my own study of shared phonetic innovations among extant Kiowa-Tanoan dialects (Ortman 2009:chap. 6) supports the traditional view that Kiowa is the most divergent dialect and thus separated earliest from Proto-Tanoan, followed by Towa from Proto-Tewa-Tiwa, Tewa from Proto-Tiwa, and finally, Northern Tiwa from Southern Tiwa (also see Davis 1959; Harrington 1909; Trager 1967).

The traditional method of estimating when major splits in a language family occurred, known as glottochronology, yields estimates that are far less precise than archaeological dating methods. In my work I have taken advantage of the precisely dated Pueblo archaeological record to estimate when the major branches of Kiowa-Tanoan formed by dating the first appearance of material culture items that have reconstructible terms in various Kiowa-Tanoan subgroups (see Ortman 2009:chap. 7). For this analysis, I used the sound correspondences worked out by Trager (1942) and Hale (1967) to identify cognates. Proto-Kiowa-Tanoan reconstructions are based on cognates in Kiowa and at least one Tanoan dialect; Proto-Tanoan reconstructions on cognates in Towa and at least one other Tanoan dialect but not Kiowa; Proto-Tewa-Tiwa, on cognates in Tewa and Tiwa but not Kiowa and Towa; and Proto-Tiwa, on cognates in Northern and Southern Tiwa but not in Kiowa, Towa, and Tewa. Archaeological dating of the material culture items thus reconstructed suggests that Proto-Kiowa-Tanoan was spoken during Basketmaker II (1500 BC–AD 450); Proto-Tanoan, Basketmaker III (450–725); Proto-Tiwa-Tewa, Pueblo I (725–920); and Proto-Tiwa, Pueblo II (980–1100) (see figure 5.2). With this framework in place, it is possible to investigate the antiquity of metaphors embedded in Kiowa-Tanoan languages using the comparative method. But before doing so, let us examine some of the metaphors Tewa people use when talking about their communities in the present.

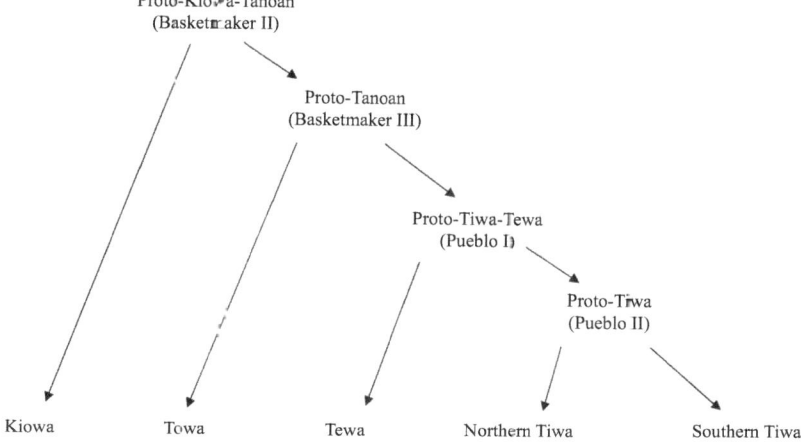

Figure 5.2. Schematic model of the Kiowa-Tanoan language family.

Community Metaphors in Discourse

If one attends a dance at a Tewa-speaking village today, one will see the elder women of the pueblo standing around the edges of the plaza, while elder men sing songs and direct the movements of the male and female dancers within. If one could also understand Tewa, one would hear in the lyrics metaphors that present the plaza and surrounding pueblo as a garden. For example, during the butterfly dance at Ohkay Owingeh in 1957, the singers chanted (Kurath 1970:152):

> In San Juan Pueblo right in the middle of the plaza outside the
>   kiva here, white corn goddess stands.
> With her living plants she stands prepared at dawn,

and during a later portion of this same dance, in 1963, the singers chanted (Kurath 1970:153):

> At (soul) village, over there where the rivers join at confluence lake.
> They come right here, carrying flowers; the oxua have flowers
>   there.
> They come to see our fields.

The first lyric presents the image of the plaza as a garden within which corn plants are growing, and the second lyric states that "right here," the pueblo where the dance is taking place, is "our fields"; the lyric describes the ancestral site across the Rio Grande as a lake from which the *ókʰùwà* 'cloud-beings' bring *okʰúwápóvi* 'cloud-flowers', or rainclouds, to water the fields.[1] Both songs thus present the village as a garden, the female dancers within the plaza as corn plants, and the male dancers who move through the plaza as clouds. THE COMMUNITY IS A GARDEN is also vividly expressed in the following poem, recorded sometime between 1909 and 1912 (Spinden 1993:95):

> Ready we stand in San Juan town,
> Oh, our Corn Maidens and our Corn Youths!
> Oh, our Corn Mothers and our Corn Fathers!
>
> Now we bring you misty water
> And throw it different ways,
> To the north, the west, the south, the east
> To heaven above and the drinking earth below!
> Then likewise throw your misty water
> Toward San Juan!
> Oh, many that you are, pour water
> Over our Corn Maidens' ears!

Here again, we see the pueblo presented as a garden, and the people as growing corn plants who beseech the *ókʰùwà* to enter the plaza and bring them life, just as rain causes corn to grow.

Community Metaphors Embedded in the Tewa Language

The etymologies and multiple senses of words in the Tewa language suggest that some of the metaphors in these Tewa songs are quite old.[2] For example, PEOPLE ARE CORN appears to be older than the Tewa language itself because at least one Proto-Tanoan maize term derives from a Proto-Kiowa-Tanoan body-part term. The relevant data are presented in table 5.1, and they show that meanings associated with Proto-Kiowa-Tanoan **kʰoy* 'skin, hide' were extended to include 'cornhusk'

Bowls to Gardens: A History of Tewa Community Metaphors

Table 5.1. People and corn in Kiowa-Tanoan context.

Reconstruction	N. Tiwa	S. Tiwa	Tewa	Towa	Kiowa
A. KT *kʰoy 'skin, hide'	xójna 'skin, hide'	kʰay 'skin'	kʰowa 'skin, bark, cornhusk'	wǽhæ 'skin, hide'	kʰɔ́y 'skin, cloth, mat'
B. PT *kʰo 'cornhusk'				hæ̂: 'cornhusk'	

Source: Ortman 2009:table 10.1.

in Proto-Tanoan times. In other words, Tanoan speakers appear to have drawn an analogy between the parts of a corn plant and the parts of a person at the time the new sense "cornhusk" became attached to the word for "skin." Additional reflexes of PEOPLE ARE CORN are scattered throughout Tanoan dialects. For example, the Tewa corn mother, a perfect ear of corn wrapped with feathers and beads, is called kʰuluŋʔaa or 'corn-clothed' (Parsons 1929:249; Robbins et al. 1916:88), and Jemez kį 'child' can also mean 'seed', 'grain', or 'bean.' These examples suggest that metaphorical relationships among people and corn, and especially women and corn, have been part of the culture of Tanoan speakers for many centuries.[3]

Details that imply the metaphor MEN ARE WATER are also clearly embedded in the Tewa language. For example, the souls of initiated Tewa men become cloud-beings after death (A. Ortiz 1969:96), a transformation reflected in the phonetic correspondence of okʰúwá 'cloud' and ókʰùwà 'cloud-being' (table 5.2). The only contrasts between these words are tonal contours that reflect the movements of clouds and souls, respectively. Clouds form high over the mountains and remain in

Table 5.2. Tonal contours and patterns of movement in Tewa.

Up	Down	Up and Down
okʰúwá 'cloud' (ʔokʰu 'down, fluff' + wá 'breath')		ókʰùwà 'cloud-being'
	pʔo: 'water, stream'	pʔô: 'trail, path'

Source: Ortman 2008b:142–143.

the sky, a pattern reflected in the high tone of *okʰúwá*. In contrast, cloud-beings are ancestral spirits that leave the bodies of the deceased, travel up to the mountains, and then return to the village in the form of rain and male impersonators. This pattern of movement is reflected in the rising-then-falling tone of *ókʰùwà* (Ortman 2008b). This same tonal pattern is apparent in words for trails, streams, and water. The water in streams only flows downhill, and thus the word for water or stream, *pʔòː*, has a low tone. In contrast, males, as the real-world counterparts of the cloud-beings, travel in both directions along trails leading to and from mountaintop shrines so as to encourage water to come down to the villages. Accordingly, the word for a trail or path is *pʔô:*, with a rising-then-falling tone. Finally, the relationship between water and males is implied by the name for the stone-lined passages at mountaintop shrines that point toward Tewa villages. Men pass through these *kwänpʔô:* or 'rain-roads' as they enter or exit the shrine enclosures (Douglass 1917; Ortman 2008b).

Given that metaphors linking women and corn, and men and water, are embedded in the Tewa language, one might expect THE COMMUNITY IS A GARDEN to be embedded in this language as well. That this is the case is demonstrated by the most commonly used word for village, *'ówîngé*. This word analyzes as 'there-standing-at,' and contains the verb *wį́nú* 'to stand' (from Proto-Tanoan **gʷin* 'stand') that is used to describe growing corn as well as female dancers in the plaza (table 5.3). *Ówîngé* also has no cognates in other Kiowa-Tanoan languages, and it thus was probably coined after Tewa became a distinct language, sometime after 920. In addition, it is likely that this word was coined prior to 1350 because the oldest Tewa Basin villages known as *'ówînkeyi* 'village ruin' were abandoned by this date (see Ortman 2009:chap. 8).

These linguistic data thus show that the metaphors expressed in songs performed during plaza ceremonies today are not recent inventions but instead reflect ideas that have been part of Tewa culture for many centuries. Also, the linguistic data suggest that the three major elements of this model came together gradually: connections between people and corn appear to predate the development of Tewa as a distinct language, but connections between men and water developed only after Tewa became distinct, and connections between villages and gardens could have developed as recently as 1300.

Table 5.3. Villages and plazas in Kiowa-Tanoan context.

Tewa	N. Tiwa	S. Tiwa	Towa	Kiowa	Reconstruction
bɛ́ 'pottery bowl, vessel, fruit' bú:'ú 'village, plaza' bɛ́:'e-bú:'ú, 'small-large, low roundish place'	mulu'une 'pottery' (tio- 'village'	búru 'pottery bowl' natiy, tiy 'community, home, pueblo'	bɨdó 'round, fat, chubby' t'a:bɨ 'sacred bowl' tú:kʷa 'village' tí:yo 'home, place where we live'	cend'ɔ'atdɔ 'clay dish' to-byu'ę 'house-circle'	PT *bɨ́ulu 'pottery (bowl), round'
pín 'heart, middle'	píana 'heart, middle'	pia 'heart' piantad 'center middle'	pɛ́ 'heart' pó:k'a 'in the middle'	t'ęn 'heart'	PT *pian- 'heart'
búpíngéh 'plaza' (bú:'ú + pín + géh 'place')	píanto 'plaza, center-middle' (lit. "heart-within")	nap'ahia 'place, town, plaza' p'ahiad 'plaza' (cf. p'ahia 'well')	pó:t'u 'plaza, middle, center' ñó:pitá 'plaza' ñó:lá 'inside a circle, in the plaza' (cf. ñó:- 'inside')	guɔn-dąm 'dance-ground'	TT *pian- 'middle, plaza' (?)
'ówínge 'village' (there-stand-at) wínú 'to stand' 'awį́n 'to grow in a standing position'	kʷínmą 'to stand'	wini 'stand up'	kʷíp'ǽ 'stand up'	pʰǫ 'to stand up'	PT *gʷí 'stand'

Source: Ortman 2009:table 10.2. Noncognate forms for each row are presented using gray text.

Yet the Tewa language also enshrines community metaphors that are not expressed in contemporary songs. For example, another Tewa word for village, *bú:ʔú*, does not derive from words related to maize agriculture but instead comes from Proto-Tanoan **búlu* 'pottery (bowl), round' (table 5.3). *Bú:ʔú* can also mean 'large, low roundish place' or 'plaza' (e.g., *Pʼoqwogeʔimbú:ʼú* 'San Ildefonso [water cuts down through] plaza' [Harrington 1916:305–306]; *búpíngéh* 'plaza' [*bú:ʼú* + *pín* 'heart, middle' + *géh* 'place']), and it is related to *be:ʔe* 'small, low roundish place' and *be:* 'pottery bowl' via sound symbolism (Harrington 1910:16). In many Tewa words, front vowels (/e/ and /a/) indicate small entities, whereas back vowels (/o/ and /u/) indicate larger entities, as shown in table 5.4. The Tewa forms *be:*, *be:ʔe* and *bú:ʔú* follow this pattern, and they thus link the imagery of pottery bowls, bowl-shaped topographical features, and villages and plazas in a series of forms that all derive from an older word for 'pottery bowl'. Finally, reflexes of Proto-Tanoan **búlu* in other Tanoan languages refer only to pottery, and not to topographical features or villages. All of this suggests there was a period of time after Tewa had become a distinct language during which Tewa speakers imagined their communities by using the metaphor THE COMMUNITY IS A SERVING BOWL.[4]

Table 5.4. Sound symbolism: Tongue position and scale in Tewa.

Front/Small	Middle/Medium	Back/Very Large
iʔpiye 'to this place'	*haeʔpiye* 'to yonder place'	*oʔpiye* 'to that remote place'
heʔe 'small groove, arroyito'		*húʔú* 'large groove, arroyo'
pʰigi 'small and flat'	*pʰagi* 'large and flat'	
be:giʔ 'small and round'		*bu:giʔ* 'large and round'
be: 'pottery bowl, vessel, fruit'	*be:ʔe* 'small low roundish place'	*bú:ʔú* 'large, low roundish place, village plaza'

Source: Ortman 2009:Chapter 10.

Bowls to Gardens: A History of Tewa Community Metaphors

For a word that originally meant 'pottery bowl' to have developed the additional sense 'village', a metaphor that linked these two domains must have been sufficiently widespread in the Tewa speech community for listeners to have understood a speaker when he or she used the word for 'bowl' in the new, figurative sense. Then this word must have been used in the figurative sense often enough that it became a second conventional meaning of the word. It is not unreasonable to expect that a metaphor pervasive enough to influence the meanings of words would have also influenced other forms of social action. Yet the metaphor implied by *be:~be:ʔe~tú:ʔú* 'pottery bowl'~'small/large low roundish place'~'plaza/village' is not only absent from contemporary Tewa songs but is also absent from the architecture of ancestral Tewa villages in northern New Mexico. These villages were neither bowl-shaped nor built in bowl-shaped settings; rather, they were rectilinear and built on terraces above major streams (see figure 5.3; also see Anschuetz 2005; Fowles 2004; Harrington 1916; Snead 2008; Snead et al. 2004). What

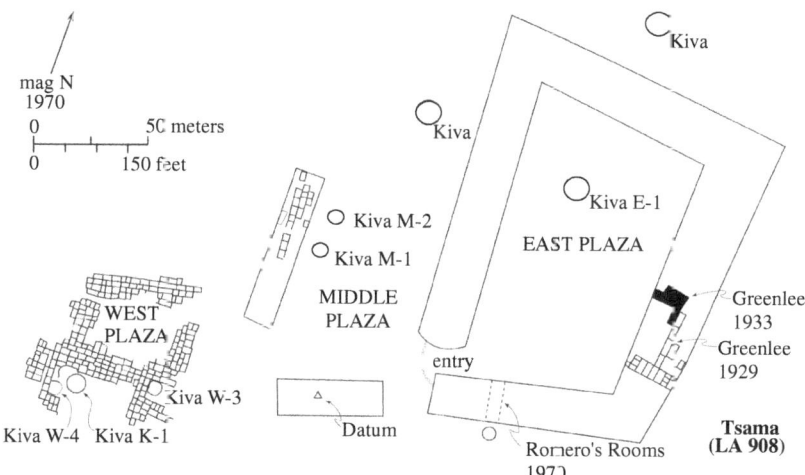

Figure 5.3. Plan map of Tsama Pueblo (*Tsáma'ówinkeyi* 'wrestling pueblo ruin'), a Tewa Basin village. The West Plaza dates to the Late Coalition–Early Classic Period (1250–1400); the Middle Plaza dates to the Early-Middle Classic Period (1350–1500); and the East Plaza dates to the Middle-Late Classic Period (1400–1600) (Windes and McKenna 2006:fig. 1; courtesy of Tom Windes).

is one to make of the absence of local archaeological expressions of these linguistic residues?

The Archaeology of Vestigial Tewa Metaphors

One possibility, given that the oldest sites with Tewa names in the northern Rio Grande date from around 1275, whereas the Tewa language was distinct as early as 920, is that Tewa was spoken somewhere else prior to 1275, and THE COMMUNITY IS A SERVING BOWL circulated among speakers in this former homeland. If Tewa was ever spoken anywhere besides the Tewa Basin, the most likely candidate would be the Mesa Verde region of southwestern Colorado and southeastern Utah. In a separate study (Ortman 2009; also see Ortman 2010), I present a range of evidence that supports this hypothesis. This evidence includes the following:

1. Population reconstructions, which show a pattern of population growth in the northern Rio Grande that is difficult to explain in terms of intrinsic population processes and is coincident in scale and timing with population decline in the Mesa Verde region;
2. Biological variation, which suggests an ancestor–descendant relationship between Mesa Verde region populations on the one hand, and ancestral Tewa populations in the northern Rio Grande on the other;
3. Paired Tewa and Northern Tiwa place-names, which contain no evidence that the Proto-Tiwa-Tewa speech community was located in the northern Rio Grande;
4. Tewa and Northern Tiwa names for archaeological sites, which indicate that Tewa cannot be documented in the northern Rio Grande prior to 1275, whereas Northern Tiwa can be documented from the late 1100s;
5. Tewa place-names for locations in the Mesa Verde region, including Sleeping Ute Mountain, the Montezuma Valley, and the archaeological site of Yucca House, a 1200s village;
6. Oral traditions, which state that Tewa ancestors lived in the Mesa Verde region prior to moving to the northern Rio Grande; and
7. Spanish documents, which indicate that knowledge of the name

and general location of the former Tewa homeland was widespread in seventeenth century New Mexico.

An additional line of evidence that is generally supportive of this hypothesis is that Mesa Verde material culture expresses a complex of "material" metaphors that are also enshrined in the Tewa language but are vestigial at best in Tewa Basin material culture. I have presented methods for reconstructing metaphors from archaeological evidence and reconstructions of specific metaphors in the Mesa Verde region archaeological record in a number of earlier studies.[5] Here I focus on the results and implications of these studies.

My previous work in this area suggests that Mesa Verde people used container imagery as a model for many diverse realms of experience. For example, the Mesa Verde design style was inspired by weaving imagery, tracked developments in weaving over time, and blended imagery from different industries in coherent ways (Ortman 2000b). In contrast, weaving imagery was not generative in Tewa Basin pottery decoration. Motifs that originated in weaving continued to be painted, but only in static and stereotyped ways (Ortman 2009:chap. 13). Yet one of the Tewa words for pottery, *nat?ú*, is a compound of *nan* 'earth, clay' and *t?ú* 'coiled baskets' and clearly expresses the metaphor POTTERY VESSELS ARE BASKETS.

Another example is that the small kivas of Mesa Verde region domestic architecture were typically constructed with cribbed and dome-shaped roofs that present an image of an overturned coiled basket, and they were also often decorated with murals that presented the lower, plastered half of the chamber as a pottery bowl (Ortman 2008a). Cribbed kiva roofs are completely absent from the Tewa Basin archaeological record, but the Tewa word for 'pitched roof', *t?úp̣ʰá?di?*, is a compound that analyzes as "coiled basket of timbers" and clearly expresses the metaphor KIVA ROOFS ARE COILED BASKETS.

Finally, and most importantly, the last villages constructed in the Mesa Verde region were built around canyon-head environments that present concave enclosures of rock and soil, and they also contained water emanating from a spring within (see figure 5.4). The houses in these canyon-rim villages were terraced down the slope, creating a settlement in which buildings faced inward, toward the low, geographical

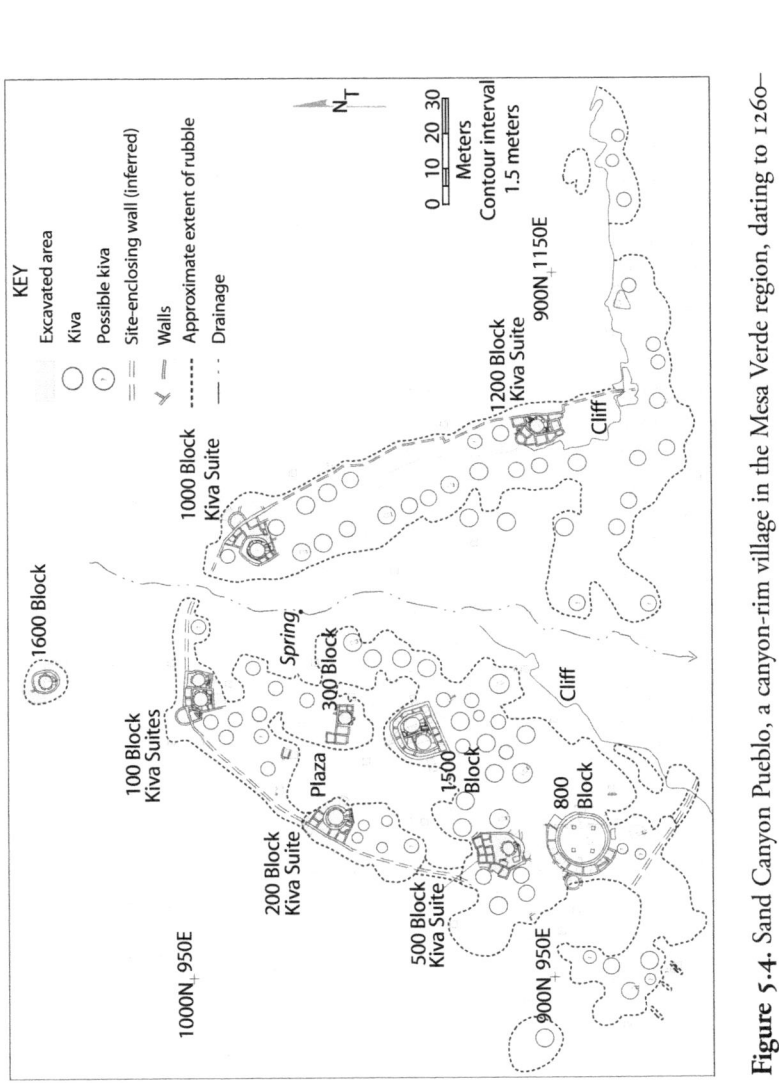

Figure 5.4. Sand Canyon Pueblo, a canyon-rim village in the Mesa Verde region, dating to 1260–1280. © Crow Canyon Archaeological Center.

center of the local built environment. In addition, communal food storage, preparation, and consumption were commonplace in these villages. The concept appears to have been that the community was a family that lived around, and shared food from, a common bowl (table 5.5; also see Lipe and Ortman 2000; Ortman and Bradley 2002; Ortman 2009:chap. 9). As mentioned earlier, villages that express this imagery were never characteristic of the Tewa Basin, but one of the Tewa words for village, *bú:'ú*, also refers to bowl-shaped things, and it actually derives from an older Proto-Tanoan word for a pottery bowl.

From this evidence, I draw two conclusions. First, Tewa-speaking peoples of the Mesa Verde region imagined their communities using metaphors that appropriated imagery of the family, the house, and do-

Table 5.5. Correspondences between pottery-serving bowls and canyon-rim villages.

Serving Bowls	Canyon-Rim Villages
Image-schematic correspondences	
1. Made of earth	1. Constructed on the ground
2. Temper	2. Building stone
3. Clay and water make paste	3. Earth and water make mortar and plaster
4. Round, open, concave interior	4. Canyon-head setting
5. Liquid collects in center	5. Spring occurs in the middle
6. Vessel holds water	6. Village contains water issuing from spring
7. Vessel contains food	7. Village contains people (PEOPLE ARE CORN)
Additional transferred structure	
1. Rim	1. Enclosing wall
2. Inward-facing band of terraced geometric designs	2. Terraced houses face inward, toward the center of the canyon-head environment
3. Center left undecorated	3. Spring area left undeveloped
4. Serves food to a family	4. Stores food for the community
5. Household eats out of a bowl	5. The community feasts in the plaza
6. Household members sit around a bowl to eat	6. Community members sit around the perimeter of the plaza to feast
7. Pottery made by mothers	7. Village layouts planned by leaders
8. Meals prepared by mothers	8. Feasts scheduled by leaders

mestic meals. Discourses involving these metaphors ceased to function as generative bases for social action when Tewa speakers migrated to New Mexico, but residues of these discourses remained enshrined in the Tewa language as semantic fossils. Second, the newer style of imagining the community as a garden, which remains active today, appears to have taken shape during the period of cultural transformation that followed migration. In the following pages, I argue that THE COMMUNITY IS A GARDEN has been an active part of Tewa culture from the early 1300s because this is when novel expressions of this concept began to appear in the archaeological record of the Tewa Basin.

Architecture and Agriculture

The first village-sized settlements that are generally agreed to have been created by Tewa speakers in the northern Rio Grande date from the middle to late 1200s and are known as plaza pueblos (Ford et al. 1972; Kohler 2004; Creamer 1993; Stubbs and Stallings 1953). The architecture and settings of these settlements probably expressed many concepts, including a communal ideology (Ortman 1998), a defensive posture (Snead 2008; Snead et al. 2004), and a worldview that emphasized cardinal regions and landforms (A. Ortiz 1969) as well as relationships between the spirit world, the earth, and the sky (Ruscavage-Barz and Bagwell 2006). Additional details of these sites suggest a number of cultural practices that encouraged new connections between architecture and agriculture. For example, kivas, the underground chambers where rituals of emergence, growth, and transformation took place, were constructed inside the plazas in these villages. As a result, ritual practices that reflect PEOPLE ARE CORN, such as the emergence of new initiates from underground, took place in public view inside the plaza. In addition, burial practices that reflect ANCESTORS ARE WATER as well as CHILDREN ARE CORN took place in public view in and around plaza-oriented sites. At Arroyo Hondo, for example, sub-adults tended to be "replanted" beneath plaza and room surfaces, whereas adults tended to be interred in extramural middens or ash piles, presumably reflecting the journey of their souls to the mountains that rim the present-day Tewa homeland (table 5.6, after Palkovich 1980:appendix B).[6] These practices related existing metaphors concern-

Table 5.6. Arroyo Hondo burial locations.

	Adults	Subadults
Extramural middens (ash piles)	16	10
Beneath plaza and room surfaces	27	58
Chi-square probability =	.006	

Source: Palkovich 1980:appendix B.

ing people, corn, and water to the new built environment of plaza-oriented villages.

The recruitment of architectural imagery for agricultural practices appears to have begun a few generations after Tewa speakers settled in the Tewa Basin. Although agricultural features are difficult to date, the development of Tewa Basin agricultural technology has been clarified by a recent study of the Truchas drainage in which Marshall and Walt (2007) identified a single-component pueblo dating from 1250 to 1325 in an area with no prior or subsequent occupation. The agricultural features associated with this pueblo are limited to cobblestone check dams and terraces constructed to retain or divert runoff and to capture soil. Similar features have been found in association with pueblos abandoned by 1375 elsewhere in the Tewa Basin, and they are common surrounding Mesa Verde region sites in the 1200s as well (Varien 1999b).

By 1400, however, more elaborate agricultural features that clearly exhibit architectural imagery were being constructed. The clearest examples are cobble-bordered fields constructed by gathering cobblestones and arranging them in grid patterns (see figure 5.5). A layer of gravel mulch was also often laid on top of the soil within the cells (Anschuetz 1998:fig. 7.4; Bugé 1984:29). The sizes and shapes of the cells in these fields are identical to those of pueblo habitation rooms. In fact, the similarities are so pronounced that some early archaeologists mistook cobble-bordered fields for pueblo wall foundations. Sylvanus Morley (1910:24), for example, described cobble-bordered fields as remains of "pre-Pajaritan" villages, stating that "in many cases the size, shape and assemblage of these enclosures are such as to strongly indicate that they were once dwelling sites." Greenlee (1933:13) also de-

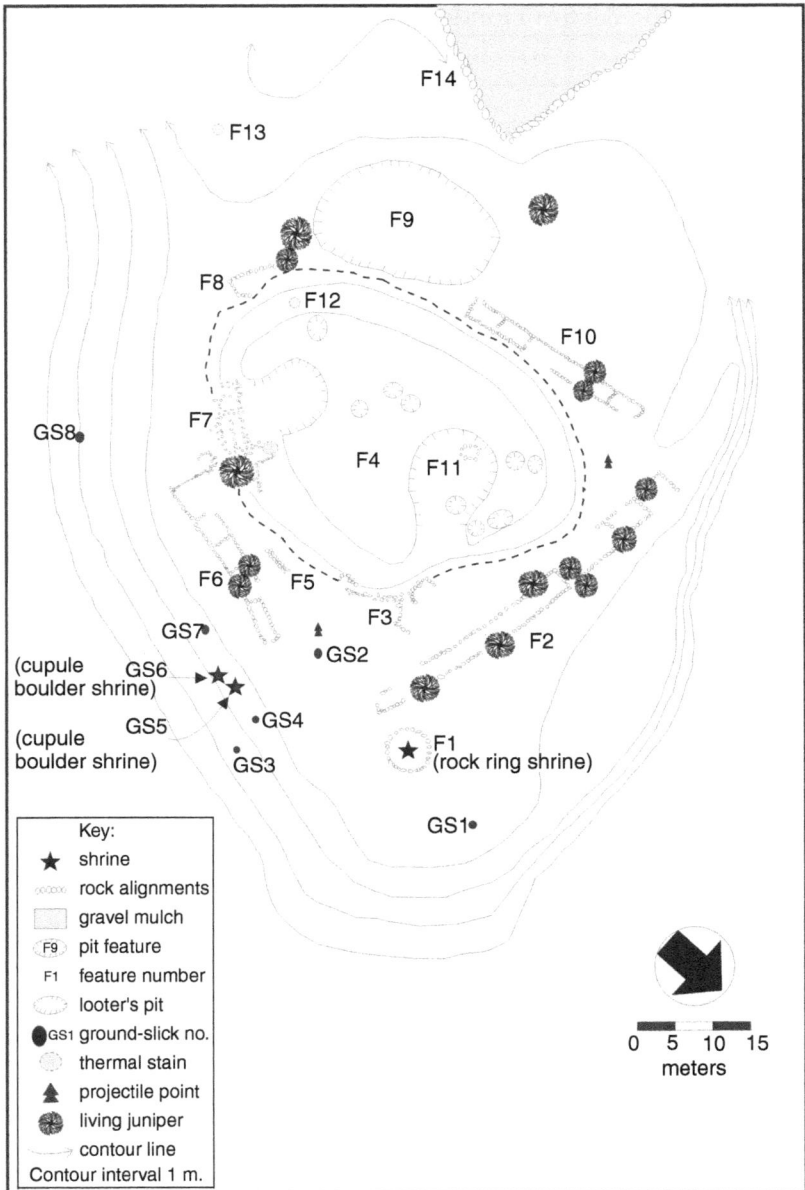

Figure 5.5. Maestas Pueblo, an early Tewa Basin village. Note the cobble-bordered gardens (F2, F6, F8, and F10) surrounding the house mound (F4). Map courtesy of Kurt Anschuetz.

scribed these fields as "foundation stone villages" in his survey of the Rio Chama. Research on lithic fields indicates that these features improved yields by retaining runoff and soil, absorbing heat and radiating it onto crops on cool evenings, and retaining soil moisture beneath the gravel mulches. Pollen studies also indicate that corn was grown in these fields along with other crops (Maxwell and Anschuetz 1992: 61–66; Marshall and Walt 2007). Thus, these features, which expressed architectural imagery, also increased the productivity of agricultural lands.

Another development in fourteenth-century Tewa Basin agriculture that may have inspired the development of cobble-bordered fields was the reuse of old habitations as gardens. On the Pajarito Plateau, farmers cleared the rubble from collapsed rooms, stacked it up to form terraces and field houses, and used the wall foundations as gridded cell borders (Gauthier and Herhahn 2005:30–31; Kohler 2004:148; Steen 1982:3–4). In the Chama, cobble-bordered fields were also constructed on top of melted adobe room blocks (Luebben 1953:13–15). In both cases, Tewa farmers took advantage of the increased soil fertility inside abandoned structures due to decomposition of the walls, roofing material, and organic refuse left over from the previous occupation. In short, people appear to have recognized that, if they planted corn inside old houses it grew better in the same way that children flourished in the context of the home. This must have provided striking support for the conceptual unity of people and corn, and of connections between architecture and agriculture.[7]

A final parallel between fields and houses appeared in the fifteenth century, when Tewa architects began building the adobe walls of houses on top of cobble-filled foundation trenches (Creamer 1993:41, 13l; Fallon and Wening 1987:19; Jeançon 1923:10–11; Luebben 1953:11; Stubbs and Stallings 1953:26; Wendorf 1953:37). These foundations look like the cells of cobble-bordered fields when the adobe melts away, and I have seen examples where the corners of gridded fields and house foundations were both marked by noticeably upright cobbles. Also, as mentioned previously, early archaeologists sometimes mistook cobble-bordered fields for pueblo wall foundations due to their similar size and shape. I suggest these correspondences in the construction of cobble-bordered fields and house foundations reflect the transfer of conceptual structure between fields and homes. In other words, parallels in the foundations of houses and fields suggest that, by the fifteenth century, Tewa people viewed families in adobe pueblos as a mirror image of planted corn kernels in the earth within cobble-bordered fields.

These observations suggest that Tewa speakers, who had viewed people and corn as reflections of each other long before moving to the Rio Grande, began to extend relationships between people and buildings to corn and fields soon after settling in the Tewa Basin. Because several new expressions of this relationship developed over time, it would appear that symbolic connections between village architecture and agricultural fields influenced thought and action in Tewa communities from the middle of the fourteenth century onward. Thus, the style of imagining the community reflected in contemporary Tewa songs appears to have developed through the encounter of existing metaphors linking people, corn, and water with embodied experience in a new landscape and in new built environments (table 5.7). In other words, the analogy *people are to villages as corn is to fields* developed as a preexisting metaphor linking people and corn confronted new experiences with plaza-oriented settlements and farming in the Tewa Basin. The resulting metaphor, THE COMMUNITY IS A GARDEN, was subsequently elaborated through practices that transferred additional structure between the realms of homes, gardens, and ritual.

Metaphors, Discourses, and History

The data and arguments presented in this chapter suggest that one of the styles through which Tewa people imagine their communities today did indeed take shape during the period of remarkable social and cultural transformation that is the focus of this volume. When Tewa speakers entered the Tewa Basin, they brought with them metaphors that related women and men to corn and water, and upon arrival these same people began constructing settlements with innovative, plaza-focused layouts. This combination of inherited metaphors linking people, corn, and water with new built environments appears to have brought into being new correspondences between architecture and agriculture that exerted a wide-ranging influence on Classic Period material culture, and these influences continue to be expressed in present-day ritual and

Table 5.7. Correspondences between cobble-bordered gardens and plaza-oriented villages.

Cobble-Bordered Gardens	Pueblo Village
Image-schematic correspondences	
1. Rectangular shape of cells	1. Rectangular shape of rooms/plazas
2. Corn germinates underground	2. Children grow in houses
3. Corn plants grow in cells	3. Women work in the village
4. Water comes from mountains	4. Men work outside the village
5. Corn planted in old houses	5. People live in current houses
6. Water follows arroyos to gardens	6. Men follow trails to village
7. Cobs grow on plants in cells	7. Corn changed to food in plazas
8. Water causes kernels to germinate	8. Men cause babies to grow
Additional transferred structure	
1. Grid cell size	1. Room size
2. Cobble border	2. Room foundation
3. Upright cobbles mark corners	3. Upright cobbles mark corners
4. Earth within cell	4. Adobe house
5. Kernels planted in earth within cells	5. Children buried in plazas/houses
6. Water comes from clouds	6. Elders buried in ash piles
7. Clouds form over mountains	7. Men pray at mountain shrines
8. Cobs grow on plants in cell	8. Corn changed to food in plaza
9. Water germinates seeds	9. Cloud-beings mingle with corn maidens in dances

song. In addition, these new experiences not only reinforced perceptual correspondences between villages and fields but they also encouraged technological innovations that furthered the adaptation of ancestral Tewa farmers to the Tewa Basin landscape. The fact that THE COMMUNITY IS A GARDEN developed in dialectical relation with agricultural technology emphasizes that transcendent religious discourses are often built up from concrete bodily experience and practical knowledge, and they remain connected to these purely temporal concerns. Thus, it would appear that culture and religion need to be viewed as connected to function and adaptation if one wishes to fully understand the histories of religious discourses. Conceptual metaphors are not merely about symbolism and meaning; they are also about practical knowledge that helps people to survive and thrive. This fundamental reality is much easier to perceive when ethnographic and linguistic data come down to earth and confront the materiality of the archaeological record.

This study also suggests that, in earlier Tewa-speaking communities of the Mesa Verde region, the community was imagined differently, using metaphors that presented the community as a group of relatives who shared from a common bowl. This is reflected in both the histories of words in the Tewa language and the archaeological record of the Mesa Verde region where the Tewa language originated. The exciting implication of this finding is that, due to the fact that the *content* of this earlier style of imagining can be specified, one can compare the imagery associated with THE COMMUNITY IS A GARDEN and THE COMMUNITY IS A SERVING BOWL to suggest ways in which Tewa religious discourses changed over time.

For example, the corn plants in a garden present an undifferentiated group, and this communal image appears to be reflected in the homogeneous pottery style and anonymous household architecture of plaza pueblos in the fourteenth-century Tewa Basin (Kohler et al. 2004). An image of social harmony is also invoked by a group of relatives eating around a common bowl, but these individuals also had different statuses, roles, and responsibilities based on their age, gender, kin relationships, and so forth. Thus, Mesa Verde village leaders could have drawn upon the imagery of the matron who controlled household food stores and served food to her family to argue, on the basis of THE COMMUNITY IS A SERVING BOWL, that it was appropriate and natural for village leaders to control agricultural surpluses. Several details of canyon-rim villages suggest that community leaders did in fact frame community life in this manner. Specifically, these villages contained D-shaped structures that functioned as elite residences as well as settings for exclusive ritual; kiva-dominated houses that lacked the normal complement of food storage rooms; and storage complexes that were not physically connected to individual residences (Lipe 2002; Lipe and Ortman 2000; Ortman and Bradley 2002). All of this suggests that religious discourses in the thirteenth-century Mesa Verde region promoted a much more hierarchical society than the one that subsequently took shape in the Tewa Basin. As a result, it is not surprising that THE COMMUNITY IS A SERVING BOWL faded from use as Tewa speakers moved to the Tewa Basin and began to construct settlements that express the ideal of a more communal and undifferentiated society.

That it appears possible to reconstruct the content of religious discourses that are no longer active through archaeolinguistic methods focused on conceptual metaphors is very exciting, but for those versed in contemporary social theory, this notion also raises important questions. For example, it is clear that THE COMMUNITY IS A SERVING BOWL was active and pervasive in thirteenth-century Mesa Verde society because this concept was expressed in many different ways, and it represents one of a family of metaphors linking actual containers and architectural forms that developed over several centuries in this region (see Ortman 2008a). In addition, the Tewa language implies that, at some point in the past, a word that originally meant 'pottery bowl' was used to refer to 'village' and 'plaza' so often that these figurative meanings became additional conventional meanings that continued to be associated with that word even after the metaphor responsible for the change ceased to function in Tewa culture.

However, to say that a metaphor was so pervasive in Mesa Verde society that it influenced the conventional meanings of words in their language is not to say that everyone in that society agreed with the way in which this metaphor framed the target domain. In fact, one could emphasize different elements of THE COMMUNITY IS A SERVING BOWL in discourse to either promote a communal society, in which generalized reciprocity was the ideal (see Ortman and Bradley 2002), or a more hierarchical society, in which certain people were entitled to more social power than others. And it is not difficult to imagine that such divergent framings based on the same root metaphor were in competition in thirteenth-century Mesa Verde society. Thus, to suggest that the embedding of a metaphor in language implies shared belief would be to lapse into an outmoded form of structuralism that has difficulty accounting for the sort of transformation that we know took place in the thirteenth century. Rather, I think it is better to view metaphors embedded in language as reflecting the *hegemonic* discourses of the dominant fractions of past speech communities. In fact, the only metaphors that are likely to be materialized in patterned ways that archaeologists can perceive are those connected to these dominant discourses. Thus, to claim that THE COMMUNITY IS A SERVING BOWL was a metaphor that framed village architecture and community life in the Mesa Verde region is not to claim that this style of imagining the community was universally shared or accepted by a harmonious social whole or that everyone seized upon the same elements of this metaphor in promoting their interests. Rather, it simply means that this metaphor was part of the hegemonic discourse of the dominant social fraction, that most people had internalized it, and that most could behave in accordance with it regardless of their opinion on the ways various social factions used it to frame community life.

This final discussion suggests that archaeology, linguistics, and social theory all have important and complementary roles to play in historical anthropology. Traditional methods, which merely project present-day concepts into the past, lead to a view of ancient Pueblo societies as being more conservative, less creative, and more harmonious than the archaeological record shows us they must have been. With newer methods, a better understanding of what the building blocks of religious discourses are, and a better understanding of the relationships between discourse and society, we have the opportunity to bring the complementary strengths of archaeological evidence and linguistic reconstruction to bear in studying religious ideologies as historical products, and ancient societies as places of social ferment and strategic action as opposed to harmonious social wholes (see Pauketat 2008). Viewing conceptual metaphors as the building blocks of religious discourses, and applying methods for deciphering metaphors in the archaeological record and in language, allows one to reconstruct metaphors that people in certain times and places used to live by, the discourses that people constructed on the basis of these metaphors, and the processes by which new metaphors and their attendant discourses developed over time. In this way, we can develop an understanding of Pueblo history that is much more dynamic and realistic than will ever be possible using ethnographic analogy or the direct historical approach in isolation.

6

Iconography, Space, and Practice
Rio Grande Rock Art, AD 1150–1600
Marit K. Munson

Rock art in the northern Rio Grande valley changed dramatically in the late AD 1200s to early 1300s. Both the style and iconography of the imagery itself shifted, especially in representation of the human form and of certain animals. At the same time, rock art sites themselves reflected a newly diverse use of space, with physical layouts that structured movement through sites and provided discrete locations for producing rock art. In this chapter, I draw on proxemics and the visual characteristics of rock art from San Cristobal Pueblo and other northern Rio Grande sites, contrasting highly restricted painted rockshelters with semipublic open-air petroglyph sites. I then turn to the implications of these site locations and layouts for ritual practice from the early 1300s on, arguing that discrete groups of artists and audiences used the imagery for varying activities and purposes, perhaps related to distinctions among religious societies or other sodalities.

Northern Rio Grande Rock Art

The northern Rio Grande region is well known for its extensive rock art, including numerous petroglyph sites in the Galisteo Basin and on the Pajarito Plateau. Located on opposite sides of the Rio Grande between present-day Albuquerque and Santa Fe, the Galisteo and the Pajarito share a broad history with the rest of the northern Rio Grande region (Snead et al. 2004). The region was lightly populated prior to the beginning of the Coalition Period (1150–1325), when immigrants from outside the region began to establish numerous small villages. By the beginning of the Classic Period (1325–1600), individuals throughout the northern Rio Grande began to aggregate into larger, plaza-oriented settlements. The Pajarito Plateau was most heavily occupied in the earlier portions of the Classic Period but was largely depopulated by 1550 (Powers and Orcutt 1999). The Galisteo Basin, in contrast, was the location of eight major plaza pueblos in the Classic Period, several of which were still inhabited following the arrival of the Spanish in the late 1500s (N. Nelson 1914).

Rock art on the Pajarito Plateau and in the Galisteo Basin includes petroglyphs and pictographs from all time periods, but it is the Classic Period imagery that is most dramatic, including large-scale rock art sites that take advantage of prominent features of the landscape. For example, literally tens of thousands of petroglyphs cover the volcanic dike known as Creston (Comanche Gap), which stretches from near the Classic village of Pueblo Blanco across the southern Galisteo Basin (Schaafsma 1992a). Other images are closely associated with Classic pueblos, such as the horned serpent at Pueblo Blanco, the "star bear" at Pueblo San Cristobal, and the numerous human faces depicted on the canyon walls above Cliff House in Frijoles Canyon (see Schaafsma 1992b).

Northern Rio Grande rock art is not limited to these prominent sites, and in fact there is great diversity in the relationship of Classic rock art to the physical and social landscapes of the Rio Grande Valley. There are numerous pictograph and petroglyph sites within rockshelters, overhangs, and other secluded locations (Munson 2003; Schaafsma 1990), as well as countless smaller petroglyph sites scattered across boulders and small outcrops throughout the region. These smaller and more peripheral sites are poorly understood; most have yet to be recorded formally.

In short, not all rock art sites are the same. There is great variability in the size, location, imagery, and intensity of use across different sites. Although many archaeologists routinely assume that rock art reflects ritual activity, I believe that it is unwise to make an assumption about religious meaning or ritual function. Ethnographically, Pueblo people produced rock art for reasons varying from depicting religious icons (Fewkes 1892) to relieving boredom while tending livestock (M. Young 1988). Indeed, to assume that all rock art is religious in nature would be as absurd as to assume that all pottery was made for ritual feasting or that all ground stone was used to prepare pigments for kiva murals. Throughout this chapter, I document several lines of evidence that sug-

Iconography, Space, and Practice: Rio Grande Rock Art   111

gest that specific rock art sites were in fact ritual in nature. This evidence includes the physical topography of a site, with its implications for access by artists and audiences, repetition of specific icons in spatially distinct contexts, and the intensity of use over time.

Dating Rock Art

Temporal control has always been a difficult issue where rock art is concerned. Although various direct dating methods are being developed, they are not yet practical for widespread use. Most rock art research still relies upon the definition of temporally significant styles, defined through relative dating (Keyser 2001). This chapter uses data from a study on the Pajarito Plateau that successfully combined stylistic seriation of images from thirty-two rock art sites with independent dates associated with those sites (Munson 2002:117–140). The chronologically significant changes in style documented on the Pajarito Plateau appear to hold true for the Galisteo Basin as well.

Pajarito rock art often occurs at cavate pueblos, which consist of masonry structures built at the base of cliffs, along with cavate rooms carved into the cliff faces behind. Much of the rock art at cavate pueblos was produced by individuals standing on rooftops two to three stories above ground level. On the central Pajarito Plateau, at sites like Long House, in Frijoles Canyon, as much as 96% of the rock art was produced by people standing on the roofs of the talus rooms built against the cliff face. The rooftops of ground-level rooms at Long House also provided access to a ledge high above the canyon floor from which artists created a large panel of petroglyphs and pictographs. In other cases, panels were accessible primarily via hand-and-toe-hold trails that are contemporaneous with the site's construction. At Tsirege, in the north-central Pajarito Plateau, some rock art was produced by artists on hand-and-toe-hold trails leading to rooftops. Once a village was no longer maintained, the rooms collapsed, stranding the rock art images above an individual's reach.

This close association of village architecture and rock art, which is quite rare worldwide, makes it possible to distinguish between rock art elements directly related to the primary occupation of village sites and those images that were added after occupation. About a fifth of the rock art in the Pajarito sample was clearly associated with primary occupations. The elements from each site's primary occupation served as the foundation for stylistic seriation of rock art elements by using correspondence analysis, an exploratory multivariate statistical method.[1] The results of the stylistic seriation ordered the sites in a sequence consistent with the Bandelier Archaeological Survey's independent dates for site occupation, established with tree-ring dates and ceramic seriation (Orcutt 1999). These dates provide chronological control by confirming the validity of the stylistic seriation, allowing it to be applied to rock art sites without associated architecture.

Shifting Styles and Iconographic Transformation in the Early 1300s

The seriation of Pajarito rock art sites documented substantial change in the mode of representing human figures through time, from solidly pecked, naturalistic images in the Coalition Period (1150–1325) to outlined, geometric figures in the Classic (1325–1600) and beyond (see figure 6.1a–b). This sweeping stylistic change in human imagery generally confirms Schaafsma's (1992b) more impressionistic chronology for northern Rio Grande rock art, at least where human figures are concerned. The analyses also suggest that animals and geometric designs do not vary enough to have clear chronological significance, although there may be some exceptions in animal iconography, as discussed later.

Naturalistic Figures in the Coalition Period, 1150–1325

Pajarito Plateau rock art from the Coalition Period, 1150–1325, is generally naturalistic in form, with solidly pecked images of unidentifiable quadrupeds and simple humans (figure 6.1a). These figures are characterized by naturalistic bodies, necks, feet, legs, and arms, which are presented in natural anatomical positions. Only about 10% of the figures have facial features, in part because they are difficult to depict on solidly pecked heads. Depictions of male genitalia are most common on Coalition Period flute players, although other individuals are also shown with penises. Ambiguous "lizard-men" that may be men with

Iconography, Space, and Practice: Rio Grande Rock Art

Figure 6.1a. Typical Coalition Period human figures (and animals) from the Pajarito Plateau. The upper image shows a "lizard-man" figure on the left, complete with hair whorls, and unidentified animals on the right. The lower image shows a small person (truncated by fill inside a cavate) aiming a bow and arrow at a long-tailed quadruped. The relative lack of detail is characteristic of Coalition Period rock art, although in this case the figures are obscured in part by a fragile plaster-on-tuff substrate that is best suited to thick lines.

long penises or lizards with tails are also a part of this tradition (Hays-Gilpin 2004). Female genitalia are seldom depicted.

Human figures from the Coalition Period are generally simple, without complex decoration or detailed accoutrements. Some individuals are shown with single feathers, paired "antennae"-like lines, or other additions on their heads. Others are depicted with projections from the sides of the head, often in the form of small circles, representing ears, or perhaps hair whorls; more distinct representations of hair whorls take the form of a stemmed "butterfly." Possible depictions of headdresses include an individual with horns with balls on the tips and a

Figure 6.1b. Human figures from the Classic Period. The two in the upper right are from the Pajarito Plateau; the "star warrior" at the left and "bird man" at lower right are from the Galisteo Basin.

figure with thick straight lines from the top of the head, like rabbit ears. Interaction between figures is uncommon, although individuals are occasionally shown in "dance lines" or hunting scenes. Flute players are quite common, always solidly pecked and shown in profile, often with a humped back and a single feather.

Coalition Period depictions of animals are seldom specific; unspecified quadrupeds and unidentified animals are the most common motifs in this category. Horned serpents and snakes without horns are quite common, as are long horizontal zigzags inside of cavates that probably represent snakes. Zigzags are by far the most common of the geometric shapes, which otherwise consist largely of lines, combined forms, and miscellaneous markings that are difficult to summarize. Spirals, + or x forms, rectangles, and circles are also present.

In a general sense, Coalition Period rock art resembles contemporaneous imagery from the San Juan, Little Colorado, and Mogollon areas (Schaafsma 1992b), some of which are suggested as potential places of origin for Coalition Period immigrants. However, Pajarito rock art lacks images common elsewhere, such as fish and mountain sheep, and many of the similarities between the Pajarito and neighboring traditions are broad enough that they cannot be traced to a specific source. There also seems to be little overlap between pre-1300s rock art and contemporaneous kiva murals. As Newsome and Hays-Gilpin (this volume) discuss, early kiva murals have relatively few representational images that are similar to rock art in style and layout other than rare flute players or quadrupeds.

Geometric Figures in the Classic Period: 1325–1600

In the late 1200s or early 1300s, during the transition from the Coalition Period to the Classic Period, artists in the Rio Grande Valley adopted a new, geometric form of human representation (figure 6.1b). Although the naturalistic style of the 1100s and 1200s persisted in low frequencies, the vast majority of human figures in the Classic Period Pajarito sample were depicted with strict geometric outlines, most noticeable in the shapes of bodies, heads, and necks. For example, almost a third of the Classic Period figures have rigidly rectangular bodies, and another 10% have square or triangular bodies. Figures are often depicted with a distinct "hollow" neck consisting of parallel lines that open directly into the body, indicating that the artist planned the configuration of the shoulders and upper body with the final neck or head shape in mind. Just half of the figures have rounded, naturalistic heads; the remainder are strict geometric shapes, such as squares, drawn with precise right angles. Triangular heads with the point downwards, flat-topped heads (rounded along the bottom and sides but truncated with a straight flat line across the top), and tapered trapezoidal heads are also typical of the Classic Period.

In contrast to the largely geometric bodies and heads, other body parts were represented in an increasingly realistic fashion; almost two-thirds of human figures from the Classic Period Pajarito Plateau are shown with details such as fingers and facial features. Artists usually depicted eyes as simple dots or short horizontal lines and mouths as a straight horizontal line. Most forms of decoration are more complex than in Coalition Period figures, although ears or hair whorls are rarer and less distinct in Classic Period images. Feathers, although occasionally shown in the Coalition single-line style, are usually depicted as a series of long parallel lines, while more complex headdresses are shown in a wide range of forms. A small number of individuals have torsos decorated with chevrons, Vs, Xs, and diagonal lines.

Most of the depictions of female genitalia are from the Classic Period. They take the form of individuals shown in frontal view, with a loop or two short parallel lines pendant from the base of the body, between the legs. Males are rarely indicated in the Classic Period; like the females, they are usually depicted in frontal view. In the Coalition Period, many of the male individuals are flute players; in the Classic Period, only a single flute player is phallic. In addition, Classic Period flute players are rendered in free, looping lines, completely unlike previous figures.

All northern Rio Grande rock art appears to undergo this stylistic transformation around the late 1200s to the early 1300s, though there is considerable geographic—and probably temporal—variation within this tradition (Saville 2001; Schaafsma 1992b; H. Smith 2002). Following the lead of Schaafsma (1992b), many researchers have assumed that this spatial variation within Rio Grande rock art reflects linguistic or ethnic group differences in the valley (e.g., Graves and Eckert 1998). My own work (Munson 2002), however, suggests that Classic rock art on the Pajarito Plateau does not reflect boundaries of such groups but rather varies on a more localized, community-focused scale. This appears to be the case in the distribution of a distinctive "loopy" style of flute players in the Tsankawi area (Munson 2002), the prevalence of shields in Frijoles Canyon (Munson 2002), and perhaps the distinctive faces of the Abo area (Saville 2003; H. Smith 2002). In the Galisteo Basin, human representations are more elaborate than those of the Pajarito Plateau. The trend toward outlined figures appears consistent, but the level of detail is greater in the Galisteo, where individuals are shown with faces divided into geometric segments or wearing horned or feathered headdresses, warriors are depicted holding weapons and elaborately decorated shields, and some individuals are represented wearing kilts and other distinctive items of clothing.[2]

The geographic variation in northern Rio Grande rock art is also visible in contemporaneous kiva murals, which include complex imagery that is related to Classic Rio Grande rock art (Crotty 1995, 2007;

Dutton 1963; Hays-Gilpin and LeBlanc 2007; Newsome and Hays-Gilpin, this volume). Kiva murals, though, are usually considerably more elaborate and detailed than rock art, with greater emphasis on narrative scenes (Schaafsma 2007b). Paintings at Pottery Mound, for example, emphasize images such as shield bearers, rattlesnakes, and stars, which have been interpreted as warfare related and may reflect influences from the Western Pueblos (Crotty 1992, 2007; Schaafsma 2000). Murals at Kuaua, in contrast, have been characterized as including more fertility-related icons such as raindrops, jars, lightning, and dancers (Crotty 1992; Dutton 1963). This geographic diversity in Classic rock art and kiva murals suggests that the inhabitants of different villages chose images within the Classic Rio Grande style that were most meaningful for their specific communities.

Changing Iconography

The changes in northern Rio Grande rock art and kiva murals in the late 1200s to early 1300s include a shift toward more iconic images, which appear to have specific referents. Although the exact meanings of these icons remain unknown, their distribution among and within Classic rock art sites suggests the presence of specialized meanings associated with specific religious or social groups. As discussed previously, entire communities may have emphasized specific icons that had especially salient meanings. At the same time, the differential distribution of icons within rock art sites or among kivas in a single village suggests that either smaller, more specialized groups were responsible for creating some of the petroglyphs and paintings or that each group of images was made for a different purpose. For example, the rock art site of Las Estrellas, on the southern Pajarito Plateau, has specific icons concentrated along the path leading to the site's core. The locations and orientations of these images suggest that they were used as a way to turn away or deter those who were not to approach the site's core (see figure 6.2), which shows intensive image-making and re-working of images over time (Munson 2003). In other words, access to this site was restricted to specific individuals, a small group of people whose presence was appropriate.

Similarly, results from preliminary fieldwork at the rock art site associated with San Cristobal in the Galisteo Basin suggest that different

Figure 6.2. One of the petroglyph panels along the entrance to Las Estrellas includes this image of a mountain lion swatting a person across the face. The mountain lion has human-like thighs and knees, feathers on the back of its head, and an apparent beak. The person is typical of Classic Period images, with rectilinear form and a nose indicated by a vertical line descending from the center of the forehead.

areas within the site emphasize different imagery. While snakes and horned serpents are constant across the site, for example, images such as owls painted in red pigment are limited to one or two locales. Another locale includes repeated large-scale images of cranes or a similar large water bird; these birds do not occur elsewhere within the site. The geographic restriction of such images suggests that any given locale was associated with specific kinds of images or icons. Each space may have been the exclusive province of a small number of artists, who either tended to repeat images or who knew which images were—and were not—appropriate.

Based on the iconography of both rock art and kiva murals, the religious changes of the late 1200s to early 1300s were apparently centered on supernaturals in human form. In sharp contrast to the Coalition Period's naturalistic portrayals of human figures, Classic Period representations are strict geometric shapes, with rigidly delineated bodies and heads. Although the naturalism of Coalition art suggests that it was produced relatively casually, the stylistic standardization and iconicity of the Classic Period implies increased societal restrictions on the mode of representation. Classic figures were usually outlined and included realistic details such as fingers and facial features, along with a wide range of headdresses, decorated torsos, and accoutrements. At the same time, the static, simplified style reduced the human form to abstraction, placing as great an emphasis on the existence of the figures themselves as on their specific clothing or narrative presence. Depictions of women, though rare, also increased in frequency. Taken together, the increasing detail, precision, and stylistic standardization of northern Rio Grande rock art in the late 1200s to early 1300s all suggest greater concern with the appropriate way to produce images, even if—as in the case of the rigidly geometric human figures—they were decidedly nonrealistic depictions.

Stylistic changes in animal representations suggest that certain animals became especially significant during the Coalition to Classic transition. Many animals carried through from earlier time periods with little stylistic change; these include unspecified quadrupeds, most birds, elk, and other animals that are represented in a solidly pecked, naturalistic form. A limited number of animals, however, changed dramatically in their mode of representation in ways that parallel the transformation of human figures from simple naturalistic images to detailed iconic representations. For example, images of snakes were transformed into specific depictions of rattlesnakes and horned serpents through the addition of rattles, horns, checkered "collars," and other details (see figure 6.3). Other animals show up in specific, outlined forms, including rigidly geometric mountain lions, badgers and bears with detailed paws and legs, or rodentlike animals with long pointed noses and striped bodies. As with human figures, these iconic images reflect similar concerns with appropriate ways of representing animals. The detailed images may reflect increasingly specific rituals relating to particular animals.

Figure 6.3. The forward-pointing horns are clearly visible on this pair of horned serpents at San Cristobal Pueblo. The individual on the left has added detail of a checked "collar" and a cross-shaped tail. These large images are carefully pecked, representing considerable time and effort for their production.

Space, Accessibility, and the Proxemics of Rock Art

Rock art and kiva murals show parallel changes in the late 1200s to early 1300s in the fluorescence of imagery overall, the focus on the human form in particular, and the use of increasing detail and iconic specificity. The murals and rock art share an additional quality that relates to changes in religious expression and practice—both occur in contexts of increasingly specialized or restricted space within which ritual activities occurred (Newsome and Hays-Gilpin, this volume). Following a brief overview of rock art site locations before and after the transition, I then draw on proxemics to discuss the implications of space and accessibility for the individuals involved in producing, viewing, and using rock art.

Coalition Site Locations, 1150–1325

Coalition Period rock art tends to occur in scattered sites at some distance from contemporaneous village sites or, on the Pajarito Plateau, inside cavate rooms. Although a few of these Coalition rock art sites may be associated with trails, most simply take advantage of locations with suitable outcrops of stone. For example, the area surrounding Burnt Corn Pueblo, a late Coalition village in the Galisteo Basin (Snead and Allen, in press), includes several small petroglyph sites. Typically incorporating just a dozen or fewer images, these sites are difficult to date but most are likely to be from the Coalition Period, given the occupation history of the immediate area. The largest and most prominent rock art site in the vicinity is Petroglyph Hill, a distinct double-peaked hill located 3.2 kilometers from Burnt Corn. The hill itself was likely the main destination for Coalition visitors, with the production of rock art a secondary but consistent activity over time (Munson and Head, in press).

In general, Coalition Period rock art sites tend to be open and relatively unrestricted in layout. There is relatively little evidence as to the nature of the artist or the audience, much less the activities (other than making petroglyphs) that might have occurred at Coalition rock art sites. The sites reflect casual production of imagery, perhaps incidental to other activities in the surrounding area. The locations of the sites hint at a general orientation to the landscape beyond the village, perhaps paralleling the outward focus of kiva murals prior to the 1300s (Newsome and Hays-Gilpin, this volume).

Classic Site Locations, 1325–1600

In comparison to Coalition sites, the diverse locations and topography of Classic rock art sites suggest increasing differentiation in the practices that led to the creation of the sites. Some are similar in setting to the earlier Coalition rock art, removed spatially from contemporaneous villages. These distant sites are often small, consisting of a few petroglyphs on boulders, usually located during archaeological surveys and described in Cultural Resource Management reports (e.g., Kurota 2006). The rare exception includes extensive outcrops such as the 27 kilometers of broken mesas and talus slope boulders included in Petroglyph National Monument (Mich 2000). Despite the differences in the sizes of these sites, their distance from contemporaneous villages suggests that they were not locations that people encountered during daily activities or that they could see or hear from the village itself. The locations of these sites reflect varied uses of the landscape beyond the village, whether the production of petroglyphs was incidental to trips made to procure resources or if the rock art was a destination in and of itself. Overall, these distant Classic rock art sites are most similar in terms of access and location to the Coalition Period rock art on scattered petroglyph boulders or at large sites like Petroglyph Hill.

In the Classic Period, unlike the Coalition, many rock art sites were created with clear physical boundaries and highly structured internal space. Such sites are of particular interest, for their limitations of physical space have implications in terms of access for artists and audiences alike (Brody 1989). I draw on proxemics and the visual characteristics of rock art at several Classic Period sites to consider differential access to rock art imagery and associated ritual practice. In particular, I contrast differences among highly restricted painted rockshelters, which were quite private, and semipublic open-air petroglyph sites. I then turn to the implications of these site locations and layouts for ritual practice from the early 1300s into the historic period, focusing on the experiences of participants and audiences.

Visual Accessibility and Proxemics

Here, I focus on two different aspects of accessibility relative to rock art sites: (1) the visibility of the rock art itself, whether petroglyphs or pictographs and (2) the visibility of individuals involved in producing or using the rock art.[3] A consideration of proxemics provides a means to assess relative degrees of visibility. Proxemics originated in studies of personal space in various cultures around the world (Hall 1966, 1968). Hall (1966) defined three general spatial categories, from intimate space (up to 1 m) to social space (about 1 to 3.5 m) to public distance (greater than about 3.5 m). Each category has implications for the kinds of information available to a viewer or audience, from the subtle details of facial expressions to the broad movements of the whole body. Various distances emphasize different modes of communication, with greater distances necessitating more conventional or stereotyped movements and vocalizations if an individual is to be able to communicate with his or her audience. Archaeologically, applications of proxemics usually center on an audience's visual access of an individual or group, such as performers, a speaker, or a religious leader. Many researchers have focused on the proxemics of plazas as ritual space, both in the Ancestral Pueblo world (Chamberlin, this volume) and elsewhere.

When considering the visibility of objects, other researchers have integrated the study of space and distance with consideration of artifacts' performance characteristics. Mills (2007), for example, looks at the size and contrast of motifs on bowls in the Mogollon Rim area that were used in the context of public feasts in open plazas. Van Keuren (2004; this volume) similarly considers the effects of distance and location of design on the visibility of interior and exterior motifs on polychrome bowls. These authors and others point out that the visibility of objects is related to qualities of size, shape, color and contrast, and brightness (Munson 2011:71–93). Such qualities are relevant in considering rock art's visibility as well, although the contrast of figure and background should be considered in terms of both color and texture. The location and intensity of light sources also make a dramatic difference in rock art's visibility, given the effects of shadows and the potential for glare.

In the Galisteo Basin, most of the rock art is on a dark desert-varnished surface that creates a high contrast between petroglyphs and the surrounding rock surface. The dark background, on the other hand, makes pictographs more difficult to see; in rockshelters, though, the relatively unweathered and nonpatinated surfaces provide a lighter substrate against which paint shows up readily. The situation is reversed on the Pajarito Plateau, where the light volcanic tuff cliffs show pigment but provide little contrast for petroglyphs. The rough surfaces of the tuff also make the petroglyphs relatively difficult to see, as the many holes and pockmarks cast shadows that may obscure the pecked lines of petroglyphs. In terms of size, the vast majority of northern Rio Grande rock art is large enough to be readily visible from a distance.[4]

Proximate Rock Art: Semipublic Locales

Many Classic rock art sites are located near villages but are slightly removed from daily life. These proximate sites are close enough that villagers might overhear activities, or perhaps view artists from a distance, but are not so close that a nonparticipant would be able to observe any details. This arrangement occurs at many locations in the northern Rio Grande: in the Tsankawi area of the Pajarito Plateau (LA 65684/65686 and LA 127636; see Munson 2002:264–270) and on the southern Plateau at Las Estrellas (Munson 2003); in the Galisteo Basin at Pueblos Blanco, Galisteo, and San Cristobal (e.g., Schaafsma 1992b); at La Cieneguilla (Steed 1976); and at central and southerly villages such as Tonque and Abo (Brody 1989; H. Smith 2002).

The rock art at San Cristobal Pueblo in the Galisteo Basin is an excellent example of a site that is proximate to a large village but is not completely public. The pueblo is situated in a shallow, spring-fed creek valley, with a mesa at its north edge. The mesa is capped with irregular cliffs, with the talus slope below consisting of a complicated maze of enormous boulders. The rock art is located on the boulders and the cliff faces, with concentrations of petroglyphs in discrete areas as well as a scattering of images on boulders across the talus slope. A few pictographs are present on the cliffs. The rock art site is highly structured internally, with boulders and cliff faces effectively dividing the mesa slope into several dozen activity areas or locales, which form outdoor "rooms" open to the sky (see figure 6.4). Despite its location adjacent to the village of San Cristobal, the rock art is visually inaccessible from the pueblo itself due to the local topography. Entry into the rock art locales is channeled through a limited number of paths, created by gaps between boulders. In many cases, locales are visible only once an individual is in close proximity.

The locales vary considerably in size and shape, but they generally fall within Hall's (1966) category of public space. Most are within the near phase of public space (roughly 3.5 to 8 m away), where a performer or participant's entire body is visible in the audience's peripheral vision, though the center of attention remains primarily on the upper body and gestures. Audiences can still register facial expressions, although they may not be able to perceive the fine details of an individu-

Figure 6.4. This enormous boulder forms the downhill side of a locale, or open-air room, at San Cristobal in the Galisteo Basin. The flat, grassy area enclosed by the facing boulders provides an area suited for public or semipublic gatherings.

al's face. A speaker is obliged to raise his or her voice in order to be heard. The dimensions of these locales suggest that the spaces have the potential to accommodate anywhere from a handful to several dozen individuals participating in producing the rock art or in any associated activities. In this sense, the physical scale and capacity of the locales is similar to that of contemporaneous kivas. A few locales approach far phase public space (a distance of 10 m or more), in which a full public speaking voice is required in order to be heard, the details of the face are difficult to observe, and the entire body is the center of attention. Audience members may register the presence or movements of other people in their peripheral vision. This suggests that the largest locales may be more akin to small plazas, placing an emphasis on the repetitive whole-body movements that are central to plaza performances (Chamberlin, this volume).

In short, access to the mesa slope rock art is not difficult, given its location adjacent to the village; within the rock art site, however, the space is highly structured in terms of movement and access to the core areas. The locales themselves are large enough to provide platforms and open spaces to accommodate gatherings of many individuals, suggesting that the pool of potential artists and audience members is relatively large. At the same time, none of the locales would suffice for gathering all of the village's inhabitants. The diversity among locales in terms of size and iconography suggests that the composition of groups producing and using rock art was also varied. There might have been one group of artists, using various parts of the site for different purposes, or perhaps there were mutually exclusive groups that had access to some locales but not others. Either way, the rock art's proximity to San Cristobal implies that those who were not themselves participants had ample opportunity to see individuals leave the village, climb the slope, and disappear among the giant boulders. Shortly after, they would likely have heard some of the activities taking place at the rock art site, whether these were the sounds of pecking or of associated music or speech.

This picture of semipublic rock art in the vicinity of San Cristobal is quite different from that of painted rockshelters in the vicinity, which are far more restricted and private. The contrast of relatively accessible proximate rock art with that of the rockshelters implies that each context involved different participants and distinctly different ritual practices.

Distant Restricted Rock Art: Painted Rockshelters

The most restricted and remote rock art sites in the Classic Period are inside rockshelters or under overhanging cliffs, such that they are completely shielded from view. These sites, including LA 60500 on the Pajarito Plateau (Munson 2002:193–194) and the Pine Tree site in the Galisteo Basin (Schaafsma 1990), are typically located at some distance from any contemporaneous villages. Rockshelter sites differ considerably from the rock art sites previously discussed in that they overwhelmingly consist of pictographs. This cannot be accounted for by preservation factors alone, because paintings have been documented on open-air cliffs on the Pajarito Plateau (Munson 2002:197) and petroglyphs are rare in rockshelter sites.

Rockshelters are, more than any other site type, restricted and private. Unlike the elevated and readily visible locations of prominent sites such as Creston (Schaafsma 1992b), the rockshelters and overhangs are unlikely to attract attention from afar; rather, one has to either know of the location or to stumble upon it (see Munson 2003). The enclosed space and the locations of the sites in side canyons effectively prevent nonparticipants from visual access in any form. In fact, residents of San Cristobal would probably be unaware of activities happening in the rockshelter sites, and they would not necessarily know who was involved. Participants setting off from the village could take advantage of the easy travel afforded by the canyon to the east of the pueblo, a route that coincided with the main protohistoric trail from San Cristobal over the mesa tops to Pecos Pueblo; even observing the direction in which people set out would not provide any real information about their intended activities. Unless participants carried obvious ritual paraphernalia or announced their intentions, most villagers would have had little to no idea of the activities taking place at the rockshelter sites. This isolation has profound implications for both the size and the composition of the audience.

The size of the rockshelters severely limits the number of individuals who can enter at any given time. At the Pine Tree site, for example, the larger of the two shelters is a fairly generous 10 meters long and 4 meters deep; the smaller is a cramped overhang about 1 meter high, 3 to 4 meters long, and less than a meter deep (Schaafsma 1990). Enclosed on three sides, as well as above, entry into a rockshelter or overhang is dictated by geography. Even an individual's posture upon entering may be determined by a low-hanging ceiling or a small entrance. The small size of such shelters falls within Hall's (1966) category of social space, where verbal communication happens in a casual or conversational voice and the upper body is in focus. Individuals can perceive fairly subtle facial gestures and use their peripheral vision to track movements of the entire body. The strict physical boundaries of these spaces severely limited the number of artists at any single time, as well as restricting the possible activities and the size of a potential audience. Making and using rock art within the shelters would have been an intensely personal experience.

The Social Implications of Ritual Practice

The changes in northern Rio Grande rock art in the late 1200s and early 1300s reflect the introduction of new ideas and styles, as well as changing societal priorities. Rock art became an increasingly important mode of religious expression within Ancestral Pueblo society, reflecting newly diverse modes of ritual practice. The physical layout and local topography of the sites, for example, imply that different groups of artists and audiences had varying levels of access to imagery and associated activities. Similarly, the variation in the size of sites and locales suggests that different modes of communication were emphasized, from personal interaction to relatively distant whole-body movement. Finally, the repetition of specific images in spatially distinct contexts and the intensity of site use over time suggest that a relatively small number of artists returned to repeat certain icons and re-work existing rock art, probably over a long period of time. For example, artists at Las Estrellas, on the southern Pajarito Plateau, frequently pecked images, then returned later to re-work them with different techniques, incising deeper lines, grinding portions of the cliff face, or adding paint to existing images (Munson 2003). The rockshelter sites near San Cristobal show extensive superpositioning, with painted images melting together to form a wash of pigment. One rockshelter contains literally dozens of overlapping stenciled handprints, attesting to repeated visits to the space.

What was the point of returning to certain locations to mark the rocks? What was it about specific spaces that drew artists time after time to repeat the same icons or renew those that were already present? The answers to these questions may lie in part with the audiences for the rock art. In particular, they relate to the *lack* of an audience. The most intensely worked, most repetitive, longest-lived rock art panels are those in the most physically restricted spaces, like Las Estrellas and the rockshelter sites near San Cristobal. These are highly structured, secluded sites, with strictly limited access and few opportunities for nonparticipants to gain knowledge about activities at these sites. Just a few individuals participated in producing, re-working, and refreshing the pictographs and petroglyphs, blurring the distinction between artists and audience. In fact, one could argue that the process of producing and working with the rock art was the most important aspect, with the imagery addressed not to the participants but to an audience that is not physically present—that is, an audience of supernaturals. Sheltered from prying eyes, limited in participation and audience, highly structured rock art sites served as sacred space in the Classic Period.

Even the semipublic locales of the rock art on the mesa slope above San Cristobal may fit this characterization. Although the topography of the slope provides a great deal of variety in the capacity and accessibility of different locales, the space was still highly structured and set apart, despite its proximity to San Cristobal. The presence of superpositioning and the emphasis on certain icons over others creates a picture of small groups of individuals using and reusing semi-enclosed "rooms" for repeated ritual activity. This suggests an increasing specialization in ritual practice, with small groups within each community taking responsibility for different rituals. The membership of these groups is not entirely clear; there may have been a single group of ritually important individuals, analogous to the Made People described by Ortiz (1969), or perhaps there were many smaller groups with more exclusive membership, akin to the religious societies and other sodalities of the historic Rio Grande Pueblos (E. Brandt 1994; Hays-Gilpin 2000; Ware 2002).

Both private and semipublic rock art sites reflect the dramatic shift toward more detailed and more rigidly geometric human figures, and probably animals, in the Classic Period. These icons represent the human form, with an emphasis on females where sex is indicated, abstract curvilinear flute players, and animals such as horned serpents, mountain lions, badgers, bears, and rodentlike animals. The contemporaneous changes in style and representation mark a significant cognitive and cultural shift, reflecting the widespread adoption of new religious ideas and practices across the Pueblo Southwest. The source of these ideas is not clear from the rock art alone (*contra* Adams 1991; Schaafsma 1994a), nor is the timing precise. This should not be surprising, for surely the conception of religious epiphany diffusing from one location to the next and down the line is overly simplistic. Instead, the iconographic and spatial variability among Classic Rio Grande–style rock art sites reflects the reality of religious transition at a local level, with details of iconography and ritual practice varying from village to village.

7

Plazas, Performance, and Symbolic Power in Ancestral Pueblo Religion

Matthew A. Chamberlin

Pueblo religion is known for the emphasis it places upon the well-being of the group and upon adherence to the rules and values of the group. In ethnographic religious performances in plazas, highly structured routines of dance, song, and prayer involving large numbers of participants stress communalism and cultural conformity. This capacity to include and organize entire communities in large religious events has led archaeologists to view the development of plazas as critical to the survival and longevity of the Pueblo groups that persist today (Adams 1991; Mills 1998).

Although the group is paramount, performances in plazas also reinforce the authority of religious leaders in ethnographic Pueblo society. Examples include dances in the Ohkay Owing eh (San Juan Pueblo) plaza, the "final tetrad" of the three-tiered Tewa cosmos, which symbolically recreate a religious hierarchy governed by leaders ("Made People") who enforce cultural values for the community (A. Ortiz 1969:20, 143). Similar observations of leaders whose authority is manifest in the preparation and conduct of religious performances in plazas occur across the Pueblo world (E. Brandt 1979; Bunzel 1992; Dozier 1958; B. Tedlock 1983), illustrating the unique dynamic in Pueblo society between communal interests and individual power (E. Brandt 1994; Feinman et al. 2000; McGuire and Saitta 1996).

This chapter considers how plazas themselves may have contributed to this tension between communality and individual power in Pueblo society, and to the rise of increasingly influential religious leaders. I focus on the development of plazas over the late pre-Hispanic period, a transformative era in Pueblo religion (Van Keuren and Glowacki, this volume). As a hallmark of this era, the enclosed plaza provided an arena for new kinds of public ritual, which involved masked dances with large numbers of participants and emphasized themes of rainfall, warfare, and fertility drawn from Mesoamerican traditions (McGuire, this volume; Plog and Solometo 1997). In scale, inclusiveness, and content, these rituals presaged ethnographic Pueblo ceremonies.

The religious events made possible by plazas would also have constituted an important new social field in which the production of culture itself could be contested. I draw on social theory to explain how, as plazas evolved, new opportunities to gain power over the definition of such unquestioned cultural ideals as the primacy of communal well-being emerged within these religious events. Of special interest here are the proxemic qualities of enclosed plazas, which emphasize collective performance while nonetheless facilitating contestation over culture through often-unspoken, kinesic dimensions of practice. Focusing on the Salinas area of New Mexico, I describe spatial changes in plazas that made possible new modes of embodied communication, which enhanced the ability of some performers to control cultural messages and possibly set the stage for greater social distinctions between leaders and followers in later eras.

Symbolic Power

The idea that culture is actively made and contested rather than simply inherited inspires a theorization of social life centered on power. Bourdieu (1985), for one, describes the everyday creation of meaning as a struggle over various kinds of capital that gives rise to social topographies or "fields" of actors—some producers of culture, others consumers—who are arrayed in opposition to one another. For Bourdieu, understanding even the most taken-for-granted elements of culture requires the study of social relations within a field, including the tensions between various field positions, the forms of capital at stake, the strategies employed in preserving or contesting the social order, and the dynamics of field conflict.

The concept of field contains within it a notion of multiple kinds of power, but most relevant here is symbolic power, "the power to produce and impose the legitimate vision of the world" (Bourdieu 1989:20). Symbolic power is manifest in just those unquestioned routines and tacit meanings noted above, which underpin a social order. According to Bourdieu (1986:243), this power is not acquired but flows from possession of embodied cultural capital, the "long-lasting dispositions of the mind and body" that determine what kinds of strategies, practices, and opportunities are accessible to (and even conceivable by) social actors. This capital differs from other kinds of cultural resources, being manifest in the self; in distinctions of attitude, taste, and ability, which include bodily practices such as dialect, dress, and deportment, but also encompass cognitive capacities to comprehend, appreciate, and carry out projects of many kinds.

Considering how symbolic power is brought into play in small-scale, egalitarian-minded societies is a major goal of this chapter. Another concept of Bourdieu's, virtuosity, may be helpful in this pursuit. Even in strongly communalistic societies, some actors will display practical mastery in a field; according to Bourdieu (1977:8), "the virtuoso who perfectly masters his 'art of living' can play off all the resources offered him by the ambiguities and uncertainties of different behaviour and situations in order to produce actions suited to every occasion." In Kabylia, for example, virtuosos in the field of gift exchange possess familiarity with the logic of gift and counter-gift that allows them to accrue honor and prestige through social and economic transactions (Bourdieu 1977).

It is worth pointing out, given the conservatism in Pueblo society, that virtuosos are in many ways conservators of tradition rather than aggrandizers or individualists. Their efficacy relies to an extent on the persistence of the status quo, in which they excel. Adherence to tradition and promotion of collective ideals are vital qualities of the virtuoso. For example, according to Bourdieu (1987:129), the religious virtuoso is one who "embodies in exemplary conduct, or gives discursive expression to, representations, feelings, and aspirations that existed before his arrival." Through this embodiment, the virtuoso gains power: "those whom the group honoured with the name of 'wise men' or 'the great'... without any official mandate, were invested with a kind of tacit delegation of its authority... to remind the group of the values it officially recognized" (Bourdieu 1990:129). This embodied authority, in turn, positions the virtuoso socially and politically to renegotiate their relations with others "by manipulating common understandings ... in their favor" (King 2000:421).

Virtuosity is not a term that is used much in the anthropology of the Southwest, but I suggest that the kind of authority just described is hinted at repeatedly in Pueblo ethnography, when religious specialists are described as having some ineffable, embodied quality. Hopi religious leaders or *mongsinom*, for example, are characterized by other Hopi as having "the dignity of chiefs," which sets them apart from "ordinary" or "common people" (R. Brandt 1954:23–24). As Richard Brandt (1954:23–24) notes, "members of the upper classes have prestige in the sense that the lower classes look up to them as 'blue bloods.'" The power of Keresan *caciques* (White 1962:125–126) and Tewa Made People (A. Ortiz 1969) is similarly documented. For these individuals, authority stems mostly from the collective acceptance of their interpretations of cultural norms, such as conventions of personal and public behavior, which they enjoy because they realize those conventions so successfully.

How can we identify and explore "virtuosity" in Pueblo religion? Certainly, the time depth of religious power in the Pueblo world is great (Plog, this volume). However, it may be the adoption of large plazas, of the kind that first appear in enclosed form in the late pre-Hispanic period and continue with some modifications through the present day, which provides the spatial conditions for the ethnographic Puebloan religious virtuoso to emerge. Specifically, the ethnographic accounts suggest that the important tension in Pueblo society between communal ideals and individual authority plays out spatially in large religious dances in plazas.

Arguably, this tension appears ethnographically in the spatial relationships and actions of performers. In some instances, virtuosos are partially hidden in the arrangement of performers; at Zuni, for example, Bunzel (1992:507–508, 512–513, 518) describes actors from whom others take their cues, and whose instruction in dance and song was vital to the success of the performance, but who were otherwise anonymous in a line of dancers. At Tesuque Pueblo too, dancers "are led by 'their father' who during the dancing in place stands off a little distance from the dancers" (Parsons 1939:836). Similarly, Jemez *caciques* supervise a formation of masked dancers, whom they follow in procession through the plaza (Reagan 1906:256–257). Sometimes, though, choreographers are more visible, such as the Zuni "dance chiefs (*otakya aamoss'ona*)" who choose and direct masked dances in winter and summer ceremonies (B. Tedlock 1983:97). Keres kiva headmen, or "dance chiefs," also prepare and direct masked dances (Lange 1979:385; Parsons 1939:834). Hopi "dance directors" are separated too, especially the Kachina chief who "shepherds" the dancers (Parsons 1939:826). As Parsons (1939:138–139) notes, "between Kachina Fathers who conduct ceremony and Kachina impersonators who merely dance there is a marked distinction." Yet distinctiveness only goes so far. Early twentieth-century photographs, for instance, show "dance fathers" at the head of, but still within, long lines of masked dancers (Frigout 1979:571). Religious leaders by and large operate within the group, their influence mediated by concerns for, and ability to reinforce, inclusivity and uniformity.

Embodied Space and the Plaza

The plaza that situates these spatial relationships is more than a container for performances. Studies of built space identify a close relationship between spatial and social embodiment; space routinizes patterns of bodily movement, perception, interaction, and communication, infusing them with tacit understandings of the social world (Bowser and Patton 2004:165; Inomata 2006:807). This quality makes plazas into the centerpieces in the contestation over cultural meanings, and the social orders that accompany them (Low 2000:128). Mesoamerican plazas, for example, situate struggle over the public representation of cultural values in part by shaping bodily practice and communication (Low 1996:876). According to Low (1993:748), town plazas "contribute to the dominance of one group over others and function as mechanisms for coding their reciprocal relationships at the level of the surveillance and control of bodily movement." It seems plausible to conceptualize the Pueblo plaza too as contributing a set of expectations of bodily practice, which compel performances that emphasize dominant cultural ideals, yet also confer certain individuals with the power to convey and implement those ideals.

How, earlier in the history of Pueblo religion, could plazas have evolved and been transformed in ways that enabled virtuosos to become the powerful religious leaders observed ethnographically? In addressing this question, I follow several authors who have argued that the larger scale of gatherings possible in plazas from AD 1275 to 1400 simultaneously fostered a sense of "hypercommunalism" (Van Keuren, this volume), and enhanced the visibility of aspiring leaders (Adams 1989a; Potter and Perry 2000). I propose that, in the Salinas area, *both* communality and individual power are outcomes of the development of a "social field" of religious performance situated in plazas. This process culminated in plazas in several villages that, in scale and configuration, may have provided a resource facilitating the control of embodied cultural messages within religious performances.

The Enclosed Plaza Pueblo in the Salinas Area

Plazas in the Salinas area developed over three phases of settlement. The earliest plazas are found in communities of dispersed jacal structures, an architectural style characterized by masonry foundations and adobe-and-thatch superstructures. These sites date primarily to the Pueblo III period (1100–1275). Major changes in plaza size and configuration occurred as larger masonry enclosed-plaza pueblos replaced jacal settlements during an episode of aggregation from 1275 to 1400. These pueblos appeared in the midst of the jacal settlements, indicating that the same groups who inhabited the dispersed sites planned and built the enclosed-plaza pueblos. Further changes to plazas occurred from 1400 to 1540 as populations concentrated into a few very large settlements (Graves and Spielmann 2000).

The early part of this trajectory is documented on Chupadera Mesa, a densely occupied zone of settlement in the Salinas area (see figure 7.1). *Jacal* settlements, first appearing in the 1000s, consist of loose-knit clusters of up to fifty- to twenty-room structures. The antecedents of enclosed space are evident in larger structures within these sites, where extensions of rooms were attached to the primary room block to create C-, L-, and F-shaped buildings that partially bound small courtyard spaces.

The first formal enclosure of plaza space occurred in the 1200s, when *jacal* structures at two sites were substantively modified. At LA 9014, four *jacal* room blocks totaling perhaps twenty rooms were arranged to enclose a small square plaza of 20 to 25 square meters; this

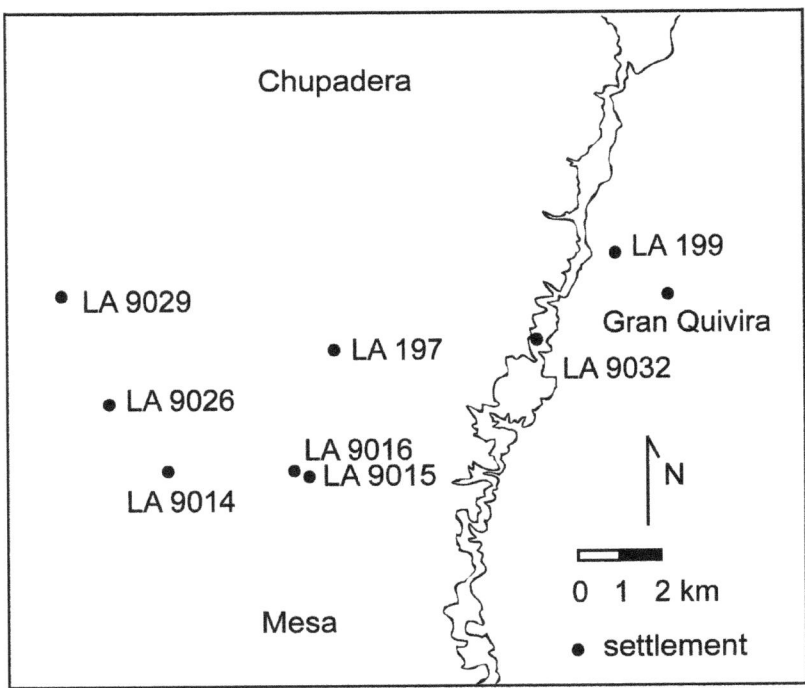

Figure 7.1. Map showing the location of the Chupadera Mesa area in the Salinas Pueblo Province, New Mexico. Major late Pueblo IV period settlements are shown.

building foreshadows the later, one-hundred-room masonry enclosed-plaza pueblo beside it, constructed in the early 1300s. At LA 9026, a fifty- to sixty-room structure, four room blocks were arranged to enclose a rectangular plaza of 200 square meters. The unique blend of architectural traditions, including three *jacal* and one full masonry room blocks (see figure 7.2), suggests a transitional stage in the evolution of the plaza within the dispersed settlement tradition that involved a qualitative shift in the scale and formal enclosure of public space.

Full masonry enclosed-plaza pueblos appeared across much of the Southwest in the 1200s and 1300s. Enclosed-plaza pueblos are planned constructions, and they thus reflect a new concern with the design and maintenance of public space (Cameron 1999; Cordell 1996; LeBlanc 1999; Preucel 2006). Examples in the Salinas area include the early

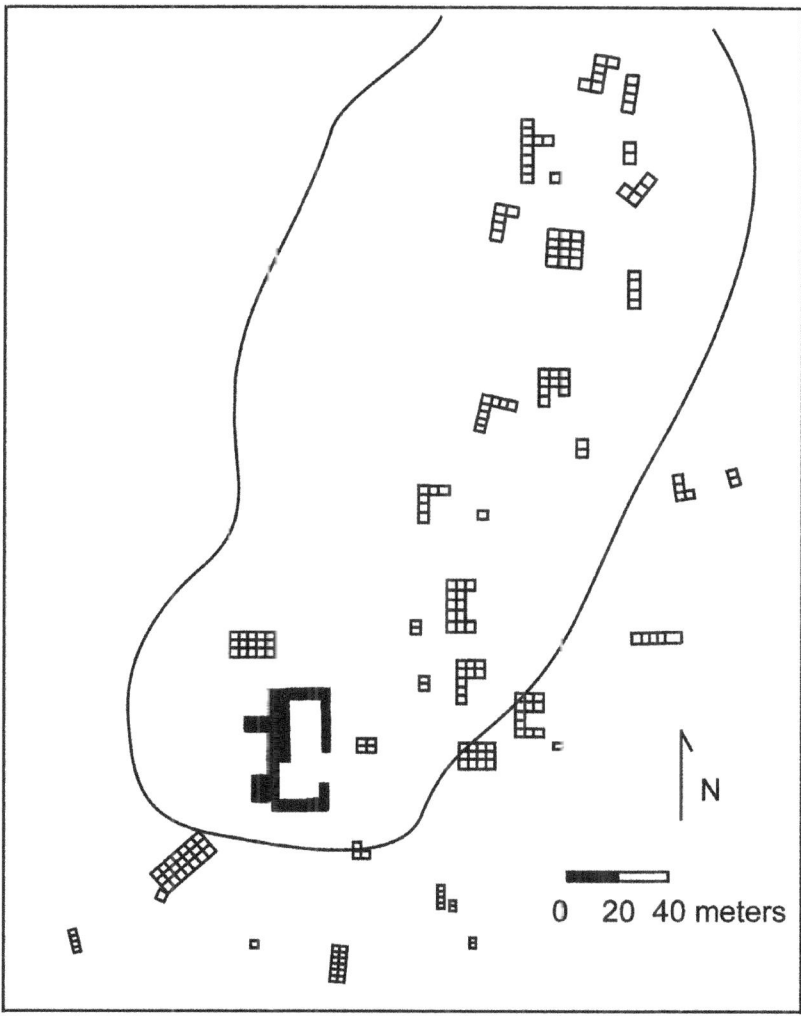

Figure 7.2. *Jacal* settlement at LA 9026 with an inset of the *jacal* structure containing an enclosed plaza.

circular pueblo at Gran Quivira, where uniform wall spacing and abutment patterns suggest rapid construction of residential architecture with the intention of enclosing a 200-square-meter plaza (Hayes 1981:15). Similar evidence of planning is recorded at Pueblo de la Mesa and Kite Pueblo, two other Salinas plaza pueblos (Rautman 2000), as is evidence for the preservation of plaza borders through multiple stages of architectural remodeling.

Enclosed-plaza pueblos on Chupadera Mesa were built in the centers of existing dispersed settlements (see figure 7.3), indicating that groups previously accustomed to unplanned, scattered settlements had radically changed their approach to village organization and to the importance of public space. Evidence for planned construction is seen at

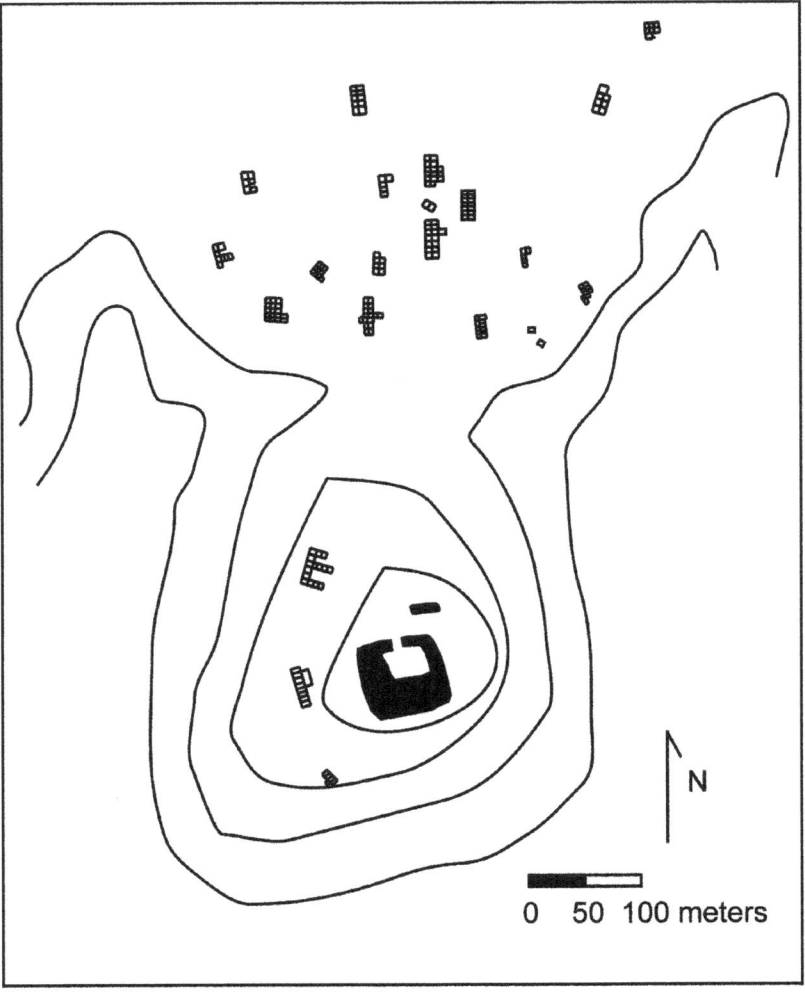

Figure 7.3. Dispersed *jacal* settlement and plaza pueblo at LA 9016.

five sites (LA 9014, LA 9029, LA 197, LA 9032, and LA 9016; Chamberlin 2008). These sites exhibit "ladder" construction, involving the initial construction of long, parallel walls of a room block, followed by the addition of short wall segments to define rooms. Use of this building technique is argued elsewhere to mean that the length and width of room blocks was determined prior to construction (Cameron 1999). It thus seems likely that each pueblo was conceived of and built in a single phase, with multiple room blocks laid out to create a bounded area. The nature of their construction suggests that the creation of plazas themselves may have been the primary motivation behind the initial design of these pueblos. Intriguingly, the shift to enclosed-plaza pueblos does not appear to have been spurred by population growth; room counts in the prior dispersed villages often exceed or equal pueblo room counts (Chamberlin 2008).

Plazas and the Religious Field

The ubiquity of enclosed plazas after 1275 also suggests the emergence of shared ideas about public spaces and religious performances (Adams 1991). One interpretation of this development is that it represents a crystallizing social field characterized by a specific set of rules, resources, appropriate strategies, and possible outcomes (Bourdieu 1990). Because enclosed plazas appeared across the Southwest and accompanied new kinds of performances with ties to more distant regions, such a field must have blended local and nonlocal elements and concerns (see McGuire, this volume). In areas such as Salinas, individual communities may have adopted the enclosed plaza and associated traditions of inclusive ceremonialism when the stakes of participation in the field became apparent; these potentially included varied forms of cultural, economic, and social capital, and involved competition both within and between communities (Chamberlin 2006:46–47).

Plazas were themselves, I suggest, resources in this field. Bourdieu (1990) contends that most competition within a field involves pursuit of objectified capital (titles, statuses, wealth), but competitors also strive to reshape or subvert the underlying "rules of the game"—the unquestioned cultural logic of the field embodied in various forms of practice. As spaces that not only situate struggle over many aspects of culture but that can also actively compel particular forms of practice, plazas constitute embodied cultural capital. Modifications to plazas that resulted in the adjustment of routines of practice, performance, and spatial interaction would thus arguably be vital ingredients to symbolic power, facilitating the imposition of what Bourdieu referred to as a "legitimate vision of the social world."

It is important to recognize that field competition only partly includes a subjective awareness of struggle and accumulation of capital. The strategies that people employ unfold in conditions not of their choosing, and these have unintended results. In the Ancestral Pueblo world, these conditions may have involved cultural notions of appropriate behavior centered on the corporate group (McGuire and Saitta 1996). It thus seems likely, too, that competition in the religious field would have initially played out through intergroup relations, with individual authority one outcome of the appearance of individual virtuosos responsible for enacting those corporate schemes. Religious personnel may have called for building larger and better plazas, or adding multiple plazas, to enhance the communal and inclusive aspects of the religious experience within their village in comparison to other villages, with enhancement of their own role an unsought result.

Variability in the plazas of the Salinas area, where significant differences are visible between villages, is consistent with this kind of corporate competition. Although villages all enclose public spaces with arrangements of residential room blocks, their plazas differ in many respects. On Chupadera Mesa, for example, plazas are all roughly rectangular, but pueblos differ in the number of plazas, area of individual plazas, percentage of total site area consisting of enclosed space, and ratio of plaza area to room count (table 7.1). For two sites (LA 9016, LA 9032), the small sizes of internal plazas appear to reflect later room additions that filled in previously open space. However, the variability in plaza scale cannot be attributed solely to later growth. This is evident at Pueblo Seco (LA 9029), a large masonry enclosed-plaza pueblo in the western portion of Chupadera Mesa, with a ceramic assemblage that indicates contemporaneity with the other enclosed-plaza pueblos in the Salinas area. Yet Pueblo Seco stands out dramatically in the number and size of its plazas (see figure 7.4). Of the pueblo's three plazas, two are

Table 7.1. Pueblo room count, pueblo area, and plaza area values. Site area measurements are based on the extent of roomblocks. Room calculations use room-count range median.

LA	Pueblo Total Rooms	Pueblo Area (m^2)	Enclosed- Plaza Area (m^2)	Percentage of Enclosed Space	Plaza Area per Room (m^2)
197	110–120	1,225	450	36.7	3.9
9014	110–120	940	336	35.7	2.9
9016	80–120	770	96	12.5	1.0
9026	50–60	630	224	35.6	4.1
9032	150–200	1,400	150	10.7	0.9
120	160–210	1,520	201	13.2	1.1
9029	200	2,240	1,050; 600; 72	76.9	8.6

the largest on the mesa; the northern plaza (1,050 m^2) is more than twice the size of any other plaza in the sample.

The size of the Seco plazas appears to be unrelated to population size; the evidence for this inference is that, despite a room count little greater than several of the other pueblos, the multiple, large plazas at Pueblo Seco result in 8.6 m^2 of plaza space per room, and nearly 77% of the overall pueblo area consists of enclosed space. The next largest value for plaza area per room is only 4.1 m^2, at LA 9026. These patterns suggest that the planned definition, enclosure, and scale of public plaza space at Pueblo Seco were driven by concerns beyond the simple need to accommodate growth.

On Chupadera Mesa early in the late pre-Hispanic period, although the plaza ideal was universally shared, the realization of it was not. Villages differed in their capacity to build and maintain plazas of a significant size, and, by extension, to hold large religious events. At LA 9029, the area devoted to plaza space would have enabled a far greater scale of public gathering than at any other settlement known in the entire Salinas area.

Even greater changes in plazas (and presumably in the scale of reli-

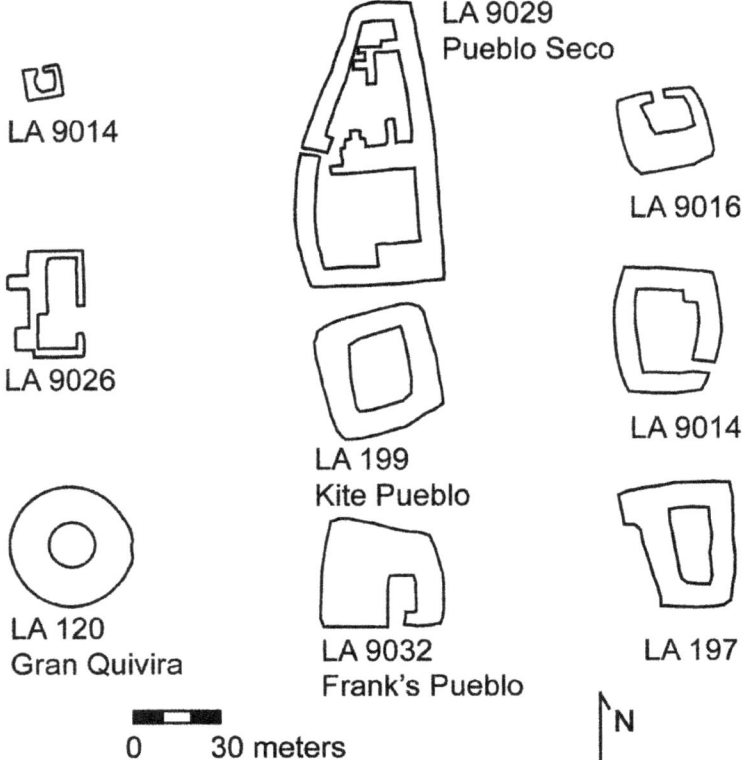

Figure 7.4. Chupadera Mesa pueblo layouts and plazas.

gious events) followed in the 1400s, when the inhabitants of most of the early plaza pueblos were abandoned. Their populations concentrated in just a few, much larger settlements, including Gran Quivira, Quarai, and Abo (Spielmann 1996); the Chupadera Mesa plaza pueblo communities probably moved to nearby Gran Quivira and Pueblo Pardo (Chamberlin 2008). These late pre-Hispanic settlements contain up to 1,000 rooms and multiple plazas, many of which are far greater in scale than those in the earlier pueblos. For example, Quarai's three plazas range from 750–1,000 m², while Pueblo Colorado's two plazas are 1,260 and 3,500 m². If Pueblo Seco's plazas represented a qualitative jump in the scale of religious gathering possible in the early part of this period, the plazas in the late pre-Hispanic sites suggest an even more dramatic leap in the numbers of performers and observers that could take part in a single event, *this* time corresponding to the concentration of larger populations within these massive communities.

In sum, the evolution of plazas in the Salinas area during the late pre-Hispanic period seems consistent with field formation: a shared concept of plazas taking hold, adopted by one village after another as the perceived importance of holding large public religious gatherings grew, with village prestige and intervillage relations motivating them. However, as noted for the ethnographic Pueblos, a strong corporate ethos ultimately coexists with powerful religious leaders. Could changes in Pueblo plazas have not only fostered highly inclusive rituals but also contributed to the rise of these leaders? Drawing on proxemic theory, I propose below that the spatial changes described above also altered the nature of communication in plazas, which gave virtuosos a new capacity to influence the transmission and interpretation of cultural information in religious performances.

The Proxemics of Public Space

Understanding how the spatial development of plazas may have impacted religious performance is aided by theory on the spatiality of human communication (Bowser 2002; Hall 1966, 1968; Mills 2007; Moore 1996). Proxemics research makes possible the identification of different modes of verbal and nonverbal communication that characterized different kinds and scales of public spaces (Moore 1996). Changes in modes of communication, in turn, may cause changes in how people interact, with far-reaching implications in a social field.

Moore's (1996) work on Andean plazas is especially useful in understanding how proxemic analysis can be applied to archaeological contexts. Drawing upon Hall's (1968) theoretical premise, Moore (1996: 790) identifies innate spatial thresholds of human communication, where the architectural parameters of spaces "suggest the modes of interaction possible . . . in contrast to other modes of action that simply could not occur." Three modes of communication are important: (1) paralinguistic ("nonverbal vocalizations, pauses, and tonal properties that provide an underlying context for speech"), (2) verbal ("speech and signs"), and (3) nonverbal ("symboling with gesture, expression, body posture, use of space").

Distance is the key variable, separating personal, social, and public categories of space. Although limits of personal space (less than 3.5 m) vary culturally, human aural and visual capacities mean that as distance between people increases, the nature of communication changes in fundamental ways (table 7.2). In personal space, communication involves many subtleties of gesture and tonality; nuances of cultural meaning are manipulated directly. In social space such nuances are lost, but the added distance means that other kinds of communication are possible, and other kinds of cultural meanings can be conveyed.

Highly significant is the transition from "near phase" (3.5- to 8-m) to "far phase" (10-m) public space, which is the maximum carrying distance of a voice. In this transition, spatial relationships between multiple persons come into view from the vantage of the observer, permitting the assessment of distinctions between them. The variability and flexibility that are characteristic of closer communication is lost and a new formality often enters the relationship between communicants.

What is most important about this transition is that as distance increases within the range of public space, communication becomes increasingly nonverbal. Physical movement, gesture, and spatial relationships among performers gain a new importance in conveying cultural messages. This is of special significance because nonverbal communication emphasizes different kinds of information altogether. As Moore (1996:791) describes it, "There is a progressive emphasis on the communication of conventional and stereotypical meanings, which rely partly on knowledge of the kinesic vocabulary."

This moment in the historical development of public space would have had an enormous impact on the role of embodied knowledge in religious performance. In modifying traditional modes of ritual communication, new ambiguities and potentialities specific to the "kinesic vocabulary" would emerge, providing risks and challenges as well as new opportunities for individuals conducting religious performances. This vocabulary would constitute a medium for the cultural message conveyed in performance, but it might also require that performers interpret and apply tradition in slightly modified form. The capacity to enact tradition through this emerging vocabulary could represent a

Table 7.2. Distance and perception (after table 1 in Moore 1996, based on data in Hall 1966).

	\multicolumn{11}{c}{Distance in Meters}										
	0	1	2	3	4	5	6	7	8	9	10
Informal distance classes	Intimate/ Personal	Social			Public						
Oral/aural	low voice	casual or consultative voice			loud voice when talking to group			full public-speaking voice; frozen style			
Detail vision	details of face visible	details of face fade; wink visible			eye color not discernible; smile vs. scowl visible			difficult to see eyes, subtle expressions			
Scanning vision	whole face visible	upper body visible; can't count fingers			upper body and gestures			whole body has space around it in visual field			
Peripheral vision	head and shoulder	whole-body movement			whole body visible			other people become important in vision			

means of either conservation or subversion of tradition among competitors in the religious field.

I suggest that a transition to "far phase" modes of communication occurred in religious performances in enclosed plazas during the late pre-Hispanic period, in the Salinas area, and elsewhere in the Southwest as well. Below, I illustrate this argument with architectural data, and I use ethnographic data to discuss the culmination of these changes in religious performances.

Architectural Data: Plazas in the Ancestral Pueblo World

Multiple attributes of plazas shape patterns of interaction within them, but scale has the greatest impact on the mode of communication among performers and observers in plaza events (Moore 1996). I use a sample of plaza area measurements recorded from Pueblo sites occupied from the late Pueblo III period to the ethnographic era in order to both illustrate the changing spatial scale of plazas, and to discuss implications for the proxemics of human communication in religious performances (see figure 7.5).

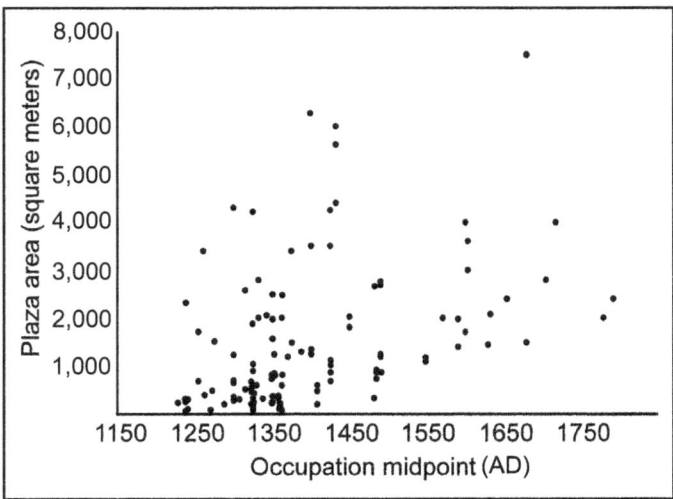

Figure 7.5. Plot of plaza-area values for sites ($n = 122$) with occupation midpoints between 1150 and 1750.

The sample includes 122 plazas from Western and Eastern Pueblo regions, including the Hopi mesas, Zuni, the Upper Little Colorado River, the Silver Creek area, and the northern, middle, and lower portions of the Rio Grande Valley, as well as the Salinas area. Because many sites have extended or multiple occupations, I used occupation midpoints in this analysis. This method is imperfect, but it captures the general trends of variability in plaza area over time.

The distribution of plaza area values reveals three major patterns. The strongest pattern is a general trend of increasing size from the mid-1200s, when plaza areas of 100 to 200 m² were common, to the ethnographic Pueblos, when most plazas were thousands of square meters in area. Although in Zuni a number of large plazas were built early in the period, the trend holds true in general for both Western and Eastern Pueblo regions. This trend suggests the increasing importance through time of religious events in which the entire community could gather, with some as performers and others as observers. This is a pattern consistent with the process of field formation discussed above.

Second, the transition from near phase to far phase public space during the late pre-Hispanic period occurs early in the life history of the enclosed plaza pueblo across much of the Southwest. The distribution of plaza area values at sites with midpoints of occupation in this interval ranges between 72 m² and 4,300 m². The precise threshold of this transition is difficult to determine, but I propose that it would begin in plazas with an area of 400 meters, where an individual located at the center of a (square) plaza would be 10 meters away from the closest observer at the plaza edge. An entire group of performers could be seen from the plaza edge at this range, although any one performer could fall within the "near phase" of public space. It is possible that "far phase" kinds of communication would begin in small plazas because in a plaza with an area of 100 m², communication across its full length would require "far phase" techniques. For example, along their long axis, linear plazas could foster "far phase" communication from certain vantage points despite a small overall area.

If this transition involved a qualitative shift toward formal and standardized kinds of communication, requiring knowledge of a kinesic cultural vocabulary, then performers already positioned socially and spatially to interpret and communicate this vocabulary would also have been well-placed to take advantage of the larger scope and scale of the plaza event. Their practical mastery in plazas would give them a special capacity to influence the communication of cultural information. While possibilities for aggrandizement were almost certainly very limited in large gatherings, influence over the public representation of collective values—symbolic power—may have emerged for religious performers. Their interpretations of collective values, ideals, and conventions would have taken on new significance, embodied in increasingly formal sequences of gesture, song, and movement through open space. They would also gain a new ability to impose their vision of common cultural values on others. Their sense of how things should be done and of how communal values should be upheld would become the proper way for others as well, communicated and instilled in the kinesic vocabulary of the plaza performance. Plazas would thus have provided a powerful basis for the differentiation of certain virtuoso performers as religious authorities.

The Salinas area appears to witness this important transition. Of seven documented early plaza pueblos on Chupadera Mesa and the immediate vicinity, only plazas at Pueblo Seco (LA 9029) are qualitatively greater than the 400 m^2 threshold (table 7.1). The crucial transition between "near phase" and "far phase" public space occurs when Seco's plazas are built. The greater distance between performers and observers in plazas, both spatially and in the formality of communication between them, may have set the stage for greater social distance as well, to the extent that performers were able to increasingly influence the cultural messages conveyed in gatherings. Such an advantage may have *initiated* the kind of embodied distinction visible in the symbolic power of virtuosos in the ethnographic pueblos.

The third pattern observed in the scatterplot (figure 7.5) involves a dramatic jump in plaza area values at a number of sites beginning after 1300. Many sites with midpoint occupations in the 1200s through to the late 1400s have plazas with areas under 1,000 m^2, but many other sites constructed much larger plazas—which themselves vary widely in size. Although this is a pan-Southwest jump, this variability also occurs *within* regions; in Salinas, area values for the largest plazas of the late pre-Hispanic period Jumanos cluster range from 750 m^2 at Quarai to 3,500 m^2 at Pueblo Colorado. This suggests that communities continued to differ significantly in their ability to develop and maintain large plazas used in religious gatherings.

This variability diminishes in the ethnographic era. Then, the largest plazas uniformly fall within the upper range of area values for all sites. Looking at only a sample of ethnographic plazas in the Rio Grande region, plaza areas of greater than 2,000 m² are typical (table 7.3). Given the spatial thresholds provided by Moore (1996), interactions in these plazas easily occupy the "far phase" of public space. Although the distance between any two persons could vary immensely, in formal religious events the distances between performers and observers in plaza interiors and perimeters, respectively, would well surpass the distance at which conversational tones would carry and facial expressions could be readily observed.

Ethnographic descriptions of dances in Eastern and Western Pueblos confirm that communication in plazas has relied on "far phase" techniques (Dozier 1958; Litvinoff 1974; Sweet 1979). Both verbal and

Table 7.3. Location and area of a sample of ethnographic Rio Grande plazas.

Location	Plaza Area (m²)	Source
Cochiti Pueblo (western plaza)	1,440	Lange (1979:367)
Isleta Pueblo (southern plaza)	1,500	Ellis (1979:352)
Santa Clara Pueblo (east plaza)	2,000	Arnon and Hill (1979:297)
Sandia Pueblo	2,400	E. Brandt (1979:344)
Santa Ana Pueblo (south plaza)	2,400	Strong (1979a:399)
Ohkay Owingeh (San Juan Pueblo) (north plaza)	2,800	A. Ortiz (1979:279)
Tesuque Pueblo	3,000	Edelman and Ortiz (1979:331)
Picuris Pueblo (north plaza)	3,600	D. Brown (1979:269)
San Felipe Pueblo	3,850	Strong (1979b:391)
Kewa (Santo Domingo Pueblo)	4,000	Lange (1979:380)
Isleta Pueblo (northern plaza)	7,500	Ellis (1979:352)

nonverbal kinds of communication are observed, but evidence of paralinguistic communication (personal and close social space) is absent; the subtleties of meaning conveyed at that scale would have been lacking. When present, verbal communication involves highly repetitive chanting in raised tones. As Weinman (1970:313–314) notes at Jemez Pueblo: "the melodic formations which underlie the chants at Jemez reflect the philosophy, purpose, and structure of the total event . . . one melodic sequence follows another in descent, always repeated on another level." Rigid, formal, and redundant in nature and in content, this form of communication offers little room for creative freedom.

The tightly orchestrated physical sequences of ethnographic dances, which follow a well-practiced path and involve highly coordinated motions and gestures (Robb 1964; Sweet 1979), also communicate ritual and cultural content to observers of plaza performances. Sweet (1979:4) describes one such Tewa dance at San Ildefonso Pueblo:

> The dancers held their torsos erect and as one unit, arms contracted three degrees or to a near 90 degree angle, and elbows usually positioned four to five inches out from the torso. They traveled with a simple alternation from right to left with an accent on the right. The legs contracted only one degree, lifting no more than three inches from the ground. The dancer rarely progressed more than six inches per alternation.

In the Tewa performance, gestures are standardized and collective, consisting of a series of group movements visible to an observer *as* a group, suggesting an intended audience located at a far enough distance that multiple performers (if not the entire group) would fall within any one observer's field of vision. This would be particularly true for an observer located on a rooftop position looking down. An observer on the ground at the perimeter of the plaza, with a partial view, might see one or more dancers at a time; however, the standardized nature of the performance would mean that even so, one would still see most elements of the entire dance. Also, dances rarely used the entire space of the plaza; as Ortiz (1969:142–143) notes, "most Tewa plaza dances are performed by one or two long lines of dancers." Two major Tewa performances, the Harvest and Matachines dances, involve long circuits of dancers that move through plazas; performers in these dances are spatially distant from observers arrayed along the plaza perimeter.

These ethnographic performances appear consistent with the communication of "conventional and stereotypical meanings," in which knowledge of a practical logic or "kinesic vocabulary" would have been vital to the transmission of cultural information. Further, this evidence suggests that the ethnographic outcome of the evolution of the plaza involved the simultaneous reinforcement of ideals of cultural uniformity and conformity in religious performance, while also providing a venue in which religious leaders are observed.

It seems significant that the sharp increase in plaza sizes around 1350 produced plazas as big, at many sites, as those observed ethnographically. The formality described in ethnographic events—a technique of communication elicited and even demanded by the distances involved—thus could have characterized performances in the late pre-Hispanic period, at which time it seems plausible that individuals with religious power comparable to those of ethnographically known groups such as the Tewa Made People, and others, emerged.

Summary

The rise of powerful religious leaders with the unique authority visible among ethnographic Pueblo groups is conceptualized here as an outcome of strategies designed primarily to enhance traditional cultural ideals of conformity and inclusivity, rather than arising purely from aggrandizing behavior. I envision these strategies as stemming from participation in the religious field during the early part of the late pre-Hispanic period, which crystallized around performances in enclosed plazas. The religious traditions adopted by villages that built and used enclosed plazas emphasized communal ideals, but they also may have fostered competition between villages. This inference of field crystallization is supported by architectural evidence in the Salinas area and elsewhere that illustrates the emergence of shared notions about the importance of plazas, yet also shows that this ideal was unevenly realized; villages were not equally able to build or maintain large plazas.

I have posited the presence of virtuosos in this explanation, an inference grounded in social theory but also supported by ethnographic descriptions of the authority and roles in performance of religious leaders. These were not (in my view) aspiring leaders so much as actors whose embodiment of collective ideals and traditions positioned them to play a key role in navigating the changes to religious performance necessitated by enclosed plaza village layouts.

The proxemic data show how the spatial development of plazas may have provided opportunities to these virtuosos that were only partially anticipated or sought after. The new ambiguities and possibilities of public religious performance in such large spaces would have fallen, in part, to these individuals to negotiate. Lacking prior experience of performance in spaces of this scale, these actors would have encountered the challenges of the new mode of "far phase" communication compelled by such large spaces. It would be up to the virtuoso to interpret and apply traditional rules and concepts in this new medium. Part of this process would have involved the definition and utilization of a "kinesic" vocabulary required to convey and translate traditional concepts.

This change may have conferred a new opportunity to shape the cultural messages conveyed in plazas in new ways—to engage in cultural production with an enormous potential for reinterpretation and transformation of fundamental cultural meanings. Refinement of a specialized body of practical, nonverbal knowledge would fall to the virtuoso, allowing not only the reinforcement of traditional norms but also the amplification of tradition, including the creation of new information, choreographed and communicated through embodied sequences of gesture, dance, and chant.

The descriptions of ethnographic dances indicate that conformity and the supremacy of the collective remained a central element in the developing "kinesic vocabulary" of religious performance. However, one new possibility for ritual choreographers would have been the representation, in the arrangement of plaza performances, of the entire spatial structure of religion and disparate elements of society, showing the relationships and relative positioning of performers of different categories, and giving those differences a new, unimpeachable public reality. This control of spatial representation may have conferred certain individuals with the symbolic power to impose a "legitimate vision" of the social world that included the distinction and higher status of religious leaders.

8

Spectatorship and Performance in Mural Painting, AD 1250–1500

Visuality and Social Integration

Elizabeth A. Newsome and Kelley Hays-Gilpin

Contexts of Vision and Spectatorship

The study of evidence for the cultural phenomenology of vision in the Southwest offers new ways to approach aspects of historic and prehistoric society and expressive culture, from visual expressions in art and architecture, to relationships between viewership and time-based media that include performance, ritual, and dance. Among the general problems this approach can address are the following: how are visual experiences manifested in material evidence for the content, scale, and context of worldview and ritual practice? What can constitute Pueblo perceptions of vision or uses of vision that pertain to power, knowledge, social arrangements, or cultural values? What is the history of development of this pattern or patterns? One of the most striking contrasts between Ancestral Pueblo styles of architectural painting before and after the migrations of the late thirteenth century is their difference in constituting visual experience. From Watson Smith (1952) to Scott Ortman (2000b, 2008a), authors have remarked on the replacement after about AD 1300 of earlier styles that emphasize abstractions closely related to decorative motifs in ceramics, baskets, and textiles with mural paintings that emphasize anthropomorphic figures and naturalistic treatments of space and form. Accompanying these stylistic changes are others that are equally dramatic and important: new subjects and settings for mural arts, new contexts of viewership, and an unprecedented emphasis on portraying dance and ritual performance.

The figurative qualities of murals preserved at such Pueblo IV period settlements as Pottery Mound, Kuaua, and the Antelope Mesa sites of Awat'ovi and Kawàyka'a are generally attributed to the spread of the Katsina religion throughout the Southwest, fueled by migration and intercultural exchange. To understand *how* mural painting related to the new ceremonial complex and its role in integrating the period's large, socially diverse communities, we shift focus from the specifics of iconography to explore particular contexts of vision and spectatorship as enduring features of Pueblo dance from late antiquity to modern times. Performance and spectatorship serve powerful cohesive functions in Pueblo communities today, transcending difference with solidarity and reinforcing corporate identities and social values. At the same time, viewership in ceremonial settings plays an equally important role in articulating differential relationships based on age, gender, clan, and sodality affiliations, as well as ceremonial knowledge and power. Pueblo ritual performance simultaneously disperses power and establishes social hierarchy, as increasing numbers of community members take part in plaza rituals and leaders move into restricted, less visible kiva spaces (Potter and Perry 2000:60, 77). Close correspondences between the kinds of visual experience emphasized in mural composition in late pre-Hispanic period kivas and dance performance in large central plazas may attest to emerging values of spectatorship from the beginning of the fourteenth century to the historic period (see Chamberlin, this volume), when Katsina ritual offered most, if not all, aggregated Pueblo communities new solutions to the challenge of aggregate communities and a dynamic social order.

Art historians have long recognized that new styles of viewership, artistic conventions, and social and ideological uses of seeing are integral to the changing worldviews and social transitions that span periods from Late Antiquity to the Middle Ages, from the Renaissance to the Baroque, and from nineteenth-century academicism to abstraction in modern art. From early scholarship that linked contrasts such as forms appealing to the tactile or optical senses (Riegl 1985, 1992), and approaches to planar and recessive space (Wölfflin 1932) with Hegelian models of historical consciousness, to later perspectives integrating an intellectual history and worldview with the problems of style (Dvorak 1967, 1984; Panofsky 1991), art historians have addressed visual practices as culturally constituted, rather than purely biological, ways of seeing and interpreting the world. T. J. Clark (1984:8) observed that "ideologies naturalize representation . . . [by presenting] constructed and disputable meanings as if they were hardly meanings at all, but rather, forms inherent in the world-out-there which the viewer is privileged to intuit directly."

We can observe the onset of a similar artistic transformation following the migration period in the Southwest, but the challenges lie in defining new methods for exploring visual practices in Pueblo history. Conceptual tools available for addressing how patterns of ideology, power, and historical change pertain to viewership and visual expression can be drawn from either art historical studies of earlier periods of Western art or from newer theories of visuality (see, for example, Sturken and Cartwright 2001) that have been largely concerned with contemporary society and mass media. Whether methods from these sources are useful for addressing visual experience in societies distant from our own is untested (but see Inomata and Coben 2006). Applying these concepts to ethnographic and archaeological research will be challenging. Yet bringing together such an unconventional union of theory and data may open the way to understanding the compelling role of vision in many different contexts of Pueblo society from prehistory to present times, and this may offer specific new insights into Pueblo ritual practices. Vision served powerful discursive functions with respect to knowledge, significance, and power: from the panoramic vision of landscape in early architectural paintings, to the heightened theatricality of Chaco Canyon's Great House complexes, to the astronomical alignments of buildings, and features that capture fleeting time in light and shadow (for example, the Fajada Butte "sun dagger" is one of many Chaco petroglyph sites that interact with light and shadow). The rhetorical power of seeing plays many roles in Pueblo society, from witnessing and concealing to negotiating social relations based on commonality and difference.

In ritual performance and observation, sight and viewership take place within a state of perceptual awareness heightened by attention to a dynamic interplay of sensations and bodily impressions, from scent to sound, the touch of ritual objects, ceremonial gestures and choreography, and the experience of different spatial scales and temporal rhythms. A number of researchers have documented descriptions of a proper mental state for taking part as participant or observer in ceremonial activities in their studies of religion and dance from Hopi, Zuni, and the Pueblos of the Rio Grande (A. Geertz 1986; Sekaquaptewa 1976; Sweet 1985; B. Tedlock 1980). In focusing on architectural painting, we explore the way that vision contributes to the aesthetic and phenomenal power of ritual to shape individual and community consciousness. Most important, we examine the way vision influences the formation of cultural subjects, who generate meaning in response to the experience of seeing (as well as hearing, moving, and feeling) in culturally structured settings.

Comparing murals painted before 1300 with later styles reveals a complex of changes that accompanied the movement from abstract to figural representations (see Munson, this volume, for similar trends in rock art). These include radical differences in the way the previous and later styles deploy meaning and reference optical experience. For example, mural paintings shift from designs that emphasize conceptual and embodied relationships between the observer and imagined landscape or cosmic settings to new styles that focus on a community of both human and spiritual actors. First, we will explain how Pueblo III period murals painted before 1300 relate the observer to landscapes and cosmology, and then explain how postmigration Pueblo IV period murals, mostly painted in the 1400s, after over a century of migration and aggregation into larger multiplaza pueblos, illustrate completely new relationships.

Pueblo III Period

A red and white geometric mural at Cliff Palace in Colorado's Mesa Verde National Park is fairly typical of the Pueblo III period, or prior to the late pre-Hispanic period (see figure 8.1). The mural, painted within a third-story room inside a rectangular four-story room block, belongs to a style of bichrome paintings that depict landscape with simple geometric forms. Occasionally, animals and flute players appear in these compositions as well. Similar murals are known from kivas across the Chaco and San Juan regions, and Scott Ortman (2008a) has noted a significant number in upper-story rooms (e.g., figure 8.1).[1] Ortman (2008a:234–235) estimates a date for the mural between 1260 and 1280, based on the area's occupation through the 1270s. Its date most likely falls near the end of Cliff Palace's occupation, because it

Spectatorship and Performance in Mural Painting 157

Figure 8.1. Mural 30, Cliff Palace, Mesa Verde, Colorado. Photo by Sally Cole.

was the last painted layer added to the walls (Ortman, personal communication, 2009). Similar murals occur at other Mesa Verde sites, including Spruce Tree House, Painted Kiva House, Balcony House, and New Fire House, and related paintings have been recorded in the McElmo and Montezuma valleys as well (see W. Smith 1952: 59–64; Cole 1996). Mathien (2003) cites examples in the Chaco Basin, where the style may have its earliest beginnings (Ortman 2008a:248; W. Smith 1952; Brody 1991). The great kivas at Aztec and Salmon ruins, between the Chaco and San Juan settlement zones, also contained landscape murals. Variants occur as far west as Canyon de Chelly, where structures such as the Antelope House Kiva feature a slightly different color scheme of bichromatic design. Reduced to a basic contrast of two colors, typically red or brown symbolizing a lower earth register and white representing an upper sky zone, the paintings depict a panoramic landscape emphasizing the separation of earth and sky (see also Newsome 2006). The horizon line is the most important defining element of these compositions, which can also incorporate additional motifs. These include clusters of triangles arranged along the "horizon" line that suggest sacred mountains, rows of dots decorating the mountain and horizon lines, and triangular breaks in the red panel that may represent cracks in the earth. Occasionally, the sky zone features motifs that may represent the sun or moon. Sometimes this zone has small flute players and zoomorphs that are similar to images in contemporaneous petroglyphs and rock paintings throughout the Ancestral Pueblo region.

As Ortman (2008a) has pointed out, landscape murals also occur in blended compositions that integrate landscape motifs with the bands of repeated geometric motifs and other abstractions derived from ceramic and textile sources. He has argued that all of these symbols reference cosmological metaphors; they establish an iconography expressing cognitive schemata that relate the built environment to cosmic order (Ortman 2000b). Time and space form a meaningful basis for these paintings, because elements such as the sun and moon designs, dotted horizon markers, and symbolic cracks in the earth probably relate to the astronomical and ritual practices used to time ceremonial events.[2] We suggest that all of these operate within a context of mythopoetic and ritualistic references that conflate landscape and time with metaphors for rainmaking, fertility, and rebirth (see also Cole 1996). Vividly poetic allusions to the figurative aspects of Pueblo cosmology and myth permeate oral and performative culture today, and they evoke images and metaphors that can also be expressed in the structural foundations of ceremonial music, choreography, and the ritual cycle. Cracks in the earth, for example (see figure 8.2), may evoke connections between the underworld and this world, as in the modern Tewa metaphor comparing the scheduling for a ceremonial to sowing a plant that will eventually bear fruit. Simon Ortiz (1977:18) wrote of the Tewa, "When the date for the ceremony is set, . . . a crack appears in the earth where the seed of the dance has sprouted. The song composing and practice sessions in preparation for the dance are viewed as being analogous to the stage of growth of the plant. The day of the dance itself is considered the day when the plant bears fruit."

Embedded in the visual construction of these images are specific perceptual and phenomenological considerations of the viewer's relationship to the expressed meanings of landscape, metaphor, and time that the murals convey. One of the most powerful conventions of this

Figure 8.2. Moon House mural showing cracks in red earthband design. Photo by Scott Van Keuren.

style is the subject position established by the observer's location within the painted room interior (although a few examples appear on exterior walls, for example, at Moon House; Bloomer 1989) circumscribed by symbolic references to landscape and calendrical cycles. Ringed on all sides by the clearly delineated geometry of horizon, mountains, earth, and sky, the viewer stands in relation to the fundamental directionality and spatiotemporal order of his or her world. The importance of murals like these in the earliest developmental phases of Ancestral Pueblo society may relate to establishing a "sense of place" as the basis for aspects of spiritual, social, and personal meaning that still resonate with Pueblo life today. We speak of "place" in the sense that Feld and Basso (1996:9) describe as "that most powerful fusion of space, self, and time" that charges a significant setting with the intense perceptual and imaginative forces that influence the formation of cultural subjects and their frameworks of spatiotemporal thought. Research relating landscape and cosmic murals to horizon astronomy (Malville and Munson 1998; Ortman 2008a) may indicate that their use coincides with the growth of calendrical ritual and solar observations to regulate agriculture and ceremonial calendars. They are also consistent with emerging symbolic values in Pueblo architecture, such as the importance of a central place, and with alignments of individual buildings and communities to local topography and sacred landscape.

Theories of landscape phenomenology address place as a construction of thought, imagination, embodiment, and lived experience. Places are formed in the imagination of the observer while his or her own self-consciousness as a thinking and perceiving subject becomes qualified through the interface between the inner world of thought and an external reality perceived in culturally specific terms, what Christopher Tilley calls "a spatialization of Being" (1994:14).

We believe that rooms painted with landscape and cosmological images enhance this spatial ontology by referencing what Tilley (1994:17) terms "existential space," "a sacred, symbolic, and mythic space replete with social meanings wrapped around buildings, objects, and features of the local topography." Produced and reproduced through human actions, existential space defines points of reference and provides the meaningful associations that connect people to significant places. Pueblo ethnographies describe existential space, for example, in their record of the way community, kinship, and sodality groups are ritually and symbolically identified with topographic sites—mesas and mountains, directions, and shrines (e.g., A. Ortiz 1969). The periphery and center, vertical and horizontal relationships determined by a gaze that intercepts the distances of horizon, earth, and sky, therefore, become incorporated in the viewer's relationship to the world and a spatial ontology that seamlessly integrates place with "Being."

Vision as a means of achieving this mental extension that both situates the observer in the landscape and internalizes its forms and features may be deeply sedimented into the way many Native Americans perceive and experience their land. N. Scott Momaday, for example, has written at length on the interplay of thought and imagination with visual experience in the way many native people conceive of living in aesthetic and spiritual unity with their environment. He emphasizes sight and a specific position and direction for viewing in his Kiowa family's oral account of the place where a woman was buried in a beautiful dress: "If you stand on the front porch of the house and look eastward . . . you know that the woman is buried somewhere within the range of your vision. But her grave is unmarked. She was buried in a cabinet, and she wore a beautiful dress. How beautiful it was! . . . That dress is still there, under the ground" (1997:36). For Momaday, gazing toward that location encapsulated the implicit understanding that the woman's presence and beauty infused the land thereafter. In this perception, "the woman, the dress, and the plain—are at last become one reality, one expression of the beautiful in nature. . . . What matters here is the translation of the woman into the landscape . . . signified by means of the beautiful dress" (36).

Pueblo authors similarly stress their cultural ethic of inseparability from the lands where they dwell, and they relate visual experience to the modes of thought and perceptual awareness that underlie those concepts. According to Paula Gunn Allen (Laguna/Lakota), "The notion that nature is somewhere over there while humanity is over here . . . is antithetical to tribal thought" (1996:246). Leslie Marmon Silko, also from Laguna, describes her people's comprehension of the environment and themselves within it as far more perceptually and intellectually encompassing than the Western idea of landscape, which relegates its image to an objectified field of vision contained within the limits of perspective:

> A "portion of territory the eye can comprehend in a single view" . . . does not correctly describe the relationship between the human being and his or her surroundings. This assumes the viewer is somehow *outside* or *separate from* the territory he or she surveys. Viewers are as much a part of the landscape as the boulders they stand on. There is no high mesa edge or mountain peak where one can stand and not immediately be part of all that surrounds. Human identity is linked with all the elements of Creation. (1996:266)

Momaday characterizes Native American relationships to nature as "a matter of reciprocal appropriation," in which "man invests himself in the landscape and at the same time incorporates landscape into his own most fundamental experience" (1976:80). He identifies this process with imagination and with vision as a way of constituting that reality. He stresses that two modes of visual experience, however, contribute to this understanding of the world: a literal perception that uses the eye, and a metaphorical way of seeing that originates in the mind, permitting figurative and mythopoetic meanings to take their place among the "range of possibilities" for perception.

The kind of visual experience evoked by the Cliff Palace mural and similar examples also parallels landscape concepts and images expressed in certain genres of ritual speech and song. For example, Alfonso Ortiz recorded these Tewa prayer verses used whenever someone addresses a spirit: "Within and around the earth, within and around the hills, within and around the mountains, your authority returns to you" (1969:23). With these words, the speaker identifies his or her personal relationship to landforms that mark successively more distant and visually prominent features of the environment, as well as the unity and parallelism that connect the human and spiritual worlds.

Jane Hill (1992) identifies landscape imagery quite similar to that of the "horizon" murals with the supreme power of song among the verbal arts of Uto-Aztecan and neighboring groups. "In song," she writes, "the trope of the 'view' appears: large-scale images of landscape celebrated for their beauty are made visible" (1992:120). Such a view, she observes, is "a vision necessarily constituted at a distance" (1992:120), consistent with the perspective of the premigration "horizon" scenes.

The song imagery that Hill describes occurs widely in the Pueblo Southwest, in contexts that direct its spiritual effectiveness toward rainmaking and earthly renewal. Allusions to the sun's annual path and its solstice movements appear frequently in these songs, traits they share with performances used today for such calendrical rites as the Zuni Shalako and Hopi Soyal. References to the movements of the sun and moon, observed against the silhouettes of mesas, mountains, and horizon, form the metaphoric content of verses from "Sayatasha's Night Chant" for the Shalako at winter solstice (see figure 8.3; M. Young 1988:109–113). The visual practice of observing solar and lunar cycles, using the horizon and reference points like mountains, mesas, and the locations of shrines is historically institutionalized in Pueblo cultures through the office of a sun priest, moiety chief, clan leader, or sodality chief (Lange 1959; Parsons 1939; Stephen 1936; Stevenson 1904; Titiev 1944; White 1932; Zeilik 1985:S4, table I). Rooms adorned with horizon murals, featuring symbols for the sun, moon, and perhaps specific references to their periodicities, may indicate the rise to prominence of earlier leaders whose knowledge of such observations empowered them

Spectatorship and Performance in Mural Painting 163

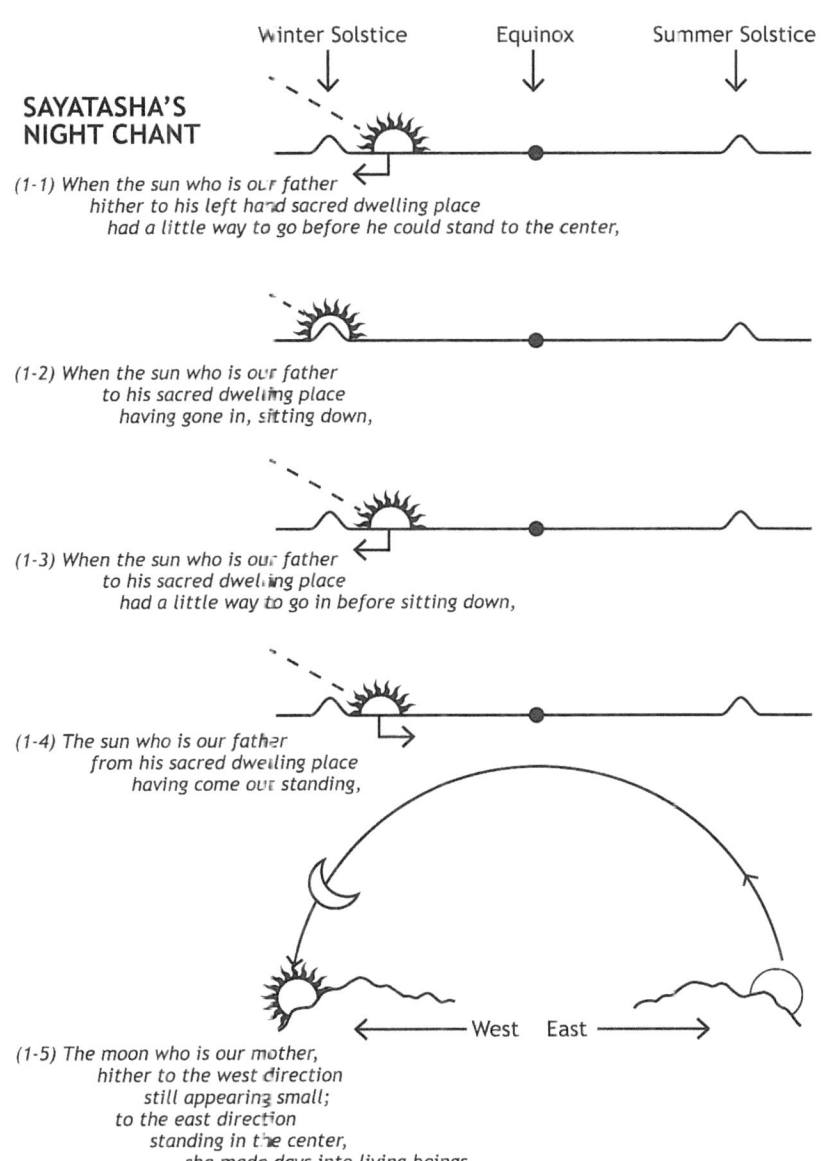

Figure 8.3. M. Jane Young's diagram of astronomical references in the verses from "Sayatasha's Night Chant," a Zuni Shalako ceremonial (adapted from Young 1988:111, fig. 45).

to control this important aspect of community ritual. Responsibility for ceremonial knowledge is not so much a matter of controlling access to specific places, at least in the western Pueblos, but of having mastered clan- and sodality-owned knowledge. Therefore, the same landscape or architectural features that are visible to everyone have deeper layers of meaning for some community members, that is, leaders. Who is watching and who is seeing is key to what is seen, or at least to what is understood.

Pueblo IV Period

Pueblo IV settlements offer a rich array of evidence for expanding and diversifying uses of public ritual (as well as private or sodality-based ritual) that include the proliferation of new architectural formats, pottery styles, and the iconography of ritual activities and paraphernalia pictured in mural designs. These mark a major shift in the scale and composition of Pueblo visual culture. Archaeological indicators that correlate with a new concern for centralized ritual and public viewership are apparent in ceramic patterns such as those that Van Keuren (this volume) discusses for the Silver Creek area, including increasing bowl size, use of exterior paintings, and a shift toward large-scale feasting in the context of more highly visible ritual performance. Making and using visually "special" vessels suggests more public and socially complex methods of circulation and display. At the same time, centralized plazas increase in scale and frequency. Chamberlin (this volume) relates these changes to strategies of public viewership that relied on mass communication through ritual performance to emphasize distinctions between participants and observers. He views this process as giving rise to new orthodoxies by using the "embodied capital" of ceremonial authority to fundamentally restructure theocratic order. Other data, however, reveal a simultaneous movement toward greater exclusivity in access to ceremonial knowledge shared in the intimate and specialized settings of kivas and the enclosed rock art locations (Munson, this volume). Growing divergence and specialization in Pueblo IV period ceremonialism seems to have generated events that were both larger and more public than at any time in the past, and activities that were more private, restricted to kiva group (sodality) initiates (see Bernardini, this volume; Potter and Perry 2000, for a discussion of such developments in the Western Pueblo/Hopi area).

Ceremonial dancers, some recognizable as Katsinas, appear among the imagery of rainmaking, fertility, and germination featured on Sikyatki Polychrome pottery (Hays-Gilpin and LeBlanc 2007). After 1375, figures of Katsinas and Katsina symbols circulated for public access and viewership on these vessels, which were widely distributed in networks of trade and ceremonial exchange. Simultaneously, images of performers and rows of dancers are featured in the more esoteric spaces of painted kivas, often shown in elaborate scenes that combine real-world and otherworldly elements, ceremonial objects, and a variety of zoomorphic and botanical forms. The florescence of this new and highly visible material culture abundant in graphic references to dance and its role in mediating between the human and spiritual worlds certainly suggests Katsina ceremonialism. The Katsina religion may have been most central to the increasing investment in dance and public performance after 1300 (Adams 1991), but the iconographic range of kiva and ceramic decoration probably indicates that these changes took place within an ever greater expansion of ceremonialism throughout Pueblo society. Munson's discussion (this volume) of Pajarito and Galisteo rock art adds weight to that perspective, suggesting that its many iconographic distinctions and different situations for viewership reflect a widening array of audiences and ritual contexts. Together with these portrayals of dance and related activities, new adaptations and specializations in architectural settings provided for staging and viewing the public and private aspects of these rites. These include the large, centrally situated plazas built for mass assembly that created a focal location for witnessing displays of regalia, choreography, and dramatic performance of the types that Pueblo IV period kiva paintings illustrate. The fully developed kiva, as E. Charles Adams (2002) notes, coincides with the plaza's appearance and is its counterpart for housing the private aspects of ceremonial society rites. In his discussions of the ancestral Hopi village at Homol'ovi II, Adams (2002:158–160) observes that kiva and plaza are paired by related symbolic allusions to the underworld and emergence, reflecting their parallelism as staging areas for esoteric or public aspects of performance. Kiva interiors, with painted images of ceremonial dance, are the private, more esoteric counterpart of spectatorship shared by a greater community in the plaza as the space for public dance.

As the confluence and merging of populations in the 1300s and 1400s led to more heterogeneous, densely populated centers, the viewership expressed in these murals and their settings shifted inward to accommodate a new emphasis on social interconnections. Kivas and plazas became sites for an existential space centrally produced by community actions on a large scale, invested with the mythic and symbolic values drawn from architectural metaphor, choreography, dramatization, and public gathering. Whereas pre-1300s architecture and painting exhibit a frequent concern with cosmology and geographical distances—landscape and horizon observations, and the alignments of sites and buildings for viewing sacred landscapes and astronomical events—their Pueblo IV period successors prioritize human agency carried out in ceremonial spaces that dominate their communities by their size and central placement.

Comparable patterns also characterize the broader distributions of both rock art and residential settlement sites, which demonstrate corresponding shifts from a focus on open lands to consolidation near expanding plaza pueblo towns. Both Munson and Chamberlin (this volume) discuss these developments for both sets of data in different parts of the Rio Grande region. Their studies reveal similar transitions: from settlements dispersed across the distances of a geographical expanse to congregation near the heart of a shared plaza space, and from isolated petroglyphs scattered among the prominent hills and outcrops of an outlying landscape to a concentration of imagery close to aggregated villages. Like Pueblo IV period murals, these changes involve establishing a central focus on dance and human performance, and in rock art, a new emphasis on the human form prevailed.

Settlement archaeology offers powerful evidence that the planning and construction of plazas exerted a magnetic influence on migration, attracting populations from outer areas to join the expanding occupation of these sites. Chamberlin observes that the development of enlarged, central plazas preceded nucleation in the Salinas area, and plaza pueblos on Chupadera Mesa appear to have been conceived and built in a single construction phase. Van Keuren (this volume) writes that plazas in the Silver Creek area appear to have dominated and even superseded the residential functions of village construction, because the first structures built in Pueblo IV villages define a plaza space. The priority assigned to plazas and their role in the "placemaking" that established and developed Pueblo IV period communities strongly implicates ideology as a key factor in the period's demographic, cultural, and sociological transformations. Ceremonialism and its combined visual and spatial frames of reference exhibit a consistent pattern of changes that can be identified for each medium of expression—rock art, mural styles, and plazas as theaters for public gathering, spectatorship, and dance.

In plazas and painted kivas, anthropomorphic portrayals and details of regalia and ritual gesture were used to communicate specific kinds of information in new ways. New features of the Pueblo IV period mural style include a diversity of dancers, priests, and supernaturals arrayed within altarlike borders or settings defined by rainbows, cloud terraces, and basebands variously interpreted as "earth altars" (Sekaquaptewa and Washburn 2006:34) and as cosmic serpents (Schaafsma and Taube 2006; Taube 2010). These figurative murals express the closeness and immediacy of figures interacting in complex evocations of narrative and performance. Their content seems closely akin to the ritual dramas performed in Pueblo plazas today, but the "near range" spatial scale of kiva painting should also be understood as involving forms of communication and information distinct from the "far range" proxemics that Chamberlin (this volume) identifies with plaza rites. The images, settings, and activities associated with kiva painting emphasized inclusion and participation within a sodality, and they differentiated its members from all others who were exposed only to its publicly presented rites. Their design implies highly structured relationships between the observer and images that may specify ritual actions and manifest powerful beings in tangible form. Human images are compositionally dominant in many paintings, with primary attention to figures that confront the viewer directly in a frontal perspective. Secondary figures appear in profile, flanking dominant frontal images or participating in scenes that suggest the dramatization of ritual or myth. The flanking figures direct their attention toward the central figure, which in turn directs the attention of the viewer there. In contrast to Pueblo III period murals that surrounded a viewer on all sides, Pueblo IV period rectangular kivas in the Hopi region, at least, were painted on only three sides. Spectators seated on the raised southern platform would have seen paintings in front and to the sides, but not behind them. The focus is on performers, depictions of performers, and backdrops for performance, rather than on fixing the viewer in a center place in a relatively static depiction of surrounding landscape.

In one Awat'ovi mural, flanking figures face each other and direct the viewer's attention upward via red lines connecting to bowls the figures hold (figure 8.4). They may illustrate specific actions and events

Figure 8.4. Mural from Awat'ovi Room 788, Left Wall Design Layer 3, showing figures holding bowls (reproduction, Harvard Peabody Museum of Archaeology and Ethnology, Catalog no. 39-97-10/23108C).

prescribed by the ceremonials conducted in these kivas, which required specific paintings for the duration of a ritual cycle. In undoubtedly multilingual postmigration communities, visual communication by image and motion might have proven more effective than verbal communication in the process of instruction and learning. Chamberlin (this volume) stresses that this formal power of image and gesture in plaza performances may have functioned to reinforce orthodox and "conventional" meanings in spatial relationships too distant to rely on the complexities of language and speech. The frequent exchange of sodality rituals between different linguistic and ethnic groups, sometimes preserved in their original languages, may have necessitated a similarly strong reliance on imagery and action to maintain kiva society rites. Pueblo IV period migrations undoubtedly accelerated such assimilations, adding to the impetus for figural murals that elaborated on the visual communication of sodality rites.

Anthropomorphic representation may span a continuum of figural representations, from humans performing ceremonial roles, such as priests and dancers, to more esoteric portrayals of spirits and deity personations. They act within spaces that interweave the tangible, sensible objects and settings of community ritual—pottery jars, shields and staffs, tiponis, and even kiva interiors—with an ideal universe of vitalizing, generative forces represented by rainbows, cloud terraces, creatures associated with rain or pollination, and depictions of flowering plants and fertile crops. In these murals, the energies of human performance are drawn together with those that sustain and renew nature, with fertility and rebirth portrayed as the result of cooperation among people, and reciprocity with a parallel community of spirits. The interblending in these compositions of the world's concrete manifestations with the expressive imagery of imagination and expectation recalls Momaday's (1976 81) description of vision in Native American cultures as the focus of two aligned visual planes: seeing with the eye combined with seeing through the mind.

Paula Gunn Allen (1996) characterizes the inclusiveness of today's ceremonialism—the merging of individuals within a community, and of the community with the esoteric world—as an integration of orders of consciousness, generating a state of experience that transcends difference and conjoins all participants within a system of harmonious relations. She writes that the purpose of a ceremony "is to integrate: to fuse the individual with his or her fellows, the community of people with that of other kingdoms, and this larger communal group with the worlds beyond this one . . . the community is not only made up of members of the tribe but necessarily includes all beings that inhabit the tribe's universe" (249). In our view, painted kivas of the late pre-Hispanic period provide clear testament to such a commingling of the tangible with the immaterial, the seen with the unseen, and the human social order with higher orders of being. An example from Kiva 2 at Pottery Mound (see figure 8.5) shows the continuity that blends a mythic world composed of cloud borders and an anthropomorphic rainbow with details that suggest the scene takes place within the kiva itself. The ceremony's supernatural participants—those whose presence is "seen with the mind" rather than beheld with the eye—institute a

Figure 8.5. Mural from Kiva 2, layer 1, north wall, Pottery Mound, showing kiva interior with cloud terraces and anthropomorphic rainbow (from Hibben 1975:fig. 14, courtesy of KC Publications).

greater framework for reciprocity and encourage the heightened ritual consciousness that supersedes dissent with commonality and bridges relationships from the human to the cosmic scale. The imagery of dance, Katsina regalia, and altars give this unseen community a visible form on painted walls, rendered immediate and comprehensible to sodality initiates or those being guided through initiation.

Conclusion

The visuality of late pre-Hispanic period mural painting strongly evokes the ideology of Katsina religion and its reliance upon anthropomorphic imagery, embodied performance, and ritual speech and song to mediate spiritual forces. It also suggests ties to the underlying dynamics of community-building and social integration that E. Charles Adams (1991) and others (e.g., Triadan 2006) have discussed for Katsina ritual, which may have helped transcend divisiveness and promote cooperation in newly forming villages. That such divisiveness was (and to some extent still is) a problem is abundantly clear in several ways. Evidence for factionalism, fissioning, and even violence is abundant both in Pueblo ethnography and archaeology (LeBlanc 1999) and in oral histories. For example, the former Hopi Tribal Chairman Ferrell Secakuku described his Hopi Snake Clan ancestors' arrival to Second Mesa as a confrontation resolved only when the resident Bear Clan leaders prevailed upon the Snake warriors to lay down their weapons and armor and turn their supernatural abilities to rainmaking instead of war (personal communication, 2006). The Hopi artist Michael Kabotie reported that his uncle related a story of a time when the Katsinas became overly coercive in their leadership, and Hopi ancestors ejected them from their villages; later, when they had learned to live humbly, they were readmitted and took on the benevolent roles they have today (personal communication, 2009).

In their discussions of Hopi ritual song, Sekaquaptewa and Washburn illustrate how deeply anthropomorphic concepts permeate Katsina theology and shape its understandings of human relationships with nature. The inherent content of these song phrases, they write, "gets across the idea that it is the katsinas that *are* the rain, not that they *bring* the rain" (2004:463). Literal translations of such song phrases, for example, yield statements by the Katsinas such as "we will arrive as rain to you" and that they "go to do dancing as rain" (Sekaquaptewa and Washburn 2004:463). These translations underscore the priority of dance and anthropomorphic representations in realizing a harmonious balance between humans and the natural world. Relationships with Katsinas are essentially social relations sustained by cooperative values and concepts that favor harmony, reciprocity, and good will. Human relations to Katsinas mirror "the fabric of Pueblo social structure" (Adams 1991:13), reinforcing its ideals and values. Although practiced in varying ways among most of today's Pueblo groups, the Katsina religion is nonetheless closely attuned to each community's organization of kinship, ceremonial, social, and political relations. Katsina practice plays crucial roles in both differentiating members within the society (based on such criteria as clan and sodality membership, ceremonial status, and gender) and separating practitioners from nonpractitioners, distinguishing its members from all outside groups (Adams 1991:12).

How, then, can people be influenced by such a system of representations to assume certain values, ideologies, and behaviors? Part of the answer, of course, is that any such effort is only partly successful. Without minimizing tensions and contradictions, we focus here on integrative processes, such as attendance at public dances and the experience of viewing them. For many Pueblo people today, attendance at dances, even without participating in them, is essential to their identities and sense of community belonging. In characterizing the communal values of Tewa dance, Jill Sweet wrote that "the most fundamental social statement is communicated simply by the act of participating in a village ritual performance. When a Tewa decides to sing or dance in, or attend, a ritual performance, he or she demonstrates a commitment to being Tewa and contributes to the cohesiveness of the social group" (1985:25). The anthropologist Alfonso Ortiz remarked that in his own community, some people insist that to remain a Tewa, one must, in some capacity, take part in village performances (Ortiz 1979:287–298). Viewership at these dances involves more than a passive attentiveness to watching; Sweet used the term "active listening" to characterize the engagement of thought, imagination, and multisensory perception that audience members contribute as they add their thoughts, hopes, and prayers to the meaning of the dance. Paula Gunn Allen alluded to this same concept of viewership in recalling that although a ceremony "may be enacted before people who are neither singing nor dancing . . . their participation is nevertheless assumed" (1956:251). Their presence, spectatorship, and contribution to the dance's success "is a matter of attention and attunement" rather than activity, equating their viewership with an intensely focused perceptual act that requires concentration, imaginative effort, and a responsive state of mind.

Hopi ceremonialism requires a specific state of mental activity identified by the word *tunatya*, which has meanings of "concentration" and "intention." *Tunatya* involves individual and group contributions to achieving a collective mood of heightened awareness that Armin Geertz (1986:49) regarded as the primary psychological foundation for all Hopi ritual expression. "The main psychological activity during all ritual contexts . . . ," he wrote, "is that of nurturing the state of mind which can maintain the holistic image of reality" that he identified with the duality and ritual interpenetration of the sacred and sensible realms. "Everyone must concentrate and do it wholeheartedly," he continued, for the rite to be efficacious in effecting "the transition mechanism between two realities, where one reality is actively pierced by another reality" (1986:49, 42). Interestingly, the phrase also assumes special importance in terminology for the sponsor of a ritual dance, called *tunatyay'taqa*, or "one who has an intention," described as an individual who "carefully pays heed, and always concentrates" so that "he will be the one to have influence on these clouds" (1986:49). For the duration of a particular ceremony, its sponsor is elevated to a supreme place in public affairs, not only as the leader of the complete ritual cycle but also as village chief, or *kikmongwi*, assuming both the political and sacred duties of this office for a period that may last up to twenty days (1986:47–49). These connections are interesting to consider in relation to Chamberlin's interpretation of the role of plaza ritual in producing social venues for the precursors of the Hopi *mongsinom*, the Tewa Made People, and similar classes of ceremonial leaders.

Mural painting before and after the thirteenth- to fourteenth-century migrations articulates the contrasted frameworks of visual experience that attended the ways of thinking, being, and generating social order that characterized these two distinct phases of Pueblo history. The role of vision was neither passive nor neutral in the key ceremonial practices of their societies. However, visual experience was and is inseparably joined to the culturally generated substrates of how Pueblo people living in these different times conceived and experienced the world. Pueblo III period painted kivas and ritual rooms placed the viewer in a center place that evoked the surrounding landscape, earth, and sky, within an orderly progression of time. In contrast, the fully specialized Pueblo IV period painted kivas were iconographically charged by the figural presences that nearly encircled the viewer's space, creating an interactive space in which the observer is an active participant.

Theories of spectatorship examine how images and visual perception help bring about an "ideal subject" that becomes part of the cultural and historical fabric of society within a certain time. The ideal subject is socially generated within a particular viewing situation, and so is a construct that transcends viewers' individual identities. Familiar examples include the use of a darkened theater, cinematic narratives, sound, character performances, and ideologies presented from a specific viewpoint that encourage spectators to identify with, and recognize themselves in, portrayals based on social class, gender, national identity, and more. In the Southwest, we can recognize changing contexts of spectatorship and its settings, and we can consider specific questions about the uses of vision to generate cultural subjects and establish shifting frameworks for ritual power. The cosmological emphasis in premigration murals suggests the importance during that era of leaders who were responsible for maintaining a ceremonial calendar by using astronomical observations. The changing ceremonial orders of the Pueblo IV period transition may have prompted a new kind of ideal subject, fostered within a community life that was expressed through public plaza rituals. Component parts of these ceremonials are the responsibility of the leaders and members of diverse sodalities who maintained esoteric kiva rituals in nonpublic contexts (Adams 1991; Potter and Perry 2000). Visual strategies associated with imagery and display may have shaped the formation of quite different cultural subjects before and after the stresses of migration, contributing to each period's distinct expression of concerns with rainmaking and fertility that persisted across that transition, and still persists today.

9

The Materiality of Religious Belief in East-Central Arizona

Scott Van Keuren

A variety of novel or refashioned religious beliefs and practices emerged across the Pueblo Southwest during the late pre-Hispanic period. These traditions appeared during a remarkable period of change, triggered by major migrations and population resettlement that eventually resulted in postmigration landscapes of large towns built around central plazas. In addition to the expansion and formalization of these ceremonial spaces, Pueblo peoples in some areas of the Southwest began to convey religious concepts through the use and display of new pottery forms. One might argue, in fact, that the most salient markers of religious change in this period are both plazas and pots. Because modern Pueblo religion is often participatory, cohesive, and devoted to enhancing the broader social collective, we assume that these archaeological signatures relate to activities that emphasized solidarity and communalism during the late pre-Hispanic period. Both a "Southwestern Cult" (Crown 1994, 1996) and early forms of the Katsina cult (Adams 1991, 1994; Hays 1989) have been associated archaeologically to the presentation of iconographic imagery on polychrome bowls and other media, the convergence of certain ceramic styles, and the expansion of plazas (Adams 1991; Chamberlin, this volume). The suggestion that pottery icons and plaza ceremonies *functioned* to reinforce or evoke communalism has broadly influenced scholarly work on the late pre-Hispanic period (e.g., Adams and Duff 2004:4; Crown 1998; Doyel 2000:290–291; Kantner 2004:228–232; Kohler 1993:297–298).

I believe we can assume that late pre-Hispanic Pueblo religious practices were designed to reinforce communalistic ideals. These religious movements were also syncretic, melding the beliefs and rituals of the diverse groups who aggregated together at large towns throughout the Southwest following the demographic upheavals and ecological crises that marked the end of the 1200s (Bernardini, this volume; Ware and Blinman 2000). What makes the late pre-Hispanic period so interesting is that these new religious traditions were expansive, evidenced by widespread similarities in the design and use of plazas and painted ceramics. In this chapter, however, I question the notion that the spread of homogeneous pottery designs and color schemes, along with similarly configured plazas, all meant that religion was conceptualized and acted upon homogeneously everywhere that these key archaeological markers appear. The "cult models" advance this pan-southwestern point of view, and in doing so, they fail to account for historical processes at local scales. More important, the complex materialities of religious experience are overlooked in these big-picture models. Should we assume, for instance, that widely circulated ceramic forms, decoration, or even technology encoded religious subject matter that was comprehended and acted upon similarly by those groups who produced and used these containers? Were large plazas and the rooms that enclose them consistently made and occupied by communities who were applying pan-southwestern religious practices and beliefs? The answer to both questions may be yes but we need to examine how painted ceramics (or other objects) and plaza spaces manifest the diverse social practices through which understandings (or misunderstandings) of religious knowledge were expressed. In my view, late pre-Hispanic painted pottery did not merely transmit religious canons but deeply resonated the ways in which bodies of knowledge were communicated, learned, and ultimately transformed. Individuals were agents in this process; they created, copied, and reconfigured. The same can be said of plazas, where the growth and configuration of ceremonial space were complex processes associated with the diverse experiences, motivations, and even memories of individuals and households. Whether we are talking about pots or plazas, the materiality of religion in the late pre-Hispanic period embodied the negotiation of power relations, social networks, identities, and perhaps differing interpretations of sacred concepts.

In this chapter I assume that the meaning of things is never set in stone, but rather must be viewed as continually recreated through social practices (Boivin 2009). When speaking of religion, these practices defined in the broadest sense are always ritual (see Pauketat, this volume), and through ritual, the meanings of religious things are situational and contingent. Ultimately "ideology is embedded in social practices" (K. Thompson 1986:72), and it is these actions that inherently "construct particular types of meanings and values" (Bell 1997:82). My focus is on ceramic and architectural meanings in a cluster of fourteenth-century villages in the Silver Creek area of east-central Arizona (see figure 9.1). This area has been noted by recent scholars (Adams 1991:133–134; Crown 1994:215) as a possible origin place for the Southwestern Cult and Katsina religion, largely based on the early appearance of Pinedale- and Fourmile-style pottery. In this area, both the crafting of polychrome bowls and the configuration of large plazas at three villages (Fourmile, Pinedale, and Shumway ruins) signal many histories in the making as Pueblo individuals, households, and other social groups expressed and transformed bodies of religious and nonreligious knowledge. Ultimately, the archaeological evidence of religious belief and expression

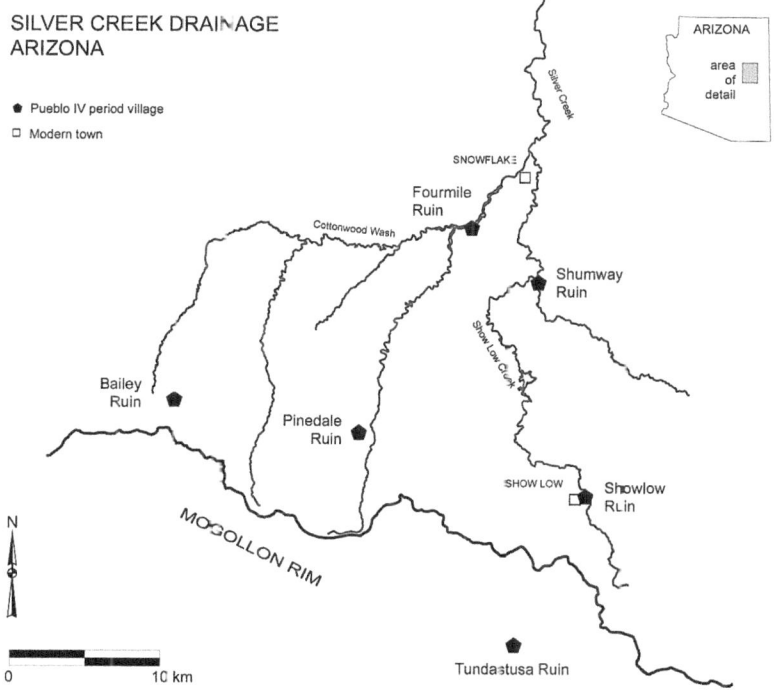

Figure 9.1. Late pre-Hispanic villages in the Silver Creek drainage, Arizona.

here neither proves nor disproves the cult models. Rather, as I argue below, it demonstrates the many unique pathways of religious belief and expression in the late pre-Hispanic period.

Religion, Materiality, and Meaning

If one wants to examine late pre-Hispanic religion in east-central Arizona, the most extant marker in the archaeological record is pottery. To be sure, ritual caches and deposits have been documented in this broader area (Mills 2004; Walker 1995), along with religious architecture (e.g., Haury 1985). Nonetheless, pots were public objects that were widely circulated and produced in large quantities, and potentially reflect the religious experience of the masses. The appearance and presentation of key icons and symbols on polychrome bowls also signal new religious ideologies by 1300. Crown (1994) examines the stylistic (and technological) changes in the transition from Pinedale to Gila-style Roosevelt Red Ware, concluding on the basis of iconographic analyses that a Southwestern Cult (or "Pinedale-style cult") emerged by the end of the thirteenth century. She draws heavily on Schaafsma's (1980) studies of rock art as well as Pueblo ethnographic data (e.g., Kenagy 1986) to chart an "iconic system" (Crown 1994:165–167). In Crown's view, icons that coded "fertility" and "weather control" were central (1994:222, 1996:243–244), and vessels adorned with these designs communicated and reified ideological doctrines. She states that the "widespread occurrence of the imagery indicates an equally widespread shared and consistent conception of the meanings behind these icons, a shared ideology" (1994:173). In a similar vein, Adams (1991, 1994) and others (Ferg 1982; Hays 1994) tie the emergence of a pre-Hispanic Katsina religion with fourteenth-century Fourmile-style pottery (along with kiva murals and other media). Adams cites painted ceramics as one part of a broader suite of archaeological changes that signal the transformation of Pueblo religion by the early 1300s. The reconfiguration of ceremonial spaces and the formalization of large plazas are also central to his model (Adams 1989, 1991:127). He implies that the Katsina religion was practiced wherever we see masks and other key signs in the visual media of archaeological sites, first in the Mogollon Rim area and spreading to adjacent areas. Although his argument is not based on ceramic evidence alone, he does imply that the origins of Katsina religion are signaled by motifs on Fourmile-style pottery produced in the Silver Creek area by the 1320s. It is worth noting that Crown disagrees with this interpretation. She suggests instead that the Katsina religion was part of the Southwestern Cult and that it originated in the Chaco and Mimbres areas well before the late pre-Hispanic period (1994:220). In his discussion of Mesoamerican connections, McGuire (this volume) makes a persuasive case for a more southern origin.

In this chapter I neither address the problematic implications of the use of the term "cult" (see Plog, this volume) nor do I discuss the debate about the origins of Katsina religion in the Southwest (see McGuire, this volume). I also do not deny that painted ceramics may have at times facilitated participatory and public ceremonies through feasts or other ritual activities by displaying religious subject-matter. My beef is specifically with the way that we read painted pottery as archaeologists. The "cult models" rely on an interpretive approach that oversimplifies the way that painted ceramics convey religious meaning, one that typically relies on an iconistic approach. To be fair, these models do not focus solely on ceramic iconography but rather a broader range of attributes on whole vessels including form, color, and layout as well as other archaeological data. However, iconicity studies assume that the way we analytically deconstruct decoration (into design elements, motifs, etc.) somehow captures the way that potters construct meaning in the painting process. The ceramic styles we discuss are defined by the presence or absence of design elements, so any statement that equates a style with an ideological movement assumes, dangerously I think, that Pueblo peoples conceptualized and read pottery decoration in our analytical terms.

Ethnoarchaeologists have shown that potters do not decorate pots by mixing and matching units or elements, and potters only vocalize their crafting in such terms when pressed by researchers (e.g., Bunzel 1929). In her classic study of Tarascan potters, Hardin (1979) demonstrated that individuals conceptualize the painting process in terms of design structure, layout, and symmetry. They are not actively cognizant of all of this artistic variability, namely the ordering of individual gestures such as the application of brushstrokes (Van Keuren 2006a). In some sense, these layers of design variability are signatures of personal expertise and expression that reflect learning histories, identity, motives, and perhaps most fundamentally, the individual's access to and understanding of specific bodies of knowledge. Thus, our archaeological typologies—originally developed for cultural and historical purposes—compel us to ignore other complex dimensions of past materiality.

The way that we infer religious beliefs on the basis of pottery decoration in the Southwest is relevant to broader debates about material symbolism and meaning. These are too numerous to engage here (see Bekaert 1998; Boivin 2009; Gell 1998; Hodder 1989; Keane 2003; Parmentier 1994). However, it is important to note that material culture studies are usually driven by an essentialist mind-set that, for instance, reduces decorative layouts to communicative motifs that are said to have encoded static meanings. Robb (1998:341) tags this notion of symbolism as the "Rosetta Stone view" and one where "interpreting a symbol involves merely identifying its literal referent." Signs certainly have such referents but these associations do not alone identify their meanings. On the topic of material meanings, Robb (1998:337) goes on to distinguish post-structural approaches to symbols as "mosaic tesserae." In this way of thinking, meaning is never fixed but inherently altered through experience (or practices, to put it another way). I argue that the most productive way to discuss meaning in southwestern ceramics is to examine how these objects were produced and transformed and, in Gell's (1998) words, to cognitively retrace the way in which objects were created. In the latter perspective, "what does late pre-Hispanic pottery decoration mean?" becomes the question, "how was decoration rendered and transformed by individual potters as they *lived* religion?"

What is really at stake here is how we access bodies of knowledge, or what Barth (2002:1–2) defines as "what a person employs to interpret and act on the world." For him, the concept has been misapplied in traditional anthropologies, which "lay out knowledge as if it were context-free—a mode that collapses historical time in acquiring knowledge, elaborates taxonomies, and prizes coherence. It simulates knowledge without knowers" (2002:2). Most attempts to discuss the meaning of objects take a static view of both knowledge and knowers. For the pottery I discuss in this chapter, meaning is often inferred through "key symbols" (*sensu* Ortner 1973), which might be identified as specific signs (cloud imagery) that encode or symbolize specific ideas ("fertility"). By discussing these key symbols, however, one neglects the individual—that is, we fall into Barth's trap by inferring Pueblo religious ideology ("knowledge") without examining the individuals ("knowers") who created and reconfigured such beliefs.

To expand the analysis of meaning in southwestern ceramic research, we need to examine how bodies of knowledge were created, exchanged, negotiated, and altered. The goal is not to measure what pots symbolized per se but rather to examine how their meanings were (re)created through social practice, and what this and other dimensions of their materiality says about broader historical processes in the past. In my view, there is significantly more meaning to be discovered through attention to how pots are painted versus what was painted on them. This requires analytical frameworks that are firmly grounded in practice theory. Hodder (1982:9) makes a critical point that is relevant to this discussion: "structuralist analyses in archaeology [have failed] to develop a theory of practice (concerning the generation of structures in social action)." Dietler and Herbich (1998:261) make a similar point and press the importance of a practice-oriented approach to inferring the contextualization of objects in social worlds. They identify the notion of *chaînes opératoires* as a "synthesizing" analytical approach, and Dobres (1999:22–23) advocates a similar program for investigating the arenas of practice. The approach is often actualized in archaeological studies as a means to infer social identity and learning through technological variation (e.g., Schiffer and Skibo 1987), but even Lechtman (1977) advocates a much broader examination of symbolic behavior in her classic essay on technological style. As Pfaffenberger (1988:249) nicely summarizes, technology, "as a social phenomenon[,] . . . marries the material, the social and the symbolic in a complex web of associations." These perspectives have reshaped analytical measures of *habitus* and other dimensions of social practice (see Dobres and Robb 2005), but have yet to influence wider archaeological discussions about meaning in the past.

A practice-oriented framework is the most effective way to measure how religious knowledge was engaged in the past. The beauty of a painted whole vessel, as one materiality of this engagement, is that it represents a glimpse of individual expression, essentially personal "depositions" (Bourdieu 1977:72) and ways of structuring the expression of shared bodies of knowledge. The vessel is also a potpourri of sorts, created in moments where potters draw upon layers of knowledge based on memories, learning, and observations. Ultimately, it is a complex embodiment of social relations and experiences, rather than a simple marker of core beliefs. My discussion of fourteenth-century religion in this chapter is primarily based on ceramic research, but the construction and configuration of plazas in the Silver Creek area is another telling aspect of religious materiality in the early 1300s. Much like pottery, plazas were spaces where religious knowledge was actively engaged, and the fact that no two pots and no two plazas were ever similarly crafted helps to point to the many ways that religious knowledge was actively transformed in the past.

Pottery and Plazas in the Silver Creek Area

The "cult models" are predicated, in part, on archaeological evidence from the Silver Creek area in the upper Little Colorado River drainage in Arizona (figure 9.1). The type sites for Pinedale- and Fourmile-style ceramics are located here, and the area may well have been the source of some of the sacred knowledge and rituals for new religious ideologies (Adams 1991:133; Crown 1994:223, 1996:247). By 1300, the occupants of this area had relocated to six major villages that form the Silver Creek cluster (Kaldahl et al. 2004).[1] This occurred roughly at the time that the Pinedale style appears on multiple, technologically distinct painted wares. The style blended decorative traditions found in areas to the north and east, and presumably it signals the arrival and mingling of migrant and local groups at Silver Creek villages (Mills 1998). During a second phase of settlement aggregation by the 1330s, several towns were expanded and even larger central plazas were constructed as another wave of migrants arrived (Van Keuren 2006b). Permanent residential occupation ended at one large town (Bailey Ruin) and possibly another (Pinedale Ruin), leaving four major villages (Fourmile, Showlow, Shumway, Tundastusa ruins) in the cluster. At roughly the same time, White Mountain Red Ware potters began producing Fourmile-style vessels (see figure 9.2). Other potters who worked with a different, organic-paint tradition began to paint much bolder stylistic elements on the Salado Polychromes (see figure 9.2). The early 1300s was thus a dynamic period in the area. Two major painted wares diverge from a unified stylistic tradition (Pinedale style), one of which blooms into a rich iconographic-style with religious subject matter (Fourmile Poly-

Figure 9.2. Painted bowl interiors: (a) Pinedale-style White Mountain Red Ware (top three vessels) and Roosevelt Red Ware/Salado Polychrome (bottom two vessels); (b) Fourmile Polychrome (top vessel) and Fourmile-style "hybrids"; and (c) Gila-style Roosevelt Red Ware/Salado Polychrome (all Gila Polychromes).

chrome). Several towns with new and larger central plazas become the focus of Pueblo occupation. In the remainder of this chapter, I briefly outline what these ceramic and architectural dimensions of religious experience suggest about how Silver Creek fits into (or out of) broader models of social change in the late pre-Hispanic period.

Painted Bowls

I have no doubt that fourteenth-century pottery materialized religion in ways that earlier ceramics had not. Red-slipped, polychrome bowls became the main serving vessels while the geometric-style bichromes that dominated earlier assemblages waned. A number of these new pottery types display iconography that likely referenced clan affiliation, mythological figures or ancestor spirits, allegories, or combinations thereof (Crown 1994; Ferg 1982; Hays 1989). Some of this imagery mimics that found on kiva murals (Hays-Gilpin and LeBlanc 2007; Newsome and Hays-Gilpin, this volume). In contrast to these concealed paintings, polychrome bowls were circulated, highly visible forms of media. Here, I focus on stylistic trends on the two primary service wares used by late pre-Hispanic period households (White Mountain and Roosevelt Red wares, see figure 9.2).

The most dynamic iconographic-style visuals appear on Fourmile Polychrome (figure 9.2b), a White Mountain Red Ware type produced in the Silver Creek area and circulated to surrounding areas. The type marked a fundamental change in the treatment of bowl interior designs, namely with the use of elaborate symbolism compared to earlier Pinedale-style vessels. Stylized depictions of macaws evoke connections to Mesoamerican beliefs (McGuire, this volume); masked icons bear a resemblance to those referenced in the modern Pueblo Katsina religion (Adams 1994). Somewhat different subject matter was painted on contemporaneous Salado Polychromes (namely Pinto/Gila and Gila Polychromes), the other primary decorated ware used by Silver Creek households (figure 9.2c). In her analysis of Salado Polychromes, Crown (1994) provides an exhaustive review of the decorative features of Pinedale-, Gila-, and Tonto-style vessels based on a large corpus of museum whole vessels, with specific attention to iconography (Crown 1994:132). My space here is too limited to review all of the important changes in imagery, color schemes, and vessel forms. However, it is worth noting that by the second or third decade of the 1300s, the primary vessel form for both wares was a hemispherical bowl with designs that wrap around the vessel exterior. I suggest elsewhere that the inherent design features were associated with specific types of ritual food consumption, including feasts (Van Keuren 2004).

Crown (1996:241) is correct when she states that the early fourteenth-century reorganization of the Pueblo world resulted in "abrupt changes in decorative and technological styles." However, her view that pottery styles "converge"—a central premise in the cult model she outlines—overlooks an important change. There was a notable uptick in variability within specific ceramic types. Two trends in particular are worth noting: first, a proliferation of stylistic variability, especially in the bowl interiors of Fourmile- and Gila-style bowls, and second, the widespread emulation of specific types (namely of Fourmile Polychrome). In earlier work, I suggested those potters who emulated the complex interiors of the "classic" Fourmile Polychrome bowls misunderstood or altogether misconstrued the underlying semantics (Van Keuren 2006a). Many of these copies (see figure 9.2b) do not present asymmetrical imagery on bowl interiors, but rather they mix older-style geometric layouts with the standard exterior of the Fourmile Polychrome. In the Grasshopper area south of the Mogollon Rim—a primary consumer area of Silver Creek White Mountain Red Ware—potters emulated the style of the Fourmile Polychrome on Grasshopper Polychromes by closely copying exterior designs and largely improvising interior layouts (figure 9.2). Fourmile-style copies are also present in the assemblages of other Mogollon sites (e.g., Point of Pines Pueblo), and similar vessels are even found in the Silver Creek area where Fourmile Polychrome was produced. At Fourmile Ruin, for instance, many examples repeat the same decorative shuffling of Grasshopper Polychrome (i.e., improvised and often symmetrical interior designs, but with Fourmile-style exterior designs). I also suspect that the emulation of Fourmile style occurred in other areas where Fourmile Polychrome bowls are present (e.g., Winslow Orange Ware in the middle Little Colorado River Valley; Hays-Gilpin et al. 1996).

Based on Crown's published images and a survey of other Gila-style Roosevelt Red Ware whole vessels in major museum collections, it appears that the same increase in intra-type variability characterizes the

Salado Polychromes (Roosevelt Red Ware), the other dominant red ware of the Silver Creek area towns and surrounding areas. These assemblages reflect a similar divergence at the point at which exterior motifs appear and interior decoration became bolder and displayed more dynamic iconography with the appearance of Gila-style vessels (figure 9.2c).[2] The period of diversification is significant because earlier Pinedale-style bowls were so remarkably uniform (across both wares). In fact, it is difficult to distinguish the decorative elements or layouts of Pinedale-style Roosevelt and White Mountain Red Wares in whole vessel collections, despite discrete differences in how each ware was produced (e.g., different clays, pigments, and firing regimes). By the 1330s, however, there is an explosion of personal expression in the painting process. White Mountain Red Ware potters began producing pots in the Fourmile style, which was copied at Grasshopper Pueblo and elsewhere (figure 9.2b). With the appearance of Salado Polychromes, Roosevelt Red Ware production extends well beyond the Silver Creek where Pinto Polychrome was likely first produced (Mills, Herr et al. 1999); the decorative schemes that follow are amazingly diverse (figure 9.2c). These changes correspond with the arrival of another wave of migrant groups into the Mogollon Rim area and the construction of the latest and largest plazas at major villages (this is the second phase of aggregation that I mentioned earlier).

When potters began to paint more elaborate religious imagery on bowls in east-central Arizona, we thus witness a proliferation of decorative variability in at least two major wares that almost defies classification. What others view as consistent production of a widely shared pottery style wherever it appears is instead, I think, the display of a range of local varieties of a broader tradition. In his classic survey of White Mountain Red Ware, Carlson (1970) combines an array of geometric- and iconographic-style bowls under the single designation of Fourmile Polychrome. Whole vessel examples that lack the correct stylistic features are designated as "Degenerate Fourmile," a phrase he never fully defines (1970:92, fig. 49). In her discussion of a Southwestern Cult, Crown (1994:79–82) handles the decorative variety of Salado Polychromes by dividing the Pinedale style into stages, but her designations are best understood as *post*-Pinedale-style Gila or Tonto styles that defy classification. For lack of a better term, some are "hybrids" that are squeezed into existing typological frameworks or occasionally attributed to the work of children (e.g., Crown 1999:42–43). In sum, potters in the Silver Creek area and likely elsewhere began to decorate polychrome containers in remarkably diverse ways. In my view, as I argue later in this chapter, these ceramic trends give us some sense—albeit indirect—of the ways that aspects of religious knowledge were created, expressed, and presumably transformed in these fourteenth-century towns.

Plaza Layouts

The reconfiguration of central plazas across the Pueblo world was unquestionably an outcome of new ceremonies and other public activities that evoked community well-being (Adams 1989, 1991; Chamberlin, this volume; Longacre 1966). The ways in which these extramural spaces were constructed and continually reconstructed also reflect religious engagement and other dimensions of social discourse. For instance, the addition of new rooms and other remodeling events continually redefined the adjacency of households to plazas as well as their access to ceremonies and other activities that took place in these spaces. The appearance of large, partially or fully enclosed plazas was a pan-southwestern event, but were these spaces all created alike? Can the "biographies" of individual plazas offer some way to gauge how the communal dimensions of late pre-Hispanic religious beliefs were practiced at local scales? Here, I briefly discuss new data on the configuration and growth of plazas at Fourmile, Shumway, and Pinedale ruins (see figure 9.3a–c)—all primary production centers for the pottery discussed above. I also draw on published architectural data from Bailey Ruin (Mills, Van Keuren et al. 1999).

Bailey Ruin aside, the three villages noted above include multiple plazas that were constructed at different stages of occupation. The latest and largest plazas were typically added at the southeast or southwest edges of the villages, with the addition of long contiguous room blocks. At Bailey Ruin, and in the earlier portions of Pinedale Ruin (around Plaza One) and Shumway Ruin (Plaza One), the room expansion was accretional, eventually filling gaps between room blocks. With the exception of Bailey Ruin, the expansion of these sites involved the addition of rooms away from the plaza, preserving the in-

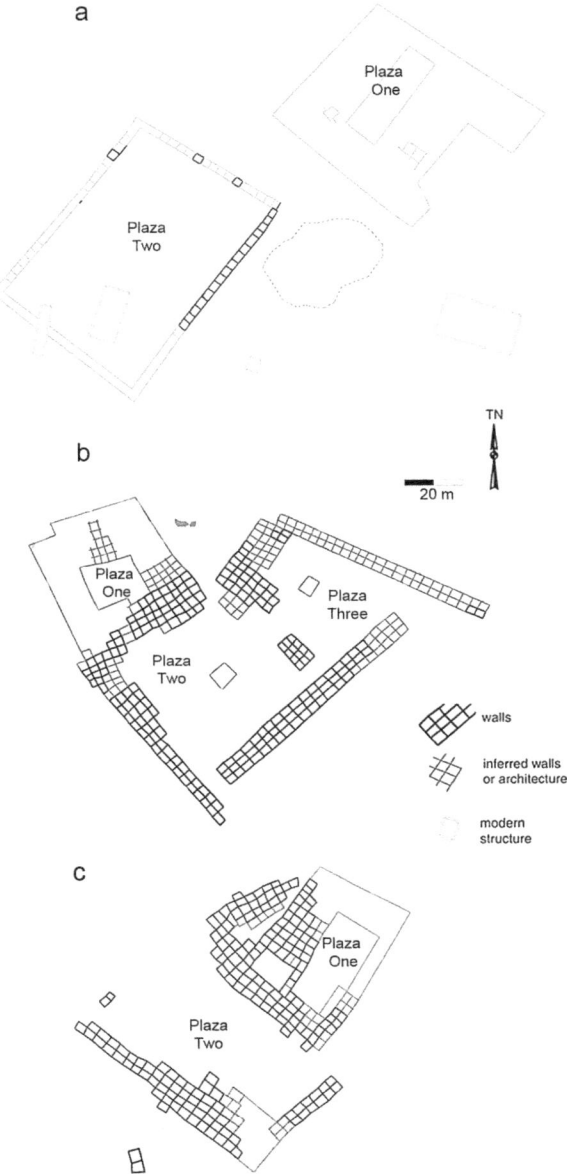

Figure 9.3. Architectural plans of three Silver Creek villages: (a) Pinedale Ruin (AZ P:12:2 ASM), (b) Fourmile Ruin (AZ P:12:4 ASM), and (c) Shumway Ruin (AZ P:12:127 ASU).

ternal boundaries of these primary spaces. Beyond this, however, plaza configuration and growth were surprisingly different at each village. At Fourmile Ruin, the long room blocks that border the southeast plazas (Plazas Two and Three) were planned and constructed in one or more construction episodes. The spaces between room blocks make it impossible to know the relative timing of these construction phases, but they were presumably designed to delineate the edges of this large rectangular plaza. The long southwest and northwest room blocks were primarily constructed of adobe brick walls that were braced by interior masonry spine walls (D. Johnson 1992). These and other room blocks surround but do not fully enclose the two latest plazas at Fourmile Ruin (Plazas Two and Three, figure 9.3b). Similarly, the late plaza at Shumway Ruin (Plaza Two, figure 9.3c) was never fully enclosed, but the rooms that delineate this space were full-standing in height and constructed of masonry (there is no evidence for adobe brick construction at the village). Shumway Ruin does not have plaza kivas, but a natural spring once emerged from a deep crevice in the center of the largest plaza. At Pinedale Ruin (figure 9.3a), the late plaza appears to be completely enclosed (Plaza Two).[3] This feature shows up on early sketch maps of the village (Spier 1919), but it was not formally mapped by Haury and Hargrave (1931). Based on its size and configuration, the plaza is unlike every other ceremonial space constructed in the Silver Creek area. The interior area is approximately 4,248 square meters, making it substantially bigger than the late plazas at Fourmile Ruin (2,356 m^2) and Shumway Ruin (2,740 m^2). The Pinedale Ruin plaza is fully enclosed by masonry rooms, but curiously, none were ever completed; walls were not full-standing and rooms tested in recent fieldwork lacked formal floors, features, and trash. Both here and at Fourmile Ruin, large plazas became the primary focus of village expansion, so much so that the completion and occupation of the rooms that surrounded these spaces lagged behind the construction and use of the plaza itself. Most if not all of the adobe brick rooms that define both Plazas Two and Three at Fourmile Ruin were also delineated by long double or triple rows of rooms added during a single construction episode. Many of the walls in these rooms are composed of four to five courses of bricks, and the lack of wall fall hints that these structures were never full-standing in height. The design of Pueblo villages in the Silver Creek area had thus fundamentally changed: the large central plaza became the focus for public ceremonies, virtually occupied before the surrounding rooms were completed or occupied. Plaza Two at Pinedale Ruin was curiously oversized, as if to allow all households to be located on the plaza itself. Here, access and adjacency to the large plaza seems to have been of chief concern to the individuals who built this structure, testifying, I think, to the primacy of this social space as well as the need for visibility (of household units) within the entire community. At Fourmile and Shumway ruins, however, the expansion of surrounding room blocks either encroached upon plaza space or moved outward (away from the plaza) through additions to existing rooms.

At Pinedale Ruin, the late plaza (Plaza Two) was physically removed from other room blocks at the village and the ceremonies that occurred in this space would have been largely invisible to individuals located outside the plaza (had the rooms ever been completed, see above). In contrast, the large plaza space at Shumway Ruin (Plaza Two) was never fully enclosed, and as I noted above, Fourmile Ruin was similarly configured, with multiple disconnected room blocks defining major plaza spaces. I suspect that the configuration of Fourmile Ruin relates to the presence of "multiple villages" within a single town, as distinct social identities were maintained when the village was expanded with the arrival of migrant groups.[4] In other words, aggregating groups preserved social distance and autonomy as they expanded around the village's central ceremonial space.

The main thrust of this very brief overview is that when we "unpack" these spaces, one finds that the Silver Creek area villages (and plazas) were crafted very differently. Part of this can be explained by the different "ethnic" makeup of these settlements and the timing of migrant arrivals at each village. For instance, evidence of migrants from the Middle Little Colorado River valley or other areas to the north is strongest at Fourmile Ruin (Mills 1998). However, I propose that the growth and configuration of plazas at these villages also relate to historical differences in religious experience, or more accurately, the ways that individuals and groups accessed and acted upon bodies of knowledge in the processes of creating and occupying these built environments.

Pots, Plazas, and Religious Practice

Rappaport (1979:179–180) identifies two categories of information associated with ritual. The first, indexical information, signals, through actions, the individual's personal identity, status, and beliefs. The second, canonical information, refers to "immutable" and consistent messages that are understood independently of the agent. For Rappaport, canonical information is enduring while indexical information is largely fluid. Both categories shape the individual's religious experience. Broadly speaking, this experience can be situational and improvised, based in other words on what people *think* they know of things and ideas (Barth 2002:2). Knowledge in practice can thus result in amazingly variable outcomes, even in cases when individuals work with bodies of what they perceive as reliable information (e.g., holy concepts). I believe that this was the case in the fourteenth-century Pueblo world, as individuals worked with and acted upon differing bodies of knowledge through ritual practices. I use the term ritual rather broadly (as does Pauketat, this volume) to embody the social practices involved in the materialization of these beliefs, not simply those activities in which objects or spaces were used for ceremonial events.

Rappaport's distinction helps reconcile how red ware pottery actively referenced widely shared ideologies through highly variable decorative layouts. The indexical information that potters were working with—that flexible part of ritual knowledge—may have distorted the canonical information or the orthodoxy of broader religious ideologies. At Fourmile Ruin, for instance, crafting, eating from, or displaying a red ware bowl may have, for some, evoked participation; for others, the use and display of these same pots could have been read or construed as exclusion, because distinctions were revealed through the exercise of indexical knowledge. The ways in which pots were crafted also conveyed social meanings to other participants, some intended, some not, regarding familiarity with ideological concepts. The potters who produced Fourmile-style copies closely mimicked the exteriors of true Fourmile Polychrome bowls, but they applied very different decorative layouts to bowl interiors. Other potters were working with lower-fired, organic-paint Salado Polychromes, producing Gila-style pots with varying results. My central argument is that many vessels—

some "hybrids"—essentially avoided, miscopied, or misconstrued the semantic content that potters were intending to reproduce. These pots were not mistakes and they did not lie at the margins of ritual; rather, we should assume they were actively in play within these fields of religious expression. In some sense, the ongoing creation of religious knowledge was thus embedded in the use histories of these red ware bowls, from the moments they were painted, through their use in food sharing, to their eventual placement in burials. At all times in between, pots were active markers in public settings, viewed by many as they moved in and out of plazas, when exchanged as gifts, and so forth. Along with the creation and growth of plazas, these pots created the context for social discourse in which religious experience played out in fourteenth-century villages. From this perspective, neither architecture nor pottery ever passively reinforced or codified shared ideologies (through ritual or other practices). Rather, these aspects of the material world, borrowing a phrase from Dobres and Robb (2005:162), "actually *constitute[d]* social relations and meaning making." Making and using painted pots and plazas in the Silver Creek area "constituted" practices that were deeply intertwined with religious experience and belief in the past.

Pots and plazas certainly facilitated new types of ceremonialism and other rituals that evoked communalistic ideas, or reinforced the commonalities among newly aggregated groups. The material evidence that I discuss in this chapter in no way contradicts this. However, when painted pottery came to express shared religious ideologies (even "cults") by the fourteenth century, individuals increasingly misread, questioned, and perhaps even subverted these shared ideals through their manufacture and use of these valued containers. At the same time, the creation of plaza spaces embodied the distinctiveness of the groups who joined these villages. I suspect that these groups conceptualized the plaza as a social space in different ways, perhaps even conflicting expectations about participation and proxemics (Chamberlin, this volume). Both aspects of fourteenth-century materiality reflected the ways in which collective bodies of religious knowledge were diversely articulated and acted upon by social groups or even specific individuals. Public rituals reinforce the histories of sodalities, the social standing of different groups within communities, and they reaffirm differences in access to important bodies of information or paraphernalia (E. Brandt 1994). As objects that display what people know and what they do not know (or even think they know), painted vessels were at what Saitta and McGuire (1998:335) call junctions of communal relations and "noncommunal" appropriation of resources. Plazas would have certainly acted as multidimensional settings in this regard (see Chamberlin, this volume). Some of these fields of social discourse undermined the cooperative principles of religious ideologies at towns as layers of meaning were altered, even manipulated. These and other historical processes have played a part in fueling factionalism and other social turmoil that have fissioned Pueblo communities in the recent past (Cameron 1992; Levy 1992). Factionalism may in fact account for the end of permanent Pueblo occupation in the Silver Creek by 1400 (Kaldahl et al. 2004).

Conclusion

I have highlighted both the diversity of plaza construction as well as the dizzying multiplicity of decorative layouts in pottery assemblages in the Silver Creek region to rethink religiosity in the late pre-Hispanic period. In the case of pottery, this diversity certainly resulted from many historical factors, not the least of which was individual creativity and experimentation (Hagstrum 1995). However, I interpret some of this patterning as inconsistencies in the expression of ritual knowledge—at least that part of ritual that evoked religious ideologies through making, seeing, eating from, and gifting painted bowls. Conventional analyses overlook this meaningful variation, driven in part by functionalistic paradigms that presuppose fixed roles for painted objects. There is no doubt that pots, display masks, macaws, and other signs that generically referenced community- or even region-wide belief systems. The more interesting question, however, is how individuals shaped these ideologies through practice. In the case of pottery, and for that matter plaza construction, individuals used these objects and spaces to negotiate ideological concepts. Some of this involved social discourse centered on purposeful agency as a few individuals perhaps proscribed the use of particular images (on pottery). So while it is an impossible task to guess what people were thinking, whole vessels reveal what people were actually doing. In the case of red ware pottery at late villages in eastern Arizona, it does not appear that everyone was doing the same thing, or even conceptualizing key ideologies in the same ways. This shift appears to coincide with both the expansion of plazas and the establishment of what I would term multicultural villages in the Silver Creek. As I see it, the archaeological evidence at hand reveals emerging tensions with respect to the practice of religion in these fourteenth-century communities.

The pioneering work by Crown (1994), Adams (1991), and others clarify the appearance and role of late pre-Hispanic religious ideologies in the Pueblo world. I would go further and say that this scholarly work has reshaped interpretative archaeology in the Southwest (Hegmon 2003:222). I remain skeptical, however, about the formula that uses iconography or symbolism to gauge shared religious beliefs or cults. First, it invites us to do the improbable, to infer semantics vis-à-vis enigmatic designs whose meanings cannot be fixed. And second, it presumes that religious movements in the late pre-Hispanic period were homogeneously understood and acted upon. I think the opposite might be true: painted ceramics and plaza construction may have embodied social practices that undermined the communal ethos of new religious beliefs. At the end of the day we will never demonstrate that a particular decorative scheme signals the Southwestern Cult, a pre-Hispanic Katsina religion, or another ideology, and we will never discover what most of these key icons meant. In my view, any notion of meaning will come from unpacking the materialities of Ancestral Pueblo religion. Meaning itself is fundamentally constituted by contingent practices and historical processes (Pauketat, this volume), and, in any cultural context, meaning is always in flux. My goal here was ultimately to examine *how* religious spaces were socially constructed rather than how they fit functionalistic expectations about the integrative role of religious rites; and to think about *how* pots were painted and viewed, versus what was painted on them. Broadly speaking, these practices reveal a great deal about how the creation, transformation, and perhaps even misreading of religion shaped the Pueblo past.

Acknowledgments

A portion of the research discussed in this chapter was supported by grants from the Wenner-Gren Foundation (Gr. 7161) and the National Science Foundation (BCS 0753156). I thank Donna Glowacki and Matt Chamberlin for detailed feedback on the chapter. The participants of the 2009 Amerind Seminar also provided insightful comments on this research. Eliot Sloan offered valuable guidance and support during the writing process.

10

North, South, and Center
An Outline of Hopi Ethnogenesis
Wesley Bernardini

The religious transformations of the fourteenth century in the American Southwest involved both novel introductions and things that were left behind. New ritual practices tied to the Katsina religion or the Southwestern Cult swept broad areas, while long-standing ways of life in places like the Mesa Verde region were let go. Efforts to reconstruct the events of this dynamic period benefit from the incorporation of Hopi oral tradition as a historical resource. These traditions provide a record of the experiences and issues deemed important enough to remember—both at the time and retroactively. Because they represent an emic view, these accounts have the potential to highlight behavioral processes and scales that are not commonly the focus of archaeological study. As such, they can spark a productive round of "tacking" (Wylie 1989) between oral and archaeological lines of evidence that produces new questions, models, and insights (e.g., Bernardini 2005).

Some Hopi discourse frames clan history in terms of a duality not previously recognized in the archaeological literature: the *Motisinom* ("first people"), who originated in the north, and the *Nùutungkwisinom* ("later people"), who came from the south. In this view, contemporary Hopi society emerged from the convergence of these two populations on the Hopi mesas and the reconciliation of their distinct religious traditions. The culture that resulted understood the Hopi mesas as *Tuuwanasavi*, the earth center, where *hopivötskwani*, the Hopi path of life, would be practiced. Elements of the reconciliation of these two religious traditions underlying Hopi society are still visible in the Hopi ritual calendar and in tensions in Hopi philosophy.

Motisinom and Nùutungkwisinom are relative, not absolute, terms; in addition to the usage cited above, they are also used to distinguish between earlier and later migrants to villages established in the twentieth century. As with much Hopi traditional knowledge, conditioned by the unique historical and ritual perspectives of different clans, there are also differences in usage across villages and mesas. Archaeologists are still working to understand the historical implications of these terms; this chapter represents one of what will necessarily be many attempts to reconcile these terms with the archaeological record. This attempt is admittedly speculative and perhaps even provocative, and it is intended to push our understanding of both Hopi traditional knowledge and the archaeological record.

With these caveats in mind, this chapter argues that understanding the nature and interactions of Motisinom and Nùutungkwisinom religious traditions is central to an understanding of Hopi ethnogenesis, and to larger patterns of migration and cultural evolution in the American Southwest. Nùutungkwisinom and Motisinom populations were the products of different historical trajectories, diverging most significantly in their participation or nonparticipation in the Chaco Phenomenon. Understanding the story of these two historical and cultural trajectories thus has the potential to shed light on broader phenomena like Chaco, the abandonment of the Colorado Plateau in the late AD 1200s, and the migrations and reorganization of populations in the late pre-Hispanic period. Because the Hopi mesas were one of only a handful of population centers into which late pre-Hispanic southwestern populations consolidated following the demographic upheavals of the thirteenth and fourteenth centuries (Adams 2004; Bernardini 2005), the story of the Motisinom and Nùutungkwisinom is important to an understanding of postcontact trends as well.

Motisinom and Nùutungqwsinom in Hopi Traditional Knowledge

The current anthropological view of Hopi social organization, derived primarily from the ethnographic work of Titiev (1944) and Eggan (1950), emphasizes three primary scales of identity: clan, village, and tribe. The clan—a totemically named, exogamous matrilineal descent group—is "the outstanding feature of social life, in Hopi eyes" (Eggan 1950:62), the primary medium through which identity is expressed in the community. Each clan has a unique migration history that recounts its origins and legitimizes its control over a particular ceremony (Bernardini 2008), though not all Hopi clans control ceremonies. Villages grew through the aggregation of clans, each of which (according to Hopi traditional knowledge) was required to demonstrate the efficacy of its ceremony before gaining entrance to the village (Eggan 1950:64; Fewkes 1900:585). Historically, each village has functioned as a largely endogamous and autonomous political, ritual, and subsistence unit, though "daughter" villages, which lack the full complement of ceremonies, are ritually dependent on "mother" villages (Connelly 1979). Above the level of the village, the Hopi population is united by a common clan and ceremonial system and a common language (except, of course, for the bilingual Tewa/Hopi speakers of First Mesa). With a few notable, postcontact exceptions (e.g., the Pueblo Revolt in 1680 and the destruction of Awat'ovi in 1700), however, there is little evidence of coordinated activity at the level of the "tribe" (what Titiev [1944:59] referred to as "the amorphous Hopi state") outside the federally organized tribal government system.

The ethnographic focus on Hopi clans has obscured a fourth scale of Hopi identity that is the focus of this study. While each Hopi clan has a unique migration history, in Hopi traditional knowledge clans are grouped into two major categories: Motisinom and Nùutungkwisinom—literally, first people and last people (Anyon 1999:41; Dongoske et al. 1997:603; Ferguson 2003:63). The Motisinom/Nùutungkwisinom distinction is thus in part chronological, with the Motisinom being conceived as original residents and the Nùutungkwisinom as later arrivals. Embedded in the categories is also a difference in origin; the Motisinom are described as "the clans that have always resided in North America" (Anyon 1999:47–48), while the Nùutungkwisinom are said to have migrated from the south, perhaps South America and Mesoamerica (Ferguson 2003:63). These cultural categories can be difficult to reconcile with traditional archaeological cultural units, as we shall see below, in part because of ambiguity about their time depth (for issues of time in oral tradition broadly, see Vansina 1985). Nùutungkwisinom immigration appears to span the time from the introduction of agriculture into the Southwest through the protohistoric period, though specific stories about movements and interactions with Motisinom are concentrated in the latter portion of this sequence. The fact that the Nùutungkwisinom label is applied in Hopi traditional knowledge both to very ancient immigrants, who may have lived in the northern Southwest (e.g., in Mesa Verde and Chaco Canyon) for many generations before moving to the Hopi mesas, and to more recent immigrants is a primary source of confusion. Another source of misunderstanding is the fact that the zones of occupation associated with the two groups overlap; as nonlinear migrations unfolded over time, for example, Nùutungkwisinom clans often occupied areas of traditional Motisinom residence, like the Flagstaff, Arizona, area. It is also unclear how large of a geographic region the term Motisinom is intended to apply to; some sources indicate a continental scale, but other usages suggest that its primary usage applies to the region surrounding the Hopi mesas. Still another source of potential confusion stems from the fact that the Motisinom and Nùutungkwisinom include groups that eventually "became Hopi" in addition to those that did not. That is, some southern immigrants to the Southwest joined different ancestral tribal populations (e.g., Zuni), just as some "original residents" of the Hopi mesas did. Both the emic and etic usages of the terms *Motisinom* and *Nùutungkwisinom* refer primarily to the people who *did* ultimately become part of the Hopi population, but given our incomplete knowledge of the archaeology and oral traditions of various ancient populations we are not always able to make this distinction.

All Hopis share a generalized origin story that describes the emergence of all peoples into the current Fourth World from a common *Sípàapuni* in *Öngtupqa,* the Grand Canyon (Ferguson et al. 1993:27; Fewkes 1907:566), from which they scattered before some of them eventually reunited on the Hopi mesas. Yet many Hopi clans also have another origin place cited in their clan-specific migration traditions, which reflects their status as Motisinom or Nùutungkwisinom. As with all histories, there are multiple Hopi accounts reflecting the different experiences and perspectives of the narrators and their ancestral groups; the account summarized below is a Third Mesa version and is not intended to be universally representative of Hopi traditions on this subject.

Motisinom clans trace origins to emergence points close to the Hopi mesas like *Kishyu'ba,* a mountain spring 50 kilometers north of Walpi (Stephen 1936:1072 n.4, 1158), or the San Francisco Peaks in Flagstaff, about 75 miles southwest of the Hopi mesas (Stephen 1936:539–540). The history of the Badger Clan, as recounted to Alexander M. Stephen by Wĕ'hĕ in the late 1800s (Stephen 1936:860 n.1), is illustrative of Motisinom traditions:

> Long ago, some of the Shoyo'hĭm kachina who dwell at Kishyu'ba came to Oraibi, and they . . . gave a typical kachina exhibition. . . . At the end of the songs Badger, Hona'ni, came up in the centre of the square, from the Below (At'kyaa). . . . He said, "I know all medicinal charms, and I have the feather for navo'chiwa, to drive away (expel) all bodily ills. All peoples have this feather and I have brought it to you."— "An'chai," the kachina all said, "now we shall change into Badger clan people (Hona'ninyümü) and you shall be chief." This and a great many of these Kachina-Badger stopped at Oraibi; then the others went on and exhibited at Shŭño'povĭ and Müsho'ñĭnovi, but none stopped at those villages. They went on to Walpi . . . and, after exhibiting, all stopped there except some considerable number who went on and stopped at Awa'tobi.

Other Badger clan traditions indicate movement from the Grand Canyon to the south of the San Francisco Peaks and the Hopi Buttes (Curtis 1922:84), or even Mesa Verde, though most are confined to northern Arizona. Hopi Motisinom traditions mention local movements but do not emphasize stories of long, chainlike migrations; the Badger story, for example, names no migration stops between Kishyu'ba and the Hopi mesas. The histories of at least some Motisinom clans are linked to particular Katsinas; both Kishyu'ba and the San Francisco Peaks are primary homes of the Katsinam.

A contrasting Nùutungkwisinom migration tradition from the *Patkingyam* (Water Clan; recounted by LaVern Siweumptewa of Musangnuvi [summarized in Ferguson and Lomaomvaya 1999:89–90]) reveals significant differences with Motisinom traditions:

> The Patkinyam . . . came to Hopi from the south. The place of origin is called Yayniwpu, and from here the Patkingyam settled at Palatkwapi, which he translated as "Watery Area." . . . Mr. Siweumptewa believes Palatkwapi is located somewhere southwest of Mexico City. . . . The Patkinyam came from Palatkwapi through the Tucson Valley to Casa Grande and the Salt-Gila Basin. . . . From there they migrated

> through Wukoskyavi, the area where Roosevelt Lake is now located....
> When the Patkinyam left Wukoskyavi, some people went straight towards Payson and Chavez Pass. Other people went towards the San Francisco Peaks.... The Patkinyam people who went towards Payson occupied three villages before they crossed over the Mogollon Rim. One of these villages is Paayusunvi (Still Water Along Cliff), and the other two have names Mr. Siweumptewa no longer remembers. These Patkingyam then moved to Nuvakwewtaqa ("Snow Belted One," Chavez Pass). The other group ... moved to Pasiovi (a.k.a., Pasiwovi, "Meeting Place," Elden Pueblo) and Wupatki, where the Snake Dance was performed.... The Patkingyam at Wupatki went to Chavez Pass, where they joined the other group of Patkingyam already there. From there the Patkingyam went to Homol'ovi ... they then moved to Siipa where Seba Dalkai is now, where they performed the Lakontiiva (Basket Society Dance). From Siipa they went to southeast of Walpi to a place called Paaqötsomo (Water Collects Hill).... From Palatkwapi, the Patkingyam brought our religious societies and knowledge. We brought six songs, which are part of the Leelant (Flute Society) rituals.... The Kwanmongwi (Agave Society Chief), soyalmongwi (Winter Solstice Society Chief), and the Lakonmongwi (Basket Society Chieftess) were all brought by our clan as well.

As is evident in this example, Nùutungkwisinom clans have elaborate migration traditions, often detailing long lists of named, sequentially occupied villages (e.g., Fewkes 1900). Nùutungkwisinom migrations also ranged over much greater distances, with origin points hundreds of miles to the south of the Hopi mesas. In further contrast to Motisinom traditions, Nùutungkwisinom clan histories are typically associated with the control of non-Katsina ceremonies (see below).

Motisinom and Nùutungqwsinom in the Archaeological Record

Hopi traditions suggest the presence of a local, autochthonous population and one or more immigrant populations that together composed the Hisatsinom, or Hopi ancestors. To what extent are these populations visible in the archaeological record? Owing to a lack of systematic survey, pre-1200 occupation on and around the Hopi mesas proper is not as well known as other areas of the northern Southwest, especially outside of nucleated pueblo contexts. Better-known areas to the north on Black Mesa and the Kayenta Valley (Dean 1996b; Powell 2002) may be considered representative of broad demographic trends, although there may be important differences due to climate and local cultural trajectories. The archaeology of northeastern Arizona records the presence of shifting populations of hunters and gatherers in the Paleoindian and Archaic periods, transitioning to a widely, if thinly, dispersed Western Basketmaker pithouse occupation exhibiting a relatively stable and homogenous material culture beginning ca. 1300 BC (Adams 1989c; Colton 1974; Plog 1986). Pithouse occupations persisted in most areas of northeastern Arizona until at least the AD 900s. A shift to aboveground masonry architecture and small-scale aggregation of population into small (ca. fifty-room) pueblos in the 900–1250 period can be largely attributed to local (i.e., Black Mesa/Kayenta region) population dynamics (Powell 2002), rather than immigration. Fine-grained population reconstructions on Black Mesa (Plog 1986) document a pattern of boom-and-bust population oscillation, but given the relative continuity in material culture these movements appear to involve "Brownian" motion of the regional population rather than directional immigration from long distances. If the Motisinom were the "local" population component of Hopi, we might equate them with the Basketmaker to early Pueblo III period populations on and around Black Mesa (see figure 10.1), roughly equivalent to the "Western" or "Kayenta" Anasazi region (Ambler 2002; Cordell and Gumerman 1989) (archaeologists have rightly abandoned use of the term "Anasazi" in favor of "Ancestral Puebloan"; I employ the term Anasazi here only to refer to historical usage).[1]

Given our concern with the organization of religious practice, it is important to note that the relatively small social scale of most pre-1200 nucleated settlements of this region—probably fewer than seventy-five people per site—would not have required elaborate decision-making structures or integrative mechanisms (e.g., G. Johnson 1978, 1982).[2] Evidence of large-scale public ritual, for example, such as feasting or plaza performances, is largely absent from pre-1200 Western Anasazi settlements. These autochthonous populations apparently did not participate in the Chaco Phenomenon of the 900s to early 1100s (Adams 1996; Dean 1996b; but see Gilpin 1989), nor in the post-Chacoan

North, South, and Center An Outline of Hopi Ethnogenesis 203

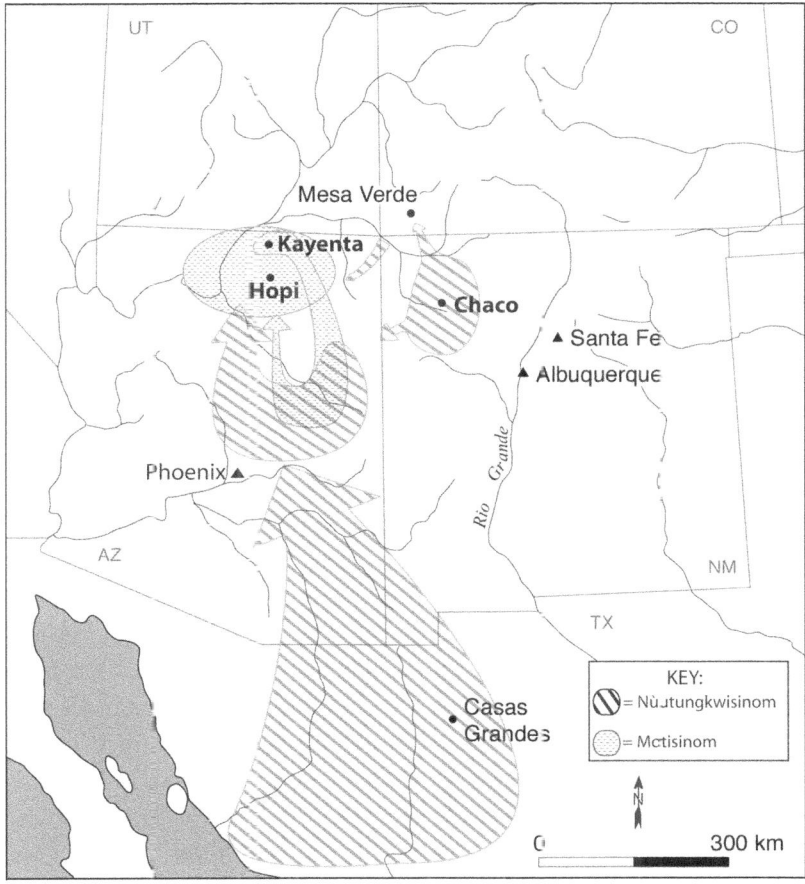

Figure 10.1. Reconstructed origins and migrations of Hopi Motisinom and Nùutungkwisinom populations.

developments of the later 1100s, unlike regions to the south (e.g., Herr 2001; Kintigh et al. 1996).

Waves of immigrants began arriving at the Hopi mesas in significant numbers beginning with the diasporic migrations from the Four Corners region in the mid- to late 1200s, including groups from the Mesa Verde, southern Utah, and especially Kayenta regions (Dean 2002:157) (figure 10.1). Larger pulses of immigration to Hopi came in the mid- to late 1300s, when groups from the Silver Creek, Homol'ovi, Chavez Pass, Sinagua, Salado, and adjacent regions migrated north (Adams

2004; Adams and LaMotta 2004; Bernardini 2005; Ferguson and Lomaomvaya 1999; Lyons 2003). Although archaeologists' understanding of the Hopi concept Nùutungkwisinom is still incomplete, it appears that Hopi use of the term refers primarily to these later waves of immigrants (largely from the south) beginning in the 1300s.[3] Complicating the picture is the fact that some Kayenta migrants in the late 1200s appear to have skipped over Hopi and moved further south into central Arizona, mixing with southern groups in variable and complex ways before circling back to Hopi (Clark 2001; Lyons 2003). The arrival of fourteenth-century immigrants had a substantial demographic impact, at least doubling population on the Hopi mesas by 1400 (Adams and LaMotta 2004; Bernardini 2005).

Compared to the autochthonous population of the Hopi region, these immigrant groups arrived with much greater experience of aggregated village life, status differences, and regional ceremonial systems. Thirteenth-century immigrant groups (primarily Nùutungkwisinom) arrived at Hopi with prior experience in living in cosmopolitan centers such as Mesa Verde, Totah, and post-Chacoan settlements, among other places (Glowacki, this volume; Plog, this volume). Chaco itself had been a locus of aggregation for Nùutungkwisinom, though it is unclear what role the San Juan Basin Motisinom played in Chacoan developments (or, for that matter, in post-Chacoan events). Immigrants who arrived at Hopi in the fourteenth century brought with them experiences of living in large aggregated settlements at Chavez Pass, Homol'ovi, and elsewhere, though by the early 1300s large nucleated villages were also common on the Hopi mesas (see below).

Religious Traditions

The distinct histories of the Motisinom and Nùutungkwisinom are reflected in their distinctive religious traditions. Some of these ritual differences are evident in the oral tradition examples discussed above. It is notable, for example, that the history of Motisinom clans is often linked to the history of Katsinas (e.g., the Badger Clan story above). In contrast, Nùutungkwisinom emphasize links between clan identity and control of a particular non-Katsina ceremony (Bernardini 2008). In fact, for Nùutungkwisinom clans, the clan name and the clan's ceremony serve as almost an interchangeable appellation for the migrating group: "The Patki clan came from where the sun rises; they had with them the Gray Flute ceremony" (Voth 1905:28–30). Important variability in ritual control does exist, especially among mesas. For example, on Third Mesa the Màasaw clan (a Motisinom clan) controls the Kwan society (controlled by Patki on First Mesa), and on Second Mesa the Parrot and Crow clans—associated with the Katsina clan (Motisinom)—control the Flute ceremony. The fact that some non-Katsina rituals are controlled by Motisinom clans could be explained by clan fusion and the inheritance of ceremonies upon clan extinction over the centuries, although these processes typically happen among partner clans who traveled similar migration paths.

Some variation in patterns of ritual control notwithstanding, the Motisinom/Nùutungkwisinom division in contemporary Hopi religion is visible in the structure of the annual ritual cycle. At each Hopi village, clan ceremonies are organized into a calendric cycle, with "a fixed time of year during which a society is expected to celebrate the observances entrusted to its care" (Titiev 1944:103). The ritual cycle, however, does not simply comprise unrelated, clan-specific ceremonies. Instead, the Hopi ceremonial calendar is divided into two distinct halves: Katsina and non-Katsina ceremonies (B. Wright 1973:258). The Katsina season is controlled by two Motisinom clans, Badger and Katsina. The non-Katsina season is controlled by a series of Nùutungkwisinom clans.

Katsina and non-Katsina ceremonies differ dramatically in their history, membership, content, performance, power, and status. Contemporary Katsina ritual is democratic, public, and benign. Katsina culture emphasizes a life of humility and hard work revolving around corn agriculture, embodied in the practice of hopivötskwani, "the Hopi path of life" (K. Hill et al. 1998:101).[4] According to Hopi traditional knowledge, the deliberately simple life of the Motisinom did not require elaborate ceremonies (Ferguson 2003:106). The power of Màasaw, the lord of the (current) Fourth World and spiritual head of the Motisinom, stems not from any special ceremonial knowledge but from his mastery of simple but essential materials: a planting stick, water, and seeds (Leigh Kuwanwisiwma, personal communication, 2005). In contemporary Hopi society, admission to the Katsina society is universal for all village members. The composition of individual Katsina performances includes members of many different clans and ceremonial societies, and Katsina performances are public, held in village plazas with large audiences. Most Katsina dances are not subject to centralized control; during the bulk of the Katsina season, dances can be sponsored by anyone in the village (Parsons 1939:138), and new Katsina songs can be written by members of the community. Both participants and the audience have relatively open access to the ceremonial content of Katsina ritual.

The non-Katsina ceremonies of the Nùutungkwisinom, in contrast, are restrictive, esoteric, and dangerously powerful. Many of these ceremonies were imported from Palatkwapi, a region whose villages collapsed in part because of the abuse of ritual power by ceremonial leaders (Leigh Kuwanwisiwma, personal communication, 2007) (additional non-Katsina ceremonies were brought from places like Tokonave [Navajo Mountain] and the Rio Grande). So great were the power and risk of non-Katsina ceremonies that Màasaw granted the Nùutungkwisinom permission to live with him only after they demonstrated that they could focus their ceremonial knowledge on the bringing of rain (Leigh Kuwanwisiwma, personal communication, 2000). Membership in many non-Katsina ceremonial societies requires sponsorship from an existing society member, and many performances are private, held in proprietary kivas. Access to knowledge is restricted even among initiates, with the esoteric knowledge required to perform non-Katsina ceremonies held closely by the core maternal household of the controlling clan. When a Hopi man is spoken of as "being initiated" (and therefore especially knowledgeable), the reference is to membership in one of the powerful non-Katsina societies.

Tension and Transition

What happened when the practitioners of these two distinct religions—north and south—met on the Hopi mesas in the thirteenth and fourteenth centuries? How did the populations reconcile different strategies of village organization, leadership, and ideology and produce a set of practices that would define that place as Tuuwanasavi, the center of the universe?

North, South, and Center: An Outline of Hopi Ethnogenesis

In the wake of the large-scale immigrations of the thirteenth century, settlement patterns on the Hopi mesas underwent significant changes. By the early 1300s large aggregated settlements of several hundred rooms came to dominate the landscape, and local pottery traditions incorporated styles from a variety of areas to the south (Adams 1996; Adams and LaMotta 2004; Hays-Gilpin and LeBlanc 2007; Lyons 2003). Occupation at Hopi by ca. 1300 consisted of seventeen main villages ranging from fifty to four hundred rooms, with Awat'ovi on Antelope Mesa probably the largest. After 1325, villages consolidated, with smaller villages disappearing and the largest villages from the preceding period increasing in size. It was during this period of initial consolidation that production of the distinctively yellow-bodied Jeddito Yellow Ware ceramics began, quickly replacing all previous black-on-white and black-on-orange wares and eclipsing all but a small handful of pottery imports. By the early 1300s all of the villages that would become the historic Hopi "mother villages" (Orayvi, Musangnuvi, Songoopavi, Walpi, and Awat'ovi) had been established,[5] and by 1450, almost all residents of the Hopi mesas were living in one of these large settlements. By ca. 1400, the total number of rooms present in Hopi villages had grown to almost twice the number of rooms present at 1325 (Adams and LaMotta 2004:9). Population levels stabilized after 1400 and actually decreased after 1500, but village consolidation continued. The occupation of several very large villages ended by the early 1500s, including the 1,000-room village of Kawàyka'a and the 600-room village of Sikyatki, leaving only the five mother villages of Awat'ovi, Walpi, Songoopavi, Musangnuvi, and Orayvi by 1540.

Tension between autochthonous and immigrant groups is recorded in Hopi traditional knowledge. As Patkingyam (Water Clan, a Nùutungkwisinom group) informants told Alexander Stephen, "We are recent comers here; when we came from Pala'tkwapi, the Wal'pitü [people of Walpi] were already here, and after we came here we had much trouble with them over the apportionment of land" (Stephen 1936:943). The archaeological record of the late 1200s and early 1300s, when large numbers of immigrants were arriving at Hopi, may reflect some of this tension. Many sites from this time period are located on defensible buttes and cliff edges, though evidence of actual physical violence has not yet been documented. A number of *Kiqötutuwutsi*, or Hopi ruin legends, which recount conflict between neighboring villages also date to this time period (e.g., the stories of the destruction of Huk'ovi and Pivanhonkyapi, both occupied ca. 1250–1300; Malotki 1993). Hopi consultants emphasize that the conflict between ancestral groups at this time was ritual in nature, rather than physical, as people struggled to reconcile different ideologies. After 1350, sites on the Hopi mesas no longer exhibit defensive positioning or layouts, suggesting resolution of high-level tensions.

Intuitively (and, often, anthropologically—see Eggan 1966:124–125), one might imagine that the earliest arrivals in a region held a certain advantage: first-comers would have gotten first shot at monopolizing key resources, building local traditions, and inscribing their ideologies into the landscape. In fact, primacy is a common theme in Hopi migration traditions, with the order of arrival at a village factoring strongly into clan status. As Eggan (1966:124–125) noted:

> at the head of the prestige hierarchy is the Bear Clan, the members of which arrived first in the Hopi region and made a compact with Masu'u, the god of life and death, in which he gave the Hopi land and crops in exchange for carrying out the proper rituals. Late-comers received portions of this estate in exchange for the performance of ceremonies for rain for the crops, but the "last" arrivals often possessed no rituals and offered their services as guards. Their position was marginal, and usually they were not assigned clan lands.

Most Hopi clan traditions recognize the Bear Clan (a Nùutungkwisi-nom group, though possibly an early arriving one [see note three]) as the first arrival at Hopi, justifying its members' hold on the office of kikmongwi, or village leader. Yet some Hopi traditional knowledge indicates that the Bear Clan did not enter an empty landscape, as the Motisinom were the original occupants of the region. When immigrants arrived at the Hopi mesas, Motisinom clans were cautious and ceded the responsibility (and prestige) of organizing the subsequent arrivals to the Bear Clan (Leigh Kuwanwisiwma, personal communication, 2007). Thus, despite the Motisinom clans' primacy of place, the original "mother" villages developed as Nùutungkwisinom communities.

The ritual power of the later arriving Nùutungkwisinom groups, and their prior experiences in large aggregated communities, likely facilitated their assumption of leadership positions in the new composite villages on the Hopi mesas. The precedent set at this early date continues in Hopi social organization today. The cardinal status division in contemporary Hopi villages is between *pavansinom* ("ruling people") and *söqavungswinom* ("common people") (Whiteley 1988:65; see also K. Hill et al. 1998:398, 530). Although there are pavansinom at the head of both Motisinom and Nùutungkwisinom clans, high-status traditional village offices (i.e., non-tribal government) are overwhelmingly held by members of Nùutungkwisinom clans, at least on Third Mesa where ethnographic evidence is most complete (table 10.1). Thus, contemporary Hopi village governance is largely in the hands of the Nùutungkwisinom.

The Nùutungkwisinom did not, however, simply settle freely at Hopi and displace the local population and religious system. According to Hopi traditional knowledge, when the Nùutungkwisinom arrived at Hopi they had to submit to Màasaw, the "lord of the Fourth [current] world" (K. Hill et al. 1998:219) and spiritual leader of the Motisinom.

Table 10.1. Clan and dual-division affiliation of village offices at the Third Mesa village of Orayvi in 1906 (clan data from Titiev 1944 and Levy 1992).

Office	Clan	Group
Soyal Officer	Rabbit	Nùutungkwisinom
Aa'alt Chief (Two-Horn Chief)	Bow	Nùutungkwisinom
Qalèetaqmongwi (War Chief)	Spider	Nùutungkwisinom
Soyal Officer	Pikyas	Nùutungkwisinom
Soyal Officer	Parrot	Nùutungkwisinom
Soyalmongwi (Soyal Chief)	Bear	Nùutungkwisinom
Taatawkyam (Singers) Chief	Parrot	Nùutungkwisinom
Tsa'akmongwi (Crier Chief)	Greasewood	Nùutungkwisinom
Wuwtsimt Chief	Sparrowhawk	Nùutungkwisinom
Kwaakwant Chief (One-Horn Chief)	Màasaw	Motisinom

Thus, two senior members of the Antelope Society (a Nùutungkwisinom ceremonial) prefaced their migration traditions with this statement: "Masau'wu possessed this land" (Stephen 1936:676). Snake Clan tradition recounts that "when the Snake clan first came to Tusayan they came down the valley on the west side and halted close beside Wàlpi mesa. Masawu'wu came and refused them leave to stay ... he made them move off southward down the valley ... Masawu' afterward relented and allowed them to come back and build a village in this locality" (Stephen 1936:141). Elsewhere, however, Stephen (1936:813–814) records Bear Clan traditional knowledge recounting the "overthrow" of Màasaw by the Bear Clan chief.

In sum, the Nùutungkwisinom dominate contemporary formal Hopi village offices, but the Motisinom contributed fundamental aspects of Hopi ideology. The principles of humility and hard work that define Hopi identity to insiders and outsiders alike are rooted in Màasaw and Katsina culture. It could be argued that the ritual submission of all Hopis to Màasaw is also reflected in contemporary Hopi society in the fact that the first ritual that any Hopi learns is Katsina. In this manner, the Katsina initiation could be viewed as a symbolic reaffirmation of all Hopi's obedience to Màasaw.

Discussion

The merging of northern and southern populations and religious traditions outlined in Hopi oral tradition presents an intriguing model that finds a level of support in the archaeological record. Some details, however, remain difficult to reconcile. Most problematic is the association of contemporary Motisinom ritual with the Katsina religion. Current archaeological perspectives on the Katsina religion point to its emergence by the 1300s, most likely in the Little Colorado River region or surrounding areas (Adams 1991, 1994), though others argue for twelfth-century origins in southwestern New Mexico prior to the late pre-Hispanic period (Lekson and Cameron 1995; Schaafsma 1994b). Given these archaeologically well supported views of Katsina origins—and especially timing—it is unclear how to make sense of traditional knowledge recounting pre-1300 Katsina practices by Motisinom populations on the Hopi mesas. It is important to keep in mind that the

North, South, and Center: An Outline of Hopi Ethnogenesis   211

nature and practice of Katsina religion need not have remained constant over time (e.g., Glowacki, this volume; Pog and Solometo 1997). It is possible, for instance, that precedents of the Katsina religion did not feature masked personages or that the Katsina religion existed but that depicting Katsina images in rock art or ceramics was proscribed prior to 1300 (e.g., Fowles 2008; Newsome and Hays-Gilpin, this volume).

It is possible to sketch a plausible, if speculative, scenario reconciling Hopi traditional knowledge with archaeological evidence. This scenario involves two rounds of ritual reconciliation merging three different religious traditions. The oldest religious tradition would be that of the autochthonous population of Black Mesa and the surrounding region, probably featuring the deity Màasaw and core cultural values of humility and hard work. There may have been little public ritual associated with Màasaw ritual, given the small scale of the groups who practiced it. This more private or individualized religious tradition may have its roots in Western Basketmaker culture. Màasaw's antiquity in Hopi cosmology is clear from traditional knowledge, which describes Màasaw as the "first denizen" of the world (Stephen 1936:xli, 525) who "goes everywhere, has always been present everywhere" (150), and who was present at the time of the Emergence to help people up from the sipapu onto the land. Màasaw is also described as "the first house builder" (150), perhaps a reference to early Basketmaker/Pueblo I period villages. In this hypothetical reconstruction, the Màasaw substrate of Motisinom religion would have persisted in some form from Basketmaker III period to the present.

One way to reconcile the original focus of Motisinom ritual practice on Màasaw with its subsequent linking to the Katsina religion is to remember that Motisinom ("original people") populations lived in places other than the Hopi mesas. Motisinom lived along the Little Colorado River, for example, and it was here that evidence of the early Katsina religion is strongest. We have good reason to believe that residents of fourteenth-century Little Colorado villages were in contact with groups living on the Hopi mesas based on the occurrence of Jeddito Yellow Ware pottery (made only on the Hopi mesas and traded southward beginning around 1300 [Bernardini 2005]) at these sites (Duff 2002: 79). Little Colorado villages may even have contained some Motisinom who had migrated south from the Kayenta region through central Arizona (Clark 2001; Lyons 2003).

These links to Hopi villages likely encouraged many Little Colorado residents to migrate to Hopi when the region was depopulated in the fourteenth century (Bernardini 2005; Duff 2002). In fact, Duff (2002: 182) suggests that Hopi villages may have actively recruited groups that controlled the Katsina ceremony from Upper Little Colorado sites (and other neighboring regions) specifically to acquire these popular rituals. A comparison of the distribution of Jeddito Yellow Ware and Katsina rock art (see figure 10.2) reveals significant overlap, suggesting that outreach by fourteenth-century Hopi villages may indeed have been focused on participants in the early Katsina religion.[6] It is important to note that there is variability in both ceramic and rock art assemblages between even neighboring villages, so we should not paint this picture with an overly broad brush.

If some Little Colorado Katsina-carrying immigrants were considered Motisinom upon their arrival at the Hopi mesas—a classification that would have been encouraged if they traveled with Kayenta-based Motisinom groups making a "return migration" (Lyons 2003)—then it was perhaps at this Motisinom "reunion" that the Katsina religion became explicitly identified as a Motisinom ceremony. The resulting Motisinom religious tradition thus combined Màasaw and the core values of humility and hard work with a public ceremony (which Màasaw ritual likely previously lacked), which would be the face of this population.

That the Katsina religion was "reinterpreted" or reassigned ownership to the local Hopi Mesa Motisinom population during this initial reconciliation may be evident in the "homes" of the Hopi Katsinas as recorded in Hopi traditional knowledge. There are four homes for Hopi Katsinam where they live during the non-Katsina portion of the ritual calendar: Nuvatukya'ovi (the San Francisco Peaks), representing the southwest cardinal direction; Kawestima (Betatakin Ruin), the Katsina home representing the northwest cardinal direction; Weenima (near the confluence of the Little Colorado and Zuni rivers), representing the southeast cardinal direction; and Kiisiw (Cliff Spring), representing the northeast cardinal direction (K. Hill et al. 1998:345). Stephen (1936: 442n1) also lists Mount Taylor in New Mexico as a northeast Katsina home,[7] and some sources indicate that Tokonave (Navajo Mountain) is

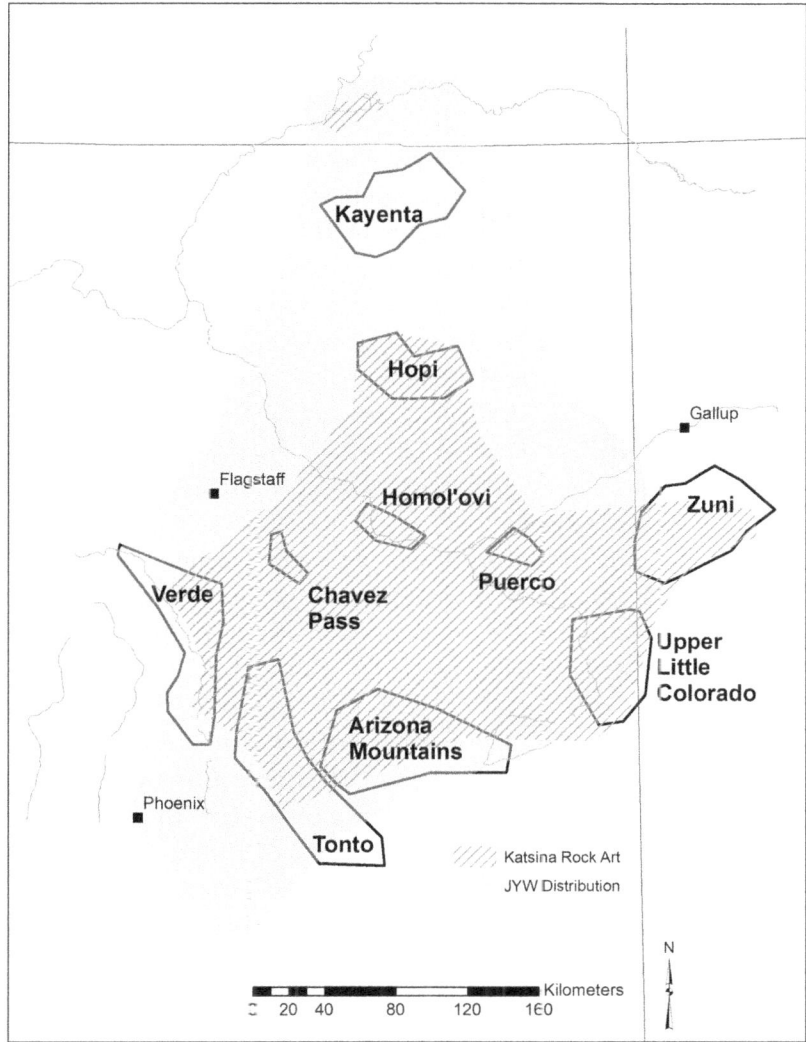

Figure 10.2. Map of the Western Pueblo area showing the distribution of Jeddito Yellow Ware pottery (data from Benitez 1998:fig. 3) and Katsina iconography (data from Nichols 2007).

also a northwest home. Stephen (1936:539–540) recorded his confusion about Katsina homes, noting that Hopi consultants told him that at the Niman ceremony (Katsina homegoing ceremony, held in July), all the Katsinam go home to the San Francisco Peaks, yet when they return to Hopi villages in late November, they return from *all* of the directional Katsina homes. One consultant (Stephen 1936:540) clarified that the San Francisco Peaks contains the hatchway or Sipaapuni to the Underworld, through which the Katsinas descend to disperse to their ancestral homes. This conflated story about Katsina homes could reflect the reassignment of nonlocal Katsinas to the most prominent landmark visible from the Hopi mesas.

A viewshed analysis[8] of the five Katsina homes (see figure 10.3) reveals that only the San Francisco Peaks and Tokonave (to a lesser extent) are visible from Hopi villages, with the remainder of the Katsina homes either so topographically subtle or so distant that they would not be visible even within an 18-kilometer radius encompassing a maximum one-day round-trip travel range.[9] Outside of the Hopi mesas and Homol'ovi regions, the only area of thirteenth- or fourteenth-century occupation in Arizona containing sites with a clear view of the San Francisco Peaks was the Verde Valley, and here only two of thirty-six villages qualify. In fact, the other Katsina homes are far enough away from the Hopi mesas—especially those at Weenima and Mt. Taylor—that they could have been seen by most occupants of the Hopi mesas only on specific pilgrimages or resource-gathering trips. Their distance and lack of visibility on the horizon from Hopi villages suggest the ritual efficacy of these places was likely brought into Hopi traditional knowledge by immigrant groups.

The Motisinom population might have been motivated to adopt the Katsina religion as its public ceremonial face as a result of the influence of Nùutungkwisinom ritual practice. Recall that Nùutungkwisinom groups were strongly affiliated with clan control of a ceremony contributed for the greater village good, a tradition that probably developed during the long migrations of Nùutungkwisinom clans. If the mother villages on the Hopi mesas were founded by Nùutungkwisinom populations who emphasized clan control of ceremonies, Motisinom groups may have adopted a strategy of group organization and identity signaling that was compatible with Nùutungkwisinom organization (Bernar-

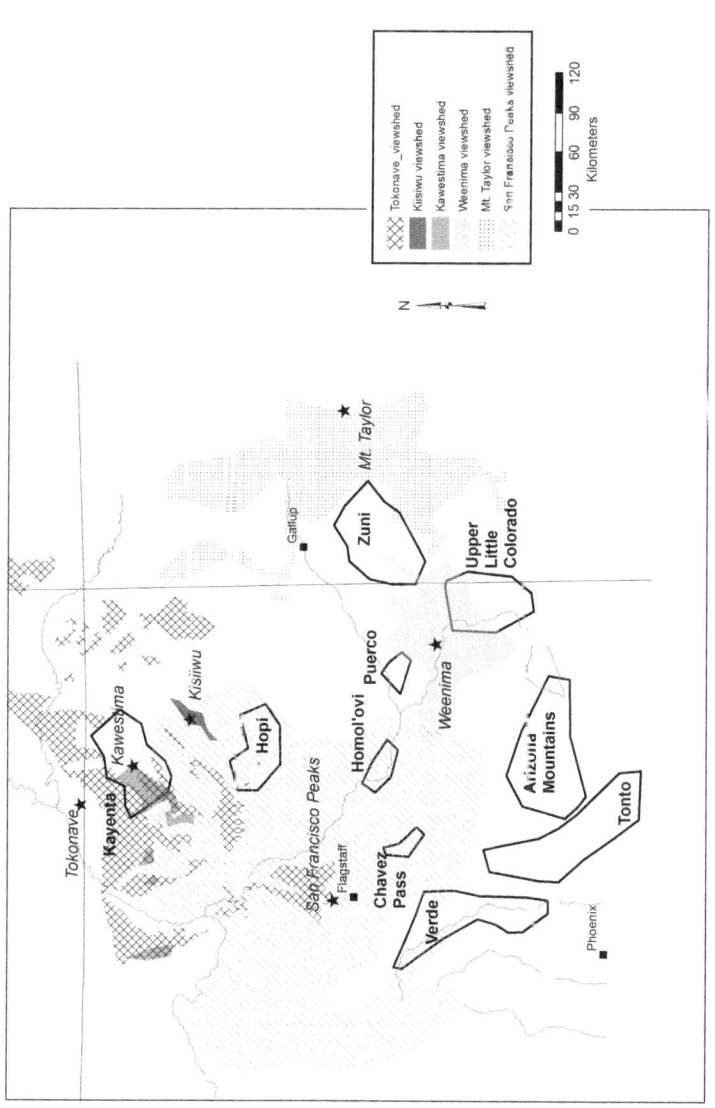

Figure 10.3. Viewsheds of the five Hopi Katsina homes. Shaded areas represent the cells from which each Katsina home is visible.

dini 2005). Perhaps Katsina religion became more formalized (and thus more materially evident), and individual Katsinam became associated (retroactively) with particular Motisinom groups as the public face of a "clan" identity. This sort of organizational and behavioral convergence has been observed between hunters and farmers in several areas of the world (Spielmann and Eder 1994). For example, in the interest of facilitating interaction with farmers, hunters typically adopt (or learn) the language of the farmers and even establish fictive kinship ties to farmer clans or other social groupings (Pederson and Waehle 1988).

Significantly, there are some indications that early Katsina religion was associated with individual clans. Katsinas, for example, are often "referred to as actual personages" (Parsons 1936:122n4), and the Katsina religion has long been considered a generalized form of ancestor worship. The class of Katsinas known as *mong* (chief) or *wuy'o* (old one, elder) Katsinas, in particular, is strongly associated with particular clans (Bunzel 1932b:848; Parsons 1936:xxxvii; Titiev 1944:109) and may have once served a more explicit role as clan ancestors. Mong Katsinas are strongly associated with directions as illustrated in the Katsina initiation ceremony, during which the Powamu Chief recites the direction from which each Mong Katsina came to Hopi and the places the Katsina stopped along the way (Kennard and Earle 1938:20). Although these recitations of directional movement are largely symbolic today, linked to color-directional symbolism, it is possible that Mong Katsinas originally served a more explicit role as clan ancestors, the historical residences of which formed the charter for each clan (cf. Bernardini 2008). The Ahul Katsina, for example, is said to have led the Katsina clan on its migrations (Parsons 1936:165). The Mong or chief Katsinas comprise most of the identifiable masked images in precontact kiva murals (Crotty 1995:261), suggesting a long time depth to the potential association between Katsinas and particular clans (Plog and Solometo 1997).

Descent Groups Versus Sodalities

The duality of Hopi ritual outlined here takes on further significance in light of Ware's (2001, 2002) discussion of descent groups and sodalities. Ware argues that an early division emerged in the American

North, South, and Center: An Outline of Hopi Ethnogenesis 217

Southwest between communities who organized control of ritual through descent groups (lineages, clans, and so on) and those who organized control through nondescent-based ritual sodalities. In Ware's model, the earliest potential sodalities are visible in northern San Juan villages in the early eighth century that featured oversize pit structures (Kane and Robinson 1988), in contrast to the rows of unit pueblos that made up contemporaneous western settlements (i.e., Arizona and south-central Utah). It has been proposed (Wilshusen and Ortman 1999) that some residents of northern San Juan villages with oversized pit structures may have constituted a distinct sociopolitical and linguistic population who moved to Chaco Canyon in the mid- to late 800s, perhaps founding the first sodality-based complex society in the Southwest (see Ware 2001). As discussed above, at least some of the ancestors of Nùutungkwisinom immigrants to Hopi had participated directly in the Chaco Phenomenon, where they (hypothetically) would have acquired the model of the sodality control of ritual. Other Nùutungkwisinom may have embraced sodality control of ritual during their long process of serial migration (Bernardini 2005), which featured just the kind of short-lived, multiethnic communities in which sodalities—with their flexible membership criteria—tend to thrive (Ware 2002). In socially and residentially unstable landscapes, when mobility disrupts long-term claims on agricultural resources, groups often reorganize around the control of portable rituals, membership, and inheritance of which need not be bound by kinship (Bernardini 2008; Mills 2004).

In contrast, most of the Western Pueblo region—notably including Hopi and Kayenta—largely opted out of participation in Chaco (Dean 1996b). Likewise, we see little evidence for serial migration among the autochthonous Western Anasazi population, either in material culture or traditional knowledge. In a landscape characterized by relative demographic and residential stability[10] prior to the waves of immigration beginning in the thirteenth century, descent groups appear to have prevailed as the preferred mechanism for maintaining control of fixed resources (i.e., land and water). Control of ceremonies in such unilineal agricultural societies tends to be held by avunculate groups—housed in this case in kivas, which provide a means for non-coresident matrilineal kin to congregate for ceremonies controlled by their matrilineage, away from the prying eyes of in-married husbands of other descent groups (Ware 2000).

In this light, the tension between autochthonous and immigrant populations over the emergent Hopi ritual order may have stemmed as much from *how* ritual was controlled as much as who controlled it. That is, perhaps the thirteenth century at Hopi was another replay of the tension between descent group and sodality hypothesized by Ware (2001) to have first played out at Chaco three centuries prior. The concessions the Nùutungkwisinom had to grant their Motisinom hosts apparently included the adoption of descent group control of ritual (the historic norm at Hopi). This change would work against the concentration of power in few hands—the primary danger of the "Palatkwapi clans" still remembered in Hopi traditional knowledge. In this scenario, the Nùutungkwisinom adopted descent group control of ritual and resources only after completing their migrations and settling permanently at the "earth center."

Conclusion

Hopi oral tradition provides an interesting model of ethnogenesis featuring the merging of two historically, geographically, and ritually distinct populations: the Motisinom of the north and Nùutungkwisinom of the south, who met at Tuuwanasavi, the earth center, to forge the Hopi identity. This traditional knowledge should not—and is not intended to—substitute for history. Instead, its utility is as a source of ideas and models about prehistoric social change, which can spark new and productive exploration of the archaeological record. The scenario sketched here is admittedly speculative and draws from a small portion of Hopi traditional knowledge relevant to understanding clan histories. It represents only a first step in what should be a lengthy process of "tacking" between ideas and evidence (Wylie 1989).

Perhaps the most intriguing avenue for further exploration concerns the downstream consequences of participation or nonparticipation in the Chaco Phenomenon for divergent patterns of social organization, centuries later and hundreds of miles afield from Chaco Canyon itself (Bernardini and Fowles 2011; Glowacki, this volume; Plog, this volume). Borrowing heavily from Ware (2001), we may speculate that the sodality model of ritual control that may have developed in Chaco could have set the stage for generations of conflict over the proper mechanism for owning and transmitting ritual knowledge—whether it should be sodalities or avunculates. Chaco is remembered by a number of southwestern tribes as a place where power was abused, a place and societal structure that was deliberately left behind. This view is prevalent in aspects of Hopi traditional knowledge about Chaco, perhaps indicating not just a memory of conflicts in Chaco Canyon proper but of recurrent rounds of conflict among descendant groups that harken back to that formative time and place.

This case study also provides a useful comparative case for cross-cultural studies. It is not often that we have the level of geographic, demographic, and cultural continuity embodied by the Hopi population (not to minimize significant cultural transformations associated with European contact), and for this reason we have the unusual opportunity to compare an ethnographically well-described contemporary situation with ancient social conditions that have been reconstructed through both archaeology and a rich body of oral tradition. One lesson, perhaps unsurprising, is that contemporary ideologies—presented as timeless to and by insiders and outsiders under a variety of motivations—are often historical layer cakes. The self-consciously agglomerative nature of the Hopi ritual calendar, which preserves individual clan's ritual contributions as discrete events, makes the palimpsest unusually clear in the Hopi case. But similar layers of historical complexity likely underlie the ritual systems of other middle-range societies that avoided inundation by state-sponsored religions. Teasing out the motivations of the various actors who contributed to the reconciliations underlying agglomerated ritual systems can be difficult, similar in some ways to historical linguistics, but it offers the potential to reconstruct generations of ritual evolution.

A second useful comparative point is to caution against exclusively materialistic motivations for conflict, given the ritual nature of the tension that appears to characterize the early immigration period on the Hopi mesas. We must broaden our view of the "things worth fighting for" to include ritual resources, and perhaps even mechanisms of social reproduction (i.e., inheritance of ritual and ritual identity by sodalities versus avunculates). This caution might be especially relevant in landscapes for which conflict is manifest archaeologically primarily through defensive site locations (as opposed to more direct evidence of physical violence)—that is, where there can be reason to question whether conflict actually (or often) came to a head.

The historical trajectories of Puebloan populations were deeply affected by the origins and outcomes of religious ideologies. Ritual was both a motivating factor behind migration, assimilation, aggregation, and conflict, and a lens through which actors understood these processes. The scales of these religious traditions—both temporal and spatial—can be surprisingly large. The ripples of early events are visible in populations many centuries and miles removed from their origins.

11

Getting Religion

Lessons from Ancestral Pueblo History

Timothy R. Pauketat

Religion may be uniquely human. It might even be that which makes human beings human (Rappaport 1979:229–230). But to what extent do religions or religious ideologies constitute human history? Answering that question is a task for archaeologists, but they often seem uncertain about their beliefs about, well, beliefs.

Fortunately, uncertainty in the study of religions or, more precisely, the relationship between humanity, history, and religious practices, rituals, places, ideologies, or cosmologies is as it should be. Any understanding of religion necessitates gaining some perspective on the matter. One does this by first stepping outside the role of believer and then by unpacking that which is asserted to be religion by those who would define it. Archaeologists often do the former, but they seldom do the latter.

This volume does the latter, and here I attempt to clarify why it matters to the larger historical and anthropological project. Importantly, neither the volume nor this essay begins with a rigid definition of Ancestral Pueblo religion (see Parsons 1939), although most analysts would undoubtedly agree that Pueblo religious practices were "animistic," not unlike those of many people worldwide (Bird-David 1999). That is, many if not all Pueblo peoples probably recognized that spirits or powers might inhabit certain people, places, things, nonhuman creatures, and any number of earthly or atmospheric phenomena (see also Ingold 2007). This is an ontological truism almost as basic as the statement above that people are inherently religious.

But it matters with respect to understanding the history of the later Pueblo world because various kinds of numinous experiences or cosmic events might have held greater significance to Pueblos than they do in the Western world today (Walker 2008). Indeed, the trends and events of the late thirteenth century hinge on understanding why this is (see Van Keuren and Glowacki, this volume). Reviewing the chapters in this book leads one to an important conclusion: the central issues of and major transformations in indigenous and later colonial history in the Southwest are fully explicable only in religious terms. Most significantly, the authors of these chapters interrogate Ancestral Pueblo rituality and religiosity (by which I mean the ritual and religious dimensions of past practices and experiences) rather than delineate Pueblo religion. By doing so, the authors in effect enable Ancestral Pueblo people to define religion for themselves. As a result, we all learn some lessons about human history (if not humanity generally) from the later Pueblo people of North America. These include the following: religion is multidimensional performance; it has an extended or networked character; and it is transferred or transmitted in ways that radically alter history.

Religious Experiences

What I mean to be saying from the very beginning may seem counterintuitive to some: an archaeology of religion is not necessarily best pursued as the study of religion, a unified body of sacred knowledge and practices surrounding some divine powers or numinous experiences (Durkheim 1965:62). Indeed, a focus on religion, understood as orthodox knowledge and practice, might lead one to assume rather than to question the religious precepts asserted to be common to some people, cultural region, or historical period. This is because studies that first isolate a religion—or an ideology, a belief system, or a cosmology—as if it were a bounded entity (be it Christianity, Islam, Buddhism, Hinduism, etc., or any one of the indigenous New World–isms), must first artificially reduce the complexities, syncretisms, or internal contradictions and conflicts of its tenets, spaces, materialities, or practitioners to an essence, an orthodoxy, or a cosmological principle. Indeed, some students of religion reduce entire historical epochs to single religious metaphors or "cosmovisions" (Carrasco 1990; Eliade 1991).

I do not mean to say that any one religion was as open, diffuse, or variable as another. Centuries of official decrees and councils and unofficial revivals of various sorts have served to syncretize some religious practices or peoples more so than others. But we must be clear that the resultant orthodoxies, key metaphors, or cosmovisions were, in reality, the historical projects of some people (say, priests) and not others (say, farmers). They were themselves constructions or projections and not necessarily norms that can be used to characterize entire peoples, epochs, or places.

Unfortunately, archaeologists are not always so careful, often deploying direct historical analogies of religious beliefs—usually as recorded by some nonnative observer—to interpret some earlier period or people. Lars Fogelin (2007, 2008) has labeled some such approaches as "structural," because they presume that deeply embedded cultural or mental structures or templates underlie people's dispositions and practices. Elsewhere, Lambros Malafouris (2004) calls them "cognitivist." Such structural or cognitivist starting points are convenient but also deceptive. On the one hand, they free analysts from seeking the often confounding and hard-won evidence of practical diversity, ideological contradictions, "hidden transcripts," and "historical silences" (Scott 1990; Trouillot 1995). On the other hand, they disguise the alternative approaches, divergent agendas, and subaltern dispositions that were commonplace in human history. Such variable dispositions were manifest simply owing to the locally disparate biographies and unintended experiences of different people.

Certainly, archaeologists from any number of epistemological stances begin their interpretations by deploying analogies. This is both a necessary and reasonable starting point (Wylie 2002). However, the lines of inferential reasonability are crossed when archaeologists argue teleologically, projecting onto the distant past a cultural or structural uniformity distilled from later accounts and, thereby, denying historical difference and divergence in that earlier period (Stahl 1993:252). For instance, instead of assuming that certain legends or myths were transmitted unchanged over centuries, or that men, women, and children shared the same belief system, or that the practices of priests and farmers were in essence the same, analysts would do better to understand the changing configurations of practices relative to larger relational webs of people, places, and things (or substances and elements). Otherwise, we create structural regularity and (re)invent religious tenets, principles, and orthodoxies where none may have existed. Structural and cognitivist approaches do just this (as argued for another North American case by Emerson and Pauketat 2008; Pauketat 2001).

How does one avoid making such an error? The answer is simple: rich, robust historical data. Structural approaches tend to be light on multiple lines of such data and heavy on interpretation, the latter often based around a few texts or a small corpus of iconographic material rather than the inevitable diversity of practices, experiences, and performances common even to the most orthodox religion today. The archaeological data to which I refer are derived from the material and spatial dimensions of past religious practices. Religious practices, that is, exist outside the human mind, in the relations between objects, elements, substances, bodies, buildings, and places. They can be experienced, cited by others, and reinterpreted. They are open to ambiguity, accommodation, contestation, and change.

Questions of Materiality

Having avoided the pitfalls of structural and cognitivist interpretations by not reconstructing a Pueblo belief system, cosmology, or religion, we must still confront head-on the question of the religious dimension of human experience. It is commonly agreed that, in many times and places, religion is inseparable from social life, a point made clearly by Stephen Plog (in this volume). For Plog, to live in or around New Mexico's Chaco Canyon, circa AD 860–1140, meant to have entangled family, community, polity, and economy with cosmic principles through ritual performance (see also Van Dyke 2008). A number of researchers of the European Neolithic have likewise considered the ritual dimensions of social life as the means whereby religious precepts were embedded in everyday experience (R. Bradley 2005; Richards 1996; Thomas 1996; Tilley 1994).

So what makes a practice religious? As recently summarized by Lars Fogelin (2007), researchers usually approach this question in two ways. First, they focus on ritual, by which is meant routinized or scripted performance, especially when such performance relates things sacred to those mundane (Bell 1997; Insoll 2004). Of course, many rituals are not primarily religious. One can easily imagine any number of annual ceremonies or life-cycle events (feasts, births, marriages, etc.) that have little religious content (Chapple and Coon 1942; Van Gennep 1960).

Similarly, many public or political rituals might primarily reference secular matters (Kertzer 1988). Of course, many of these yet incorporate some degree of religiosity, which is to say that they have a religious dimension. And the religiosity of rituals varies according to the performative context.

Second, these researchers usually adopt some form of practice-theoretic or phenomenological point of view that, in turn, is based on a theory of materiality (R. Bradley 2000; Joyce and Lopiparo 2005; Knappett and Malafouris 2008; Meskell 2004a, 2004b; Miller 2005; Mills and Walker 2008; Pauketat 2001; Renfrew 2004). Without reviewing their varied approaches, suffice it to say that these researchers posit that the material dimension of social experience and cultural practice or performance—which subsumes in seamless experiential fields the corporeality of human bodies, the thingness of portable objects, and the physicality and spatiality of landscapes—entangles people, places, and things in ways that produce lasting historical effects on those fields. In other words, that which people do—indeed their very being as people—is contingent on the external world as previously configured by themselves, by other people, and by other causal forces. The way that people think, once supposed to be a mental process within the body, is now commonly argued to be an embodied experience. People think through their bodies. They engage the world through their senses (Gell 1998; Hurcombe 2008; Robb 2004).

In short, saying that the cultural worlds of people are based in the materialities of experience is the same as saying that one's objective knowledge and subjective dispositions are virtually one and the same. In like manner, mind and body, thought and action, continuity and change, or structure and agency are inseparable (Gosden 1994; Ingold 2000). To assume otherwise would constitute a Cartesian bifurcation: an analytical separation of mind and body that often inappropriately privileges the former, implying that beliefs preexist as shared traditions, norms, cultural schemas, or even religious ideologies as if these are not continuously negotiated, contested, and changed through practice and performance.

In other words, from the perspective of theories of materiality, even religious "beliefs" are not safely tucked away in the minds of people to be later transmitted or materialized relatively unchanged down through the generations. Memories are, instead, closely associated with experience and, even as inscribed into some landscape of experience (poorly described as "collective memory"), are to a varying degree always creatively remembered in ways that select, emphasize, or silence some memories vis-à-vis others (Halbwachs 1992).

Movements Toward Answers

As it turns out, many Native Americans do not consider their religions to be frozen systems of belief either. Instead, they have some sense of religion as performance. It is about doing, not thinking. It is in ritual. It is in ceremony. "We don't believe our religion," according to one Plains performer, "we dance it!" (J. Brown 1977:123).

That sentiment extends to many non-Western people around the world, who "seem to think of their religion 'as encapsulated in . . . discrete performances which they [can] exhibit to visitors and to themselves'" (Geertz 1973:113). Indeed, there is an argument to be made that beliefs, in general, are not held in the mind first to be materialized second. Rather, they are always embodied and externalized; they are put in motion. To believe anything is to experience something. Thus, religions are experiential and experiences, in turn, are contingent on the disposition of and histories of movement through landscapes by bodies, objects, and various other forces, seen and unseen.

According to David Morgan (2005:8), who analyzes the visuality of religions, belief "does not exist in an abstract, discursive space, in an empyrean realm of pure proclamation, 'I Believe.'" Rather, "belief happens in and through things and what people do with them." It is only with Western Christianity, Morgan says, that people were made to "profess" their faith, to put it into abstract conceptual terms as if it was held in the mind—a Western mind that not incidentally needed to discipline and punish the body for failing to live up to beliefs (Foucault 1977).

Such an unabashedly Cartesian separation of mind and body is no more evident than among contemporary Christian and Muslim sects that beat and whip their own bodies or those of their families or community members (Aragon 2006; Moghissi 2005). As earlier noted, such a mind-body separation is recapitulated by other analytical dualisms: culture and history, structure and agency, or continuity and change.

In more subtle ways, it also underwrites structural- and symbolic-anthropological approaches that treat core symbols, key metaphors, or cultural schemas as mental templates with lasting integrity (Ortner 1973; Turner 1974). The same is true at a considerably smaller scale of poststructural notions of *doxa* and *habitus*, which assert that individualized sets of cultural dispositions are routinely exposed through practice but reside largely in the mind (cf. Bourdieu 1977; Miller 2005).

Certainly, this separation of history or action from culture or religious tradition underlies Anthony Wallace's (1956, 2003) original formulation of "revitalization movements" (cf. Glowacki, this volume). As he described them, these movements were perturbations in a functioning society that followed a predictable course of events and, eventually, returned social life to a steady state. In denying to them or their participants long-term cause and effect, Wallace's scheme ultimately dehistoricized such movements (see also Van Keuren's and Munson's concerns about artificially homogenizing diversity, this volume). And while his structural-functional approach is untenable today, revitalization movements were real and had important historical effects, as argued by Donna Glowacki (this volume).

Indeed, once we abandon the rigid Cartesian separation of culture and history or continuity and change that underwrote Wallace's analysis, we can appreciate that many of the major changes in the Southwest can be usefully analyzed as social or religious movements. To be clear, a movement is simply a pervasive rearrangement of a field of social relationships at any scale articulated around a person, place, thing, substance, element, or practice. Wallace (1956, 2003) examined a series of well-known historical cases, in North America focusing on the many prophets and prophecies of the historic era (Pauketat 2009). In the Southwest, one could easily imagine the formation of Chaco, with its periodic flurries of construction, to have taken shape as a series of revitalizations. Certainly the place was all about experience (Van Dyke 2008).

But there is no reason to believe that such large-scale movements were always qualitatively distinct from smaller-scale practical reinventions of culture. Every practice—whether a speech event in a Pueblo plaza or a painted pot used to serve a meal—is a potential point of articulation for some distinct set of religious practices and practitioners that might reinvent tradition (see also Dorsey 1894; Durkheim 1965). Of course, certain reinventions based on religious experiences may have been potentially more transformative than others (consider Hobsbawm and Ranger 1983). Pueblo construction events, whether at Chaco or Chupadera Mesa, are possibly good examples of such revitalizations that literally replaced religious practices in different ways and at different scales. On the one hand, the scale and configuration of a Chaco might have involved proactive conversions of distant people. On the other hand, Chupadera Mesa's conversions might have been limited to, say, training the young. The differences are as much matters of scale as of kind.

One might imagine any number of agents or attractors that might have been at the core of such movements: the sun and the moon, a supernova, a prominent butte, or the bones of ancestors (see Plog, this volume). Thus, let us call these points of articulation in such movements "nodes" (Plog, this volume; see also Ingold 2006; Knappett and Malafouris 2008; Pauketat 2011). Doing this moves us toward more complex, relational theories of agency that understand agents or "mediators" in social networks to result from as much as to cause change (Ingold 2006; Latour 2005). Importantly, such nodes or mediators include nonhuman as well as human entities. People, places, substances, and things have "affordant" qualities, which is to say that they induce or impede relationships (Ingold 2000). Likewise, they may be connected to each other via eventful conjunctions, or "happenings," which likewise afford certain relationships (Gell 1998). Every supernova, lunar standstill, drought, eclipse, or other such happening—whether viewed as a crisis or an opportunity—was a happening that might initiate a movement and rearrange a relational network.

In fact, depending on the rate and scale of such movements, they might themselves be perceived as happenings. For instance, certain large-scale plaza events are both movements of a sort and happenings. So too are large-scale or rapid migrations—of obvious importance in the ancient Southwest—happenings that are simultaneously physical movements and social movements (much like the Israelites who followed their leader Moses out of Egypt or the Mormons who followed theirs to Utah). And in the same way, as inferred from Chamberlin's (this volume) discussion of Pueblo plaza construction, pilgrimages are part and parcel of religious movements, literally and figuratively.

Perhaps then, and consistent with the sensibilities of various indigenous viewpoints, we might begin to think of southwestern religion as religion-in-motion. There was no single organized or orthodox set of religious practices involving deities or some form of holy mystery. But there were movements in that direction, ranging from collecting the clay to make a pot to pecking a petroglyph to building a pueblo to gathering at Chaco Canyon when the sun and moon were in proper alignment.

Lessons

The thing is, if there is a religious dimension to so much of what people do, then religious practices are continuously exposed to the circumstances and agendas of networks or landscapes in flux. And this historical process means that structuralist or cognitivist positions, often borrowed from ethnology via analogy, can no longer be allowed to spill into interpretations of the Southwest. People do not put structures, meanings, or templates into action per se; these always and necessarily exist simultaneously outside the mind in the spatiality and materiality of bodies, landscapes, and objects, along with other elements, sensations, or unseen forces that are all potentially part of larger relational fields or networks. They engage webs of relationships and, in turn, those webs engage people.

So we are talking about thickly entangled relationships, such that agents and structures, or nodes and networks, become inseparable. For example, Latour (1991) rhetorically asks about handguns in contemporary times. Do they kill people, or do people using guns kill people? Which is the structure and which is the agent? Similarly, we might conceive of a mountain as an inanimate piece of a larger landscape, not an agent. But it does act as an obstacle, in a sense affording certain movements of animals, people, clouds, and winds. And if that mountain happened to also be a volcano that sometimes erupted, then people might reasonably consider it to be a more active interlocutor of human affairs. After all, it moves, makes noise, and changes people's lives. So too might various other animals, clouds in the sky, lightning and rain, and so on. Are these not all causal agents of change or mediators of relationships of a sort, at least as broadly conceived (Latour 2005)?

Regardless of one's specific answers to this question, we should all be able to agree that, minimally, experience—especially that within thick overlaid multidimensional social fields—entangles intentionality, affordance, and causality to the point of inseparability. By the later pre-Hispanic period, this is an apt description of the Southwest. By then, a petroglyph was powerful because of its place as a point of articulation in a complex and historically contingent field wherein people, places, spirit beings, and rocks, among other things, connect (Basso 1996; Munson, this volume). Likewise, the ancestral remains in Room 33 at Pueblo Bonito, described by Plog (this volume), probably had great power over people. They afforded a certain kind of history. They had agency, as did the other things in the room, the room itself, and all of Pueblo Bonito, if not the entire canyon and the moving beings in the sky and on the ground that defined this center place. Clearly the same is true of other people, places, and things in similarly fractal ways (e.g., Heckenberger 2005). History, community, gender, and religion were performed in plazas (Chamberlin, this volume; Low 2000). Bones used in ceremonies or dancers in costumes evoked the presence of ancestors. Plays of light and shadow on walls witnessed the convergence of powerful forces in some place, at some time, with some people.

Thus our first lesson from the later pre-Hispanic Southwest: the ability to afford certain movements, relationships, or effects resides variously in people, places, things, organisms, substances, and the elements. Any number of things, then, can have power (i.e., the ability to constrain the biographies or histories of other things). To take this another obvious step, we might note that the concentration of these powers is powerful. All places, for instance, are not created equal, if spirits happen to reside in one and not the others. All people, too, are not equally agentic, if one has greater access than others to the powers of certain places, elements, or beings. Chamberlin (this volume) would call the latter individual a "virtuoso." But virtuosity here is heavily contingent on the emergent properties of the field within which one woman or man might step into the role of virtuous mediator.

In regard to this second example, there seems little good reason to separate political power from religious powers, as it were. The latter are the bases of political power, at least of the sort sanctioned by some community as authority. Political power, that is, was not based in some abstract human essence but instead on the articulation of affordances and agencies that were otherwise dispersed across the landscape or located in the heavens and earth. Emplace those powers in a Great House, contain them in a pot, or weave them into a piece of fabric worn on the body, and one might be said to be exercising political power.

Dimensionality

This first lesson is actually an aspect of a much larger and more important lesson about the dimensionality of religious practice. Marit Munson, Matthew Chamberlin, and Elizabeth Newsome and Kelley Hays-Gilpin (this volume) all analyze distinctly different datasets to derive some insights into how visual, audible, and tactile senses were engaged by religious practices with distinctive material and spatial properties. Munson (this volume) establishes a Coalition to Classic Period transition that, in correlating formal rock art styles with site locations and sensory qualities, points to pervasive pan-regional changes in relationships between hosts and audiences, with some local variation. In much the same way, Chamberlin (this volume) delineates the dialectical performative dimensions of late thirteenth- and fourteenth-century plaza pueblos in the Salinas area. Both, in different ways, show that community, as experienced or defined vis-à-vis outsiders and ancestors, was undergoing profound changes.

Understanding this relationship of community and change might require some rethinking of the notion of community itself. It is my contention that community, broadly conceived, was (and is) neither simply a "natural" place nor an "imagined" identity (Anderson 1983), but an ever emergent and performed dimension of social experience (Pauketat 2008). Certain people, places, or things embodied community, which is to say that they afforded communal senses of self or personhood in relation to other people, places, and things (see also Fowler 2004). The people brought to bear, the spaces afforded, or the things commemorated social relationships and collective identities. A plaza might engender community, a pot could serve up community, or a particular individual could personify it. The point is that community, as a dimension of experience, was contingent on the materiality and spatiality of that experience. It was open and fluid, and subject to large extent on the potential vagaries of who and what was gathered in some space. In other words, community might change depending on the configuration of relationships between the people, places, things, substances, and other powers in the fields of human experience.

In the present volume, the dénouement of this argument is Newsome and Hays-Gilpin's recognition of visual culture changes from the Pueblo III to the Pueblo IV period. Later in time, there was a notable shift away from the outward-looking, all-encompassing visual culture of Chaco and its Pueblo III period descendants toward the inward-turned, centripetal visual culture of the Pueblo IV period. Earlier, there seems to have been a privileging of the skyward gaze of a few, perhaps with a religious zeal that included carrying the message far afield. Given the ways in which the celestial realm was "gathered" by a few religious leaders in the earlier period, one might surmise that many experiences possessed a celestial temporality, giving human experience a tempo consistent with annual and multiyear cycles of solar, lunar, planetary, and stellar movements.

Later in time there seems to have been an inclusive conflation between organizer, performer, and audience. These more consistently human rhythms of the later late pre-Hispanic period probably would have contrasted greatly with the earlier experience of a Chaco-ized regional landscape and cosmic field of view. It was as if people who used to look *to* the gods in the sky (and at Chaco) later were being visited *by* the gods in their pueblos. There would have been large-scale and long-term implications of the repeated performance of the different temporalities of experience (Newsome and Hays-Gilpin, this volume). The Pueblo III period experiences would have engendered a "historical ontology" different from that associated with continued practices of the Pueblo IV period sort (Robb and Pauketat 2009). In other words, history itself—as a process of the cultural construction of relationships—would have unfolded at different rates and in different ways during the ninth through twelfth centuries as opposed to the thirteenth through early sixteenth centuries, contingent on who, what, and where such relationships were being practiced, performed, and embodied.

Network-Based Relationships

How to understand such complex, weblike fields of experience (i.e., history) is tricky, but Wes Bernardini, Stephen Plog, Randall McGuire, Scott Ortman, and Scott Van Keuren (all in this volume) each have elements of an approach. It begins with Bernardini's recognition of "histories of practice" or what McGuire understands as "relations between" happenings and agents. History, as a dynamic web of cultural constructions of and through relationships, must be understood genealogically (Mills and Walker 2008).

Such a networking process is absolutely a metaphorical one, as Ortman (this volume) argues (Lakoff and Johnson 1980). Importantly, such metaphors are always embodied or externalized. They have a materiality, as noted earlier, and are not wedded to underlying cultural structures because they—the networked material metaphors—are themselves the structures. That is, extending Van Keuren's argument (this volume)—red ware pots or black-and-white bowls are not expressions of ideologies or metaphors; they are themselves ideologies or metaphors in action. They physically and materially relate people, spaces, and other referents through their production, use, and disposal. Likewise, the Room 33 bones in Pueblo Bonito are not there because of a Chacoan identity, they and the structured earth in Room 32 (among other things) are Chacoan identity as it was continuously performed (see Plog, this volume). One would have connected to the past figuratively and literally by visiting Pueblo Bonito, if not by entering the dark quarters of the ancestors, perhaps leaving an offering behind. Presumably, that identity was actively constructed by Mesa Verde priests and pilgrims long after the significant depopulation of Chaco Canyon. Their sense of self and community probably depended on Chaco still being there.

That is, such citations or metaphors are not deep and inaccessible but, instead, surficial, everyday, and repeated through ritual action. In this way they would become thoroughly enmeshed with each other and would continuously associate one person, place, object, substance, or element with another. Each is a node in an ephemeral network of associations always in the process of becoming. No citation or metaphor existed by itself, nor could one long stand on its own, limited by the ephemeral character of human memories (see Connerton 1989). Instead, they were enmeshed with others as parts of larger fields, milieus, or gestalts (Gell 1998; Lakoff and Johnson 1980; Latour 2005).

Understanding how this works is helped by introducing some notion of the bundle (Pauketat 2011). Here, we must turn first to Suzanne Küchler's (2002) work with religious art objects in the South Pacific, so-called *Malanggan* carvings. These images depicted various qualities or entities being tied together, which led her to propose that meanings or coassociations are created by "binding" image-making practices together, both literally and figuratively. Webb Keane (2005) has said that this same principle, which he called "bundling," applies to all material culture. One thing references or cites another and the associations of things are, therefore, always multiple and dynamic. One metaphor is meaningless outside the larger and continuously changing field of metaphors (Lakoff and Johnson 1980). It is the binding or bundling of relational fields that knots up or combines aspects of agents or nodes in ways that, in turn, afford them causal powers to affect the disposition of the larger fields of relationships.

Of course, particular bundled relationships might be more or less durable, depending on the material medium involved and the rate at which some practice was repeated. Owing to its masonry constructions, many southwestern places retain a remarkable degree of citationality still today. And because of the durability of the genealogies of some combinations or bundled networks, the past appears more present than in other parts of the world. But it is not more deeply embedded in the traditions of people; it is more tightly wrapped in the living traditions of people.

Transfer

Elsewhere, I have argued that bundled fields of relationships have another quality that bears consideration in terms of how rapid, large-scale change occurred in history: certain bundles can be transferred (Pauketat 2011). A bundle transfer is the movement of some whole set of relationships from one field of human experience to another. Architectural designs can be moved from one place and emplaced elsewhere (see Chamberlin, this volume). A Mexican object may be traded north (McGuire, this volume). A Katsina image might be transferred from one medium to another (Munson, this volume). A virtuoso who embodies some distinctive community genealogy might migrate to a new home. All of these are bundle transfers.

In terms of religious practices in Native North America, including the Southwest, this process is exemplified by actual medicine bundles or fetishes (see Parsons 1939; for an extensive description of Plains bundles, see Zedeño 2008). These sacred objects are actually assemblages of other objects wrapped up in a common package and associated with thickly liturgical practices memorized by a few and repeated with great care on ritual occasions. In some cases, all ritual knowledge resides in the bundle, making it a powerful container of the most sacred information and identity of a people.

Yet, infrequently, the medicine bundle and its knowledge must be transferred to another human being or place where it will be cared for. Such transfers were not done casually or simply, because they entailed accommodating entire suites of biographical information, practices, and associations extracted from one context and emplaced into a new context. In the Plains, for instance, transferring the special knowledge, ritual songs and verses, and proper order of religious practices from one man to another or parent to offspring often entailed weeks, months, or even years of training (e.g., Murie 1981; Wissler 1912). Such training ensured continuity of a sort. Then again, on the Plains, such bundle transfers were also the mechanisms whereby entire religious movements spread across the continent's vast interior: the Sun Dance, Tobacco societies, Sweet Grass ceremonies, and so on (e.g., Archambault 2001). Prophets too "revitalized" their traditions by carefully manipulating bundles (Pauketat 2009, 2011).

As the medicine bundles exemplify, movements of the mediating and agentic knotted or packaged entities matter. Even if the transfer of a bundle—and here we include all network mediators, from site plans and objects to human beings and celestial objects in the sky—was intended to maintain or share some traditional knowledge, its movement also entailed potentially radical change in some localities, the recipients needing to realign all of their relationships to accommodate the new bundle or to convert others to their relational viewpoint. The effect was similar to an artist's corpus of work, the entirety of which may be revalued or reappraised with each new piece (Gell 1998). The results might be histories of practices and genealogies of places that appear to bespeak change and continuity. This is because of the ways in which knotted fields of relationships—bundles—could be transferred from time to time and place to place.

Big Historical Processes in the Southwest

Bundle transfers are, technically, movements at a small scale with potentially large-scale implications. These larger-scale implications include revitalizations and religious movements (Glowacki, this volume). Movements are experiential. They are, as previously noted, religion in motion. They can have dramatic historical effects. Such movements exemplify the ways in which bundle transfers, then, might have produced radical changes in southwestern history, if often in the guise of local continuity.

Such big historical effects probably stemmed from relations between Mesoamerica and the Southwest (McGuire, this volume). The Pueblo Southwest was not, of course, isolated from the indigenous happenings in Mesoamerica. However, the historical implications of such relationships have never been clear in large part, from my way of thinking, owing to the deficiencies of our own understanding of history and religion. Adopting McGuire's (this volume) relational view helps us to appreciate that Ancestral Pueblo knowledge of Mesoamerica, or at least of northern Mexico, was always locally bundled, either with the aid of actual foreign things (chocolate drinks, macaws, copper bells) or via images and site plans (e.g., Tláloc in rock art, the colonnades at Chaco's Chetro Ketl) meant to be reanimated and experienced in local settings (cf. Munson, this volume; Plog, this volume).

And as bundles of thickly interreferential religious practices, Mesoamerican influences were indirect and, yet, arguably, profound. They might have been experienced as movements by way of the actual movement or transfer of exotic things (bundles of associations needed to be reconnected locally) or the occasional traveler (technically also a bundle, a body with added knowledge that would enable linkages with and reinventions of the cultural worlds of others). Local agents rearticulated or reconfigured their networks by alternately adding or subtracting, remembering or forgetting, and concentrating or dispersing referents and metaphors in ways that can be conceived as bundle transfers.

Radical realignments of histories of practice and webs of relations also occurred through and as migrations. Recognizing that certain Hopi clans ended up with some practices but not others, or that some Ancestral Puebloan peoples avoided elements of Chacoan religion, shows that people transferred some but not all of their relational networks in the process (Bernardini, this volume; Glowacki, this volume). Upon arrival, the establishment of an ordered landscape might have centered on a pueblo, often aligned to the sun or citing shrines atop sacred hills, all necessary foundational acts that completed the transfer of identity bundles to new homelands. But other relations might have been forgotten, not transferred or reconnected to a new location.

Thus, the construction of cultural continuity was oddly contingent to some degree on constructing discontinuities (Trouillot 1995). Similarly, it was probably equally contingent on the bundling of certain lateral relationships by ignoring others. Is it a historical coincidence, for instance, that the anomalous Pueblo town of Paquimé, at the heart of the Casas Grandes phenomenon, emerged as a political powerhouse at roughly the same time as the start of the late pre-Hispanic period? As the crow flies, Paquimé is located 645 kilometers due south of the Salinas pueblos, a small "city" of two thousand people (Lekson 1999; Whalen and Minnis 2001). But it is only 193 kilometers southwest of the Rio Grande, the same river that runs past these same pueblos and, presumably, the source for the macaws and bells found therein (McGuire, this volume). By comparison, Mesa Verdeans lived 145 kilometers north of Chaco Canyon, the presumed destination of certain periodic pilgrimages during the Pueblo III period.

The question remains, to what extent were the large-scale and long-term changes described in this volume entangled with the religious performances bundled with places like Paquimé and with the associated things or the related journeys to and from them? Arguably, many Coalition Period and Pueblo III period experiences yet cited and transferred into their towers and kivas notions of an ancient centerplace: Chaco (à la Newsome and Hays-Gilpin, this volume). But those practices seem to have ended with the movements away from Mesa Verde and elsewhere to the south and west, and with it the ways in which (and the tempo at which) history unfolded changed as well. Defensive, inward-turned, and occasionally burned pueblos testify to the dramatic changes. Were they connected to Paquimé?

Conclusion

In other words, can we connect Pueblo religious experience, performance, or practice with the big historical events, happenings, or trends in the Southwest? For present purposes, merely posing the question is enough. The ultimate point of the question is not the answer, but the implications of the asking. Large-scale and long-term changes in human history are contingent on understanding the religious practices of people. This is because all such practices involved bundled fields. The specificities of the repeated knotting or mediating of those fields and the transference of relationships across space and through time—via long-distance exchange, large-scale migration, or everyday social movement on the one hand or experiential histories of practices involving costumed bodies, painted pots, ordered landscapes, and so on, on the other—constructed the great social webs and experiential networks differently. Before the late 1200s, the historicity of experiences (which is to say the rates and ways in which history might play out) was expansive, cosmic, and cosmopolitan. Later, it turned inward (following Newsome and Hays-Gilpin, this volume).

The two eras are defined in essence by divergent historical ontologies, different ways of being human that extended to and were constructed repeatedly by the fields of experience (Robb and Pauketat 2009). What had changed? Everything. This includes religion, although not in the strict orthodox sense, but in the larger relational sense. All relations were mediated religiously. Indigenous Pueblo history is religion, so to speak.

Moreover, the big lesson of the Southwest is this. Seen in the abstract as a process of relating to one's world, creating sense from nonsense or meaning from chaos, religion is not only human. It is humanity. And an archaeology of religion, understood as the study of religious practices, reveals that major changes in human history—especially the great transformation of earlier Pueblo networks into later pre-Hispanic webs of divergent tendencies wrapped within bundles of continuity—are to be understood *as* religion and *through* religion.

Notes

Chapter 3

1. Van Dyke (2008:108) argues that "archaeologists cannot glean much specific information about the nature and meanings of Chaco ceremonies, nor should we necessarily try." Most recently, Lekson (2009:278) bluntly asserts that "attempting to determine the principles of an ancient religion—gone for almost a thousand years—is probably a waste of time."

2. "Probably 90% of the excavated 'storage' rooms at Chaco were empty" (Lekson 2007:14). "The little bits of evidence that do exist from Chaco Canyon and outlying great houses suggest that great house rooms were almost always empty, infrequently had hearths, and on rare occasions conceal unusual artifacts such as painted wooden objects or oddly shaped pottery" (Kantner 2006:32).

3. The numbers listed are minimum frequencies.

4. Judd almost always labeled such forms "ducks" while Pepper consistently used the more generic "bird."

5. Only Judd uses the specific phrase "cloud blower." Pepper never refers to anything other than "pipes," perhaps because he was not aware of the use of pipes to generate smoke that symbolizes clouds.

Chapter 4

1. Chaco-based ideologies were not completely abandoned, however, as Chacoan history and associated beliefs were, and are, deeply embedded in Pueblo traditions and ideology.

Chapter 5

1. Tewa speakers refer to the ancestral rain beings known as Katsinas in most other pueblos as *ókʰùwä* 'cloud-beings.' Unless otherwise noted, all Tewa forms in this paper are written in the orthography of Esther Martinez's dictionary of the San Juan Tewa dialect (1982).

2. All Kiowa-Tanoan reconstructions in this paper are from Ortman (2009:appendix 3).

3. Of course, the metaphor PEOPLE ARE CORN is widespread among maize-growing peoples of North America. For example, it is documented in the ethnographic literatures of the Hopi (Black 1984), Tewa (A. Ortiz 1969), Huichol (Shelton 1996), Nahua (Sandstrom 1991), Mixtec (Monaghan 1995), and Maya (Carlsen 1997).

4. There may be evidence for an even older community metaphor. In table 5.3, specifically, the Tewa word for 'plaza', *búpíngéh*, also contains *pín* 'heart, middle', a form that is cognate with Taos *píana* 'heart, middle', and derives from Proto-Tanoan **pian-* 'heart'. This suggests that people who spoke Proto-Tiwa-Tewa (AD 725–920) may have imagined the community as a person, and they may have viewed the plaza as the heart or center of this person.

5. This method uses generalizations on the structure of figurative language identified through cognitive linguistic research to develop expectations for the structure of material expressions of a proposed metaphor in the archaeological record. For case studies of the method, see Ortman 2000b, 2008a, 2009.

6. Stubbs and Stallings (1953:143) note that middens, abandoned rooms, and subfloor pits were also used as burial locations at Pindi, but they do not tabulate the ages of individuals buried in these contexts.

7. In an unpublished conference paper, Head and Snead (1992) suggest that the reuse of old house sites for farming may also represent a symbolic response to competition over resources. Even under this scenario, however, farmers would have chosen to plant within old houses to demonstrate claims to agricultural land, thus reinforcing symbolic connections between people, corn, and architecture.

Chapter 6

1. First used in archaeological research in the late 1970s (see Baxter 1994:110–139), correspondence analysis (CA) can be used to identify and describe the relationships between variables. It may be thought of as a form of Principal Components Analysis that is appropriate for discrete data, such as frequency counts (Baxter 1994:100–101). Similar to a chi-square test, CA is based on the distances between cell values in a contingency table. Unlike the chi-square, though, CA is an exploratory technique that describes how the rows and columns are related, rather than testing a hypothesis of row and column independence. CA is appropriate for discrete, nonnegative data, including frequency counts, percentages, or presence/absence data. The analyses described here use frequency counts of the occurrence of stylistic traits, rather than of defined types, at each site.

2. On the other hand, the greater elaboration may indicate that some portion of the Galisteo rock art extends into the historic period, after 1600. My Pajarito Plateau research indicates that historic period rock art shows little change from that of the late Classic (Munson 2002), although most of the trends in the Classic are somewhat strengthened. Regardless of the exact timing, the data clearly show that rock art throughout the northern Rio Grande changed dramatically in style over time, beginning in the late 1200s or early 1300s and extending through the Classic Period into the early historic.

3. In addition to the typical archaeological emphasis on vision, other senses were likely equally important (Edwards et al. 2006; Magowan 1998). In plaza dances, being able to hear music was surely important, just as the sounds coming from within a kiva would alert villagers to the activities taking place. Likewise, the

sounds associated with ritual practice at petroglyph sites were surely of interest to villagers, whether in the form of speaking or singing or simply the percussive sound of pecking a petroglyph (Ouzman 2001; Rainbird 2002b).

4. The exception is finely scratched images made with faint lines. These obscure images are often overlooked because they are so difficult to see, though J. J. Brody (2007) and colleagues have documented extensively scratched images on the Galisteo Dike.

Chapter 8

1. Ortman (2008:242–245) reports surveying forty-three landscape and horizon bichrome murals across the northern San Juan drainage. Of his sample, most occurred in building interiors, with only five examples painted on exterior pueblo walls. Of seventeen landscape murals painted in rectangular rooms, nine occur in second- or third-story structures. Ortman suggests that these contexts support the association of these murals with calendrical observations based on horizon astronomy, as proposed by Malville and Munson (1998). Ortman further suggests that an upper-story room featuring a landscape mural with a door, window, or peephole that admitted light from a low position on the horizon could substitute for a panoramic horizon view.

2. Malville and Putnam (1993) and Malville and Munson (1998) have discussed various aspects of the Cliff Palace mural in relation to what they believe was a complex system of solar and lunar observations that were connected to a calendar of rituals at Mesa Verde. Their interpretations relate the mural's imagery and the third-story room where it is situated to patterns of astronomical observation that use the horizon to calculate solstices and lunar cycle dates.

Chapter 9

1. The Silver Creek area designates an archaeological district in the Upper Little Colorado River drainage that is bounded by the Mogollon Rim to the south. However, I designate the "Silver Creek village cluster" to include Tundastusa Ruin (south of the Mogollon Rim) with the other Pueblo IV period towns in the drainage (Bailey, Pinedale, Fourmile, Shumway, and Showlow ruins).

2. I adopt "Gila style" to designate the decorative layout and elements that appear in the transition from Pinto to Gila Polychrome, which Crown (1994:79–82) alternatively labels "Stage 4, 5, and 6" Pinedale style.

3. The end date of permanent Pueblo occupation at Pinedale Ruin is difficult to estimate. Fewkes excavated five classic Pinedale-style whole vessels in 1896. A very small portion of the undocumented whole vessels that were recovered by looters in the 1970s include *post*-1330 types (Fourmile Polychrome, Tonto Polychrome), but there is no way to confirm that all of the vessels in these photos were recovered from Pinedale Ruin alone. Based on ceramic and tree-ring dating, Haury and Hargrave (1931) confirm that the main occupation dated prior to 1330, but

they do note the presence of later types (including Jeddito Yellow Ware). My excavations in and around the large southern plaza in 2005 revealed only trace amounts of post–Pinedale style types. I conclude that the village was abandoned at a time when the occupants at Fourmile and Shumway ruins to the north (and possibly Showlow Ruin, see [Haury and Hargrave 1931:61–62]) continued to expand.

4. Evidence of migrants includes adobe brick construction and locally produced pottery painted with nonlocal decorative styles. Fourmile Ruin is the only archaeological site in the Silver Creek area where adobe brick construction was apparently utilized.

Chapter 10

1. Making such an equation glosses differences in architecture and ceramics between the Hopi mesas and the Kayenta Valley, which indicate important social variability within the region (e.g., Colton 1955; Dean 1996).

2. A recently recorded, kilometer-long Pueblo I period site (Bernardini n.d.) near Low Mountain, Arizona, suggests that some pithouse villages around the Hopi mesas were bigger than previously suspected.

3. There are as-yet poorly understood (by archaeologists) references in Hopi traditional knowledge to earlier waves of migration north by Nùutungkwisinom groups, potentially complicating the chronological separation from Motisinom populations. The migration of the Bear Clan is particularly difficult to reconcile with first/last divisions. Most traditions agree that Bear was first to arrive at Hopi, arriving from the vicinity of the San Francisco Peaks (typically associated with Motisinom groups). But some traditions recount that prior to living near the San Francisco Peaks the Bear Clan lived at Palatkwapi (e.g., Saufkie 1998) and followed a northward migration similar to other Palatkwapi clans. Bear is still distinguished by being the first of the southern clans to find its way to Hopi, but in this recounting the clan would be classified as Nùutungkwisinom.

4. Plog and Solometo (1997) argue that Katsina symbolism indicates an earlier emphasis on war and conflict that has been suppressed since the time of Spanish contact.

5. The villages of Musangnuvi, Songoopavi, and Walpi all shifted from the valley floor to the mesa top following the Pueblo Revolt in 1680, but the distances moved were short (a few hundred meters) and demographic continuity appears to have been maintained.

6. Table Rock Pueblo, however, contains no rock art (and thus no Katsina petroglyphs), and it has not yielded any ceramics with Katsina depictions (Nichols 2007).

7. Mount Taylor is in fact southeast of the Hopi mesas rather than northeast. The discrepancy in the directional association of this Katsina home is likely due to the fact that the direction was originally measured from the Upper Little Colorado region, before its occupants immigrated to Hopi.

8. The viewshed analysis was conducted with the Viewshed tool in ArcGis 9.2 on a 30-meter DEM, taking the earth's curvature into account in the calculations.

9. Of course, much longer trips for resource collection, hunting, and ceremonial purposes would have been common, if less frequent.

10. However, recall the boom-bust cycles documented by Plog (1986) for Black Mesa.

REFERENCES

Adams, E. Charles
- 1989a Changing Form and Function in Western Pueblo Ceremonial Architecture from A.D. 1000 to A.D. 1500. In *The Architecture of Social Integration*, edited by W. Lipe and M. Hegmon, pp. 155–160. Cortez, CO: Crow Canyon Archaeological Center Occasional Paper No. 1.
- 1989b Western Anasazi and Western Pueblo Ceremonial Architecture: Contrasting Patterns in Form and Function A.D. 1000 to A.D. 1500. In *Seasons of the Kachina*, edited by S. B. Vane, pp. 41–50. Hayward, CA: Ballena Press.
- 1989c Hopi Use, Occupancy, and Possession of the Indian Reservation Defined by the Act of June 14, 1934: An Archaeological Perspective. Report prepared for the 1934 Case Litigation. The Hopi Tribe, Kykotsmovi, Arizona.
- 1991 *The Origin and Development of the Pueblo Katsina Cult*. Tucson: University of Arizona Press.
- 1994 The Katsina Cult: A Western Pueblo Perspective. In *Kachinas in the Pueblo World*, edited by Polly Schaafsma, pp. 35–46. Albuquerque: University of New Mexico Press.
- 1996 The Pueblo III–Pueblo IV Transition in the Hopi Area, Arizona. In *The Prehistoric Pueblo World, A.D. 1150–1350*, edited by M. A. Adler, pp. 48–58. Tucson: University of Arizona Press.
- 2002 *Homol'ovi: An Ancient Pueblo Settlement Cluster*. Tucson: University of Arizona Press.
- 2004 Homol'ovi: A 13th–14th Century Settlement Cluster in Northeastern Arizona. In *The Protohistoric Pueblo World, A.D. 1275–1600*, edited by E. C. Adams and A. I. Duff, pp. 119–127. Tucson: University of Arizona Press.

Adams, E. Charles, and Andrew I. Duff
- 2004 Settlement Clusters and the Pueblo IV Period. In *The Protohistoric Pueblo World, A.D. 1275–1600*, edited by E. C. Adams and A. I. Duff, pp. 3–16. Tucson: University of Arizona Press.

Adams, E. Charles, and Vincent M. LaMotta
- 2004 Hopi Settlement Clusters Past and Present. In *The Protohistoric Pueblo World, A.D. 1275–1600*, edited by E. C. Adams and A. I. Duff, pp. 128–136. Tucson: University of Arizona Press.
- 2006 New Perspectives on an Ancient Religion: Katsina Ritual in the Ar-

chaeological Record. In *Religion in the Prehispanic Southwest,* edited by C. S. VanPool, T. L. VanPool, and D. A. Phillips Jr., pp. 53–66. Lanham, MD: AltaMira.

Aguilar-Moreno, Manuel
 2007 *Handbook to Life in the Aztec World.* Oxford: Oxford University Press.

Ahlstrom, Richard V. N., Carla R. Van West, and Jeffrey S. Dean
 1995 Environmental and Chronological Factors in the Mesa Verde–Northern Rio Grande Migration. *Journal of Anthropological Archaeology* 14:125–142.

Akins, Nancy J.
 1986 *A Biocultural Approach to Human Burials from Chaco Canyon, New Mexico.* Santa Fe, NM: US Department of Interior, National Park Service.
 2001 Chaco Canyon Mortuary Practices: Archaeological Correlates of Complexity. In *Ancient Burial Practices in the American Southwest,* edited by D. R. Mitchell and J. L. Brunson-Hadley, pp. 167–190. Albuquerque: University of New Mexico Press.
 2003 The Burials of Pueblo Bonito. In *Pueblo Bonito: Center of the Chaco World,* edited by J. E. Neitzel, pp. 94–126. Washington, DC: Smithsonian Books.

Allen, Paula Gunn
 1996 The Sacred Hoop: A Contemporary Perspective. In *The Ecocriticism Reader: Landmarks in Literary Ecology,* edited by C. Glotfelty and H. From, pp. 241–263. Athens: University of Georgia Press.

Ambler, J. R.
 2002 Hopi and Keres Origins. Paper presented at The Transition from Prehistory to History in the Southwest, Albuquerque, New Mexico, February 1998, and the Annual Meeting of the Society for American Archaeology, March 2002.

Anderson, Benedict
 1983 *Imagined Communities: Reflections on the Origin and Spread of Nationalism.* New York: Verso.

Anschuetz, Kurt F.
 1998 Not Waiting for the Rain: Integrated Systems of Water Management by Pre-Columbian Pueblo Farmers in North-Central New Mexico. Ph.D. dissertation, University of Michigan, Ann Arbor.
 2005 Landscapes as Memory: Archaeological History to Learn from and Live By. In *Engaged Anthropology: Research Essays on North American Archaeology, Ethnobotany, and Museology,* edited by M. Hegmon and B. S. Eiselt, pp. 52–72. Anthropological Papers, Number 94, Museum of Anthropology, University of Michigan, Ann Arbor.

Anyon, Roger
 1999 Migrations in the South: Hopi Reconnaissance in the Barry M. Gold-

water Range. Report prepared for the Hopi Cultural Preservation Office, Kykotsmovi, Arizona.

Aragon, Ray John de
    2006   *The Penitentes of New Mexico: Brothers of the Light.* Santa Fe, NM: Sunstone Press.

Archambault, JoAllyn
    2001   Sun Dance. In *Handbook of North American Indians, Plains, Part 2 of 2,* edited by R. J. DeMallie, pp. 983–995. Washington, DC: Smithsonian Institution.

Arnold, Denise Y., and Christine A. Hastorf
    2008   *Heads of State: Icons, Power, and Politics in the Ancient and Modern Andes.* Walnut Creek, CA: Left Coast Press.

Arnon, Nancy, and W. W. Hill
    1979   Santa Clara Pueblo. In *Handbook of North American Indians.* Vol. 9. *Southwest,* edited by A. Ortiz, pp. 296–307. Washington, DC: Smithsonian Institution.

Asad, Talal
    1983   Anthropological Conceptions of Religion: Reflections on Geertz. *Man* 18(2):237–259.
    1993   *Genealogies of Religion: Disciplines and Reasons of Power in Christianity and Islam.* Baltimore: Johns Hopkins University Press.

Ashmore, Wendy
    2007   Building Social History at Pueblo Bonito. In *The Architecture of Chaco Canyon, New Mexico,* edited by S. H. Lekson, pp. 179–198. Provo: University of Utah Press.

Barth, Fredrik
    2002   An Anthropology of Knowledge. *Current Anthropology* 43(1):1–18.

Basso, Keith H.
    1996   *Wisdom Sits in Places: Landscape and Language among the Western Apache.* Albuquerque: University of New Mexico Press.

Baxter, M. J.
    1994   *Exploratory Multivariate Analysis in Archaeology.* Edinburgh: Edinburgh University Press.

Beals, Ralph
    1944   Relations between Mesoamerica and The Southwest. In *El Norte de México y el Sur de Estados Unidos,* pp. 245–252. Mexico City: Sociedad Mexicana de Antropología.

Beck, Robin A., Jr., Douglas J. Bolender, James A. Brown, and Timothy K. Earle
    2007   Eventful Archaeology: The Place of Space in Structural Transformation. *Current Anthropology* 48(6):833–860.

Bekaert, Stefan
    1998   Multiple Levels of Meaning and the Tension of Consciousness. *Archaeological Dialogues* 5(1):6–29.

Bell, Catherine
　1997　*Ritual: Perspectives and Dimensions*. Oxford: Oxford University Press.
Benitez, Alexander V.
　1998　*Refining 14th Century Jeddito Yellow Ware Chronology and its Distribution in Central Arizona*. Unpublished Master's thesis, Department of Anthropology University of Texas, Austin.
Benson, Larry, Kenneth Petersen, and John Stein
　2007　Anasazi (Pre-Columbian Native American) Migrations During the Middle-12th and Late-13th Centuries—Were They Drought Induced? *Climatic Change* 83:187–213.
Bernardini, Wesley
　1996　Transitions in Social Organization: A Predictive Model from Southwestern Colorado. *Journal of Anthropological Archaeology* 15:372–402.
　1998　Conflict, Migration, and the Social Environment: Interpreting Architectural Change in Early and Late Pueblo IV Aggregations. In *Migration and Reorganization: The Pueblo IV Period in the American Southwest*, edited by K. A. Spielmann, pp. 91–114. Anthropological Research papers, No. 51. Tempe: Arizona State University.
　2005　*Hopi Oral Tradition and the Archaeology of Identity*. Tucson: University of Arizona Press.
　2008　Identity as History: Hopi Clans and the Curation of Oral Tradition. *Journal of Anthropological Research* 64:483–509.
　n.d.　The 2008 Ancestral Hopi Villages Mapping Project Progress Report. Report on file at the Hopi Cultural Preservation Office, Kykotsmovi, Arizona.
Bernardini, Wesley, and Severin Fowles
　2011　Becoming Hopi, Becoming Tewa: Two Pueblo Histories of Movement. In *Movement, Connectivity, and Landscape Change in the Ancient Southwest*, edited by M. C. Nelson and C. Strawhacker. Boulder: University Press of Colorado.
Billman, Brian R., Patricia M. Lambert, and Banks L. Leonard
　2000　Cannibalism, Warfare, and Drought in the Mesa Verde Region During the Twelfth Century A.D. *American Antiquity* 65(1):145–178.
Bird-David, Nurit H.
　1999　"Animism" Revisited: Personhood, Environment, and Relational Epistemology. *Current Anthropology 40 (supplement)*:67–91.
Black, Mary E.
　1984　Maidens and Mothers: An Analysis of Hopi Corn Metaphors. *Ethnology* 23:279–288.
Blinman, Eric
　1989　Potluck in the Protokiva: Ceramics and Ceremonialism in Pueblo I Villages. In *The Architecture of Social Integration in Prehistoric Pueblos*,

edited by W. D. Lipe and M. Hegmon, pp. 113–124. Cortez, CO: Occasional Papers of the Crow Canyon Archaeological Center, No. 1.

Bloomer, W. W.
   1989   Moon House: A Pueblo III Cliff Dwelling Complex in Southeastern Utah. Master's thesis, Department of Anthropology, Washington State University.

Boivin, Nicole
   2009   Grasping the Elusive and Unknowable: Material Culture in Ritual Practice. *Material Religion* 5(3):266–287.

Boone, Elizabeth H., and Michael E. Smith
   2003   Postclassic International Styles and Symbol Sets. In *The Postclassic Mesoamerican World*, edited by M. E. Smith and F. F. Berdan, pp. 186–193. Salt Lake City: University of Utah Press.

Bourdieu, Pierre
   1977   *Outline of a Theory of Practice*. Translated by R. Nice. Cambridge: Cambridge University Press.
   1985   The Social Space and the Genesis of Groups. *Theory and Society* 14(6):723–744.
   1986   The Forms of Capital. In *Handbook of Theory and Research for the Sociology of Education*, edited by John G. Richardson, pp. 241–258. New York: Greenwood Press.
   1987   Legitimation and Structured Interest in Weber's Sociology of Religion. In *Max Weber, Rationality, and Modernity* edited by S. Whimster and S. Lash, pp. 119–136. London: Allen and Unwin.
   1989   Social Space and Symbolic Power. *Sociological Theory* 7(1):14–25.
   1990   *The Logic of Practice*. Stanford: Stanford University Press.

Bowie, Fiona
   2006   *The Anthropology of Religion: An Introduction*. Second ed. Malden, MA: Blackwell.

Bowser, Brenda J.
   2000   From Pottery to Politics: An Ethnoarchaeological Study of Political Factionalism, Ethnicity, and Domestic Pottery Style in the Ecuadorian Amazon. *Journal of Archaeological Method and Theory* 7(3):219–248.
   2002   The Perceptive Potter: An Ethnoarchaeological Study of Pottery, Ethnicity, and Political Action in Amazonia. Unpublished Ph.D. dissertation, Department of Anthropology, University of California, Santa Barbara.

Bowser, Brenda J., and John Patton
   2004   Domestic Spaces as Public Places: An Ethnoarchaeological Case Study of Houses, Gender, and Politics in the Ecuadorian Amazon. *Journal of Archaeological Method and Theory* 11(2):157–181.

Bradley, Bruce A.
　1996　Pitchers to Mugs: Chacoan Revival at Sand Canyon Pueblo. *Kiva* 61(3):241–256.

Bradley, Richard
　2000　*An Archaeology of Natural Places*. London: Routledge.
　2005　*Ritual and Domestic Life in Prehistoric Europe*. London: Routledge.

Bradley, Ronna
　1993　Marine Shell Exchange in Northwest Mexico and the Southwest. In *The American Southwest and Mesoamerica: Systems of Prehistoric Exchange*, edited by J. Ericson and T. G. Baugh, pp. 121–158. New York: Springer.

Brand, Donald D., Florence M. Hawley, and Frank C. Hibben
　1937　*Tseh So, A Small House Ruin, Chaco Canyon, New Mexico*. Albuquerque: University of New Mexico Press.

Brandt, Elizabeth A.
　1979　Sandia Pueblo. In *Handbook of North American Indians*. Vol. 9. *Southwest*, edited by A. Ortiz, pp. 343–350. Washington, DC: Smithsonian Institution.
　1980　On Secrecy and the Control of Knowledge: Taos Pueblo. In *Secrecy: A Cross-Cultural Perspective*, edited by S. K. Tefft, pp. 123–146. New York: Human Sciences Press.
　1994　Egalitarianism, Hierarchy, and Centralization in the Pueblos. In *The Ancient Southwestern Community: Models and Methods for the Study of Prehistoric Social Organization*, edited by W. H. Wills and R. D. Leonard, pp. 9–23. Albuquerque: University of New Mexico Press.

Brandt, Richard
　1954　*Hopi Ethics: A Theoretical Analysis*. Chicago: University of Chicago Press.

Braniff, Beatriz
　1974　Sequencias Arqueológicas en Guanajuato y la Cuenca de México: Intento de Correlación. In *Teotihuacan: XI Mesa Redonda*, pp. 273–323. Mexico City: Sociedad Mexicana de Antropología.

Breternitz, David A., Arthur H. Rohn, and Elizabeth A. Morris
　1974　*Prehistoric Ceramics of the Mesa Verde Region*. Museum of Northern Arizona, Ceramic Series No. 5. Flagstaff: The Northern Arizona Society of Science and Art.

Brew, J. O.
　1943　On the Pueblo IV and on the Katchina-Tlaloc Relations. In *El Norte de Mexico y El Sur de Estados Unidos, Tercera Reunión de Mesa Redonda sobre Problemas Antropológicos de México y Centro América*, pp. 241–245. Mexico City: Sociedad Mexicana de Antropologia.

Broda, Johanna Prucha
　2004　Paisajes Rituales Entre Los Indios Pueblo y Mexica: Una Comparación.

In *Desierto y Fronteras: El Norte de México y Otros Contextos*, edited by H. Salas and R. Pérez, pp. 265–295. México, DF: Plaza y Valdes

Brody, J. J.
- 1989 Site Use, Pictorial Space, and Subject Matter in Late Prehistoric and Early Historic Rio Grande Pueblo Art. *Journal of Anthropological Research* 45:15–28.
- 1991 *Anasazi and Pueblo Painting.* Santa Fe, NM: School of American Research Press.
- 2007 A Preliminary Analysis of the Petroglyphs of the Creston and Galisteo Dikes, Galisteo Basin, New Mexico. Paper presented at the New Mexico Archaeological Council Fall Conference, Albuquerque.

Brown, Donald
- 1979 Picuris Pueblo. In *Handbook of North American Indians*. Vol. 9. *Southwest*, edited by A. Ortiz, pp. 268–277. Washington, DC: Smithsonian Institution.

Brown, Emily J.
- 2005 Instruments of Power: Musical Performance in the Rituals of the Ancestral Puebloans of the American Southwest. Ph.D. dissertation, Department of Anthropology, Columbia University.

Brown, Gary, Thomas C. Windes, and Peter J. McKenna
- 2008 Animas Anamnesis: Aztec Ruins or Anasazi Capital? In *Chaco's Northern Prodigies: Salmon, Aztec, and the Ascendancy of the Middle San Juan Region After A.D. 1100*, edited by P. F. Reed, pp. 231–250. Salt Lake City: University of Utah Press.

Brown, Joseph Epes
- 1977 *The Spiritual Legacy of the American Indian*. New York: Crossroad Publishing.

Bugé, David E.
- 1984 Prehistoric Subsistence Strategies in the Ojo Caliente Valley New Mexico. In *Prehistoric Agricultural Strategies in the Southwest*, edited by S. K. Fish and P. R. Fish, pp. 27–34. Anthropological Research Papers 33. Tempe: Arizona State University.

Bunzel, Ruth L.
- 1929 *The Pueblo Potter: A Study of Creative Imagination in Primitive Art*. New York: Columbia University Press.
- 1932a "Zuni Origin Myths" and "Zuni Ceremonialism." In *Forty-Seventh Annual Report of the Bureau of American Ethnology*, pp 467–835. Washington, DC: Government Printing Office.
- 1932b "*Zuñi Katcinas*." In *Forty-Seventh Annual Report of the Bureau of American Ethnology Annual Report*, pp. 837–1086. Washington, DC: Government Printing Office.
- 1992 *Zuni Ceremonialism*. Albuquerque: University of New Mexico Press.

Cameron, Catherine M.
- 1992 An Analysis of Residential Patterns and the Oraibi Split. *Journal of Anthropological Archaeology* 11:173–186.
- 1995 Migration and the Movement of Southwestern Peoples. *Journal of Anthropological Archaeology* 14(2):104–124.
- 1999 Room Size, Organization of Construction, and Archaeological Interpretation in the Puebloan Southwest. *Journal of Anthropological Archaeology* 18:201–239.
- 2005 Exploring Archaeological Cultures in the Northern Southwest: What Were Chaco and Mesa Verde? *Kiva* 70(3):227–254.

Cameron, Catherine M., and Andrew I. Duff
- 2008 History and Process in Village Formation: Context and Contrasts from the Northern Southwest. *American Antiquity* 73(1):29–58.

Campbell, L.
- 1998 *Historical Linguistics: An Introduction.* Cambridge, MA: MIT Press.

Carlsen, Robert S.
- 1997 *The War for the Heart and Soul of a Maya Town.* Austin: University of Texas Press.

Carlson, Roy L.
- 1970 *White Mountain Redware: A Pottery Tradition of East-Central Arizona and Western New Mexico.* University of Arizona Anthropological Papers 19. Tucson: University of Arizona Press.

Carot, Patricia
- 2001 *Le site de Loma Alta, Lac de Zacapu, Michoacan, Mexique.* Paris Monographs in American Archaeology 9, BAR International Series 920. Oxford: Archaeopress.

Carot, Patricia, and Marie-Areti Hers
- 2008 Epic of the Toltec Chichimec and Purépecah in the Ancient Southwest. In *Archaeology without Borders: Contact, Commerce, and Change in the US Southwest and Northwestern Mexico*, edited by L. D. Webster and M. E. McBrinn, pp.301–334. Boulder: University Press of Colorado.

Carpenter, John P.
- 1996 El Ombligo en la Labor: Differentiation, Interaction and Integration in Prehistoric Sinaloa. Ph.D. dissertation, Department of Anthropology, University of Arizona.
- 2008 El Conjunto Mortuorio de el Ombligo: Su Análisis e Interpretación. In *Excavaciones en Gusave, Sinaloa,* by G. F. Ekholm, pp. 149–181, Mexico: Siglio XXI Editores.

Carrasco, David
- 1990 *Religions of Mesoamerica: Cosmovision and Ceremonial Centers.* Prospect Heights, IL: Waveland Press.

Chamberlin, Matthew
    2008   Evaluating the Cultural Origins of Complexity in the Ancestral Pueblo World. Ph.D. dissertation, Department of Anthropology, Arizona State University.
    2006   Symbolic Conflict and the Spatiality of Traditions in Small-scale Societies. *Cambridge Archaeological Journal* 16(1):39–51.

Chapple, Eliot D., and Carleton S. Coon
    1942   *Principles of Anthropology*. New York: Henry Holt.

Chilton, Elizabeth S. (editor)
    1999   *Material Meanings: Critical Approaches to the Interpretation of Material Culture*. Salt Lake City: University of Utah Press.

Chuipka, Jason, and Jerry Fetterman
    2009   Examining Orthodoxy in the Upper San Juan Region of the Northern Southwest. Paper presented in at the 74th Annual Society for American Archaeology Meeting, Atlanta.

Churchill, Melissa J., Kristin A. Kuckelman, and Mark D. Varien
    1998   Public Architecture in the Mesa Verde Region, A.D. 900 to 1300. Paper presented at the 63rd Annual Meeting of the Society for American Archaeology, Seattle.

Clark, Jeffrey
    2001   *Tracking Prehistoric Migrations: Pueblo Settlers among the Tonto Basin Hohokam*. Tucson: University of Arizona Press.

Clark, Jeffrey, Patrick D. Lyons, J. Brett Hill, Anna A. Neuzil, and William H. Doelle
    2008   Immigrants and Population Collapse in the Southern Southwest. *Archaeology Southwest* 22(4).

Clark, T. J.
    1984   *The Painting of Modern Life: Paris in the Art of Manet and His Followers*. New York: Knopf.

Cole, Sally J.
    1996   Imagery and Tradition: Murals of the Mesa Verde Region. In *The Mesa Verde World: Explorations in Ancestral Pueblo Archaeology*, edited by David Grant Noble, pp. 93–100. Santa Fe, NM: School of American Research Press.

Colton, Harold
    1955   *Pottery Types of the Southwest: Tusayan Gray and White Wares, Little Colorado Gray and White Wares; Wares 8A, 8B, 9A, 9B*. Ceramic Series No. 3A. Flagstaff: Museum of Northern Arizona.
    1974   Hopi History and Ethnobotany. In *Hopi Indians*, edited by D. A. Horr. New York: Garland.

Connelly, John C.
    1979   Hopi Social Organization. In *Handbook of North American Indians*,

Vol. 9, edited by Alfonso Ortiz, pp. 539–553. Washington, DC: Smithsonian Institution.

Connerton, Paul
  1989   *How Societies Remember*. Cambridge: Cambridge University Press.

Cordell, Linda S.
  1996   Big Sites, Big Questions: Pueblos in Transition. In *The Prehistoric Pueblo World, AD 1150–1350*, edited by M. Adler, pp. 228–240. Tucson: University of Arizona Press.
  2000   Aftermath of Chaos in the Pueblo Southwest. In *Environmental Disaster and the Archaeology of Human Response*, edited by Garth Bawden and Richard M. Reycraft, pp. 179–193. Maxwell Museum of Anthropology, Anthropological Papers No. 7. Albuquerque: University of New Mexico.

Cordell, Linda S., and George J. Gumerman
  1989   Cultural Interaction in the Prehistoric Southwest. In *Dynamics of Southwestern Prehistory*, edited by L. S. Cordell and G. J. Gumerman, pp. 1–17. Washington, DC: Smithsonian Institution Press.

Cordell, Linda S. and Fred Plog
  1979   Escaping the Confines of Normative Thought: A Reevaluation of Puebloan Prehistory. *American Antiquity* 44(3):405–429.

Cordell, Linda S., H. Wolcott Toll, Mollie S. Toll, and Thomas C. Windes
  2008   Archaeological Corn from Pueblo Bonito, Chaco Canyon, New Mexico: Dates, Contexts, Sources. *American Antiquity* 73:1–21.

Cordell, Linda S., Carla R. Van West, Jeffrey S. Dean, and Deborah A. Muenchrath
  2007   Mesa Verde Settlement History and Relocation: Climate Change, Social Networks, and Ancestral Pueblo Migration. *Kiva* 72:379–405.

Creamer, Winifred
  1993   *The Architecture of Arroyo Hondo Pueblo, New Mexico*. Arroyo Hondo Archaeological Series 7. Santa Fe, NM: School of American Research Press.

Crotty, Helen K.
  1992   Protohistoric Anasazi Kiva Murals: Variation in Imagery as a Reflection of Differing Social Contexts. In *Archaeology, Art, and Anthropology: Papers in Honor of J. J. Brody*, edited by M. S. Duran and D. T. Kirkpatrick, pp. 51–61. Papers of the Archaeological Society of New Mexico, Vol. 18. Albuquerque: Archaeological Society of New Mexico.
  1995   Anasazi Mural Art of the Pueblo IV Period, A.D. 1300–1600: Influences, Selective Adaptation, and Cultural Diversity in the Prehistoric Southwest. Unpublished Ph.D. dissertation, Department of Art History, University of California, Los Angeles.
  2007   Western Pueblo Influences and Integration in the Pottery Mound

Painted Kivas. In *New Perspectives on Pottery Mound Pueblo*, edited by Polly Schaafsma, pp. 85–107. Albuquerque: University of New Mexico Press.

Crown, Patricia L.
1994 *Ceramics and Ideology: Salado Polychrome Pottery*. Albuquerque: University of New Mexico Press.
1996 Change in Ceramic Design Style and Technology in the 13th to 14th Century Southwest. In *Interpreting Southwestern Diversity: Underlying Principles and Overarching Patterns*, edited by P. R. Fish and J. J. Reid, pp. 241–247. Anthropological Research Papers 48. Tempe: Arizona State University.
1998 Changing Perspectives on the Pueblo IV World. In *Migration and Reorganization: The Pueblo IV Period in the American Southwest*, edited by Katherine A. Spielmann, pp. 293–299. Arizona State University Anthropological Research Papers 51. Tempe: Arizona State University.
1999 Socialization in American Southwest Pottery Decoration. In *Pottery and People: A Dynamic Interpretation*, edited by J. M. Skibo and G. M. Feinman, pp. 25–43. Salt Lake City: University of Utah Press.

Crown, Patricia L., and W. Jeffrey Hurst
2009 Evidence of Cacao Use in the Prehispanic American Southwest. *Proceedings of the National Academy of Science* 106:2110–2113.

Curtis, Edward S.
1922 *The North American Indian*. Vol. 12, *The Hopi*. New York: Aperture.

Cushing, Frank H.
1886 A Study of Pueblo Pottery as Illustrative of Zuni Culture Growth. In *Fourth Annual Report of the Smithsonian Institution*. Washington, DC: Government Printing Office.

Davis, Irvine
1959 Linguistic Clues to Northern Rio Grande Prehistory. *El Palacio* 66 (June):73–84.

Dean, Jeffrey S.
1996a Demography, Environment, and Subsistence Stress. In *Evolving Complexity and Environmental Risk in the Prehistoric Southwest*, edited by J. A. Tainter and B. Bagley Tainter, pp. 25–26. Santa Fe Institute Studies in the Sciences of Complexity, Proceedings Volume 24. Reading, MA: Addison-Wesley Publishing.
1996b Kayenta Anasazi Settlement Transformations in Northeastern Arizona, A.D. 1150 to 1350. In *The Prehistoric Pueblo World, A.D. 1150–1350*, edited by M. A. Adler, pp. 29–47. Tucson: University of Arizona Press.
2002 Late Pueblo II–Pueblo III Kayenta-Branch Prehistory. In *Prehistoric Change on the Colorado Plateau: 10,000 Years on Black Mesa*, edited by S. Powell, pp. 121–157. Tucson: University of Arizona Press.

2010   Environmental, Demographic, and Behavioral Context of the Thirteenth Century Depopulation of the Northern Southwest. In *Time of Peril, Time of Change: Explaining Thirteenth Century Pueblo Migrations*, edited by Timothy A. Kohler, Mark D. Varien, and Aaron M. Wright. Tucson: University of Arizona Press.

Dean, Jeffrey S., Robert C. Euler, George J. Gumerman, Fred Plog, Richard H. Hevly, and Thor N. V. Karlstrom
1985   Human Behavior, Demography, and Paleoenvironment on the Colorado Plateaus. *American Antiquity* 50(3):537–554.

Dean, Jeffrey S., and John C. Ravesloot
1993   The Chronology of Cultural Interaction in the Gran Chichimeca. In *Culture and Contact, Charles C. Di Peso's Gran Chichimeca*, edited by A. I. Woolsey and J. C. Ravesloot, pp. 83–103. Albuquerque: University of New Mexico Press.

Dietler, Michael, and Ingrid Herbich
1998   Habitus, Techniques, Style: An Integrated Approach to the Social Understanding of Material Culture and Boundaries. In *The Archaeology of Social Boundaries*, edited by M. L. Stark, pp. 232–263. Washington, DC: Smithsonian Institution Press.

Di Peso, Charles C.
1974   *Casas Grandes: A Fallen Trade Center of the Gran Chichimeca*. Vols. 1–3. Flagstaff, AZ: Northland Press.

Di Peso, Charles C., John B. Rinaldo, and Gloria J. Fenner
1974   *Casas Grandes: A Fallen Trading Center of the Gran Chichimeca*. Vol. 8. Flagstaff, AZ: Northland Press.

Dobres, Marcia-Anne
1999   Of Paradigms and Ways of Seeing: Artifact Variability as If People Mattered. In *Material Meanings: Critical Approaches to the Interpretation of Material Culture*, edited by E. S. Chilton, pp. 7–23. Salt Lake City: University of Utah Press.

Dobres, Marcia-Anne, and John Robb
2005   "Doing" Agency: Introductory Remarks on Methodology. *Journal of Archaeological Method and Theory* 12(3):159–166.

Dongoske, Kurt, M. Yeatts, Roger Anyon, and T. J. Ferguson
1997   Archaeological Cultures and Cultural Affiliation: Hopi and Zuni Perspectives in the American Southwest. *American Antiquity* 62(2):600–608.

Dorsey, James Owen
1894   A Study of Siouan Cults. In *Eleventh Annual Report of the Bureau of Ethnology*, pp. 351–554. Washington, DC: Government Printing Office.

Douglass, William B.
1917   Notes on the Shrines of the Tewa and Other Pueblo Indians of New

Mexico. In *Proceedings of the 19th International Congress of Americanists*, edited by E. W. Hodge, pp. 344–378. Washington, DC: U.S. National Museum.

Dowd, Gregory Evans
 1992 *A Spirited Resistance: The North American Indian Struggle for Unity, 1745–1815*. Baltimore: John Hopkins University Press.

Doyel, David E.
 2000 Salado in Chihuahua. In *Salado*, edited by J. S. Dean. Dragoon, AZ: Amerind Foundation.

Dozier, Edward P.
 1958 Cultural Matrix of Singing and Dancing in Tewa Pueblos. *International Journal of American Linguistics* 24(4):268–272.
 1970 *The Pueblo Indians of North America*. New York: Holt, Rinehart, and Winston.

Driver, Jonathan C.
 2002 Faunal Variation and Change in the Northern San Juan Region. In *Seeking the Center Place: Archaeology and Ancient Communities in the Mesa Verde Region*, edited by M. D. Varien and R. H. Wilshusen, pp. 143–160. Salt Lake City: University of Utah Press.

Duff, Andrew I.
 2002 *Western Pueblo Identities: Regional Interaction, Migration, and Transformation*. Tucson: University of Arizona Press.

Duff, Andrew I., and Richard H. Wilshusen
 2000 Prehistoric Population Dynamics in the Northern San Juan Region, A.D. 950–1300. *Kiva* 66(1):167–190.

Durkheim, Emile
 1965 *The Elementary Forms of the Religious Life* (originally published 1912). New York: Free Press.

Dutton, Bertha P.
 1963 *Sun Father's Way*. Albuquerque: University of New Mexico Press.

Dvorak, Max
 1967 *Idealism and Naturalism in Gothic Art*. Translated by Randolph J. Klawiter. South Bend, IN: University of Notre Dame Press. Originally published as *Idealismus und Naturalismus in der gottischen Skulptur und Malerei, Historische Zeitschrift* CXIX (1918), pp. 1–62.
 1984 *The History of Art as the History of Ideas*. Translated by John Hardy. London: Routledge and Kegan Paul. Originally published as *Kunstgeschichte als Geistesgeschichte*, Munich, 1924.

Edelman, Sandra, and Alfonso Ortiz
 1979 Tesuque Pueblo In *Handbook of North American Indians*. Vol. 9. *Southwest*, edited by Alfonso Ortiz, pp. 330–335. Washington DC: Smithsonian Institution.

Edwards, Elizabeth, Chris Gosden, and Ruth B. Phillips (editors)
    2006   *Sensible Objects: Colonialism, Museums and Material Culture.* New York: Berg.

Eggan, Fred
    1950   *Social Organization of the Western Pueblos.* Chicago: University of Chicago Press.
    1966   *The American Indian: Perspectives for the Study of Social Change.* Chicago: Aldine.

Eliade, Mircea
    1991   *The Myth of the Eternal Return or, Cosmos and History* (originally published 1954). Princeton, NJ: Princeton University Press.

Emerson, Thomas E., and Timothy R. Pauketat
    2008   Historical-Processual Archaeology and Culture Making: Unpacking the Southern Cult and Mississippian Religion. In *Belief in the Past: Theoretical Approaches to the Archaeology of Religion*, edited by D. S. Whitley and K. Hays-Gilpin, pp. 167–188. Walnut Creek, CA: Left Coast Press.

Evans-Pritchard, E. E.
    1965   *Theories of Primitive Religion.* Oxford: Clarendon Press.

Fallon, Denise, and Karen Wening
    1987   *Howiri: Excavations at a Northern Rio Grande Biscuit Ware Site.* Laboratory of Anthropology Notes 261b. Santa Fe: Museum of New Mexico.

Feinman, Gary, Kent Lightfoot, and Steadman Upham
    2000   Political Hierarchies and Organizational Strategies in the Puebloan Southwest. *American Antiquity* 65(3):449–470.

Feld, Steven, and Keith H. Basso (editors)
    1996   *Senses of Place.* Santa Fe: School of American Research Press.

Ferg, Alan
    1982   14th Century Kachina Depiction on Ceramics. In *Collected Papers in Honor of J. W. Runyon*, edited by G. X. Fitzgerald, pp. 13–29. Papers of the Archaeological Society of New Mexico, No. 7. Albuquerque: Archaeological Society of New Mexico.

Ferguson, T. J.
    2003   Yep Hisat Hoopoq'yaqam Teesiwa (Hopi Ancestors Were Once Here): Hopi-Hohokam Cultural Affiliation Study. Report prepared for the Hopi Cultural Preservation Office, Kykotsmovi, Arizona.

Ferguson, T. J., Kurt Dongoske, Leigh Jenkins, Eric Polingyouma, and Michael Yeatts
    1993   Working Together: The Roles of Archaeology and Ethnohistory in Hopi Cultural Preservation. *CRM 16* (Special Issue):27–37.

Ferguson, T. J., and M. Lomaomvaya
    1999   Hoopoq'uaqam niqw Wukoskyavi (Those Who Went to the Northeast and Tonto Basin): Hopi-Salado Cultural Affiliation Study. Report pre-

pared for the Hopi Cultural Preservation Office, Kykotsmovi, Arizona.

Fewkes, Jesse Walter
- 1891 A Few Summer Ceremonials at Zuñi Pueblo. *Journal of American Ethnology and Archæology* 1:1–62.
- 1892 A Few Summer Ceremonials at the Tusayan Pueblos. *Journal of American Ethnology and Archæology* 2:1–161.
- 1900 Tusayan Migration Traditions. In *19th Annual Report of the Bureau of American Ethnology for the Years 1897–1898*, Pt. 2, pp. 573–634. Washington, DC: Government Printing Office
- 1904 Two Summers' Work in Pueblo Ruins. In *22nd Annual Report of the Bureau of American Ethnology, Part 1*, pp. 1–196. Washington, DC: Government Printing Office.
- 1907 Hopi. In *Handbook of American Indians North of Mexico*, edited by F. Hodge, pp. 550–567. Smithsonian Institution, Bureau of American Ethnology, Bulletin 30. Washington, DC: Government Printing Office.
- 1909 *Antiquities of the Mesa Verde National Park: Spruce Tree House*. Bureau of American Ethnology Bulletin No. 49, Washington, DC: Government Printing Office.

Fiero, Kathleen
- 1999 *Balcony House: A History of a Cliff Dwelling*. Mesa Verde National Park Archeological Research Series Number Eight-A. Cortez, CO: Mesa Verde Museum Association, Inc., Mesa Verde National Park.

Firth, Raymond
- 1996 *Religion: A Humanist Interpretation*. New York: Routledge.

Florance, Charles A.
- 1985 Recent Work in the Chupícuaro Region. In *The Archaeology of West and Northwest Mesoamerica*, edited by M. S. Foster and P. C. Weigand, pp. 9–46. Boulder, CO: Westview Press.

Fogelin, Lars
- 2007 The Archaeology of Religious Ritual. *Annual Review of Anthropology* 36:55–71.
- 2008 Methods for the Archaeology of Religion. In *Religion, Archaeology, and the Material World*, edited by L. Fogelin, pp. 1–14. Occasional Paper No. 36, Center for Archaeological Investigations. Carbondale: Southern Illinois University.

Ford, Richard I., Albert H. Schroeder, and Stewart L. Peckham
- 1972 Three Perspectives on Puebloan Prehistory. In *New Perspectives on the Pueblos*, edited by Alfonso Ortiz, pp. 19–39. Albuquerque: University of New Mexico Press.

Foster, Michael S.
- 1982 The Loma San Gabriel-Mogollon Continuum. In *Mogollon Archaeol-

　　　　　ogy: Proceedings of the 1980 Mogollon Conference, edited by P. H. Beckett and K. Silverbird, pp. 251–261. Ramona, CA: Acoma Books.
　　1999　The Azatlán Tradition of West and Northwest Mexico and Casas Grandes. In *The Casas Grandes World*, edited by C. F. Schaafsma and C. L. Riley, pp. 149–163. Provo: University of Utah Press.

Foucault, Michel
　　1977　*Discipline and Punish: The Birth of the Prison*. London: Penguin.

Fowler, Chris
　　2004　*The Archaeology of Personhood: An Anthropological Approach*. London: Routledge.

Fowles, Severin
　　2004　Tewa versus Tiwa: Northern Rio Grande Settlement Patterns and Social History, A.D. 1275 to 1540. In *The Protohistoric Pueblo World, A.D. 1275–1600*, edited by E. C. Adams and A. I. Duff, pp. 17–25. Tucson: University of Arizona Press.
　　2008　Steps toward an Archaeology of Taboo. In *Religion, Archaeology, and the Material World*, edited by L. Fogelin. Center for Archaeological Investigations, Occasional Paper No. 36. Carbondale: Southern Illinois University.

Frigout, Arlette
　　1979　Hopi Ceremonial Organization. In *Handbook of North American Indians*. Vol. 9. *Southwest*, edited by A. Ortiz, pp. 564–576. Washington, DC: Smithsonian Institution.

Fritz, John
　　1978　Paleopsychology Today: Ideational Systems and Human Adaptation in Prehistory. In *Social Archaeology: Beyond Subsistence and Dating*, edited by C. L. Redman, E. V. Curtain, W. T. Langhorn, N. M. Versaggi, and J. C. Wanser, pp. 37–59. New York: Academic.

Furst, Peter T.
　　1973　West Mexican Art: Secular or Sacred? In *The Iconography of Middle American Sculpture*, edited by I. Bernal, M. D. Coe, G. Kubler, G. R. Willey, and J. E. Thompson, pp. 99–133. New York: Metropolitan Museum of Art.

Gauthier, Rory, and Cynthia Herhahn
　　2005　Why Would Anyone Want to Farm Here? In *The Peopling of Bandelier: New Insights from the Archaeology of the Pajarito Plateau*, edited by R. P. Powers, pp. 27–34. Santa Fe, NM: School of American Research Press.

Geertz, Armin
　　1986　A Typology of Hopi Indian Ritual. *Temenos* 22: 41–56.

Geertz, Clifford
　　1973　*The Interpretation of Cultures*. New York: Basic.

Gell, Alfred
　　1998　*Art and Agency: An Anthropological Theory*. Oxford: Clarendon Press.

Gilpin, Dennis
   1989   Great Houses and Pueblos in Northeastern Arizona. Paper presented at the 1989 Pecos Conference, Los Alamos, New Mexico.

Glowacki, Donna M.
   2006   The Social Landscape of Depopulation: the Northern San Juan, A.D. 1150–1300. Unpublished Ph.D. dissertation, Department of Anthropology, Arizona State University, Tempe.
   2010   The Social and Cultural Contexts of the Central Mesa Verde Region During the Thirteenth-Century Migrations. In *Leaving Mesa Verde: Peril and Change in the 13th Century Southwest*, edited by T. Kohler, M. D. Varien and A. Wright. Tucson: University of Arizona Press.

Glowacki, Donna M., and Scott G. Ortman
   In press Characterizing Community Center (Village) Formation in the VEP Study Area, A.D. 600–1280. In *Emergence and Collapse of Early Villages: Models of Central Mesa Verde Archaeology*, edited by T. A. Kohler and M. D. Varien. Berkeley: University of California Press.

Gonlin, Nancy, and John C. Lohse (editors)
   2007   *Commoner Ritual and Ideology in Ancient Mesoamerica*. Boulder: University Press of Colorado.

Gosden, Chris
   1994   *Social Being and Time*. Oxford: Blackwell.

Graves, William M.
   2002   Power, Autonomy, and Inequality in Rio Grande Puebloan Society, A.D. 1300–1672. Unpublished Ph.D. dissertation, Department of Anthropology, Arizona State University, Tempe.

Graves, William M., and Suzanne L. Eckert
   1998   Decorated Ceramic Distributions and Ideological Developments in the Northern and Central Rio Grande Valley, New Mexico. In *Migration and Reorganization: The Pueblo IV Period in the American Southwest*, edited by K. A. Spielmann, pp. 263–283. Anthropological Research Papers. Vol. 51. Tempe: Arizona State University.

Graves, William M., and Katherine Spielmann
   2000   Leadership, Long Distance Exchange, and Feasting in the Protohistoric Rio Grande. In *Alternative Leadership Strategies in the Prehispanic Southwest*, edited by B. J. Mills, pp. 45–59. Tucson: University of Arizona Press.

Graves, William M., and Scott Van Keuren
   2011   Ancestral Pueblo Villages and the Panoptic Gaze of the Commune. *Cambridge Archaeological Journal* 21(2):263–282.

Greenlee, Robert
   1933   *Archaeological Sites in the Chama Valley, and Report on Excavations at Tsama, 1929–1933*. Manuscript on file (P651), Laboratory of Anthropology, Santa Fe: Museum of New Mexico.

Gregory, David A., and David R. Wilcox
2007   A New Research Design for Studying Zuni Origins. In *Zuni Origins: Toward a New Synthesis of Southwestern Archaeology*, edited by D. A. Gregory and D. R. Wilcox. Tucson: University of Arizona Press.

Haas, Jonathan, and Winifred Creamer
1993   Stress and Warfare among the Prehistoric Kayenta Anasazi of the Thirteenth Century. *Fieldiana: Anthropology 21*. Chicago: Field Museum of Natural History.

Habicht-Mauche, Judith A.
1993   *The Pottery from Arroyo Hondo Pueblo, New Mexico: Tribalization and Trade in the Northern Rio Grande*. Arroyo Hondo Archaeological Series 8. Santa Fe, NM: School of American Research Press.
2006   The Social History of Southwestern Glaze Wares. In *The Social Life of Pots: Glaze Wares and Cultural Dynamics in the Southwest, AD 1250–1680*, edited by J. A. Habicht-Mauche, D. L. Huntley, and S. L. Eckert, pp. 3–16. Tucson: University of Arizona Press.

Hagstrum, Melissa B.
1995   Creativity and Craft: Household Pottery Traditions in the Southwest. In *Ceramic Production in the American Southwest*, edited by B. J. Mills and P. L. Crown, pp. 281–299. Tucson: University of Arizona Press.

Halbwachs, Maurice
1992   *On Collective Memory*. Translated by L. Coser. Chicago: University of Chicago Press.

Hale, Kenneth L.
1967   Toward a Reconstruction of Kiowa-Tanoan Phonology. *International Journal of American Linguistics* 33(2):112–120.

Hale, Kenneth L., and David Harris
1979   Historical Linguistics and Archeology. In *Handbook of North American Indians*. Vol. 9. *Southwest*, edited by A. Ortiz, pp. 170–177. Washington, DC: Smithsonian Institution.

Hall, Edward T.
1966   *The Hidden Dimension*. Garden City, NY: Doubleday.
1968   Proxemics. *Current Anthropology* 9(2/3):83–108.

Hammond, George P., and Agapito Rey
1966   *The Rediscovery of New Mexico, 1580–1594*. Albuquerque: University of New Mexico Press.

Hardin, Margaret Ann
1979   The Cognitive Basis of Productivity in a Decorative Art Style: Implications of an Ethnographic Study for Archaeologists' Taxonomies. In *Ethnoarchaeology: Implications of Ethnography for Archaeology*, edited by C. Kramer, pp. 75–101. New York: Columbia University Press.

Harkins, Michael E.
2004   Revitalization as History and Theory. In *Reassessing Revitalization Move-

ments: Perspectives from North America and the Pacific Islands, edited by M. E. Harkins, pp. xv–xxxvi. Lincoln: University of Nebraska Press.

Harrington, John P.
- 1909 Notes on the Piro Language. *American Anthropologist* 11(4):563–594.
- 1910 An Introductory Paper on the Tiwa Language, Dialect of Taos, New Mexico. *American Anthropologist* 12:11–48.
- 1916 Ethnogeography of the Tewa Indians. In *29th Annual Report of the Bureau of American Ethnology*, pp. 29–618. Washington, DC: Government Printing Office.

Haury, Emil W.
- 1950 A Sequence of Great Kivas in the Forestdale Valley, Arizona. In *For the Dean*, edited by Eric K. Reed and Dale S. King, pp. 29–39. Sante Fe: Hohokam Museums Association and the Southwestern Monuments Association.
- 1976 *The Hohokam: Desert Farmers and Craftsmen.* Tucson: University of Arizona Press.
- 1985 *Mogollon Culture in the Forestdale Valley, East-central Arizona.* Tucson: University of Arizona Press.

Haury, Emil W., and Lyndon L. Hargrave
- 1931 *Recently Dated Pueblo Ruins in Arizona.* Smithsonian Miscellaneous Collections Vol. 82, No. 11. Publication 3069. Washington, DC: Government Printing Office.

Hawkes, Christopher
- 1954 Archeological Theory and Method: Some Suggestions from the Old World. *American Anthropologist* 56(2):155–168.

Hayes, Alden
- 1981 *Excavation of Mound 7, Gran Quivira National Monument, New Mexico.* Publications in Archaeology No. 16. Washington, DC: National Park Service.

Hays, Kelley A.
- 1989 Katsina Depictions on Homol'ovi Ceramics: Toward a Fourteenth-Century Pueblo Iconography. *Kiva* 54(3):297–313.
- 1994 Kachina Depictions on Prehistoric Pueblo Pottery. In *Kachinas in the Pueblo World*, edited by P. Schaafsma, pp. 47–62. Albuquerque: University of New Mexico Press.

Hays-Gilpin, Kelley A.
- 2000 Gender Ideology and Ritual Activities. In *Women and Men in the Prehispanic Southwest: Labor, Power, and Prestige*, edited by P. L. Crown, pp. 91–135. Santa Fe, NM: School of American Research Press.
- 2004 *Ambiguous Images: Gender and Rock Art.* Walnut Creek, CA: AltaMira.
- 2006 Icons and Ethnicity: Hopi Painted Pottery and Murals. In *Religion in the Prehispanic Southwest*, edited by C. S. VanPool, T. L. VanPool, and D. A. Phillips, pp. 67–80. Lanham, MD: AltaMira.

2008   Life's Pathways: Geographic Metaphors in Ancestral Puebloan Material Culture. In *Archaeology without Borders: Contact, Commerce and Change in the US Southwest and Northwestern Mexico*, edited by L. Webster and M. McBrinn, pp. 257–270. Boulder: University Press of Colorado.

Hays-Gilpin, Kelley A, Trixi D. Bubemyre, and Louise Senior
  1996   The Rise and Demise of Winslow Orange Ware. In *River of Change: Prehistory of the Middle Little Colorado River Valley, Arizona*, edited by E. C. Adams, pp. 53–74. Arizona State Museum Archaeological Series 185. Tucson: Arizona State Museum.

Hays-Gilpin, Kelley A., and Jane Hill
  2000   The Flower World in Prehistoric Southwest Material Culture. In *The Archaeology of Regional Interaction: Religion, Warfare, and Exchange Across the American Southwest and Beyond*, edited by M. Hegmon, pp. 411–428. Boulder: University Press of Colorado.

Hays-Gilpin, Kelley A., and Steven A. LeBlanc
  2007   Sikyatki Style in Regional Context. In *New Perspectives on Pottery Mound Pueblo*, edited by P. Schaafsma, pp. 109–136. Albuquerque: University of New Mexico Press.

Head, Genevieve, and James E. Snead
  1992   Recycling the Cultural Landscape: Prehistoric Site Reuse on the Pajarito Plateau, New Mexico. Paper presented at the 57th annual meeting of the Society for American Archaeology, Pittsburgh, Pennsylvania.

Heckenberger, Michael J.
  2005   *The Ecology of Power: Culture, Place, and Personhood in the Southern Amazon, A.D. 1000–2000*. New York: Routledge.

Hegmon, Michelle
  1991   Six Easy Steps to Dating Pueblo III Ceramic Assemblages: Working Draft. Manuscript on file, Crow Canyon Archaeological Center, Cortez, Colorado.
  2003   Setting Theoretical Egos Aside: Issues and Theory in North American Archaeology. *American Antiquity* 68(2):213–243.
  2010   Mimbres Society: Another Way of Being. In *Mimbres Lives and Landscape*, edited by M. C. Nelson and M. Hegmon. Santa Fe, NM: School of American Research.

Hegmon, Michelle (editor)
  2000   *The Archaeology of Regional Interaction: Religion, Warfare, and Exchange Across the American Southwest and Beyond*. Boulder: University Press of Colorado.

Heitman, Carrie C.
  2011   Architectures of Inequality: Evaluating Houses, Kinship and Cosmology in Chaco Canyon, New Mexico A.D. 800–1200. Ph.D. dissertation, Department of Anthropology, University of Virginia, Charlottesville.

Helms, Mary
  1998 *Access to Origins: Affines, Ancestors, and Aristocrats*. Austin: University of Texas Press.
Herr, Sarah
  2001 *Beyond Chaco: Great Kiva Communities along the Mogollon Rim Frontier*. Anthropological Papers 66 of the University of Arizona. Tucson: University of Arizona Press.
Hers, Marie-Areti
  2001 Zacatecas y Durango, Los Confines Tolteca-Chichimecas. In *La Gran Chichimeca: El Lugar de las Rocas Secas*, edited by B. Braniff, pp. 113–154. Milán: Jaca Books.
Hibben, Frank C.
  1975 *Kiva Art of the Anasazi at Pottery Mound*. Las Vegas, NV: KC Publications.
Hill, J. Brett, Jeffrey Clark, William Doelle, and Patrick Lyons
  2004 Prehistoric Demography in the Southwest: Migration, Coalescence, and Hohokam Population Decline. *American Antiquity* 69(4):689–716.
Hill, Jane H.
  1992 The Flower World of Old Uto-Aztecan. *Journal of Anthropological Research* 48:117–144.
Hill, K. C., Sekaquaptewa, E., Black, M. E., Malotki, E., and Lomatuway'ma, M.
  1998 *Hopi Dictionary = Hopìikwa Lavàytutuveni: A Hopi-English Dictionary of the Third Mesa Dialect with an English-Hopi Finder List and a Sketch of Hopi Grammar*. Tucson: University of Arizona Press.
Hirschfelder, Arlene B.
  1999 *Encyclopedia of Native American Religions: An Introduction*. New York: Facts on File.
Hobsbawm, Eric, and Terrance Ranger (editors)
  1983 *The Invention of Tradition*. Cambridge: Cambridge University Press.
Hodder, Ian
  1982 Theoretical Archaeology: A Reactionary View. In *Symbolic and Structural Archaeology*, edited by I. Hodder, pp. 1–16. Cambridge: Cambridge University Press.
Hodder, Ian (editor)
  1989 *The Meaning of Things: Material Culture and Symbolic Expression*. London: Unwin Hyman.
Hodder, Ian, and Scott Hutson
  2003 *Reading the Past: Current Approaches to Interpretation in Archaeology*, 3rd ed. Cambridge: Cambridge University Press.
Hurcombe, Linda
  2008 A Sense of Materials and Sensory Perception in Concepts of Materiality. *World Archaeology* 39(4):532–545.

Ingold, Tim
   2000   *The Perception of the Environment: Essays in Livelihood, Dwelling and Skill.* London: Routledge.
   2006   Rethinking the Animate, Re-Animating Thought. *Ethnos* 71(1):9–20.
   2007   Earth, Sky, Wind, and Weather. *Journal of the Royal Anthropological Institute (N.S.)*:S19–S38.

Inomata, Takeshi
   2006   Plazas, Performers, and Spectators: Political Theaters of the Classic Maya. *Current Anthropology* 47(5):805–842.

Inomata, Takeshi, and Lawrence S. Coben (editors)
   2006   *The Archaeology of Performance: Theaters of Power, Community, and Politics.* Lanham, MD: AltaMira.

Insoll, Timothy
   2004   *Archaeology, Ritual, Religion.* London: Routledge.

Isbell, William H.
   2000   What We Should Be Studying: The "Imagined Community" and the "Natural Community." In *The Archaeology of Communities: A New World Perspective,* edited by M. A. Canuto and J. Yaeger, pp. 243–266. London: Routledge.

James, Susan
   2002   Mimetic Rituals of Child Sacrifice in the Hopi Kachina Cult. *Journal of the Southwest* 44:337–357.

Jeançon, Jean A.
   1923   Excavations in the Chama Valley, New Mexico. Bureau of American Ethnology Bulletin 81. Washington, DC: Government Printing Office.

Jett, Stephen C., and Peter B. Moyle
   1986   The Exotic Origins of Fishes Depicted on Prehistoric Mimbres Pottery from New Mexico. *American Antiquity* 51(4):688–720.

Johnson, Anna Stofer
   1958   Similarities in Hohokam and Chalchihuites Artifacts. *American Antiquity* 24(2):126–130.

Johnson, C. David, Timothy A. Kohler, and Jason Cowan
   2005   Modeling Historical Ecology, Thinking about Contemporary Systems. *American Anthropologist* 107:96–108.

Johnson, D. A.
   1992   Adobe Brick Architecture and Salado Ceramics at Fourmile Ruin. In *Proceedings of the Second Salado Conference, Globe, Arizona, 1992,* edited by R. C. Lange and S. Germick, pp. 131–138. Phoenix: Arizona Archaeology Society.

Johnson, Gregory
   1978   Information Sources and the Development of Decision-making Organizations. In *Social Archaeology: Beyond Subsistence and Dating,* edited

by C. L. Redman, M. J., Berman, E. V. Curtin, W. T. Langhorne Jr., and N. M. Versaggi, pp. 87–112. New York: Academic Press.

1982 Organizational Structure and Scalar Stress. In *Theory and Explanation in Archaeology*, edited by C. Renfrew, M. Rowlands, and B. A. Segraves, pp. 389–421. New York: Academic Press.

Joyce, Rosemary A., and Jeanne Lopiparo
2005 Postscript: Doing Agency in Archaeology. *Journal of Archaeological Method and Theory* 12(4):365–374.

Judd, Neil M
1924 Letters to John LaGorce, National Geographic Society, July 6 and 31, 1924. Papers of Neil M. Judd, National Anthropological Archives, Smithsonian Institution, Washington, DC. Available at http://www.chacoarchive.org/media/pdf/000066.pdf and http://www.chacoarchive.org/media/pdf/000067.pdf. Accessed February 27, 2009.
1954 *The Material Culture of Pueblo Bonito*. Smithsonian Miscellaneous Collections Volume 124. Washington, DC: Smithsonian Institution.
1964 *The Architecture of Pueblo Bonito*. Smithsonian Miscellaneous Collections Volume 147, no. 1. Washington, DC: Smithsonian Institution.

Judge, W. James
1993 Resource Distribution and the Chaco Phenomenon. In *The Chimney Rock Archaeological Symposium*, edited by J. McKim Malville and Gary Matlock, pp. 35–36. USDA Forest Service General Technical Report RM-227. Ft. Collins, CO: Rocky Mountain Forest and Range Experimental Station, USDA.

Kaldahl, Eric J., Scott Van Keuren, and Barbara J. Mills
2004 Migration, Factionalism, and the Trajectories of Pueblo IV Period Clusters in the Mogollon Rim Region. In *The Protohistoric Pueblo World: A.D. 1275–1600*, edited by E. C. Adams and A. I. Duff, pp. 85–94. Tucson: University of Arizona Press.

Kane, Allen E. and C. T. Robinson
1988 *Dolores Archaeological Program: Anasazi Communities at Dolores: McPhee Village*. Denver: USDI Bureau of Reclamation, Engingeering, and Research Center.

Kantner, John
2004 *Ancient Puebloan Southwest*. Cambridge: Cambridge University Press.
2006 Religious Behavior in the Post-Chaco Years. In *Religion in the Prehispanic Southwest*, edited by C. S. VanPool, T. L. VanPool, and D. A. Phillips Jr., pp. 31–51. Lanham, MD: AltaMira.

Keane, Webb
2003 Semiotics and the Social Analysis of Material Things. *Language & Communication* 23:409–425.
2005 Signs Are Not the Garb of Meaning: On the Social Analysis of Material

Things. In *Materiality*, edited by D. Miller, pp. 182–205. Durham, NC: Duke University Press.

Kelley, Isabel T.
   1938   *Excavations at Chametla, Sinaloa.* Ibero-America 14. Berkeley: University of California Press.

Kelley, J. Charles
   1966   Mesoamerica and the Southwestern United States. In *Handbook of Middle American Indians.* Vol. 4. *Archaeological Frontiers and External Connections*, edited by G. F. Ekholm and G. R. Willey, pp. 95–110. (Robert Wauchope, general editor.) Austin: University of Texas Press.
   1976   Alta Vista: Outpost of Mesoamerican Empire on the Tropic of Cancer. In *Las Fronteras de Mesoamérica: XIV Mesa Redonda*, pp. 21–40. Mexico City: Sociedad Mexicana de Antropología.

Kenagy, Susan Gandell
   1986   Ritual Pueblo Ceramics: Symbolic Stylistic Behavior as a Medium of Information Exchange. Ph.D. dissertation, University of New Mexico.

Kennard, Edward A. and Edwin Earle
   1938   *Hopi Kachinas.* New York: J. J. Augustin.

Kertzer, David I.
   1988   *Ritual, Politics and Power.* New Haven, CT: Yale University Press.

Keyser, James D.
   2001   Relative Dating Methods. In *Handbook of Rock Art Research*, edited by D. S. Whitley, pp. 116–138. Walnut Creek, CA: AltaMira.

Kidder, Alfred V.
   1962   *An Introduction to the Study of Southwestern Archaeology, with a Preliminary Account of the Excavations at Pecos.* Department of Archaeology, Phillips Academy, Andover. New Haven, CT: Yale University Press. [Originally published 1924; reprinted with a new introductory chapter by Yale University Press, 1962]

King, Anthony
   2000   Thinking with Bourdieu against Bourdieu: A "Practical" Critique of the Habitus. *Sociological Theory* 18(3):417–433.

Kintigh, Keith W.
   1985   *Settlement, Subsistence, and Society in Late Zuni Prehistory.* Anthropological Papers of the University of Arizona. Tucson: University of Arizona Press.

Kintigh, Keith W., Todd L. Howell, and Andrew I. Duff
   1996   Post-Chacoan Social Organization at the Hinkson Site, New Mexico. *Kiva* 61:257–274.

Knappett, Carl, and Lambros Malafouris (editors)
   2008   *Material Agency: Towards a Non-Anthropocentric Approach.* New York: Springer.

Kohler, Timothy A.
- 1993 News from the Northern American Southwest: Prehistory on the Edge of Chaos. *Journal of Archaeological Research* 1:267–321.
- 2010 A New Paleoproductivity Reconstruction for Southwestern Colorado, and Its Implications for Understanding Thirteenth-Century Depopulation. In *Leaving Mesa Verde: Peril and Change in the 13th Century Southwest*, edited by T. A. Kohler, M. D. Varien, and A. Wright. Tucson: University of Arizona Press.

Kohler, Timothy A. (editor)
- 2004 *Archaeology of Bandelier National Monument: Village Formation on the Pajarito Plateau, New Mexico*. Albuquerque: University of New Mexico Press.

Kohler, Timothy A., Stephanie VanBuskirk, and Samantha Ruscavage-Barz
- 2004 Vessels and Villages: Evidence for Conformist Transmission in Early Village Aggregations on the Pajarito Plateau, New Mexico. *Journal of Anthropological Archaeology* 23:100-118.

Kohler, Timothy A., Sarah Cole, and Stanca Ciupe
- 2009 Population and Warfare: A Test of the Turchin Model in Pueblo Societies. In *Pattern and Process in Cultural Evolution*, edited by Stephen Shennan, pp. 277–295. Berkeley: University of California Press.

Kohler, Timothy A., Mark D. Varien, Aaron M. Wright, and Kristin A. Kuckelman
- 2008 Mesa Verde Migrations. *American Scientist* 96:146–153.

Kövecses, Zoltan
- 2002 *Metaphor: A Practical Introduction*. New York: Oxford University Press.

Kowalski, Jeff Karl, and Cynthia Kristan-Graham (editors)
- 2007 *Twin Tollans: Chichén Itzá and the Epiclassic to Early Post Classic Mesoamerican World*. Cambridge, MA: Harvard University Press.

Kroskrity, P. V.
- 1993 *Language, History, and Identity: Ethnolinguistic Studies of the Arizona Tewa*. Tucson: University of Arizona Press.

Küchler, Suzanne
- 2002 *Malanggan: Art, Memory and Sacrifice*. Oxford: Berg.

Kuckelman, Kristin A.
- 2002 Thirteenth-Century Warfare in the Central Mesa Verde Region. In *Seeking the Center Place: Archaeology and Ancient Communities in the Mesa Verde Region*, edited by M. D. Varien and R. H. Wilshusen, pp. 233–253. Salt Lake City: University of Utah Press.

Kuckelman, Kristin A., Grant D. Coffey, and Steve R. Copeland
- 2009 Interim Descriptive Report of Research at Goodman Point Pueblo (5MT604), Montezuma County, Colorado, 2005–2008. http://crowcanyon.org/ResearchReports/GoodmanPoint/interim_reports/2005_2008/GPP_interim_report_2005_2008.pdf

Kuckelman, Kristin A., Ricky R. Lightfoot, and Debra L. Martin
    2000   Changing Patterns of Violence in the Northern San Juan Region. *Kiva* 66(1):147–166.
Kurath, Gertrude P., with Antonio Garcia
    1970   *Music and Dance of the Tewa Pueblos.* Museum of New Mexico Research Records No. 8. Santa Fe, NM: Museum of New Mexico Press.
Kurota, Alexander
    2006   Class III Cultural Resources Inventory of 435 Acres in Pueblo Blanco Country, Galisteo Basin, New Mexico. Office of Contract Archaeology, University of New Mexico. OCA-185-880.
Lakoff, George, and Mark Johnson
    1980   *Metaphors We Live By.* Chicago: University of Chicago Press.
LaMotta, Vincent Michael
    1996   *The Use of Disarticulated Human Remains in Abandonment Ritual at Homol'ovi.* Master's thesis, Department of Anthropology, University of Arizona, Tucson.
Lange, Charles H.
    1959   *Cochiti: A New Mexico Pueblo Past and Present.* Austin: University of Texas Press.
    1979   Santo Domingo Pueblo. In *Handbook of North American Indians.* Vol. 9. *Southwest,* edited by A. Ortiz, pp. 366–378. Washington, DC: Smithsonian Institution.
Latour, Bruno
    1991   *We Have Never Been Modern.* Translated by C. Porter. Cambridge, MA: Harvard University Press.
    2005   *Reassembling the Social: An Introduction to Actor-Network Theory.* Oxford: Oxford University Press.
Lave, Jean, and Etienne Wenger
    1996   Practice, Person, Social World. In *An Introduction to Vygotsky*, edited by H. Daniels, pp. 143–150. London: Routledge.
LeBlanc, Steven A.
    1999   *Prehistoric Warfare in the American Southwest.* Salt Lake City: University of Utah Press.
    2000   Regional Interaction and Warfare in the Late Prehistoric Southwest. In *The Archaeology of Regional Interaction: Religion, Warfare, and Exchange Across the American Southwest and Beyond*, edited by M. Hegmon, pp. 41–70. Boulder: University Press of Colorado.
    2008   The Case for Early Farmer Migration into the Greater American Southwest. In *Archaeology without Borders: Contact, Commerce, and Change in the US Southwest and Northwestern Mexico,* edited by L. D. Webster and M. E. McBrinn, pp. 107–144. Boulder: University Press of Colorado.
Lechtman, Heather
    1977   Style in Technology—Some Early Thoughts. In *1975 Proceedings of the*

American Ethnological Society, edited by H. Lechtman and R. Merrill, pp. 3–20. 1975 Proceedings of the American Ethnological Society. St, Paul, MN: West Publishing.

Lekson, Stephen H.
- 1999 *The Chaco Meridian: Centers of Political Power in the Ancient Southwest*. Walnut Creek, CA: AltaMira.
- 2006 Chaco Matters: An Introduction. In *The Archaeology of Chaco Canyon, An Eleventh-Century Pueblo Regional Center*, edited by S. H. Lekson, pp. 3–44. Santa Fe, NM: School of American Research Press.
- 2007 Great House Form. In *The Architecture of Chaco Canyon, New Mexico*, edited by Stephen H. Lekson, pp. 7–44. Provo: University of Utah Press.
- 2009 *A History of the Ancient Southwest*. Santa Fe NM: School for Advanced Research Press.

Lekson, Stephen H., and Catherine M. Cameron
- 1995 The Abandonment of Chaco Canyon, the Mesa Verde Migrations, and the Reorganization of the Pueblo World. *Journal of Anthropological Archaeology* 14:184–202.

Lepowsky, Maria
- 2004 Ritual Violence and Revitalization in California and New Guinea. In *Reassessing Revitalization Movements: Perspectives from North America and the Pacific Islands*, edited by M. E. Harkins, pp. 1–60. Lincoln: University of Nebraska Press.

Levy, Jerrold
- 1992 *Orayvi Revisited: Social Stratification in an "Egalitarian" Society*. Santa Fe, NM: School of American Research Press.

Liebmann, Matthew, and Robert W. Preucel
- 2007 The Archaeology of the Pueblo Revolt and the Formation of the Modern Pueblo World. *Kiva* 73(2):195–218.

Lincoln, Bruce
- 2006 *Holy Terrors: Thinking about Religion After September 11*. 2nd ed. Chicago: University of Chicago Press.

Lipe, William D.
- 1989 Social Scale of Mesa Verde Anasazi Kivas. In *The Architecture of Social Integration in Prehistoric Pueblos*, edited by W. D. Lipe and M. Hegmon, pp. 53–71. Occasional Paper No. 1. Cortez, CO: Crow Canyon Archaeological Center.
- 1995 The Depopulation of the Northern San Juan: Conditions in the Turbulent 1200s. *Journal of Anthropological Archaeology* 14:143–169.
- 2002 Social Power in the Central Mesa Verde Region, A.D. 1150–1290. In *Seeking the Center Place: Archaeology and Ancient Communities in the Mesa Verde Region*, edited by M. D. Varien and R. H. Wilshusen, pp. 203–232. Salt Lake City: University of Utah Press.
- 2006 Notes from the North. In *The Archaeology of Chaco Canyon: An 11th*

Century Regional Center, edited by S. Lekson, pp. 261–313. Santa Fe, NM: School of American Research Press.

2010 Lost in Transit: The Central Mesa Verde Archaeological Complex. In *Leaving Mesa Verde: Peril and Change in the 13th Century Southwest*, edited by T. A. Kohler, M. D. Varien and A. Wright. Tucson: University of Arizona Press.

Lipe, William D., and Stephen Lekson

2001 Mesa Verde Pueblo Migrations and Cultural Transformations, A.D. 1250–1350. Paper presented at the 66th annual meeting of the Society for American Archaeology, New Orleans.

Lipe, William D., and Scott G. Ortman

2000 Spatial Patterning in Northern San Juan Villages, A.D. 1050–1300. *Kiva* 66(1):91–122.

Lipe, William D., and Mark D. Varien

1999 Pueblo III (A.D. 1150–1300). In *Colorado Prehistory: A Context for the Southern Colorado River Basin*, edited by W. D. Lipe, M. D. Varien, and R. H. Wilshusen, pp. 290–352. Denver: Colorado Council of Professional Archaeologists, Colorado Historical Society.

Litvinoff, Valentina

1974 Lessons from the Dancing Ground to the Studio: Implications of Pueblo Indian Dance for Modern Dance. *Journal of Aesthetics and Art Criticism* 32(3):397–407.

Longacre, William A.

1966 Changing Patterns of Social Integration: A Prehistoric Example from the American Southwest. *American Anthropologist* 68:94-101.

López Austin, Alfredo, and Leonardo López Luján

2001 *Mexico's Indigenous Past*. Norman: University of Oklahoma Press.

Low, Setha M.

1993 Cultural Meaning of the Plaza: Origin and Evolution of the Spanish-American Gridplan-Plaza Urban Design. In *The Cultural Meaning of Urban Space*, edited by G. McDonogh and R. Rotenberg, pp. 75–94. Amherst: Bergin and Garvey.

1996 Spatializing Culture: The Social Production and Social Construction of Public Space in Costa Rica. *American Ethnologist* 23(4):861–879.

2000 *On the Plaza: The Politics of Public Space and Culture*. Austin: University of Texas Press.

Luebben, Ralph A.

1953 Leaf Water Site. In *Salvage Archaeology in the Chama Valley, New Mexico*, assembled by F. Wendorf, pp. 9–33. Monographs of the School of American Research, Number 17. Santa Fe, NM: School of American Research Press.

Lyons, Patrick

2003 *Ancestral Hopi Migrations*. Anthropological Papers of the University of Arizona. Tucson: University of Arizona Press.

Mabry, Jonathan B., John P. Carpenter, and Guadalupe Sanchez
    2008   Archaeological Models of Early Uto-Aztecan Prehistory in the Arizona-Sonora Borderland. In *Archaeology without Borders: Contact, Commerce, and Change in the US Southwest and Northwestern Mexico*, edited by L. D. Webster and M. E. McBrinn, pp. 155–184. Boulder: University Press of Colorado.

Magowan, Fiona
    1998   Singing the Light: Sense and Sensation in Yolngu Performance. *Res: Anthropology and Aesthetics.* 34:192–204.

Malafouris, Lambros
    2004   The Cognitive Basis of Material Engagement: Where Brain, Body and Culture Conflate. In *Rethinking Materiality: The Engagement of Mind with the Material World*, edited by E. DeMarrais, C. Gosden, and A. C. Renfrew, pp. 53–62. Cambridge: MacDonald Institute for Archaeological Research.

Malotki, E.
    1993   *Hopi Ruin Legends*. Lincoln: University of Nebraska Press.

Malville, J. McKim, and Nancy J. Malville
    2001   Pilgrimage and Periodic Festivals as Processes of Social Integration in Chaco Canyon. *Kiva* 66:329–344.

Malville, J. McKim, and Gregory Munson
    1998   Pecked Basins of the Mesa Verde. *Southwestern Lore* 64(4): 1–35.

Malville, J. McKim, and Claudia Putnam
    1993   *Prehistoric Astronomy in the Southwest*. Rev. ed. Boulder, CO: Johnson Books.

Marcus, Joyce
    1989   Zapotec Chiefdoms and the Nature of Formative Religions. In *Regional Perspectives on the Olmec*, edited by Robert J. Sharer and David C. Grove, pp. 148–197. Cambridge: Cambridge University Press.

Marden, Kerri Ann
    2009   Interpretation of the Variation in Mortuary Behavior in Chaco Canyon. Paper presented at the 74th annual meeting of the Society for American Archaeology, Atlanta.

Marshall, Michael P., and Henry Walt
    2007   *The Eastern Homeland of San Juan Pueblo: Tewa Land and Water Use in the Santa Cruz and Truchas Watersheds: An Archaeological and Ethnogeographic Study*. Prepared for Ohkay Owingeh (San Juan) Pueblo. Corrales, NM: Cibola Research Consultants Report No. 432.

Martinez, Esther
    1982   *San Juan Pueblo Tewa Dictionary*. San Juan Pueblo Bilingual Program, San Juan Pueblo, New Mexico.

Mathien, Francis J.
    2003   Pueblo Wall Decorations: Examples from Chaco Canyon. In *Climbing the Rocks: Papers in Honor of Helen and Jay Crotty*, edited by R. N.

Wiseman, T. C. O'Laughlin, and C. T. Snow, pp. 111–126. Papers of the Archaeological Society of New Mexico 29. Albuquerque: Archaeological Society of New Mexico.

Mathiowetz, Michael

2009a The Mountain of Dawn: Sacred Landscape and Political Power at Paquimé, Chihuahua, México. Paper presented at the 53rd meeting of the International Congress of Americanists, México City.

2009b The Son of God Who Is in the Sun: Political Authority and the Personified Sun God in Ancient West and Northwest Mexico. Paper presented at the annual meeting of the Society for American Archaeology, Atlanta.

Maxwell, Timothy D., and Kurt F. Anschuetz

1992 The Southwestern Ethnographic Record and Prehistoric Agricultural Diversity. In *Gardens in Prehistory: The Archaeology of Settlement Agriculture in Greater Mesoamerica,* edited by T. W. Killion, pp. 35–68. Tuscaloosa: University of Alabama Press.

McGuire, Randall H.

1980 The Mesoamerican Connection in the Southwest. *Kiva* 46(1–2):3–38.

1986 Economies and Modes of Production in the Prehistoric Southwestern Periphery. In *Ripples in the Chichimec Sea: New Considerations of Southwestern-Mesoamerican Interactions,* edited by F. J. Mathien and R. H. McGuire, pp. 243–269. Carbondale: Southern Illinois University Press.

1989 The Greater Southwest as a Periphery of Mesoamerica. In *Centre and Periphery: Comparative Studies in Archaeology,* edited by T. C. Champion, pp. 40–66. London: Unwin and Hyman.

1991 From the Outside Looking In. In *Changing Views of Hohokam Archaeology,* edited by G. Gumerman, pp. 347–382. Albuquerque: University of New Mexico Press.

McGuire, Randall H., E. Charles Adams, Benjamin A. Nelson, and Katherine Spielmann

1994 Drawing the Southwest to Scale: Perspectives on Macroregional Relations. In *Themes in Southwestern Prehistory: Grand Patterns and Local Variations Culture Change,* edited by G. Gumerman and M. Gell-Mann. Santa Fe, NM: School for American Research Press.

McGuire, Randall H., and Dean Saitta

1996 Although They Have Petty Captains, They Obey Them Badly: The Dialectics of Prehispanic Western Pueblo Social Organization. *American Antiquity* 61(2):197–216.

McGuire, Randall H., and Elisa Villalpando

2007 The Hohokam and Mesoamerica. In *The Hohokam Millennium,* edited by S. K. Fish and P. R. Fish, pp. 57–64. Santa Fe, NM: School for Advanced Research Press.

Meighan, Clement W.
 1999 The Mexican West Coast and the Hohokam Region. In *The Casas Grandes World*, edited by C. F. Schaafsma and C. L. Riley, pp. 206–212. Provo: University of Utah Press.

Mendiola, Francisco
 2006 Posibles Representaciones de Tlác y Quetzalcóatl en el Arte Rupestre de Sinaloa, Chihuahua y Suroeste de Estados Unidos. In *Los Petroglifos del Noret de México*, edited by V. J. Santos and R. Viñas, pp. 32–43. Mexico City: INAH.

Mera, H. P.
 1935 *Ceramic Clues to the Prehistory of North Central New Mexico*. Laboratory of Anthropology Technical Series, Bulletin 8. Santa Fe, NM: Laboratory of Anthropology.

Meskell, Lynn
 2004a Divine Things. In *Rethinking Materiality: The Engagement of Mind with the Material World*, edited by E. DeMarrais, C. Gosden, and C. Renfrew, pp. 249–259. Cambridge: McDonald Institute for Archaeological Research.
 2004b *Object Worlds in Ancient Egypt: Material Biographies Past and Present*. London: Berg.

Meslin, Michel
 1985 From the History of Religions to Religious Anthropology: A Necessary Reappraisal. In *The History of Religions: Retrospect and Prospect*, edited by J. M. Kitagawa, pp. 31–52. New York: Macmillan.

Mich, Kerri
 2000 *A Spatial Analysis of Petroglyph Locations at Petroglyph National Monument*. Unpublished Master's thesis, University of New Mexico, Albuquerque.

Miller, Daniel (editor)
 2005 *Materiality*. Durham, NC: Duke University Press.

Mills, Barbara J.
 1998 Migration and Pueblo IV Community Reorganization in the Silver Creek Area, East-central Arizona. In *Migration and Reorganization: The Pueblo IV Period in the American Southwest*, edited by K. A. Spielmann, pp. 65–80. Arizona State University Anthropological Research Papers 51. Tempe: Arizona State University.
 1999 Ceramics and the Social Contexts of Food Consumption in the Northern Southwest. In *Pots and People: A Dynamic Interaction*, edited by J. Skibo and G. Feinman, pp. 99–114. Salt Lake City: University of Utah Press.
 2004 The Establishment and Defeat of Hierarchy: Inalienable Possessions and the History of Collective Prestige Structures in the Puebloan Southwest. *American Anthropologist* 106(2):238–251.

    2007   Performing the Feast: Visual Display and Suprahousehold Commensalism in the Puebloan Southwest. *American Antiquity* 72(2):210–239.

Mills, Barbara J., and T. J. Ferguson
    2008   Animate Objects: Shell Trumpets and Ritual Networks in the Greater Southwest. *Journal of Archaeological Method and Theory* 15:338–361.

Mills, Barbara J., Sarah H. Herr, Susan L. Stinson, and Daniela Triadan
    1999   Ceramic Production and Distribution in the Silver Creek Area. In *Living on the Edge of the Rim: Excavations and Analysis of the Silver Creek Archaeological Research Project 1993–1998*, edited by B. J. Mills, S. H. Herr, and S. Van Keuren, pp. 295–324. Arizona State Museum Archaeological Series 192(2). Tucson: Arizona State Museum, University of Arizona.

Mills, Barbara J., Scott Van Keuren, Susan L. Stinson, William M. Graves, III, Eric J. Kaldahl, and Joanne M. Newcomb
    1999   Excavations at Bailey Ruin. In *Living on the Edge of the Rim: Excavations and Analysis of the Silver Creek Archaeological Research Project, 1993–1998*, edited by B. J. Mills, S. A. Herr, and S. Van Keuren. Arizona State Museum Archaeological Series 192(1). Tucson: Arizona State Museum, University of Arizona.

Mills, Barbara J., and William H. Walker
    2008   Memory, Materiality, and Depositional Practice. In *Memory Work: Archaeologies of Material Practices*, edited by B. J. Mills and W. H. Walker, pp. 3–23. Santa Fe, NM: School for Advanced Research Press.

Mithen, Steven
    1998   The Supernatural Beings of Prehistory and the External Storage of Religious Ideas. In *Cognition and Material Culture: The Archaeology of Symbolic Storage*, edited by C. Renfrew and C. Scarre, pp. 97–106. Cambridge: McDonald Institute for Archaeological Research.

Moghissi, Haideh (editor)
    2005   *Women and Islam: Critical Concepts in Sociology*. New York: Routledge.

Momaday, N. Scott
    1976   Native American Attitudes to the Environment. In *Seeing with a Native Eye*, edited by Walter Holden Capps, pp. 79–85. New York: Harper & Row.

    1997   *The Man Made of Words: Essays, Stories, Passages*. New York: St. Martin's.

Monaghan, John
    1995   *The Covenants with Earth and Rain: Exchange, Sacrifice, and Revelation in Mixtec Sociality*. Norman: University of Oklahoma Press.

Moore, Jerry D.
    1996   The Archaeology of Plazas and the Proxemics of Ritual: Three Andean Traditions. *American Anthropologist* 98(4):789–802.

Morgan, David
   2005   *The Sacred Gaze: Religious Visual Culture in Theory and Practice*. Berkeley: University of California Press.

Morley, Sylvanus G.
   1910   The Excavations at Ojo Caliente. In *Ojo Caliente Journal, Rio Grande Expedition*. Manuscript on file, Fray Angelico Chavez History Library, Santa Fe, NM.

Morris, Earl H.
   1924   *Burials in the Aztec Ruin*. Anthropological Papers of the American Museum of Natural History Vol. XXVI, Parts III. New York: American Museum of Natural History.
   1939   *Archaeological Studies in the La Plata District, Southwestern Colorado and Northwestern New Mexico*. Publication No. 519. Washington, DC: Carnegie Institution of Washington.

Morris, Earl H., and F. Burgh
   1941   *Anasazi Basketry: Basket Maker II through Pueblo III*. Publication 533. Washington, DC: Carnegie Institution of Washington.

Muir, Robert J., and Jonathan C. Driver
   2002   Scale of Analysis and Zooarchaeological Interpretation: Pueblo III Faunal Variation in the Northern San Juan. *Journal of Anthropological Archaeology* 21:165–199.

Munson, Marit K.
   2002   On Boundaries and Beliefs: Rock Art and Identity on the Pajarito Plateau. Unpublished Ph.D. dissertation, Department of Anthropology, University of New Mexico, Albuquerque.
   2003   Rock Art Imagery and the Power of Place at Las Estrellas, New Mexico. In *Climbing the Rocks: Papers in Honor of Helen and Jay Crotty*, edited by R. N. Wiseman, T. C. O'Laughlin, and C. T. Snow. pp. 127–136, vol. 29. Albuquerque: Archaeological Society of New Mexico.
   2011   *The Archaeology of Art in the American Southwest*. Lanham, MD: AltaMira.

Munson, Marit K., and Genevieve Head
   in press   Surveying Petroglyph Hill: Cultural Landscapes of the Galisteo Basin. In *Conflagration and Conflict: Burnt Corn Pueblo and the Galisteo Basin in the 14th Century AD*, edited by J. E. Snead and M. Allen. Anthropological Papers of the University of Arizona 74. Tucson: University of Arizona Press.

Murie, James R.
   1981   *Ceremonies of the Pawnee, Part I: The Skiri*. Smithsonian Contributions to Anthropology, Number 27. Washington, DC: Smithsonian Institution Press.

Naranjo, Tessie
   1995   Thoughts on Migration by Santa Clara Pueblo. *Journal of Anthropological Archaeology* 14(2):247–250.

Neitzel, Jill E.
   2003   The Organization, Function, and Population of Pueblo Bonito. In *Pueblo Bonito: Center of the Pueblo World*, edited by Jill E. Neitzel, pp. 143–149. Washington, DC: Smithsonian Press.

Nelson, Ben
   1995   Complexity, Hierarchy, and Scale: A Controlled Comparison between Chaco Canyon, New Mexico and La Quemada, Zacatecas. *American Antiquity* 60(4):597–618.
   1997   Chronology and Stratigraphy at La Quemada, Zacatecas, Mexico. *Journal of Field Archaeology* 24(1):85–109.
   2000   Aggregation, Warfare, and the Spread of the Mesoamerican Tradition. In *The Archaeology of Regional Interaction*, edited by M. Hegmon, pp. 317–340. Boulder: University Press of Colorado.
   2006   Mesoamerican Objects and Symbols in Chaco Canyon Contexts. In *The Archaeology of Chaco Canyon: An Eleventh Century Pueblo Regional Center*, edited by Stephen H. Lekson, pp. 339–421. Santa Fe, NM: School of American Research, Advanced Seminar Series.
   2007   The Crafting of Places: Mesoamerican Monumentality in Cerros de Trincheras and Other Hilltop Sites. In *Enduring Borderlands Traditions: Trincheras Sites in Time, Space, and Society*, edited by S. K. Fish, P. R. Fish, and M. E. Villalpando, pp. 230–245. Tucson: University of Arizona Press.

Nelson, Ben A., J. A. Darling, and D. A. Kice
   1992   Mortuary Patterns and the Social Order at La Quemada, Zacatecas. *Latin American Antiquity* 3(4):298–315.

Nelson, Nels C.
   1914   *Pueblo Ruins of the Galisteo Basin*. Anthropological Papers of the American Museum of Natural History, Volume 5, Pt. 1. New York: American Museum of Natural History.

Newsome, Elizabeth
   2006   Weaving the Sky: The Cliff Palace Painted Tower. In *We Are Here: Pueblo Paintings and Place* (Plateau 2/2), edited by P. Schaafsma et al. Flagstaff, AZ: Museum of Northern Arizona.

Nichols, Elizabeth
   2007   Regional Patterns in Prehistoric Katsina Iconography in the Western Pueblo Province. Unpublished Master's thesis, Department of Anthropology, Northern Arizona University, Flagstaff.

Nichols, Debora L., and Patricia L. Crown (editors)
   2008   *Multidisciplinary Approaches to Social Violence in the Prehispanic American Southwest*. Tucson: University of Arizona Press.

Nordby, Larry V.
   2001   *Prelude to Tapestries in Stone: Understanding Cliff Palace Architecture*. Mesa Verde National Park Archaeological Research Series, Ar-

chitectural Studies, No. 4. Mesa Verde National Park Division of Research and Resource Management. Colorado: Mesa Verde National Park.

Orcutt, Janet D.
- 1999 Chronology. In *The Bandelier Archeological Survey*, edited by R. P. Powers and J. D. Orcutt, pp. 85–116. Intermountain Cultural Resources Management Professional Paper. vol. 57. Intermountain Region: National Park Service.

Ortiz, Alfonso
- 1969 *The Tewa World: Space, Time, Being, and Becoming in a Pueblo Society*. Chicago: University of Chicago Press.
- 1979 San Juan Pueblo. In *Handbook of North American Indians*. Vol. 9. *Southwest*, edited by A. Ortiz, pp. 278–295. Washington, DC: Smithsonian Institution.

Ortiz, Simon
- 1977 *Song, Poetry, and Language—Expression and Perception*. Occasional Papers, Vol. III (Music and Dance Series) No. 5, 1st edition. Tsaile, AZ: Navajo Community Press.

Ortman, Scott G.
- 1998 Corn Grinding and Community Organization in the Pueblo Southwest, A.D. 1150–1550. In *Migration and Reorganization: The Pueblo IV Period in the American Southwest*, edited by K. A. Spielmann, pp. 165–192. Anthropological Research Papers 51. Tempe: Arizona State University.
- 2000a Artifacts. In *The Archaeology of Castle Rock Pueblo: A Thirteenth-Century Village in Southwestern Colorado* [HTML title], edited by K. A. Kuckelman. Available: http://www.crowcanyon.org/castlerock. Accessed May 3, 2002.
- 2000b Conceptual Metaphor in the Archaeological Record: Methods and an Example from the American Southwest. *American Antiquity* 65(4):613–645.
- 2002 Artifacts. In *The Archaeology of Woods Canyon Pueblo: a Canyon-rim Village in Southwestern Colorado* [HTML title], edited by M. J. Churchill. Available: http://www.crowcanyon.org/woodscanyon. Accessed April 11, 2005.
- 2006 Ancient Pottery of the Mesa Verde Country: How Ancestral Pueblo People Made It, Used It, and Thought about It. In *The Mesa Verde World*, edited by D. G. Noble, pp. 101–110. Santa Fe, NM: School of American Research Press.
- 2008a Architectural Metaphor and Chacoan Influence in the Northern San Juan. In *Archaeology without Borders: Contact, Commerce, and Change in the US Southwest and Northwestern Mexico*, edited by L. Webster and M. E. McBrinn, pp. 227–255. Boulder: University Press of Colorado.

2008b   Action, Place and Space in the Castle Rock Community. In *The Social Construction of Communities: Studies of Agency, Structure and Identity in the Southwestern U. S.*, edited by M. D. Varien, and J. M. Potter, pp. 125–154. Walnut Creek, CA: AltaMira.

2009   Genes, Language and Culture in Tewa Ethnogenesis, A.D. 1150–1400. Ph.D. dissertation, Department of Anthropology, Arizona State University.

2010   Evidence of a Mesa Verde Homeland for the Tewa Pueblos. In *Leaving Mesa Verde: Peril and Chance in the Thirteenth Century Southwest*, edited by T. A. Kohler, M. D. Varien and A. Wright, pp. 222–261. Tucson: University of Arizona Press.

Ortman, Scott G., and Bruce A. Bradley

2002   Sand Canyon Pueblo: The Container in the Center. In *Seeking the Center Place: Archaeology and Ancient Communities in the Mesa Verde Region*, edited by M. D. Varien, and R. H. Wilshusen, pp. 41–78. Salt Lake City: University of Utah Press.

Ortner, Sherry B.

1973   On Key Symbols. *American Anthropologist* 75(5):1338–1346.

Ouzman, Sven

2001   Seeing Is Deceiving: Rock Art and the Non-Visual. *World Archaeology* 33(2):237–256.

Palkovich, Ann M.

1980   *The Arroyo Hondo Skeletal and Mortuary Remains*. Santa Fe, NM: School of American Research Press.

Panofsky, Erwin

1991   *Perspective as Symbolic Form*. New York: Zone Books. Originally published as "Die Perspektive als symbolische Form" in *Vortrage der Bibliotek Warburg, 1924–25*, 1927, pp. 258–330.

Parks, James A., and Jeffrey S. Dean

1997   Interpretation of Tree-ring Dates from Spring House and 20-1/2 House, Mesa Verde National Park, Colorado. Manuscript on file at the Laboratory of Tree-Ring Research, University of Arizona, Tucson.

Parmentier, Richard J.

1994   *Signs in Society: Studies in Semiotic Anthropology*. Bloomington: Indiana University Press.

Parsons, Elsie Clews

1917   *Notes on Zuni, Part I*. Lancaster, PA: American Anthropological Association.

1929   *The Social Organization of the Tewa of New Mexico*. American Anthropological Association Memoir 36.

1933   Some Aztec and Pueblo Parallels. *American Anthropologist* 35:611–631.

1939   *Pueblo Indian Religion*. Volumes I and II. Chicago: University of Chicago Press.

Pauketat, Timothy R.
- 2001 Practice and History in Archaeology: An Emerging Paradigm. *Anthropological Theory* 1:73-98.
- 2008 The Grounds for Agency in Southwestern Archaeology. In *The Social Construction of Communities: Agency, Structure, and Identity in the Prehispanic Southwest*, edited by M. D. Varien and J. M. Potter, pp. 233–249. Walnut Creek, CA: AltaMira.
- 2009 Of Leaders and Legacies in Native North America. In *The Evolution of Leadership and Complexity*, edited by J. Kanter, K. Vaughn, and J. Eerkins. Santa Fe, NM: School for Advanced Research Press.
- 2011 *An Archaeology of the Cosmos*. Manuscript in preparation.

Pederson, J., and E. Waehle
- 1988 The Complexities of Residential Organization among the Efe (Mbuti) and the Bagombi (Baka): A Critical View of the Notion of Flux in Hunter-Gatherer Societies. In *Hunters and Gatherers*. Vol. 1. *History, Evolution, and Social Change*, edited by T. Ingold, D. Riches, and J. Woodburn, pp. 75–90. Oxford: Berg.

Pepper, George H.
- 1905 Ceremonial Objects and Ornaments from Pueblo Bonito, New Mexico. *American Anthropologist* 7(2):183–197.
- 1909 The Exploration of a Burial Room in Pueblo Bonito, New Mexico. In *Putnam Anniversary Volume: Anthropological Essays, presented to Frederic Ward Putnam in Honor of his Seventieth Birthday*, April 16, 1909, by his Friends and Associates, pp. 196–252. New York: G. E. Steckhert.
- 1920 *Pueblo Bonito*. Anthropological Papers of the American Museum of Natural History, Vol. 27. New York: American Museum of Natural History.

Pérez, V. R., B. A. Nelson, and D. L. Martin
- 2008 Veneration or Violence? A Study of Variations in Human Bone Modification at La Quemada. In *Social Violence in the Prehispanic American Southwest*, edited by D. L. Nichols and P. L. Crown, pp. 123–142. Tucson: University of Arizona Press.

Pfaffenberger, Bryan
- 1988 Fetishised Objects and Humanised Nature: Towards an Anthropology of Technology. *Man* 23:236–252.

Phillips, David, A., Christine S. VanPool, and Todd L. VanPool
- 2006 The Horned Serpent Tradition in the North American Southwest. In *Religion in the Prehispanic Southwest*, edited by C. S. VanPool, Todd L. VanPool, and D. A. Phillips, pp. 17–29. Lanham, MD: AltaMira.

Pinker, Stephen
- 2007 *The Stuff of Thought: Language as a Window into Human Nature*. New York: Penguin.

Plog, Stephen
   2003   Exploring the Ubiquitous through the Unusual: Color Symbolism in Pueblo Black-on-White Pottery. *American Antiquity* 68:665–695.
   2010   Reflections on the State of Chacoan Research: A Review Essay. *Kiva* 75: 373–391.

Plog, Stephen (editor)
   1986   *Spatial Organization and Exchange: Archaeological Survey on Northern Black Mesa*. Publications in Anthropology, Center for Archaeological Investigations. Carbondale: Southern Illinois Press.

Plog, Stephen, and Carrie Heitman
   2010   Hierarchy and Social Inequality in the American Southwest, A.D. 800–1200. *Proceedings of the National Academy of Sciences* 107:19619–19626.

Plog, Stephen, and Julie P. Solometo
   1997   The Never-Changing and the Ever-Changing: The Evolution of Western Pueblo Ritual. *Cambridge Archaeological Journal* 7(2):161–182.

Potter, James M.
   1997   Communal Ritual and Faunal Remains: An Example from the Dolores Anasazi. *Journal of Field Archaeology* 24(3):353–364.
   2000   Pots, Parties, and Politics: Communal Feasting in the American Southwest. *American Antiquity* 65(3):471–492.
   2002   Community, Metaphor, and Gender: Technological Changes across the Pueblo III to Pueblo IV Transition in the El Morro Valley, New Mexico. In *Traditions, Transitions, and Technologies: Themes in Southwestern Archaeology*, edited by S. H. Schlanger, pp. 332–349. Boulder: University Press of Colorado.

Potter, James M., and Scott G. Ortman
   2004   Community and Cuisine in the Prehispanic American Southwest. In *Identity, Feasting, and the Archaeology of the Greater Southwest*, edited by B. J. Mills, pp. 173–191. Boulder: University Press of Colorado.

Potter, James M., and Elizabeth M. Perry
   2000   Ritual as a Power Resource in the American Southwest. In *Alternative Leadership Strategies in the Prehispanic Southwest*, edited by B. J. Mills, pp. 60–78. Tucson: University of Arizona Press.

Powell, Shirley (editor)
   2002   *Prehistoric Culture Change on the Colorado Plateau: Ten Thousand Years on Black Mesa*. Tucson: University of Arizona Press.

Powers, Robert P., and Janet D. Orcutt (editors)
   1999   *The Bandelier Archeological Survey*. 57. 2 vols. Santa Fe, NM: National Park Service.

Preston Blier, S.
   1987   *The Anatomy of Architecture: Ontology and Metaphor in Batammaliba Architectural Expression*. Chicago: University of Chicago Press.

Preucel, Robert W.
　2006　*Archaeological Semiotics*. Oxford: Blackwell.

Putsavage, Kathryn J.
　2008　Mesa Verde Style Mugs: An Analysis of Domestic and Ritual Functions. Unpublished Master's thesis, Department of Museum and Field Studies, University of Colorado, Boulder.

Rainbird, Paul
　2002a　A Message for Our Future? The Rapa Nui (Easter Island) Ecodisaster and Pacific Island Environments. *World Archaeology* 33(3): 436–451.
　2002b　Making Sense of Petroglyphs: The Sound of Rock-Art. In *Inscribed Landscapes: Marking and Making Place*, edited by B. David and M. Wilson, pp. 93–103. Honolulu: University of Hawaii.

Rakita, Gordon
　2009　*Ancestors and Elites: Emergent Complexity and Ritual Practices in the Casas Grandes Polity*. Walnut Creek, CA: AltaMira.

Rappaport, Roy A.
　1979　*Ecology, Meaning, and Religion*. Berkeley, CA: North Atlantic Books.

Rautman, Alison
　2000　Population Aggregation, Community Organization, and Plaza-Oriented Pueblos in the American Southwest. *Journal of Field Archaeology* 27(3): 271–284.

Reagan, Albert
　1906　Dances of the Jemez Pueblo Indians. *Transactions of the Kansas Academy of Science* 20:241–272.

Reed, Erik K.
　1958　*Excavations in Mancos Canyon, Colorado*. Anthropological Papers, No. 35. Salt Lake City: University of Utah.

Reid, J. Jefferson, and Barbara K. Montgomery
　1999　Ritual Space in the Grasshopper Region, East-central Arizona. In *Sixty Years of Mogollon Archaeology: Papers from the Ninth Mogollon Conference 1996*, edited by S. M. Whittlesey, pp. 23–29. Tucson: SRI Press.

Renfrew, Colin
　2001　Production and Consumption in a Sacred Economy: The Material Correlates of High Devotional Expression at Chaco Canyon. *American Antiquity* 66:14–25.
　2004　Towards a Theory of Material Engagement. In *Rethinking Materiality: The Engagement of Mind with the Material World*, edited by E. DeMarrais, C. Gosden, and A. C. Renfrew, pp. 23–32. Cambridge: MacDonald Institute for Archaeological Research.
　2007　The Archaeology of Ritual, of Cult, and of Religion. In *The Archaeology of Ritual*, edited by Evangelos Kyriakidis, pp. 109–122. Los Angeles: Cotsen Institute of Archaeology, University of California.

Reyman, Jonathan E.
- 1971 Mexican Influence on Southwestern Ceremonialism. Ph.D. dissertation, Department of Anthropology, Southern Illinois University.
- 1989 The History of Archaeology and the Archaeological History of Chaco Canyon. In *Tracing Archaeology's Past: The Historiography of Archaeology*, edited by Andrew L. Christenson, pp. 41–53. Publications in Archaeology, Carbondale: Southern Illinois University Press.

Richards, Colin
- 1996 Henges and Water: Towards an Elemental Understanding of Monumentality and Landscape in Late Neolithic Britain. *Journal of Material Culture* 1(3):313–336.

Riegl, Alois
- 1985 *Late Roman Art Industry*. Translated by R. Winkes. Rome: G. Bretschneider. Originally published as *Die spatromische Kunst-Industrie*, Vienna, 1901.
- 1992 *Problems of Style: Foundations for a History of Ornament*. Translated by Evelyn Kain. Princeton, NJ: Princeton University Press. Originally published as *Stilfragen*, Berlin, 1893.

Riley, Carroll L.
- 1963 Color-Direction Symbolism: An Example of Mexican-Southwestern Contacts. *America Indigena* 23:49–60.
- 1995 *Rio Del Norte: People of Upper Rio Grande from Earliest Times to Pueblo Revolt*. Provo: University of Utah Press.
- 2005 *Becoming Azatlan: Mesoamerican Influence in the Greater Southwest, AD 1200–1500*. Provo: University of Utah Press.

Ringle, William M.
- 2004 On the Political Organization of Chichen Itza. *Ancient Mesoamerica* 15:167–218.

Ringle, William M., Tómas Gallareta Negrón, and George J. Bey III
- 1998 The Return of Quetzalcoatl: Evidence for the Spread of a World Religion During the Epiclassic Period. *Ancient Mesoamerica* 9:182–232.

Robb, John Donald
- 1964 Rhythmic Patterns of the Santo Domingo Corn Dance. *Ethnomusicology* 8(2):154–160.

Robb, John E.
- 1998 The Archaeology of Symbols. *Annual Review of Anthropology* 27:329–346.
- 2004 The Extended Artefact and the Monumental Economy: A Methodology for Material Agency. In *Rethinking Materiality: The Engagement of Mind with the Material World*, edited by E. DeMarrais, C. Gosden, and A. C. Renfrew, pp. 131–140. Cambridge: MacDonald Institute for Archaeological Research.

Robb, John E. and Timothy R. Pauketat
- 2009 From Moments to Millennia: Scale and Change in Human History. Paper presented at School for Advanced Research Seminar, September 26–October 2, 2009, Santa Fe NM.

Robbins, Wilfred W., John P. Harrington, and Barbara Freire-Marreco
- 1916 *Ethnobotany of the Tewa Indians*. Bureau of American Ethnology Bulletin 55. Washington, DC: Government Printing Office.

Robinson, Hugh L.
- 2005 Feasting, Exterior Bowl Design and Public Space in the Northern San Juan, A.D. 1240–1300. Unpublished Master's thesis, Department of Anthropology, Washington State University, Pullman.

Ruscavage-Barz, Samantha, and Elizabeth Bagwell
- 2006 Gathering Spaces and Bounded Places: The Religious Significance of Plaza-oriented Communities in the Northern Rio Grande, New Mexico. In *Religion in the Prehispanic Southwest*, edited by C. VanPool, T. L. VanPool, and D. A. Phillips, Jr., pp. 81–101. Lanham, MD: AltaMira Press.

Saitta, Dean J., and Randall H. McGuire
- 1998 Dialectics, Heterarchy, and Western Pueblo Social Organization. *American Antiquity* 63(2):334–336.

Sandstrom, Alan R.
- 1991 *Corn Is Our Blood: Culture and Ethnic Identity in a Contemporary Aztec Indian Village*. Norman: University of Oklahoma Press.

Saville, Dara
- 2001 Regional Variations of Kachina Iconography in Eastern Pueblo Rock Art. Unpublished Master's thesis, University of New Mexico, Albuquerque.
- 2003 Rock art, Kachinas, and the Landscape at Cerro Indio, New Mexico. In *Climbing the Rocks: Papers in Honor of Helen and Jay Crotty*, edited by R. N. Wiseman, T. C. O'Laughlin, and C. T. Snow, pp. 177–187. Papers of the Archaeological Society of New Mexico, Vol. 29. Albuquerque: Archaeological Society of New Mexico.

Schaafsma, Polly
- 1980 *Indian Rock of the Southwest*. Santa Fe, NM: School of American Research.
- 1990 The Pine Tree Site: A Pueblo IV Shrine in the Galisteo Basin, New Mexico. In *Clues to the Past: Papers in Honor of William M. Sundt*, edited by M. S. Duran and D. T. Kirkpatrick. Papers of the Archaeological Society of New Mexico. Vol. 16. Albuquerque: Archaeological Society of New Mexico.
- 1992a Imagery and Magic: Petroglyphs at Comanche Gap, Galisteo Basin, New Mexico. In *Archaeology, Art, and Anthropology: Papers in Honor of*

              J.J. Brody, edited by R. A. Bice, M. S. Duran, and D. T. Kirkpatrick, pp. 157–174. Papers of the Archaeological Society of New Mexico, Vol. 18. Albuquerque: Archaeological Society of New Mexico.

1992b   *Rock Art in New Mexico*. Santa Fe: Museum of New Mexico Press.

1994a   The Prehistoric Kachina Cult and Its Origins as Suggested by Southwestern Rock Art. In *Kachinas in the Pueblo World*, edited by Polly Schaafsma, pp. 63–79. Albuquerque: University of New Mexico Press.

1994c   Introduction. In *Kachinas in the Pueblo World*, edited by Polly Schaafsma, pp. 1–6. Albuquerque: University of New Mexico Press.

1999   Tlalocs, Kachinas, Sacred Bundles and Related Symbolism in the Southwest and Mesoamerica. In *The Casas Grandes World*, edited by C. F. Schaafsma and C. L. Riley, pp.164–192. Provo: University of Utah Press.

2000   *Warrior, Shield, and Star: Imagery and Ideology of Pueblo Warfare*. Santa Fe, NM: Western Edge Press.

2001   Quetzalcoatl and the Horned and Feathered Serpent of the Southwest. In *The Road to Azatlan: Art From a Mythic Homeland*, edited by V. M. Fields and V. Zamudio-Taylor, pp. 138–149. Los Angeles: Los Angeles County Museum of Art.

2007b   The Pottery Mound Murals and Rock Art: Implications for Regional Interaction. In *New Perspectives on Pottery Mound Pueblo*, edited by P. Schaafsma, pp. 137–166. Albuquerque: University of New Mexico Press.

Schaafsma, Polly (editor)

1994b   *Kachinas in the Pueblo World*. Albuquerque: University of New Mexico Press.

2007a   *New Perspectives on Pottery Mound Pueblo*. Albuquerque: University of New Mexico Press.

Schaafsma, Polly, and Karl Taube

2006   Bringing the Rain: An Ideology of Rain Making in the Pueblo Southwest and Mesoamerica. In *A Pre-Columbian World*, edited by J. Quilter and M. E. Miller, pp. 231–286. Washington, DC: Dumbarton Oaks Research Library and Collection.

Schachner, Gregson

2001   Ritual Control and Transformation in Middle-Range Societies: An Example from the American Southwest. *Journal of Anthropological Archaeology* 20:168–194.

Schiffer, Michael B., and James M. Skibo

1987   Theory and Experiment in the Study of Technological Change. *Current Anthropology* 28:595–622.

Schroeder, Albert H.

1979   Pueblos Abandoned in Historic Times. In *Handbook of North American Indians, Volume 9: Southwest*, edited by A. Ortiz, pp. 236–254. Washington, DC: Smithsonian Institution.

Scott, James C.
- 1990 Domination and the Arts of Resistance: Hidden Transcripts. New Haven, CT: Yale University Press.

Sekaquaptewa, Emory
- 1976 Hopi Indian Ceremonies. In *Seeing with a Native Eye*, edited by Walter Holden Capps, pp. 35–43. New York: Harper & Row.

Sekaquaptewa, Emory, and Dorothy Washburn
- 2004 They Go Along Singing: Reconstructing the Hopi Past from Ritual Metaphors in Song and Image. *American Antiquity* 69(3): 457–486.
- 2006 Metaphors of Meaning in Murals, Pottery, and Ritual Song. *Plateau* 3(1): 26–47. Flagstaff: Museum of Northern Arizona.

Senter, Donovan
- 1937 Burials from Mound 50 and Mound 51. In *Tseh So, A Small House Ruin, Chaco Canyon, New Mexico*, edited by Donald D. Brand, Florence M. Hawley, and Frank C. Hibben, pp. 140–162. Albuquerque: University of New Mexico.

Sewell, William H., Jr.
- 2005 *Logics of History: Social Theory and Social Transformation*. Chicago: University of Chicago Press.

Shelton, Anthony A.
- 1996 The Girl Who Ground Herself: Huichol Attitudes toward Maize. In *People of the Peyote: Huichol Indian History, Religion, and Survival*, edited by S. B. Schaefer and P. T. Furst, pp. 451-467. Albuquerque: University of New Mexico Press.

Shore, Bradd
- 1996 *Culture in Mind: Cognition, Culture, and the Problem of Meaning*. Oxford: Oxford University Press.

Silko, Leslie Marmon
- 1996 Landscape, History, and the Pueblo Imagination. In *The Ecocriticism Reader: Landmarks in Literary Ecology*, edited by C. Glotfelty and H. From, pp. 264–275. Athens: University of Georgia Press.

Slingerland, Edward
- 2004 Conceptual Metaphor Theory as Methodology for Comparative Religion. *Journal of the American Academy of Religion* 72(1):1–31.

Smith, H. Denise
- 2002 History Recorded in Stone: The Rock Art of Abo Pueblo. In *Forward into the Past: Papers in Honor of Teddy Lou & Francis Stickney*, edited by R. N. Wiseman, T. C. O'Laughlin, and C. T. Snow, pp. 109–118. Vol. 28. Albuquerque: Archaeological Society of New Mexico.

Smith, Michael E.
- 2003 Information Networks in Postclassic Mesoamerica. In *The Postclassic Mesoamerican World*, edited by M. E. Smith and F. F. Berdan, pp. 181–185. Salt Lake City: University of Utah Press.

2007 Tula and Chichén Itzá: Are We Asking the Right Questions? In *Twin Tollans: Chichén Itzá, Tula, and the Epiclassic to Early Postclassic Mesoamerican World*, edited by J. K. Kowalski and C. Kristan-Graham, pp. 579–617. Washington, DC: Dumbarton Oaks.

Smith, Michael E., and Francis F. Berdan (editors)
2003 *The Postclassic Mesoamerican World*. Provo: University of Utah Press.

Smith, Michael E., and Cynthia Heath-Smith
1980 Waves of Influence in Postclassic Mesoamerica? A Critique of the Mixteca-Puebla Concept. *Anthropology* 4:15–50.

Smith, Watson
1952 *Kiva Mural Decorations at Awatovi and Kawaika-a, With a Survey of Other Walls Paintings in the Pueblo Southwest*. Papers of the Peabody Museum of Archaeology and Ethnology No. 37. Cambridge, MA: Harvard University.

Snead, James E.
2008 *Ancestral Landscapes of the Pueblo World*. Tucson: University of Arizona Press.

Snead, James E., and Mark Allen (editors)
in press *Conflagration and Conflict: Burnt Corn Pueblo and the Galisteo Basin in the 14th Century AD*. Tucson: University of Arizona Press.

Snead, James E., Winifred Creamer, and Tineke Van Zandt
2004 "Ruins of Our Forefathers": Large Sites and Site Clusters in the Northern Rio Grande. In *The Protohistoric Pueblo World, A.D. 1275–1600*, edited by E. C. Adams and A. I. Duff, pp. 26–34. Tucson: University of Arizona Press.

Spielmann, Katherine A.
1996 Impressions of Pueblo III Settlement Trends among the Rio Abajo and Eastern Border Pueblos. In *The Prehistoric Pueblo World AD 1150–1350*, edited by M. Adler, pp. 177–187. Tucson: University of Arizona Press.
1998 Ritual Influences on the Development of Rio Grande Glaze A Ceramics. In *Migration and Reorganization: The Pueblo IV Period in the American Southwest*, edited by K. A. Spielmann, pp. 253–261. Arizona State University Anthropological Research Papers 51. Tempe: Arizona State University.
2004 Communal Feasting, Ceramics, and Exchange. In *Identity, Feasting, and the Archaeology of the Greater Southwest*, edited by B. J. Mills, pp. 210–232. Boulder: University Press of Colorado.

Spielmann, Katherine A., and James Eder
1994 Hunters and Farmers: Then and Now. *Annual Review of Anthropology* 23:303–323.

Spier, Leslie
1919 *Notes on Some Little Colorado Ruins*. Anthropological Papers of the

References

American Museum of Natural History, vol. 18, pt. 5. New York: American Museum of Natural History.

Spinden, Herbert
 1993 [1936] *Songs of the Tewa*. Santa Fe, NM: Sunstone Press.

Spiro, Melford E.
 1963 Religion: Problems of Definition and Explanation. In *Anthropological Approaches to the Study of Religion*, edited by M. Banton, pp. 85–126. New York: Frederick A. Praeger.

Stahl, Ann B.
 1993 Concepts of Time and Approaches to Analogical Reasoning in Historical Perspective. *American Antiquity* 58(2):235–260.

Steed, Paul P.
 1976 Rock Art at La Cienega Mesa. In *American Indian Rock Art*, edited by A. J. Bock, F. Bock, and J. Cawley, pp. 115–119. Vol. 3. Whittier, CA: American Rock Art Research Association.

Steen, Charlie R.
 1982 Pajarito Plateau Archaeological Surveys and Excavations, II. Los Alamos. Los Alamos National Laboratory Report LA-8660-NERP. Los Alamos National Laboratory, Los Alamos.

Stein, John R., and Stephen H. Lekson
 1992 Anasazi Ritual Landscapes. In *Anasazi Regional Organization and the Chaco System*, edited by David E. Doyel, pp. 87–100. Anthropological Papers No. 5, Maxwell Museum of Anthropology. Albuquerque: University of New Mexico.

Stephen, Alexander M.
 1936 *Hopi Journal of Alexander M. Stephen*, edited by E. C. Parsons. New York: Columbia University Press.

Stevenson, Matilda Cox
 1904 The Zuni Indians: Their Mythology, Esoteric Societies, and Ceremonies. *Bureau of American Ethnology 23rd Annual Report*. Washington, DC: Government Printing Office.

Strong, Pauline
 1979a Santa Ana Pueblo. In *Handbook of North American Indians*. Vol. 9. *Southwest*, edited by A. Ortiz, pp. 398–406. Washington, DC: Smithsonian Institution.
 1979b San Felipe Pueblo. In *Handbook of North American Indians*. Vol. 9. *Southwest*, edited by A. Ortiz, pp. 390–397. Washington, DC: Smithsonian Institution.

Stubbs, Stanley A., and W. S. Stallings Jr.
 1953 *The Excavation of Pindi Pueblo, New Mexico*. Santa Fe: Monographs of the School for American Research and the Laboratory of Anthropology, No. 18.

Sturken, Marita, and Lisa Cartwright
   2001   *Practices of Looking: An Introduction to Visual Culture*. New York: Oxford University Press.

Sugiyama, Saburo
   2005   *Human Sacrifice, Militarism, and Rulership: Materialization of State Ideology at the Feathered Serpent Pyramid, Teotihuacan*. Cambridge: Cambridge University Press.

Suina, Joseph H.
   2002   The Persistence of the Corn Mothers. In *Archaeological of the Pueblo Revolt: Identity, Meaning, and Renewal in the Pueblo World*, edited by Robert W. Preucel, pp. 212–216. Albuquerque: University of New Mexico Press.

Sweet, Jill D.
   1979   Play, Role Reversal, and Humor: Symbolic Elements of a Tewa Pueblo Navaho Dance. *Dance Research Journal* 12(1):3–12.
   1985   *Dances of the Tewa Pueblo Indians*. Santa Fe, NM: School of American Research Press.

Sweetser, Eve
   1990   *From Etymology to Pragmatics: Metaphorical and Cultural Aspects of Semantic Structure*. Cambridge: Cambridge University Press.

Taube, Karl
   2001   The Breath of Life: The Symbolism of Wind in Mesoamerica and the American Southwest. In *The Road to Aztatlan: Art From a Mythic Homeland*, edited by V. M. Fields and V. Zamudio-Taylor, pp. 102–123. Los Angeles: Los Angeles County Museum of Art.
   2010   Gateways to Another World: The Symbolism of Supernatural Passageways in the Art and Ritual of Mesoamerica and the American Southwest. In *Painting the Cosmos: Metaphor and Worldview in Images from the Southwest and Mesoamerica*, edited by K. Hays-Gilpin and P. Schaafsma, pp. 73–120. Flagstaff: Museum of Northern Arizona Bulletin 67.

Tedlock, Barbara
   1980   Songs of the Zuni Kachina Society: Composition, Rehearsal, and Performance. In *Southwestern Indian Ritual Drama*, edited by Charlotte J. Frisbee, pp. 7–35. Albuquerque: University of New Mexico Press.
   1983   Zuni Sacred Theater. *American Indian Quarterly* 7(3):93–110.

Tedlock, Dennis
   1994   Stories of Kachinas and the Dance of Life and Death. In *Kachinas in the Pueblo World*, edited by Polly Schaafsma, pp. 161–174. Albuquerque: University of New Mexico Press.

Thomas, Julian
   1996   *Time, Culture and Identity*. London: Routledge.

Thompson, Kenneth
    1986   *Beliefs and Ideology*. London: Tavistock.
Thompson, Marc
    2007   Pre-Columbian Venus, Celestial Twins and Icons of Duality. In *Religion in the Prehispanic Southwest*, edited by C. S. VanPool, T. L. VanPool, and D. A. Phillips, pp. 165–183. Lanham, MD: AltaMira.
Tilley, Christopher
    1994   *A Phenomenology of Landscape: Places, Paths, and Monuments*. Oxford: Berg.
    1999   *Metaphor and Material Culture*. London: Blackwell.
Titiev, Mischa
    1944   *Old Oraibi: A Study of the Hopi Indians of Third Mesa*. Papers of the Peabody Museum of American Archaeology and Ethnology 22(1). Cambridge, MA: Harvard Museum.
Toll, H. Wolcott
    1993   The Role of the Totah in Regions and Regional Definitions. Paper presented at the 5th Occasional Anasazi Symposium, San Juan College, Farmington, New Mexico.
Trager, George L.
    1942   The Historical Phonology of the Tiwa Languages. *Studies in Linguistics* 1(5):1–10.
    1967   The Tanoan Settlement of the Rio Grande Area: A Possible Chronology. In *Studies in Southwestern Ethnolinguistics*, edited by D. H. Hymes and W. E. Bittle, pp. 335–350. The Hague: Mouton & Co..
Traugott, E. C.
    1989   On the Rise of Epistemic Meanings in English: An Example of Subjectification in Semantic Change. *Language* 65(1):31–55.
Triadan, Daniela
    2006   Dancing Gods: Ritual, Performance, and Political Organization in the Prehistoric Southwest. In *The Archaeology of Performance: Theaters of Power, Community, and Politics*, edited by T. Inomata and L. S. Coben, pp. 159–186. Lanham, MD: AltaMira.
Trouillot, Michelle-Rolph
    1995   *Silencing the Past: Power and the Production of History*. Boston: Beacon.
Turner, Victor
    1967   *The Forest of Symbols*. Ithaca, NY: Cornell University Press.
    1974   *Dramas, Fields, and Metaphors: Symbolic Action in Human Society*. Ithaca, NY: Cornell University Press.
Tyler, Hamilton A.
    1964   *Pueblo Gods and Myths*. Norman: University of Oklahoma Press.
Upham, Steadman
    1989   East Meets West: Hierarchy and Elites in Pueblo Society. In *The Socio-*

political Structure of Prehistoric Southwestern Societies, edited by S. Upham, K. G. Lightfoot, and R. A. Jewett, pp. 77–102. Boulder, CO: Westview.

Upham, Steadman, and Lori S. Reed
- 1989 Regional Systems in the Central and Northern Southwest: Demography, Economy, and Sociopolitics Preceding Contact. In *Columbian Consequences*, Vol. 1, edited by D. H. Thomas, pp. 57–76. Washington, DC: Smithsonian Institution Press.

Van Dyke, Ruth M.
- 2004 Memory, Meaning, and Masonry. The Late Bonito Chacoan Landscape. *American Antiquity* 69:413–431.
- 2008 *The Chaco Experience: Landscape and Ideology at the Center Place*. Santa Fe, NM: School for Advanced Research Press.

Van Gennep, Arnold
- 1960 *The Rites of Passage*. Originally published 1909. Translated by M. B. Vizedom and G. L. Caffee. Chicago: University of Chicago Press.

Van Keuren, Scott
- 2004 Crafting Feasts in the Prehispanic Southwest. In *Identity, Feasting, and the Archaeology of the Greater Southwest*, edited by B. J. Mills, pp. 192–209. Boulder: University Press of Colorado.
- 2006a Rethinking "Cult" Movements in the Late Pre-Hispanic Southwest. Paper presented at the 10th Biennial Southwest Symposium, Las Cruces, New Mexico.
- 2006b Shumway Ruin and the Late Pre-Hispanic Period in East-Central Arizona. *Contributions to Science* 508:1–19.

VanPool, Christine S.
- 2003 The Shaman-Priests of the Casas Grandes Region, Chihuahua, Mexico. *American Antiquity* 68:696-717.

VanPool, Christine, and Todd VanPool
- 2007 *Signs of the Casas Grandes Shamans*. Provo: University of Utah Press.

VanPool, Christine S., Todd L. VanPool, and David A. Phillips Jr.
- 2006a Introduction: Archaeology and Religion. In *Religion in the Prehispanic Southwest*, edited by C. S. VanPool, T. L. VanPool, and D. A. Phillips Jr., pp. 1–16. Lanham, MD: AltaMira.
- 2006b *Religion in the Prehispanic Southwest*. Lanham, MD: AltaMira.

Vansina, Jan
- 1985 *Oral Tradition as History*. Madison: University of Wisconsin Press.

Van West, Carla R., and Jeffrey S. Dean
- 2000 Environmental Characteristics of the A.D. 900–1300 Period in the Central Mesa Verde Region. *Kiva* 66(1):19–44.

Vargas, Victoria D.
- 1995 *Copper Bell Trade Patterns in the Prehispanic US Southwest and North-*

west Mexico. Arizona State Museum Archaeological Series 187. Tucson: Arizona State Museum.

Varien, Mark D.
- 1999a *Sedentism and Mobility in a Social Landscape: Mesa Verde and Beyond*. Tucson: University of Arizona Press.
- 1999b Regional Context: Architecture, Settlement Patterns, and Abandonment. In *The Sand Canyon Archaeological Project: Site Testing* [HTML title], edited by M. D. Varien, chap. 21. Available: http://www.crowcanyon.org/sitetesting

Varien, Mark D., William D. Lipe, Michael A. Adler, Ian M. Thompson, and Bruce A. Bradley
- 1996 Southwestern Colorado and Southeastern Utah Settlement Patterns: A.D. 1100 to 1300. In *The Prehistoric Pueblo World A.D. 1150–1350*, edited by M. A. Adler, pp. 86–113. Tucson: University of Arizona Press.

Varien, Mark D., Scott G. Ortman, Timothy A. Kohler, Donna M. Glowacki, and C. David Johnson
- 2007 Historical Ecology in the Mesa Verde Region: Results from the Village Project. *American Antiquity* 72(2):273–299.

Varien, Mark D., Carla Van West, and G. Stuart Patterson
- 2000 Competition, Cooperation, and Conflict: Agricultural Production and Community Catchments in the Central Mesa Verde Region. *Kiva* 66(1): 45–65.

Vivian, R. Gordon
- 1949 Pre-historic Handy Man. *New Mexico Magazine* 27(6):14, 39–41.
- 1959 *The Hubbard Site and Other Tri-wall Structures in New Mexico and Colorado*. Archaeological Research Series Number Five. National Park Service, US Department of the Interior. Washington, DC: Government Printing Office.

Vivian, Gordon, and Tom W. Mathews
- 1964 *Kin Kletso: A Pueblo III Community in Chaco Canyon, New Mexico*. Globe, AZ: Southwestern Monuments Association.

Vivian, R. Gwinn
- 1984 Agricultural and Social Adjustments to Changing Environment in the Chaco Basin. In *Prehistoric Agricultural Strategies in the Southwest*, edited by Suzanne K. Fish and Paul R. Fish, pp. 242–257. Anthropological Research Papers No. 33. Tempe: Arizona State University.
- 1992 Chacoan Water Use and Managerial Decision Making. In *Anasazi Regional Organization and the Chaco System*, edited by David E. Doyel, pp. 45–57. Anthropological Papers No. 5, Maxwell Museum of Anthropology. Albuquerque: University of New Mexico.
- 2004 Puebloan Farmers of the Chacoan World. In *In Search of Chaco, New*

Approaches to an Archaeological Enigma, edited by David Grant Noble, pp. 7–13. Santa Fe, NM: School of American Research Press.

Vivian, R. Gwinn, Dulce N. Dodgen, and Gayle H. Hartmann
- 1978 *Wooden Ritual Artifacts from Chaco Canyon New Mexico: The Chetro Ketl Collection*. Anthropological Papers of the University of Arizona 32. Tucson: University of Arizona Press.

Vokes, Richard
- 2007 Rethinking the Anthropology of Religious Change: New Perspectives on Revitalization and Conversion Movements. *Reviews in Anthropology* 36:311–333.

Voth, Henry R.
- 1905 *The Traditions of the Hopi*. Field Columbian Museum Publication 96, Anthropological Series, Vol. 8. Chicago: Field Museum.

Walens, S.
- 1981 *Feasting with Cannibals: An Essay in Kwakiutl Cosmology*. Princeton, NJ: Princeton University Press.

Walker, William H.
- 1995 Ceremonial Trash? In *Expanding Archaeology*, edited by J. M. Skibo, W. H. Walker, and A. E. Nielsen, pp. 67–79. Salt Lake City: University of Utah Press.
- 2008 Practice and Nonhuman Social Actors: The Afterlife Histories of Witches and Dogs in the American Southwest. In *Memory Work: Archaeologies of Material Practices*, edited by B. J. Mills and W. H. Walker, pp. 137–158. Santa Fe, NM: School for Advanced Research Press.

Walker, William H., Vincent M. LaMotta, and E. Charles Adams
- 2000 Katsinas and Kiva Abandonment at Homol'ovi. In *The Archaeology of Regional Interaction: Religion, Warfare, and Exchange Across the American Southwest and Beyond*, edited by M. Hegmon, pp. 341–360. Boulder: University Press of Colorado.

Wallace, Anthony F. C.
- 1952 Handsome Lake and the Great Revival in the West. *American Quarterly* 4(2):149–165.
- 1956 Revitalization Movements. *American Anthropologist* 58(2):264–281.
- 2003 *Revitalizations and Mazeways, Essays on Culture Change, Volume 1*, edited by Robert S. Grumet. Lincoln: University of Nebraska Press.
- 2004 Foreword. In *Reassessing Revitalization Movements: Perspectives from North America and the Pacific Islands*, edited by M. E. Harkins, pp. vii–xii. Lincoln: University of Nebraska Press.

Ware, John A.
- 2001 Chaco Social Organization: A Peripheral View. In *Chaco Society and Polity: Papers from the 1999 Conference*, edited by L. S. Cordell, W. J. Judge, and J. Piper, pp. 79–93. New Mexico Archeological Council

Special Publication 4. Albuquerque: New Mexico Archeological Council.

2002   Descent Group and Sodality: Alternative Pueblo Social Histories. In *Traditions, Transitions, and Technologies: Themes in Southwestern Archaeology in the Year 2000*, edited by S. H. Schlanger, pp. 94–112. Boulder: University Press of Colorado.

Ware, John A., and Eric Blinman

2000   Cultural Collapse and Reorganization: The Origin and Spread of Pueblo Ritual Sodalities. In *The Archaeology of Regional Interaction: Religion, Warfare, and Exchange across the American Southwest and Beyond*, pp. 381–405. Boulder: University Press of Colorado.

Watkins, Laurel

1984   *A Grammar of Kiowa*. Studies in the Anthropology of North American Indians. Lincoln: University of Nebraska Press.

Webster, Laurie D.

2008   An Initial Assessment of Perishable Artifact Relationships among Salmon, Aztec, and Chaco Canyon. In *Chaco's Northern Prodigies: Salmon, Aztec, and the Ascendancy of the Middle San Juan Region After A.D. 1100*, edited by P. F. Reed, pp. 167–189. Salt Lake City: University of Utah Press.

Weigand, Phillip C.

2007   States in Prehispanic Western Mesoamerica. In *The Political Economy of Ancient Mesoamerica: Transformations During the Formative and Classic Periods*, edited by V. Scarborough and J. Clark, pp. 101–113. Albuquerque: University of New Mexico Press.

2008   Turquoise: Formal Economic Interrelationships between Mesoamerica and the North American Southwest. In *Archaeology without Borders: Contact, Commerce, and Change in the US Southwest and Northwestern Mexico*, edited by L. D. Webster and M. E. McBrinn, pp. 343–354. Boulder: University Press of Colorado.

Weinman, Janice

1970   The Influence of Pueblo Worldview on the Construction of Its Vocal Music. *Ethnomusicology* 14(2):313–315.

Wendorf, Fred

1953   *Salvage Archaeology in the Chama Valley, New Mexico*. Monographs of the School of American Research, Number 17. Santa Fe, NM: School of American Research.

Whalen, Michael L., and Paul E. Minnis

2001   *Casas Grandes and Its Hinterland: Prehistoric Regional Organization in Northwest Mexico*. Tucson: University of Arizona Press.

2003   The Local and the Distant in the Origin of Casa Grandes, Chihuahua, Mexico. *American Antiquity* 68:314–332.

White, Leslie A.
- 1932　The Acoma Indians. *47th Annual Report of the Bureau of American Ethnology*, pp. 17–192. Washington, DC: Government Printing Office.
- 1962　*The Pueblo of Sia, New Mexico*. Bureau of American Ethnology, Bulletin 184. Washington, DC: Smithsonian Institution.

Whiteley, Peter
- 1988　*Deliberate Acts: Changing Hopi Culture through the Oraibi Split*. Tucson: University of Arizona Press.
- 1998　*Rethinking Hopi Ethnography*. Washington, DC: Smithsonian Institution Press.
- 2008　*The Orayvi Split: A Hopi Transformation*. Anthropological Papers of the American Museum of Natural History, No. 87. New York: American Museum of Natural History.

Whitley, David S.
- 2001　Science and the Sacred: Interpretive Theory in US Rock Art Research. *Theoretical Perspectives in Rock Art Research*:124–151.
- 2008　Archaeological Evidence for Conceptual Metaphors as Enduring Knowledge Structures. *Time & Mind* 1(1):7–30.

Whitley, David S., and Kelley Hays-Gilpin (editors)
- 2008a　*Belief in the Past: Theoretical Approaches to the Archaeology of Religion*. Walnut Creek, CA: Left Coast Press.
- 2008b　Religion Beyond Icon, Burial and Monument: An Introduction. In *Belief in the Past: Theoretical Approaches to the Archaeology of Religion*, edited by D. S. Whitley and K. Hays-Gilpin, pp. 11–21. Walnut Creek, CA: Left Coast Press.

Whittlesey, Stephanie M.
- 2009　Mountains, Mounds and Meaning: Metaphor in the Hohokam Cultural Landscape. In *The Archaeology of Meaningful Places*, edited by B. J. Bowser and M. N. Zedeno, pp. 73–89. Salt Lake City: University of Utah Press.

Wilcox, David R.
- 1987　Frank Midvale's Investigations at the Site of La Ciudad. Anthropological Field Studies 19. Office of Cultural Resource Management. Tempe: Arizona State University.
- 2008　Ancient Cultural Interplay of the American Southwest and the Mexican Northwest. *Journal of the Southwest* 50(12):103–135.

Williams, Eduardo
- 2009　Prehispanic West México: A Mesoamerican Culture Area. FAMSI, http://www.famsi.org/research/williams/wm_epiclassic.html. Accessed August 24, 2009.

Wills, W. H.
- 2000　Political Leadership and the Construction of Chacoan Great Houses, A.D. 1020–1140. In *Alternative Leadership Strategies in the Prehispanic*

Southwest, edited by Barbara J. Mills, pp. 19–44. Tucson: University of Arizona Press.

Wilshusen, Richard H., and Scott G. Ortman
  1999 Rethinking the Pueblo I Period in the San Juan Drainage: Aggregation, Migration, and Cultural Diversity. *Kiva* 64(3):369–399.

Windes, Thomas C., and Eileen Bacha
  2008 Sighting along the Grain: Differential Structural Wood Use at the Salmon Ruin. In *Chaco's Northern Prodigies*, edited by Paul F. Reed, pp. 113–139. Salt Lake City: University of Utah Press.

Windes, Thomas C., and Peter J. McKenna
  2006 The Kivas of Tsama (LA 908). In *Southwestern Interludes: Papers in Honor of Charlotte J. and Theodore R. Frisbie*, edited by R. M. Wiseman, T. C. O'Laughlin, and C. T. Snow, pp. 233–253. vol. 32. Albuquerque: Archaeological Society of New Mexico.

Wissler, Clark
  1912 *Ceremonial Bundles of the Blackfoot Indians*. Anthropological Papers of the American Museum of Natural History, Vol. 7, Part 2. New York: American Museum of Natural History.

Wölfflin, Heinrich
  1932 *Principles of Art History. The Problem of the Development of Style in Later Art*, Translated from 7th German Edition (1929) into English by M D Hottinger (Dover Publications, New York 1932 and reprints).

Woodbury, Richard, and Nathalie F. S. Woodbury
  1966 Decorated Pottery of the Zuni Area. In *Excavation of Hawikuh by Frederick Webb Hodge: Report of the Hendricks-Hodge Expedition*, edited by W. Smith, R. Woodbury, and N. F. S. Woodbury, pp 302–306. 20th ed. Contributions from the Museum of the American Indian. New York: Museum of the American Indian.

Wright, Aaron M.
  2010 The Climate of the Depopulation of the Northern Southwest. In *Leaving Mesa Verde: Peril and Change in the 13th Century Southwest*, edited by T. A. Kohler, M. D. Varien, and A. Wright. Tucson: University of Arizona Press.

Wright, Baron
  1973 *Hopi Kachinas*. Flagstaff, AZ: Northland Press.

Wylie, Alison
  1989 Archaeological Cables and Tacking: The Implications of Practice for Bernstein's 'Options Beyond Objectivism and Relativism." *Philosophy of the Social Sciences* 19(1): 1–18.
  2002 *Thinking from Things: Essays in the Philosophy of Archaeology*. Berkeley: University of California Press.

Yoffee, Norman
  2001 The Chaco "Rituality" Revisited. In *Chaco Society and Polity: Papers

from the 1999 Conference, edited by Linda S. Cordell, W. James Judge, and June-el Piper, pp. 63–78. New Mexico Archaeological Council Special Publication 4. Albuquerque: New Mexico Archaeological Council.

Young, Jon Nathan
    1982   Salado Polychrome Pottery. In *Collected Papers in Honor of John W. Runyan*, edited by G. X. Fitzgerald, pp. 31–57. Papers of the Archaeological Society of New Mexico 7. Albuquerque: Archaeological Society of New Mexico.

Young, Mary Jane
    1988   *Signs from the Ancestors: Zuni Cultural Symbolism and Perceptions of Rock Art*. Albuquerque: University of New Mexico Press.

Zedeño, María Nieves
    2008   Bundled Worlds: The Roles and Interactions of Complex Objects from the North American Plains. *Journal of Archaeological Method and Theory* 15:362–378.

Zeilik, Michael
    1985   The Ethnoastronomy of the Historic Pueblos, 1: Calendrical Sun Watching. *Archaeoastronomy, Journal for the History of Astronomy,* Supplement to Volume 16:S1–S24.

About the Contributors

WESLEY BERNARDINI is Associate Professor of Anthropology at the University of Redlands in California. His collaborative research with the Hopi Tribe attempts to trace the movement and development of social groups through time and space. His recent fieldwork has concentrated on documenting large fourteenth- and fifteenth-century villages on the Hopi mesas. His current work focuses on building virtual three-dimensional tools to explore ancient social landscapes, both for academic and educational uses, supported by funding from the W. M. Keck Foundation.

MATTHEW A. CHAMBERLIN received his Ph.D. from Arizona State University in 2008 and is Assistant Professor in the Interdisciplinary Liberal Studies department at James Madison University, Virginia. His current research explores population aggregation, conflict, and identity in the Salinas area of New Mexico. He has codirected an archaeological field school in the Salinas area from 2006 to 2010, a project centering on the excavation of three early plaza pueblos on the Chupadera Mesa.

DONNA M. GLOWACKI is the John Cardinal O'Hara CSC Assistant Professor of Anthropology at the University of Notre Dame, a senior researcher on the Village Ecodynamics Project, and a long-time research associate with Crow Canyon Archaeological Center. Her current research focuses on village formation and on issues of religious change and the social processes involved in the regional depopulation of the northern San Juan region at the end of the 1200s. She has conducted fieldwork at sixty-three of the largest sites in the central Mesa Verde region. She is currently engaged in fieldwork at Mesa Verde National

Park that focuses on village formation and aggregation at Spruce Tree House cliff dwelling and other large sites throughout the park.

KELLEY HAYS-GILPIN is Professor of Anthropology at Northern Arizona University and Curator of Anthropology at the Museum of Northern Arizona. Recent publications include *Ambiguous Images: Gender and Rock Art* (AltaMira), which won the 2005 Society for American Archaeology book award, and *Painting the Cosmos: Metaphor and Worldview in Images from the Southwest and Pueblos and Mexico* (Museum of Northern Arizona), with Polly Schaafsma. Her current research focuses on the long-term history of the Hopi region and on how archaeologists and Hopi communities can work together to facilitate culturally appropriate use of museum collections.

RANDALL H. MCGUIRE is Distinguished Professor of Anthropology at Binghamton University in Binghamton, New York. He received his B.A. from the University of Texas and his M.A. and Ph.D. from the University of Arizona. He has taught at the Universitat Autònoma de Barcelona and at the Esquela Nacional de Antropología y Historia in México City. He has published extensively on Marxist theory and indigenous archaeology. From 1996 to 2007, he and Dean Saitta of the University of Denver directed the Archaeology of the Colorado Coal Field War, 1913–1914 project near Trinidad, Colorado. He has worked with Elisa Villalpando of the Centro INAH, Sonora, for 28 years investigating the Trincheras Tradition of northern Sonora, México. The Spanish summary of their excavations at Cerro de Trincheras, *Entre Muros de Piedra*, was published in Hermosillo, Sonora, in 2010. The full site report on the excavations is currently in press at the Arizona State Museum. His latest books include *Archaeology as Political Action*, *The Archaeology of Class War* with Karin Larkin, and *Ideologies in Archaeology* with Reinhard Bernbeck. He has been thinking and writing about the Mesoamerican connection in the Southwest/Northwest since he took a seminar on southwestern archaeology with Emil Haury in 1978.

MARIT K. MUNSON is Associate Professor of Anthropology at Trent University (Ontario, Canada) and director of TUARC, the Trent University Archaeological Research Centre. Her research explores issues of identity, gender, and ritual practice in Ancestral Pueblo rock art of the northern Rio Grande Valley and Mimbres iconography from southern New Mexico. These interests were formed during her time as a graduate student at the University of New Mexico and were shaped by a short stint at the Smithsonian's National Museum of Natural History and by her experience teaching courses on the anthropology of art and native art of North America. She recently completed *The Archaeology of Art in the American Southwest* (AltaMira), a book that attempts to bridge the gap between archaeological, art historical, and anthropological perspectives on ancient art.

ELIZABETH A. NEWSOME is Associate Professor in the Visual Arts Department at the University of California at San Diego. She holds an M.A. and Ph.D. in the history of art from the University of Texas at Austin, where she specialized in Precolumbian and Native American art history. Newsome's studies have addressed various aspects of Maya architecture, stone sculpture and hieroglyphic writing, with active field research in Mexico, Guatemala, and Honduras. Her research and teaching explore methodologies that bridge art history and other disciplines, including philosophy, linguistics, and the social sciences. Her present works include a monograph on the fire-related mythology and rituals of the ancient Maya (*The Bundle Altars of Copan: A New Perspective on their Meaning and Archaeological Contexts*, Ancient America Monograph No. 4) and a forthcoming book titled *The Song of Painted Walls: Ancient Mural Painting in the Pueblo Southwest*. She has also authored articles on Southwest Indian painting and murals for *American Indian Culture and Research Journal* and *Plateau* among others.

SCOTT G. ORTMAN is an Omidyar Fellow at the Santa Fe Institute and the Lightfoot Fellow at Crow Canyon Archaeological Center. He received his Ph.D. in anthropology from Arizona State University in 2009 and is a former fellow of the American Council of Learned Societies/Andrew W. Mellon Foundation. He has conducted archaeological research in the US Southwest since 1990, initially in the Zuni and Mesa Verde regions and more recently in the Rio Grande region. His research focuses on historical anthropology, evolutionary culture theory, cognitive and historical linguistics, and material culture studies. Among his honors are the Fowler Prize in Anthropology from the University of Utah Press, the SAA Student Paper Award, and the Firestone Medal for excellence in undergraduate research from Stanford University.

TIMOTHY R. PAUKETAT is an archaeologist and is Professor of Anthropology at the University of Illinois in Urbana-Champaign, having previously taught at the University of Oklahoma and the State University of New York at Buffalo. He studies the relationship between religion, materiality, identity, and polity among the Woodland and Mississippian peoples in pre-Columbian eastern North America, and advocates alternative (practice-based, phenomenological, and historical) approaches in archaeology. The author or editor of eight books and numerous journal articles and book chapters, he has also directed large-scale excavations of settlements and ritual deposits associated with the pre-Columbian city of Cahokia, in southwestern Illinois, and its northern outposts in Wisconsin. His ongoing projects focus on ancient missionization, bundling, and cosmologies-in-the-making.

STEPHEN PLOG received his B.A. from the University of Michigan in 1971 and his Ph.D. in 1977. He has taught at the University of Virginia since 1978 where he is the David A. Harrison Professor of Archaeology. He has supervised fieldwork in east-central and northeastern Arizona and his interests focus on Pueblo social and ritual organization, demography, and the history of archaeology. Most recently he has supervised the creation of the Chaco Research Archive (www.chacoarchive.org) through the support of the Andrew Mellon Foundation, the National Science Foundation, the National Park Service, and the Institute for Advanced Technology in the Humanities at the University of Virginia.

SCOTT VAN KEUREN is Assistant Professor of Anthropology at the University of Vermont. Prior to arriving at UVM, he served as Curator of North American Archaeology at the Museum of Natural History of Los Angeles County, and taught courses both at the University of Southern California and California Institute of Technology. He recently completed excavations at Fourmile Ruin and two other fourteenth-century towns in the Silver Creek area, Arizona, supported by funding from the Wenner-Gren Foundation and the National Science Foundation. The project examines the origins and production of iconographic-style polychrome pottery from east-central Arizona. His ongoing research investigates the economic and political organization of late pre-Hispanic Pueblo settlements in east-central Arizona.

Volume contributors in Dragoon, Arizona, while attending the Amerind Seminar, *Religious Ideologies in the Pueblo Southwest, A.D. 1250–1540*. Front row (*left to right*): Tim Pauketat, Elizabeth Newsome, Steve Plog, Kelley Hays-Gilpin, Marit Munson, and Randy McGuire. Back row (*left to right*): Matt Chamberlin, Wes Bernardini, Scott Van Keuren, Donna Glowacki, and Scott Ortman. Not pictured: John Ware, who took the photograph.

INDEX

acculturation, 73
actors, 13, 25, 131–133, 151–152, 156, 219–220
Adams, E. Charles, 8, 10, 46, 165, 171, 178, 194
adaptations, 79, 105, 165
adobe brick, 189, 242
aesthetics, 32, 39, 41, 156, 160
agency, 15, 166, 193, 225–226, 228, 230, 231
aggrandizers, 132
aggregation, 3, 13, 19, 50, 66, 68, 72–73, 75, 80, 135, 156, 182, 186, 198, 202, 204, 220
agriculture (or agricultural), 30–31, 57–58, 66, 68, 71, 86, 94, 100–101, 103–106, 159, 198, 205, 217, 240
Allen, Paula Gunn, 161, 169, 172
altars, 48, 167, 171
Alta Vista, 33, 35
anthropomorphic, 32, 153, 167, 169–172
Archaic period, 202
architecture, 21, 26, 50, 53, 72, 75–78, 81, 84, 86, 95, 97, 100, 103–104, 106, 108, 111–112, 137, 153, 160, 166, 178, 192, 202, 240, 242
Arizona, 31–32, 44, 83, 86, 175, 177–179, 181–183, 185–187, 189, 191, 193–195, 199–200, 202, 204, 212, 214, 217, 242
Arroyo Hondo, 100–101
artistic, 154–155, 179
artists, 109, 111, 115, 118, 121–122, 124, 126–128, 171, 235
Asad, Talal, 4–6
assimilation, 169, 220
astronomy (or astronomical), 27, 155, 158–159, 163, 166, 174, 241

Awat'ovi, 153, 168, 198, 207
Aztatlán, 33–34, 37–39
Aztec, 25–27, 48–49, 56, 71–72, 76, 78, 80, 157

ball courts, 32, 35, 38, 42
ball games, 28
Basketmaker period, 88, 202, 211
baskets (or basketry), 78, 97, 153, 201
beads, 91
Beals, Ralph, 41
beings, 90–92, 105, 167, 170, 221, 230, 235, 239
beliefs, 1, 3–13, 15–17, 19–23, 25–26, 29, 39–40, 43–44, 46–48, 52, 60, 65, 68, 70, 107, 175–185, 187, 189, 191–195, 221–226, 239
belief systems, 10, 52, 193, 222–224
bells (copper), 15, 25, 33, 37–43, 45, 70, 177, 224, 236–237
Betatakin, 212
bichrome, 9, 156, 241
blessings, 28, 49
blood, 47–48
Boone, Elizabeth H., 34
Bourdieu, Pierre, 131–132, 139–140
bowls (pottery), 9, 16, 20, 72, 77, 80, 84–85, 89, 91, 93–97, 99, 101, 103, 105–107, 123, 164, 168, 175, 177–178, 183–186, 191–193, 233
Bradley, Bruce, 71, 77
Bradley, Ronna, 43
Brandt, Richard, 133
Braniff, Beatriz, 31
bundles, 21, 234–238
burials, 42–44, 53, 60–64, 78, 100–101, 192
butterflies, 27, 40, 47, 89, 113

cacao, 38, 77
caches, 15, 55–56, 59, 178
calendar (or calendric), 35, 160, 174, 196, 205, 212, 219, 241
Caracol, 25
Carot, Patricia, 32
Casa Grande, 200
Casas Grandes (Paquimé), 23–26, 37, 40, 42–44, 46–48, 55, 61, 237
Castle Rock Pueblo, 77
cave, 27, 78
celestial, 39, 43, 69, 232, 235
cemeteries, 61
center place, 41, 168, 174, 230
ceremony (or ceremonial), 1, 8, 10–12, 17, 20–21, 28, 54, 57, 59, 64, 75–78, 134, 154–155, 158, 163–166, 169–170, 172–176, 178, 189–191, 198, 204–206, 210, 212, 214, 216, 226, 243
Chacmools, 35
Chaco Canyon (or Chacoan), 15, 29, 33, 38–39, 50–53, 55–57, 60, 63–65, 67, 71, 73, 76–77, 80, 155, 199, 202, 204, 217–219, 224, 229, 233, 237, 239
Chaco Research Archive, 53
Chalchihuites, 30–33, 35, 37–39, 43
chants, 150, 152, 162–163
Chavez Pass, 201, 203–204
Chetro Ketl, 56, 236
chevrons, 116
Chichén Itza, 25
Chihuahua, 31–32
Chihuahuan polychromes, 40, 42
choreography, 155, 158, 165–166
chronology, 30, 112
Chupadera Mesa, 135–136, 138, 140–142, 148, 166, 228
Chupícuaro, 31
clans, 73, 154, 162, 164, 171–172, 184, 196–201, 204–210, 214, 216–219, 237
Cliff Palace, 75, 156–157, 162, 241
clouds, 27–28, 55, 58–59, 90–92, 105, 167, 169–170, 173, 181, 229–230, 239
clowns, 28–29
Cochiti, 149
cognition (or cognitive), 5, 18, 85, 129, 132, 158, 240
colonnades, 35, 38, 236

Colorado, 31–32, 40, 46, 77, 96, 114, 142, 147–148, 156–157, 182, 185, 190, 197, 210–212, 241–242
Colorado Plateau, 32, 77, 197
colors, 15, 27, 29, 55–57, 60, 123, 145, 157, 176, 179, 184, 216
communalism, 10, 130, 175
complexities, 7, 15, 169, 219, 222
conch trumpets, 40, 45
conformity, 130, 151–152
consultants, 214, 208, 214
contingencies, 3, 4, 11, 13, 19, 49, 68, 79, 82
cooperation, 10, 19, 169, 171
copper, 25, 33, 37–43, 45, 70, 236
corn. *See* maize
cosmology (or cosmological), 23, 25–27, 29, 30–31, 34, 37, 39, 40, 42–44, 46–48, 50–61, 63–65, 156, 158, 160, 166, 174, 211, 221–222, 224
cotton, 28
Crown, Patricia L., 9–11, 44, 178–179, 184–186, 194
cruciforms, 27, 41
cults, 8–11, 15, 20, 24, 29, 34, 39–45, 50–52, 60, 65–67, 70–71, 78, 81, 96, 101, 107, 111–112, 114, 121, 123, 125–126, 145, 147, 175–179, 182, 185–186, 192, 194, 196, 198, 210, 219, 241–242
cylinder vessels, 38, 60, 64

dances, 28, 30, 89–90, 93, 105, 114, 130, 133–134, 149–150, 152–155, 158, 165–167, 171–173, 201, 206, 226, 235, 240
deities, 43, 55–56, 169, 211, 229
demography, 53
depopulation, 1, 3, 64, 66–71, 73, 75, 77–79, 81–83, 233
deposits, 1, 3, 15, 52, 62, 178
descendants, 45, 96, 219, 232
dialectic, 7, 76
Di Peso, Charles, 42
directionality, 159
discourses, 4–6, 16, 84–85, 89, 100, 104–108, 187, 192–193, 196
doxa, 227
drought, 66, 69, 71–72, 78, 81–82, 228
D-shape, 76
duality, 173, 196, 216

Index

eagles, 76
Early Post-Classic International Symbol Set, 34, 36–37, 39–40, 44–45
Eastern Pueblo, 10, 22, 147
egalitarianism, 28
emulation, 185
environments, 97, 99, 101, 104, 158, 160–162, 190
esoteric knowledge, 28, 47, 206
ethics, 161
ethnographic (or ethnographies), 1–5, 8, 10, 16, 41, 54, 63, 65, 84, 86, 106, 108, 130–131, 133, 143, 146–152, 155, 160, 171, 178, 197–198, 229, 239

falcons, 76
famine, 69
farming, 28, 104, 240
feasts, 99, 123, 179, 185, 224
feathered or horned serpents, 26–27, 36, 38–40, 43–44, 48, 58, 110, 114, 118–120, 129
feathers, 28, 40, 48, 91, 113–115, 118, 200
fertility, 10, 26–27, 34, 43–44, 47, 57–58, 60, 64–65, 103, 117, 131, 158, 165, 169, 174, 178, 181
Fewkes, Jesse Walter, 63
Flower World, 27, 31, 43
foods, 29, 47–48, 57, 75, 77, 99, 105–106, 185, 192
Formative Period, 30
Fourmile Ruin, 185, 188–191, 242
Fourmile style, 9–10, 177–179, 183, 185–186, 191

Galisteo Basin, 78, 86, 109–111, 114, 116–117, 121, 123–126
Geertz, Clifford, 4
gender, 106, 154, 172, 174, 230
genealogies, 234–235, 236
Gila style, 178, 183, 185–186, 191, 241
glaze wares (pottery), 40, 46
Gran Quivira, 137, 142
great houses, 50–52, 55–56, 60, 64, 71–72, 80, 155, 231, 239

habitus, 181, 227
harmony, 10–11, 106, 172

Hays-Gilpin, Kelley, 9, 18–19, 30, 115, 153, 231–232
hematite, 56
hermeneutic, 18
Hers, Marie-Areti, 32
hierarchies, 6, 28, 130, 154, 208
Hill, Jane, 9, 30, 162
Hisatsinom, 201
Hohokam, 31–33, 37–41, 45–46
Homol'ovi, 165, 201, 203–204, 214
Hopi, 17, 26, 40, 48, 54, 58–59, 86–87, 133–134, 147, 155, 162, 165, 168, 171, 173, 196–219, 237, 239, 242
households, 17, 20, 48, 57, 73, 99, 106, 176–177, 184, 187, 190, 206
human sacrifice, 26, 28, 34–35, 38, 42–43, 46, 48
humped-back flute player, 38, 114

iconography, 9–10, 12, 20, 23, 25–29, 32, 34, 37–38, 40, 42–43, 46, 52–53, 64, 70, 109, 111–113, 115, 117–119, 121, 123, 125–127, 129, 154, 158, 164, 179, 184, 186, 194, 213
ideologies (or ideological), 2, 4–7, 9–11, 13, 15–20, 23–24, 31, 45, 68, 70–73, 80–82, 100, 108, 154–155, 167, 171–172, 174, 177–179, 181–182, 191–194, 206, 208, 210, 219–223, 225, 233, 239
imagery, 2, 8–10, 18, 38, 40, 70, 84, 94, 97, 99, 101, 103, 106, 109–110, 112, 114, 116, 118, 120–122, 128–129, 162, 165–166, 169, 171, 174–175, 178, 181, 184–186, 241
immigrations, 69, 73, 198, 202–203, 207, 217, 219
integration (or integrative), 10, 73, 75, 153, 169, 171–172, 194, 202
interpretation (or interpretive), 1–2, 6, 12–13, 19, 42, 68, 139, 143, 173, 179, 224
iron pyrite mirrors, 37–38

jacal, 135–138
Jalisco, 30–32
James, Susan, 48
Jeddito Yellow Ware, 46, 207, 211–213, 242
jewelry, 31–32, 38, 43
Jornada Mogollon, 46

Kabotie, Michael, 171
Katsina ceremonies, 201, 205–206, 212
Katsina religion, 20, 24, 26, 29, 40–42, 44, 46–48, 67, 70, 82, 153, 165, 171–172, 177–179, 184, 196, 210–212, 214, 216
Katsinas, 8, 10, 19–20, 24, 26, 29, 40–42, 44, 46–50, 56, 58, 60, 67, 70, 82, 153–154, 165, 171–172, 175, 177–179, 184, 194, 196, 200–201, 204–206, 210–216, 234, 239, 242
Kayenta, 44–45, 202–204, 212, 217, 242
Keane, Webb, 234
Keresan, 133
kinship, 54, 160, 172, 216–217
kiva murals, 10, 58, , 50, 56, 58–59, 70, 110, 115–118, 120–121, 178, 184, 216
kivas, 2, 8–10, 25–26, 50, 55–56, 58–59, 70, 74–78, 81, 89, 95, 97–98, 100, 106, 110, 115–118, 120–121, 125, 134, 154, 156–157, 164–167, 169–170, 174, 178, 184, 189, 206, 216–217, 237, 240
Kuwanwisiwma, Leigh, 205–206, 208

landscapes, 15, 18, 20, 22, 30, 39, 43, 55–56, 65, 79–80, 104–105, 110, 121–122, 155–162, 164, 166, 168, 174–175, 207–208, 217, 225–226, 229, 231–232, 237–238, 241
languages, 29–30, 85–92, 94, 96–97, 100, 106–108, 169, 198, 216, 240
La Quemada, 29, 33, 35, 63
Late Post-Classic International Symbol Set, 35–36, 42, 46
leadership, 64, 73, 171, 206, 209
lightning, 58, 117, 230
Lincoln, Bruce, 6
linguistics, 16, 18, 30, 85–86, 92, 96, 106, 108, 116, 169, 217, 219, 240
Little Colorado River, 40, 46, 147, 182, 185, 190, 210–211, 241

Made People (Tewa), 129–130, 133, 151, 173
Maestas Pueblo, 102
maize, 29, 48–49, 56–58, 89–92, 94, 99–101, 103–106, 121, 169, 205, 239–240
Mathiowetz, Michael, 42, 46
Maya (or Mayan), 25, 33, 239
meanings, 2, 4–5, 7, 9, 12–13, 17–19, 52, 90, 95, 105, 107, 110, 117, 131, 134, 144, 150–152, 154, 156, 158–160, 162, 169, 172–173, 176–181, 191–194, 229, 234, 239
memories, 15, 81, 176, 182, 219, 226, 234
Mesa Verde, 15–16, 66–69, 71–73, 75–83, 85, 87, 96–99, 101, 106–108, 156–157, 196, 199–200, 203–204, 233, 237, 241
Mesoamerica, 12, 16, 21, 23–26, 28–30, 32–35, 37–39, 41–43, 45–46, 48–49, 55, 60, 62, 77, 198, 236
metaphor, 29, 48, 60, 91, 94–95, 97, 104, 107–108, 158, 166, 233–234, 239–240
Michoacán, 30, 32
migrations, 1, 3, 11, 13, 15, 25, 27, 34, 41–42, 45, 66–67, 70–71, 82, 86, 100, 153, 155–156, 166, 169, 173–175, 197–201, 203, 205, 207–208, 210, 212, 214, 216–218, 220, 228, 237–238, 242
Mimbres, 33, 38–41, 45–46, 179
Mixteca-Puebla horizon, 33
Mogollon, 31–32, 39–40, 44, 46, 114, 123, 178–179, 185–186, 201, 241
Momaday, N. Scott, 160–161, 169
Monte Alban, 31, 33, 41
Montezuma, 27, 47, 96, 157
Moon House, 159
Moore, Jerry D., 143–144, 149
mortuary, 60
mosaics, 40, 45, 180
motifs, 38, 97, 114, 123, 153, 157–158, 179–180, 186
Motisinom (Hopi), 196–205, 208–212, 214, 216, 218, 242
murals, 10, 18–19, 50, 56–59, 70, 97, 110, 115–118, 120–121, 153–159, 161–171, 173–174, 178, 184, 216, 241
myths, 26, 158, 167, 223

narratives, 2, 6, 11–12, 21, 55, 66, 117, 119, 167, 174
naturalism, 119
Navajo, 57, 206, 212
Nayarit, 39
Nelson, Ben, 29, 38–39
networks, 13, 20–21, 23, 33, 37, 39–41, 49, 69, 79–80, 165, 176, 228–229, 233–238
New Fire Ceremony, 28

Index

New Mexico, 17, 31–32, 40, 44–46, 50, 86, 95, 97, 100, 131, 136, 210, 212, 224
Northwest Mexico, 23
Nùutungkwisi'nom (Hopi), 196–201, 203–210, 214, 217–218, 242

Oaxaca, 32
Olmec, 25
ontology, 160 232, 238
Oraibi (or Orayvi), 200, 207, 209
orthodoxies, 50, 164, 191, 222–223
Ortman, Scott, 16, 84, 153, 156–158, 233

Pajarito Plateau, 103, 109–117, 121, 123–124, 126, 128, 240
Paquimé. *See* Casas Grandes
parrots, 27, 38–40, 44, 205, 209
Parsons, Elsie Clews, 5, 54, 59, 134
performances, 7–8, 12–13, 17–18, 20–21, 79, 123, 125, 130–131, 133–135, 137, 139–141, 143–144, 146–155, 157, 159, 161–169, 171–174, 202, 205–206, 208, 222, 224–226, 232, 237–238
petroglyphs, 109–111, 117–118, 121–124, 126, 128, 155, 158, 166, 229–230, 241–242
phenomenology (or phenomenological), 18, 153, 158, 160, 225
Phoenix Basin, 38, 40, 44–45
pictographs, 110–111, 122–124, 126, 128
pigments, 56–57, 110, 118, 123, 128, 186
pilgrimages, 34, 52, 214, 229, 237,
Pinedale style, 9–10, 178, 182–184, 186, 241–242
pipes, 58–59, 239
plazas, 1–2, 8, 10, 17, 19–21, 29, 31, 38, 49, 55, 75–76, 82, 89–90, 92–95, 98–101, 104–107, 110, 123, 125, 130–131, 133–143, 146–152, 154, 164–167, 169, 173–178, 182, 184, 186–187, 189–194, 202, 206, 227–231, 240, 242
pochteca, 42
Post-Classic International Style, 35, 37–39, 46
pottery, 8–10, 18–19, 30–32, 34, 37–40, 42, 44, 57–58, 61–62, 72, 77–78, 93–95, 97, 99, 106–107, 110, 112, 117, 140, 153, 158, 164–165, 169–170, 175–182, 184–187, 192–194, 207, 211–213, 239, 241–242

309

Pottery Mound, 117, 153, 170
Powamu rituals, 48
practice theory, 181
prayers, 28, 48, 58–59, 130, 162, 172
priests, 28–29, 33–34, 39, 43, 47–49, 162, 167, 169, 223, 233
prophets, 227, 235
proxemics, 18, 77, 109, 120, 122–123, 131, 143, 146, 152, 167, 192
Pueblo Alto, 55
Pueblo Seco, 140–142, 148

Quetzalcoatl, 26, 29, 34, 37, 40, 43–44

rainbows, 167, 169–170
red-on-buff pottery, 31, 38
religious societies, 68, 70, 72, 75, 78, 109, 129, 201
revitalization, 15, 68–71, 78–82, 227
Rio Grande, 18, 26, 40, 86, 88, 90, 96, 100, 104, 109–113, 115–117, 119, 121, 123–125, 127–129, 147, 149, 156, 166, 206, 237, 240
ritual practices, 2, 5, 12–13, 17, 100, 109, 122, 126, 128–129, 153, 155, 158, 191, 196, 211, 214, 241
rituals, 1–8, 10–13, 15, 17–21, 23, 25–30, 35, 39, 41–48, 50–55, 57, 59–61, 63–65, 67, 70–71, 75–81, 100, 104, 106, 109–111, 119–120, 122–123, 126–131, 143–144, 150, 152–156, 158–159, 162, 164–165, 167, 169, 171–176, 178–179, 182, 185, 191–193, 196–198, 201–202, 204–206, 208, 210–212, 214, 216–222, 224–226, 233, 235, 241
roads, 38, 50, 55, 92
rock art, 9–10, 18, 37, 46, 50, 58, 78, 109–129, 156, 164–167, 178, 211–212, 231, 236, 240, 242
Roosevelt Red Ware, 10, 178, 183, 185–186. *See also* Salado Polychromes

sacred, 3, 5–7, 15, 18, 29, 47, 55, 58, 64, 93, 129, 158, 160, 166, 173, 176, 182, 222, 224, 235, 237
Salado Polychromes, 10, 40, 44–45, 183–186, 191
San Cristobal Pueblo, 109, 120, 124
San Pedro River Valley, 44–45

Schaafsma, Polly, 26, 29, 46, 56, 58, 78, 112, 116, 178
Secakuku, Ferrell, 171
Sekaquaptewa, Emory, 171
serpents, 26–27, 29, 36, 38–40, 43–44, 48, 58, 110, 114, 118–120, 129, 167
shields, 10, 78, 116–117, 169
shrines, 34, 55, 92, 102, 105, 160, 162, 237
Sikyatki Polychrome, 165
Sikyatki style, 9
Silko, Leslie Marmon, 161
Silver Creek, 19–20, 147, 164, 166, 177, 179, 182, 184–190, 192–194, 203, 241–242
Smith, Michael, 34
smoke, 59, 239
snakes, 28, 38, 58, 114, 118–119, 171, 201, 210
Snaketown, 38
sodalities, 10, 29, 73, 78, 109, 129, 154, 160, 162, 164, 167, 169, 171–172, 174, 192, 216–219
solstice, 162, 201
songs, 55, 58, 85, 89–90, 92, 94–95, 104–105, 130, 133, 148, 158, 162, 171, 200–201, 206, 235
Sonoran Desert, 32, 37
Southwestern Cult, 9–11, 20, 24, 50, 60, 175, 177, 186, 194, 196
Southwest/Northwest, 23–26, 29–34, 37–46, 49
specialists (or specialization), 129, 133, 164
spectatorship, 18, 153–155, 157, 159, 161, 163, 165–167, 169, 171, 173–174
spiritual, 1, 156, 159–160, 162, 165, 171, 205, 209
Stephen, Alexander, 56, 58–59, 200, 207, 210, 212, 214
supernatural, 6, 170–171
symbolize, 181
symbols (or symbolic), 2, 4–6, 11, 28–30, 34–37, 39–42, 44–46, 55–56, 58, 64, 84, 104, 130–133, 135, 137, 139–141, 143, 147–149, 151–152, 158–160, 162, 165–166, 176, 178, 180–181, 210, 216, 227, 240
symmetry, 31

Tanoan, 86, 88–94, 99, 239
Taos, 26, 88, 240
Taube, Karl, 25, 56, 58
Tewa, 16–17, 54–55, 84–97, 99–107, 130, 133, 150–151, 158, 162, 172–173, 198, 239–240
textiles, 153, 158
theatrical, 13, 17
Tilley, Christopher, 160, 224
Tlaloc, 26, 37–38, 40, 236
Tonto Basin, 44–45
traders, 23, 25, 34, 42
trails, 91–92, 105, 111, 121, 127
trincheras, 32, 37
turquoise, 33, 37, 40–41, 45, 50, 57, 59, 61
twins, 25–27, 29, 38, 48

underworlds, 26–27, 34, 43, 48, 55, 58, 60, 64, 158, 165, 214
Uto-aztecan, 30, 162

VanPool, Christine, 43
VanPool, Todd, 43
Vargas, Victoria, 43
viewership, 153–155, 164–166, 172–173
violence, 34, 41, 66, 71, 78–79, 81–82, 171, 207, 220
visibility, 55, 122–123, 135, 190, 214
visuality, 153, 155, 171, 226

Walpi, 200–201
Washburn, Dorothy, 171
weather, 10, 44, 178
weaving, 97
Webster, Laurie, 78
Western Pueblo, 9, 17, 20, 40, 117, 149, 164–165, 213, 217
White Mountain Red Ware, 40, 46, 182–186
worldviews, 3, 6, 18, 100, 153–154
Wupatki, 201

Yucatán, 26

zoomorphs (or zoomorphic), 32, 58, 158, 165
Zuni, 40, 58–59, 87, 133, 147, 155, 162–163, 199, 212